They Sang for Horses

They Sang for

THE IMPACT OF THE HORSE

A REVISED EDITION

Horses

ON NAVAJO & APACHE FOLKLORE

WITH A NEW EPILOGUE & PHOTOGRAPHS

LaVerne Harrell Clark

University Press of Colorado

Copyright © 2001 by the University Press of Colorado
International Standard Book Number 0-87081-496-6

Published by the University Press of Colorado
5589 Arapahoe Avenue, Suite 206C
Boulder, Colorado 80303

The University of Arizona Press edition, 1966.

The University Press of Colorado is a cooperative publishing enterprise supported, in part, by Adams State College, Colorado State University, Fort Lewis College, Mesa State College, Metropolitan State College of Denver, University of Colorado, University of Northern Colorado, University of Southern Colorado, and Western State College of Colorado.

The paper used in this publication meets the minimum requirements of the American National Standard for Information Sciences—Permanence of Paper for Printed Library Materials. ANSI Z39.48-1992

Library of Congress Cataloging-in-Publication Data

Clark, LaVerne Harrell.
   They sang for horses : the impact of the horse on Navajo and Apache folklore / by LaVerne Harrell Clark.—New ed.
       p. cm.
Includes bibliographical references and index.
   ISBN 0-87081-496-6 (pbk. : alk. paper)
   1. Navajo Indians—Folklore. 2. Apache Indians—Folklore. 3. Navajo Indians—Religion. 4. Apache Indians—Religion. 5. Horses—Southwest, New. I. Title.

E99.N3 C535 2001
398.2'089'972—dc21

                                                                        00-012667

Text design by Daniel Pratt
Cover design by Laura Furney

10   09   08   07   06   05   04   03   02   01   10   9   8   7   6   5   4   3   2   1

This new edition is dedicated to Frances Gillmor,
May 21, 1903–October 28, 1993,
friend and professor.

It is rededicated to James Boyce Harrell,
November 2, 1905–September 6, 1966,
and to Belle Bunte Harrell,
May 8, 1906–January 23, 1992,
for the continual privilege of being their own . . .
but especially to L.D., who believed . . . and who gave me
the power of the Clark's crow.

Contents

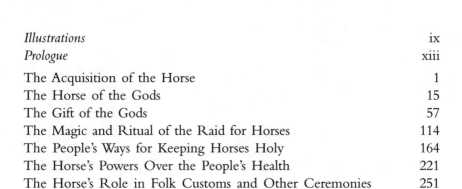

Illustrations	ix
Prologue	xiii
The Acquisition of the Horse	1
The Horse of the Gods	15
The Gift of the Gods	57
The Magic and Ritual of the Raid for Horses	114
The People's Ways for Keeping Horses Holy	164
The Horse's Powers Over the People's Health	221
The Horse's Role in Folk Customs and Other Ceremonies	251
Epilogue	278
Bibliography	318
Index	331

Illustrations

Unless otherwise noted, photographs are by LaVerne Harrell Clark.

Southern Athapascans (map)	xi
Linguistic Divisions of the Southern Athapascans (chart)	xix
Present Locations of the Navajo and Apache (chart)	xx
Western Apache Groups, ca. 1850 (map)	xxi
Navajo Reservation and Adjacent Areas (map)	xxii–xxiii
Navajo and Apache Reservations and Settlements	xxiv–xxv
Santa Fe pageant depicting the entrance of Don Juan de Oñate into the southwestern United States, 1598	2
Puye Cliffs near Española, New Mexico	5
Salt River Canyon boundary	9
A conical tepee at Mescalero	11
White Mountain horseman on palomino	16
Apaches believed in supernatural powers for horses	19
Frank Mitchell, 1881–1967, Blessing Way singer of Chinle, Arizona (courtesy David P. McAllester)	25
The pinto was the most favored mount	45
Two mounted young Apache call to mind the Twins' visit to Father Sun	58
Navajo sacred mountain Debentsa	65
Charlie Mitchell and Atta-kai-bi-tzu-ih, 1884 (photo by Ben Wittick, courtesy the Museum of New Mexico, neg. #15726)	68
Navajo Mountain Range, the Chuskas	78

Forked stick hogan behind buckboard wagon   81
San Carlos puberty maiden dances with girl companion   104
John Rope, former White Mountain Apache scout (photo by   115
    Grenville Goodwin, courtesy Arizona State Museum, photo
    #18257)
Arizona Apache horseman mounting a fast horse   136
San Carlos puberty maiden with scratch stick and tube of cane   147
Youngsters at Whiteriver, Arizona, know Dirty Boy tales   152
More Navajo women now practicing rites   165
Cibecue Apache medicine man Bosnic Lupe with his horse   173
    (courtesy Arizona Historical Society/Tucson, photo
    AHS #53771)
Trappings that can serve as Apache ceremonial offerings   178
A typical Navajo corral   187
White Mountain Apache horsemen watering their horses   200
Sam Yazzie, Navajo singer, 1972   222
Western Apache also use the conical frame   237
Navajo horseman at Round Rock, Arizona   244
Apache parents and their tiny girl in camp dress   252
Older female directs adolescent girl on sacred deerskin   254
The burden basket and Apache marriage customs   263
Homemade Apache saddle from Eve Ball collection   271
St. Michael's Franciscan Mission, Window Rock, Arizona   280
Shiprock landmark and stories about Changing Woman   283
Frank Mitchell singing the Blessing Way at the 1957   289
    puberty cermony for his granddaughter (photo by the
    late Mabel Bosch Denton, courtesy Charlotte J. Frisbie
    and David P. McAllester)
Hogan blessing rite and four main directional supports   295
San Carlos Apache cattle on range, Black River Crossing,   306
    Arizona
Today's Navajo and Apache reservation rodeos date from   308
    the 1920s
Navajo chicken pull, 1913. Photo by Dwight Franklin   310
    (courtesy Special Collections, University of Arizona
    Library/Tucson)

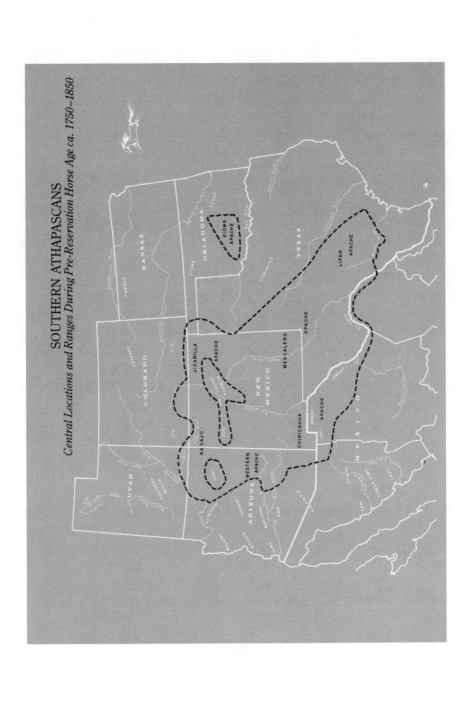

SOUTHERN ATHAPASCANS

Central Locations and Ranges During Pre-Reservation Horse Age ca. 1750–1850

Prologue

URING THE GREAT HORSE AGE—an age that began in the seventeenth
century and that for the most part was over by the 1970s—the
Navajo and Apache placed more emphasis on the horse in their
culture than did any of the other Indian tribes living in the southwestern
United States, with the exception of those Plains Indian peoples who also
inhabited parts of this region. Like other American Indians, the Navajo
and Apache had not known about the horse's existence before the coming of the white man. According to paleontologists, America may have
been the cradle of the horse, but it had completely disappeared from the
Western Hemisphere while in its prehistoric form. Columbus, arriving
in the West Indies on his second trip to the New World in 1493, introduced the animal in its present form to the Americas, and Cortés transported it first to the mainland of this continent, to Mexico in 1519. When
the Navajo and Apache received their first horses more than a century
later from those brought into the southwestern United States by other
Spaniards, the previously unknown animal wrought more changes on
their old way of life than did any other possession they ever acquired
from the white man.

My purpose in this work is to examine for the first time at any length
the impact of the horse upon traditional forms of Navajo and Apache
folklore during more than three centuries of influence, to penetrate as far
as possible the obscurity enveloping the horse in its ritualistic and supernatural manifestations. Throughout this study, I try to emphasize the adoption of the horse into the myths, tales, and other legendary lore of the
Navajo and Apache by providing illustrations and interpretations of their
mythical expressions of it. I also attempt to show how these Indians have

shaped their recent acquisition into other forms of their folklore by defining or clarifying the horse's symbolic significance in ceremony, song, prayer, custom, and belief. To communicate to the reader some knowledge of how oral and visual transmission operate with forms of folklore, I have made an effort to capture something of the creative process by which Navajo and Apache storytellers, singers, medicine people—even painters—have transformed the new elements in their religion and folklore after the likeness of the old.

In the fulfillment of my purpose, I have gathered recorded material relating to the Navajo and the various Apache groups that compose the Southern Athapascan linguistic family. In my endeavor to arrive at a comprehensive view, I treat extensively the similarities and differences of equine lore existing among all these peoples.

The seven linguistically and ethnically related members of the Southern Athapascan family are now scattered across the Southwest from Arizona to Oklahoma. Besides the Navajo, they are the Chiricahua Apache, Jicarilla Apache, Kiowa-Apache, Lipan Apache, Mescalero Apache, and the five Western Apache groups, which following the classification of many modern anthropologists, I consider here as one unit. First designated Western Apache by the late Grenville Goodwin, a leading authority on them, these peoples of eastern and central Arizona are now the Cibecue, White Mountain, and San Carlos. Because until recent years the designation also included the Northern and Southern Tonto and the references to them in this work all fall within the period when they went by that name, they are still included here as belonging to the Western Apache. Today, however, because of their heavy intermarriage and common interests with the Yavapai, they have now come to be classified with them as Yavapai.

Many readers of this book will make distinctions between the term "Navajo" and the term "Apache," perhaps thinking of them as applying to two separate and roughly equal groups. But it is important to remember that all the Apache and the Navajo are of Southern Athapascan heritage; and while it is true that the Navajo differ more from other Southern Athapascan peoples than the Apache groups, with the possible exception of the Kiowa-Apache, do from each other, Navajo folk patterns cannot be effectively studied apart from their Southern Athapascan origins. The use of the names "Navajo" and "Apache" in this book, therefore, does not imply two distinctly different types of folklore.

Dr. Harry Hoijer, foremost linguistic scholar of the Southern Athapascans, divides them into two language subfamilies: the Eastern and the Western Apachean peoples. A chart, which follows Hoijer's plan, is reproduced on a later page of this work to assist the reader in placing each of the Southern Athapascan groups within the language family. Maps are also provided indicating the present and the pre-reservation locations of all groups, as well as place names of mythical significance.

I recount first in this work what history records of how the horse came to the Southern Athapascans and how it revolutionized their mode of living. The next section explores the concept of the supernatural horse— that creature in possession of the Navajo and Apache deities long before it came to earth—as it appears in myth, tale, song, and painting. Following this, I turn to the myths, folk tales, and legends in which the culture heroes and other deities made the gift of horses to the people. My attention then turns to the rituals and magical powers upon which the Navajo and Apache depended during their raids for horses. Next this study illustrates and explains the ceremonies, songs, folk remedies, taboos, and other magical potencies relating to the daily care of the horse. In detail I consider the supernatural powers of the horse and its agents to heal in ceremonies those who suffer from injury or illness, as well as their powers to engage in various acts of witchcraft or to afflict those who offend them. Succeeding this, I deal with the horse's role in ceremonies other than healing and in folk customs surrounding the life of an individual from birth to death.

Without the aid and encouragement of my professors, guides, and friends on the faculty and staff of the University of Arizona, as well as by those at some other institutions, this book could never have been written. Without the understanding, comfort, and good faith given me by family, relatives, and friends so many times in so many places, I would certainly have abandoned my task long ago.

While acknowledgment by name to all those who have made indirect contributions to this work would be impossible, I do wish to take advantage of this opportunity to express my deepest gratitude to the following people for the special ways in which they have contributed:

To my late professor and cherished friend, Dr. Frances Gillmor, University of Arizona professor and distinguished author of books on Navajos and Aztecs, for her perpetual enthusiasm, encouragement, and belief in this work from its beginning as a term paper in her folklore class through its time as a thesis under her direction, this acknowledgment with my grateful and loving remembrance always. Without the use of her extensive library and ready introductions to faces, places, and opportunities, dating from 1956 and the Wetherills among others in Kayenta and Ganado, through the days of fiestas in Mexico in 1968, with many others in Spain in 1969, and lacking the perpetual interest she extended until her death in 1993, both this study and I would have been the losers.

To the late Harry T. Getty, my former Professor of Anthropology at the University of Arizona, who in his courses on the ethnology of the Southwestern Indians gave me kind and helpful aid toward understanding the social organization and lifeways of the Navajo and Apache, and who during his writing about the San Carlos people's cattle industry also offered me invaluable suggestions and introductions.

To the late Eve Ball, a one-of-a-kind author and oral historian for the Chiricahua, Mescalero, and Warm Springs Apache. Although we met after this book was already several years old, and became friends through our mutual interests in the Apache people, the research I continued to conduct among them—especially at Mescalero—was greatly enhanced by our steady friendship and exchanges dating from around 1970 throughout the remainder of her life. Especially am I indebted to her for her continuing interest in all my projects, her numerous introductions, and her gracious hospitality to me on the several occasions when I was a guest—one sometimes accompanied by my grateful husband, too—at her interesting home in Ruidoso.

To my inspiring undergraduate mentor—still an esteemed, dear friend—Eleanor James, Professor Emerita of English, Texas Woman's University, for starting me in the field of folklore and for the indispensable first training she provided me in the methods of research.

To the American Philosophical Society for awarding me a grant from the Penrose Fund in 1967 for research among Southwestern Indian groups. Due to surgery, I had to delay most of the work until 1969 and the early 1970s when the grant helped me take many of the photographs of Navajos and Apaches and their country, which are included here for the first time. It also enabled me to witness certain feats of horsemanship these people adopted from the Spaniards like those exhibited at the chicken pulls described in the epilogue.

To Nanibah Dodge Grogan, my friend since the day her late father, the talented Navajo painter Adee Dodge, brought her as a young girl to meet me at a Phoenix signing, with my continuing friendship and deep gratitude for encouraging me and assisting the University Press of Colorado and me in again featuring her father's brilliant painting "The Emergence" in this new edition, where this time, it is on the cover. Also to my friends Randall Platt and Helen Shakelford for their kind assistance in helping me locate various Dodge paintings.

To David P. McAllester and Charlotte Frisbie, whose numerous contributions to the study of Navajo religion and ceremonies I profoundly admire, for granting me permission to use the photograph of Frank Mitchell conducting the Blessing Way, which was made by the late Mabel Brosch Denton, and to David, again, for providing and letting me use the photo of Mitchell alone from his collection.

To the late Agapito Rey, for his friendship and encouragement with the work I continued to do, after the initial publication, on the Spanish horses that Southwestern Indians acquired. Through his introductions to the Archivo General de Indias in Seville, I was able more than once to finally hold in my hands Juan Jaramillo's handwritten account of the Coronado Expedition from Mexico to the Southwestern United States. I am also grateful to Don Agapito for his suggestions, as well as for those of my friends in Madrid, the late Nieves Hoyos Sancho of the Museo del Pueblo Español, who was also the distinguished author of numerous books of Spanish folklore, and Maria Montoya, cousin of our dear friend, the late Carlos Montoya, who was a gracious hostess to us at several wonderful dinners and evenings in her home. The direction and help of these Castilian friends enabled me to witness various exhibitions of the kind of horsemanship the Spanish *conquistadores* introduced to the Americas and therein to the Navajo and Apache. I am indebted, too, to the late Wigberto Jiménez Moreno of the Escuela Nacional de Antropología e Historia and to the anthropologist-author Isabel Kelly, both of Mexico City, for similar assistance in locating other such exhibitions in that city and in Guadalajara. My further gratitude to the late Keith Aubrey for devoting a number of Saturday and Sunday afternoons to helping L.D. and me translate various of the documents not available in English at the time—all of them regarding the spread of the horse from the time of Cortés in Mexico north through the period marking the entry of Don Juan de Oñate into the southwestern United States and during the latter's early days of colonization.

To the library of the University of Arizona and to all the librarians serving there who made a pleasure of much of the research involved, first for this study, and later for much of what is now in the epilogue appending it, especially Lutie L. Higley, Lois Olsrud, Maria Segura Hoopes, and the entire staff of Special Collections—particularly the late Phyllis Ball, and more recently the assistants in the photo archives who helped me locate various of their photograhic holdings. My additional gratitude to Special Collections for granting me permission to use here those photographs credited to them, and special thanks to Roger Myers, Manuscripts Curator, for help at the last minute in connection with other photographic needs.

Further thanks, too, to the other libraries and librarians who frequently offered me additional, beneficial help—particularly those at Columbia University and others at the University of New Mexico and the Smithville, Texas, Public Library, especially those in Inter-Library Loan Services. I also appreciate the help of the late T. M. Pearce, former professor and folklorist at the University of New Mexico, for his assistance with archival collections in Santa Fe and Albuquerque.

My additional gratitude to the late Donald M. Powell for initially assisting me in compiling this work's index and to Erwin Acuntius and Edwin N. Wilmsen for their skillful touches in shaping my drafts of the maps included here and rendering them into works of art.

To the Arizona Historical Society and Susan Sheehan, Photo Librarian, thanks for their help and permission to use the photo included here from their collection. My further thanks to the Arizona State Museum and Kathleen E. Hubenschmidt, Photo Collections Curator, and to the Museum of New Mexico and their staff for their aid and permission to use the photos credited to their collections, too.

To the Navajo and Apache who appear in the lines and photographs of these pages, as well as to those who assisted with the research but preferred not to be identified or photographed, my deepest gratitude for cooperating with me and for joining me in my long effort to present, and therein preserve, an accurate picture about certain traditions that have already faded from the lifeways of your people, or are beginning to.

Finally, thanks to all those at the University Press of Colorado who have seen this revised edition through the editing, design, and production stages involved in producing it, but especially to Yashka K. Hallein, former Acquisitions Editor; Lucienne Wu, former Assistant Editor; Luther Wilson, former Director; Darrin Pratt, present Director; and particularly to Laura Furney, Managing Editor and my chief editor and consultant from start to finish; my thanks for their careful and knowledgeable readings, suggestions, and many kindnesses. Most of all, though, I remain grateful to my dear L.D., who through thick and thin has always been in the wings. Without his support, patience, kindness, optimism, and above all companionship—once for a whole summer in a cramped camper and nearly always, too, in uncharted country and unfamiliar circumstances—I could never have joined the Navajo and Apache for such a long period of time in this perpetual search and song for horses.

LaVerne Harrell Clark
Smithville, Texas

LINGUISTIC DIVISIONS OF THE SOUTHERN ATHAPASCANS[*]

THE WESTERN APACHEAN PEOPLES

NAVAJO

Western Apache-Chiricahua-Mescalero

The Western Apache Groups[†]
  San Carlos Apache
  White Mountain Apache
  Cibecue Apache
  Southern Tonto Apache
  Northern Tonto Apache

Chiricahua-Mescalero
  Chiricahua Apache
  Mescalero Apache

THE EASTERN APACHEAN PEOPLES

Jicarilla-Lipan
  Jicarilla Apache
  Lipan Apache

Kiowa-Apache

---

[*] Based upon a chart in Harry Hoijer's "The Southern Athapascan Languages," in *American Anthropologist,* new series, XL, No. 1 (January–March 1938), p. 86.

[†] Although Hoijer identifies these Apache as the San Carlos Apache groups rather than as the Western Apache groups, Goodwin's designation is used here and throughout this work to avoid confusion with the individual Western Apache group called the San Carlos Apache, as well as with the San Carlos Apache Reservation. See Grenville Goodwin, "The Social Divisions and Economic Life of the Western Apache," *American Anthropologist,* new series, XXXVII, No. 1 (January–March 1935), pp. 55–64.

PRESENT LOCATIONS OF THE NAVAJO AND APACHE

Reservation	Group
Camp Verde (Arizona)	Northern Tonto Apache Southern Tonto Apache
Canoncito (New Mexico)	Navajo
Fort Apache (Arizona)	Cibecue Apache White Mountain Apache
Fort McDowell (Arizona)	Southern Tonto Apache
Jicarilla (New Mexico)	Jicarilla Apache
Mescalero (New Mexico)	Chiricahua Apache Lipan Apache Mescalero Apache
Navajo (Arizona, New Mexico, and Utah)	Navajo
Puertocito (New Mexico)	Navajo
San Carlos (Arizona)	San Carlos Apache Northern Tonto Apache Southern Tonto Apache White Mountain Apache

OFF-RESERVATION SETTLEMENTS IN ARIZONA

Community	Group
Clarkdale, Cottonwood, and farms in Upper Verde Valley	Northern Tonto Apache
Gisela, Pine, and Payson	Southern Tonto Apache

OFF-RESERVATION SETTLEMENTS IN OKLAHOMA

Apache	Chiricahua Apache Kiowa-Apache
Fort Cobb	Kiowa-Apache

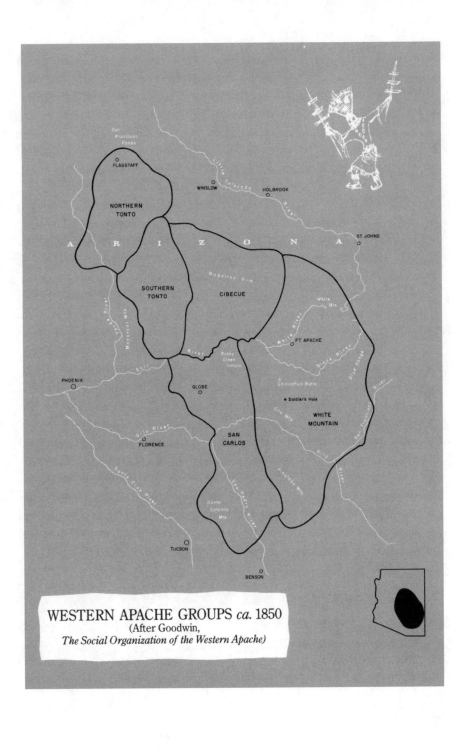

WESTERN APACHE GROUPS *ca.* 1850
(After Goodwin,
The Social Organization of the Western Apache)

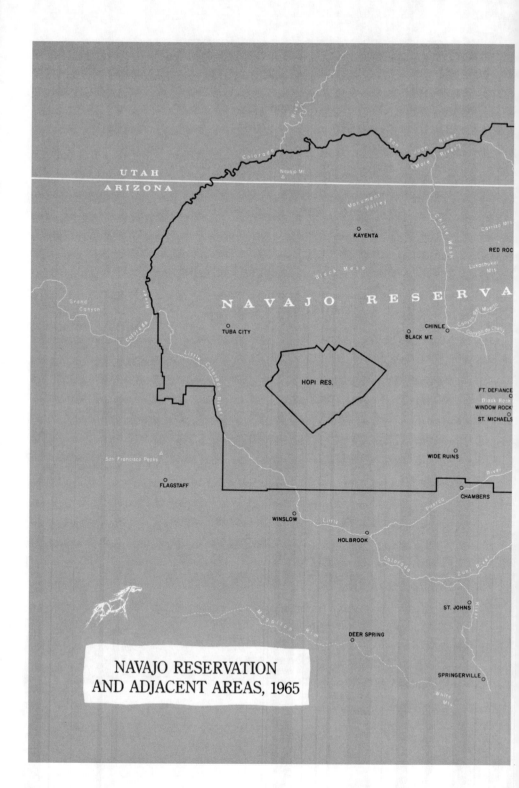

NAVAJO RESERVATION
AND ADJACENT AREAS, 1965

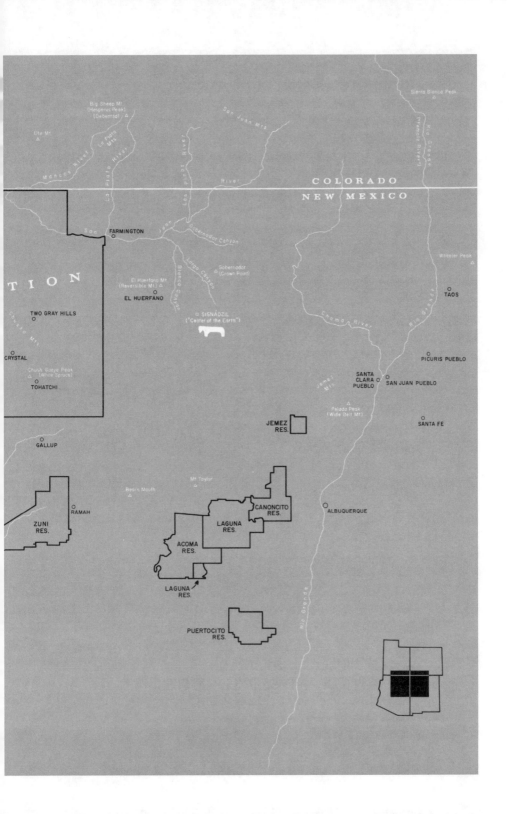

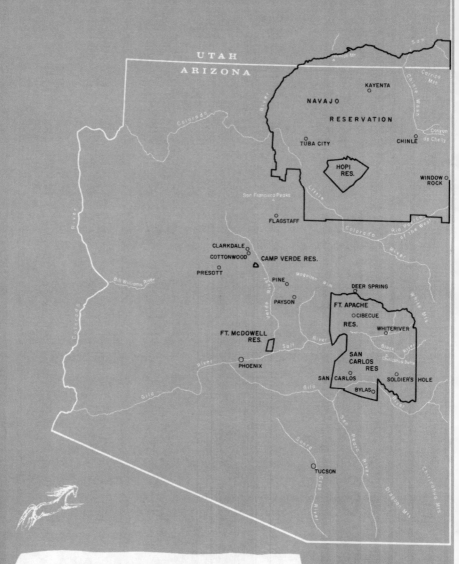

UTAH
ARIZONA

NAVAJO

RESERVATION

KAYENTA

TUBA CITY

CHINLE

HOPI
RES.

WINDOW
ROCK

FLAGSTAFF

CLARKDALE
COTTONWOOD
PRESOTT

CAMP VERDE RES.

PINE

PAYSON

DEER SPRING

FT. APACHE
CIBECUE
RES.

WHITERIVER

FT. MCDOWELL
RES.

SAN
CARLOS
RES

PHOENIX

SAN CARLOS

BYLAS

SOLDIER'S HOLE

TUCSON

NAVAJO AND APACHE
RESERVATIONS AND SETTLEMENTS
and those of Neighboring Indians, 1965

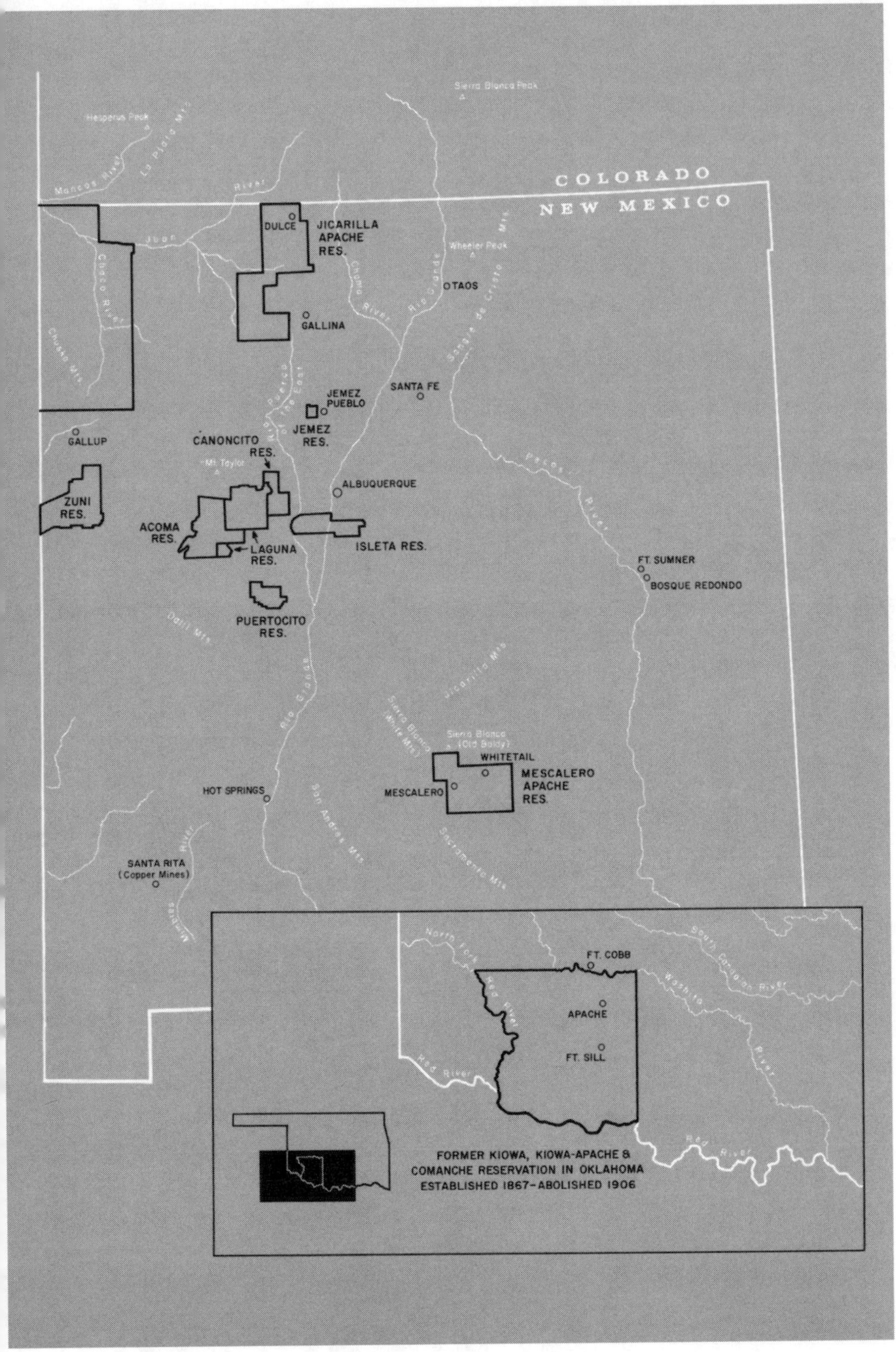

COLORADO
NEW MEXICO
Sierra Blanca Peak
Hesperus Peak
La Plata Mts.
Mancos River
River
Juan
Chaco River
Chuska Mts.
DULCE
JICARILLA
APACHE
RES.
Wheeler Peak
Chama River
Rio Grande
TAOS
Sangre de Cristo Mts.
GALLINA
Rio Puerco of the East
JEMEZ
PUEBLO
SANTA FE
JEMEZ
RES.
GALLUP
CANONCITO
RES.
Mt. Taylor
Pecos River
ALBUQUERQUE
ZUNI
RES.
ACOMA
RES.
LAGUNA
RES.
ISLETA RES.
FT. SUMNER
BOSQUE REDONDO
PUERTOCITO
RES.
Datil Mts.
Jicarilla Mts.
Sierra Blanca (White Mts.)
Sierra Blanca (Old Baldy)
WHITETAIL
MESCALERO
APACHE
RES.
MESCALERO
HOT SPRINGS
San Andres Mts.
Sacramento Mts.
SANTA RITA
(Copper Mines)
Mimbres River
North Fork
Red River
FT. COBB
Washita
South Canadian River
APACHE
FT. SILL
Red River
River
FORMER KIOWA, KIOWA-APACHE &
COMANCHE RESERVATION IN OKLAHOMA
ESTABLISHED 1867–ABOLISHED 1906

They Sang for Horses

The Acquisition of the Horse

The First Look at Horses

A LTHOUGH HISTORICAL RECORDS DO NOT ASSURE US of the date when the Southern Athapascan people first saw horses, we can be fairly certain that the Querecho Indians that Francisco Vázquez de Coronado and his army met in 1541 on the expedition through the Southwest in a fruitless search for Gran Quivira were bands of Plains Apache hunting buffalo. Eminent Southwestern historians, among them Herbert E. Bolton, Frederick Webb Hodge, George Hammond, and Agapito Rey, endorse this opinion. Two separate *rancherías* of these Querecho Indians were seen on two different occasions by Coronado's men between the Canadian River near the present New Mexico–Texas line and were described by Coronado's chroniclers, Pedro de Castañeda and Captain Juan Jaramillo.[1] If we accept Hodge's identification of the term "Querecho," the Apache people whom Coronado and his men saw may have been Jicarilla, Lipan, or possibly an eastern band of the Mescalero, who were at that time the buffalo-hunting Apache of eastern New Mexico, northwestern Oklahoma, and western Texas.[2] Bolton suggests they were called "Querechos" because of their trade with the nearby pueblos of the Keres (Queres) Indians of New Mexico.[3] Hodge believes the word "Querecho" is derived from the extinct Pecos Indians' terms for the Apache and the Navajo.[4]

We also have definite information from Pedro de Castañeda's chronicle on what the reactions of these Apache were toward Coronado's horses when first they saw them crossing the buffalo plains of the Southwest. How unlike the reactions of the Pueblo peoples, who had earlier seen these same horses, were those of the Apache! The Hopi, who had heard

Santa Fe Pageant depicting the entrance of Don Juan de Oñate into the southwestern United States, 1598.

that the Zuñi "had been conquered by very fierce men who rode animals that ate people," were astonished into a fast submission upon first seeing the mounted Spaniards and hearing their "Santiago" shout of attack.[5] The idea that horses were anthropophagous had frightened Indians all over Mexico, and the belief spread among the Indians of the Southwest as soon as the first horses entered that territory. The Acoma Indians had come down to the valley from their majestic mesa in a warlike mood, but, according to Castañeda, had "made their peace ceremonies by approaching the horses, taking their sweat, and anointing themselves with it." Though Castañeda took this action by the Acoma Indians to be merely a symbol of submission because the Indians "made crosses with the fingers of their hands," there may have been more behind their anointing themselves with the horses' sweat than met Castañeda's eyes.[6] I am more inclined to agree with Hartley B. Alexander, who surmises: "The Pueblo tribes, equally amazed with the unknown animal . . . smeared their own bodies with the fluid, doubtless with the idea of transferring to themselves something of the magic of the Great Dog of the white men."[7]

The buffalo-hunting Apache took the Spanish horses pretty calmly that memorable day on the plains near the Canadian River. Perhaps their reactions were a sign predicting the early Apache mastery of the horse, for unlike the Pueblo Indians of New Mexico, who were the first Southwestern Indians to acquire horses in sizeable numbers, the Apache and their Navajo relatives were the first to develop into a real horse people. The Apache reactions greatly surprised Castañeda, who recorded the scene as follows:

> Although they saw our army, they did not move away or disturb themselves in the least. On the contrary, they came out of their tents to scrutinize us. Then they spoke to the advance guard and asked what the army was. The general [Coronado] spoke to them, but as the Indians had already spoken to the Turk [Coronado's treacherous Wichita Indian guide], who came with the advance guard, they agreed with him in everything he said. These people were so skillful in the use of signs that it seemed as if they spoke.[8]

Perhaps there were other reasons why the Apache responded so equably in their encounter with Coronado's caravan. We can never know for certain, but historians would have us believe that the Indians were not altogether taken by surprise. For one thing, the Spaniards had wintered at Tiguex, a now-extinct pueblo of the Tiwa Indians of New Mexico. The Querecho Apache may have been in trade communication with the Tiwa people and have learned from them the true nature of horses. At any rate, the Querecho Apache had been given adequate time to receive news about the Spanish visitors and their mounts. But it is most likely that the information that the Querecho Apache received from Coronado's traitor Indian guide, called the Turk by the Spaniards, was the real reason behind their reactions. It later turned out that the Turk was involved in a plot started by the Tiguex Indians and their neighbors, the Towa Indian people of the now-extinct Pecos Pueblo, to rid themselves forever of the Spanish intruders. Their plan was for the Turk, whom Coronado believed to be guiding him to Gran Quivira, to lose the *conquistador* and his army on the plains of Texas and New Mexico, where it was hoped that these unwanted guests and their horses would die from hunger and thirst. Another Indian guide, named Sopete, who also accompanied the expedition, later declared to Coronado that his rival and enemy, the Turk, "had primed the Querechos" before they gave Coronado directions on the whereabouts of Quivira.[9]

A few days after the Turk had talked with the first group of Querecho, who disappeared quietly in the opposite direction the day after the interview, Coronado and his men met the second group. It was this group who led them on the famous wild-goose-chase into the barren Texas Panhandle. Coronado described the frustration he experienced on that trip in a letter to the King of Spain: "For five days I went wherever they led me, until we reached some plains as bare of landmarks as if we were surrounded by the sea. Here the guides lost their bearings . . ." and here, strikingly enough, the Querecho Apache also took leave of the Spaniards. According to Coronado, their fate was then to wander "aimlessly over these plains" until they met the Querechos' enemies, the "Teyas" (Texas) Indians, who told them the bitter truth about Quivira.[10]

The animals that these Apache saw pass over the plains that spring day in 1541 and fade away like a mirage were never to be possessed by them, nor by their children. Perhaps some of their grandchildren rode a hundred years later when the first Apache had acquired horses. Until then, it was their destiny to continue, as Castañeda described them, going "about like nomads with their tents and with packs of dogs harnessed with little pads, pack-saddles, and girths. When the dogs' loads slip to the side, they howl for some one to come and straighten them."[11]

The Dates of Acquisition

Numerous scholars, since the time of Clark Wissler's famous article upon the Plains Indians' acquisition of horses, have speculated about the dates of this event.[12] Most of them endorse Francis Haines's theory that the Plains Indians acquired horses some time after 1600, with the center of distribution around Santa Fe, New Mexico. Pioneering this theory, Haines abolished Wissler's thesis that horses may have been available to the Plains Indians as early as 1541 from the strays lost on the Coronado and DeSoto expeditions. Haines wrote that the distribution of horses among the Plains Indians "proceeded rather slowly; none of the tribes becoming horse Indians before 1630, and probably not until 1650."[13]

The first basic research on the actual spread of horses that focused on the Southwest was done by D. E. Worcester, who agreed basically with Haines's thesis that the Plains Indians obtained most of their horses from

The Puye Cliffs near Española, New Mexico, mark the area where the Navajo were living when they first came into historic reference in 1626.

Southwestern Indians, who in turn acquired them in raids on the ranches of New Mexico, and also from those of Sonora, Chihuahua, Nueva Vizcaya, and Coahuila. Worcester's general conclusion about the Apache Indians of New Mexico is that they "began using horses otherwise than for food . . . between 1620 and 1630; possibly earlier, but certainly not later."[14] He does not attempt to designate the specific Apache groups that first acquired horses from New Mexican or northern Mexican ranches, nor to date the Navajo acquisition of the horse. Both of these tasks are almost impossible, for while historical documents on early New Mexico are full of material concerning Apache raids, little if any effort was made to designate specific Apache groups. That the name Navajo was not applied to

the raiding group meant little either. The Navajo did not come into specific historical reference until 1626 when Fray Gerónimo de Zárate-
Salmerón wrote of the "Apaches de Nabajú."[15] They were not referred to
by name again until 1630 and 1634, when Fray Alonso de Benavides
called them "the Apaches of Navajó."[16]

More recent and detailed research on the spread of horses in the
Southwest has been done by Jack D. Forbes. Offering the thesis that the
Indians of the Southwest had begun to acquire horses before the colonization of New Mexico was initiated in 1598 by Don Juan de Oñate, Forbes
writes:

> The appearance of the mounted Indian in northern Mexico began
> in the 1550s; by 1600 most of the Indians of that area (with the
> exception of Sonora) probably had horses. The spread of riding
> animals into the southwestern United States apparently began in
> 1574 at La Junta and in 1590 farther to the east. After 1600 the
> northward movement of the horse continued, being greatly facili-
> tated by the actual transporting of animals into New Mexico by the
> Spanish.[17]

Deciding upon a much earlier date than Worcester, Forbes concludes:
"Thus it is clear that by 1606–1609 the Athapaskans of New Mexico were
acquiring herds of horses and that they were cooperating with refugee
Pueblo Indians who probably had experience with handling livestock."[18]
In this statement, Forbes includes not only the Apache of New Mexico,
but the Navajo as well. While it is possible, of course, that the Navajo had
begun to acquire horses as early as 1606 to 1609, Forbes does not give
concrete evidence that they had. His theory is that the Navajo were the
principal allies of the Jemez Indians "from 1606 until the late 1620s" and
that through this alliance, "the Navaho and the Indians of Jemez were the
principal opponents of the Spanish and therefore the principal raiders for
livestock."[19]

Forbes's ideas about a Jemez-Navajo alliance at this time seem feasible to me when viewed in the light of the Navajo's earlier geographical
location as neighbors of the Jemez Indians. His belief that they were the
principal raiders of the region, however, still needs to be developed more
fully before we can accept it. In a later work, Forbes calls attention to John
P. Harrington's statements that the Tewa Indians of New Mexico, neighbors of the Jemez Indians, who are the last surviving members of the
Towa linguistic family, still refer to the Navajo as the "Jemez Apache."[20]
Then, citing the Southwestern historian France V. Scholes as his source,

Forbes writes that in 1606–1607, the Spaniards in the territory of the Jemez sent out several expeditions against the Apache in this area. He identifies these as the "Jemez Apache," or Navajo Apache.[21] However, Scholes makes no such identification; he only refers to the warriors as "marauding Apaches."[22] The evidence that they were definitely Navajo and not some other Apache group living in the same general area seems to me sketchy. Further, there is nothing in Scholes' statements to show that these Apaches, even if they were the Navajo, were acquiring "herds of horses" at that time, as Forbes asserts they were. [23]

Concerning the Apache of Texas, Forbes says that horses began to spread northward into the western part of Texas from the La Junta area—located near the modern Texas-Chihuahua border in the vicinity of the town of Presidio at the juncture of the Rio Conchos and the Rio Grande—sometime after 1574 and from the lower Rio Grande region into eastern Texas sometime after the 1590s.[24] He deduces that "the La Junta region served as a gateway for the transmission of traits from New Spain to Texas and the vehicle for this movement was the Jumano Apache."[25] Forbes may well have a point in his belief that the people he calls the "Jumano Apache" were the most important agents in spreading horses into Texas. Before the Spaniards began attempting to establish missions in Texas at the close of the seventeenth century, the Lipan and some of the other Eastern Apachean groups are said to have "pestered," as the historian William Edward Dunn notes, "the frontiers of Nueva Vizcaya and Coahuila."[26] It is quite possible that some of these Apache also frequented the La Junta region in what is now Chihuahua and acquired some horses there at some early date after 1574; it is possible too that the Spaniards writing at that time identified some of these Apache by the term Jumano.

However, because the term "Jumano" (Jumane) is conflicting in itself, there is still no way of being certain that Forbes's "Jumano Apaches" actually were Apache people and not people belonging to some other Indian group or groups. Although the Spaniards sometimes applied the name "Jumano" to certain Apache groups, more frequently they attached it to more than one group of Indians, often employing it for Indian peoples distinctly different from one another.[27] According to Dunn, they used it "most commonly" to identify "Indians living in southwestern Texas near the Rio Grande." Concerning relationships and alliances between "Jumanes" groups and the Texas Apache, Dunn writes: "In the later seventeenth century the Jumanes of southwestern Texas had been the enemies of the Apaches. These Jumanes, it seems, in the eighteenth century became allies of the Apaches, while the northern Jumanes, or Taovayases, remained hostile." He contends that it was after the year 1731—the year in which a "Jumanes" group was reported to have engaged in a fight near San Antonio, Texas, as the allies of the Pelones (Lipan) Apache—that a "Jumanes" group was spoken of as an important division of the Texas Apache, adding that by 1746 some "Apache Jumanes" were reported to be "living just north of the Rio Grande." "But after the middle of the eighteenth century," he says, "Jumane was a name applied in New Mexico to the Indians called in Texas the Taovayases—Wichita Indians always hostile to the Apaches."[28]

Although Forbes does not attempt to assign any actual date for the acquisition of horses by the Indians that he identifies as the "Jumano Apache," he believes it to have been sometime after their Mexican allies, the Julimes, came to own them and offers proof that the Julimes had them by the year 1677.[29] Only two years earlier—in 1675—the Spanish expedition of Fernando del Bosque had traveled through Texas from the mouth of the Conchos River northeastward to the vicinity of the modern Edwards County without encountering any horses, much less Indians on horseback. But in 1684, the Mendoza-López expedition met Indians with horses north of the Big Bend country in Texas on the Pecos River, and recorded that the Apache stole some of their mounts.[30] By 1691, we know from an account found in Father Damian de Massanet's diary that the Lipan Apache of Texas were experienced horsemen and practiced armored horse warfare.[31]

With Eastern Apachean groups like the Kiowa-Apache, the matter of when they acquired horses is equally uncertain. The earliest definite reference I have found of their possession of them occurs in a report of the French explorer La Salle, written in 1682 and based upon information obtained at St. Louis from a captive Pawnee youth. Identifying the Kiowa-Apache by the name "Gattacka" and their allies, the Kiowa, as the "Manrhoat," he described these Indians as living south of their confederates, the Pawnees. Of them he wrote that they

> sell horses which they apparently steal from the Spanish in New Mexico. These horses, I expect, will be quite useful to us. The savages use them in war, in hunting, and in transporting everything, but they are not in the habit of giving them shelter, rather allowing them to sleep outside, even in the snow, and giving them nothing else to eat except what they are allowed to graze. This kind of horse must be very strong and long-winded, for it is said that one can carry the meat from two bulls, which weighs almost a thousand pounds. What makes me think they get these horses from the Spaniards is that

The Salt River Canyon forms a boundary between the two Western Apache reserva-tions: the San Carlos and the White Mountain (or Fort Apache). From 1638 on, historical documents contain much material about Apache raids for horses.

although they go naked, when they ride a horse they wear a hat of tanned hides which they make themselves.[32]

The dates of acquisition by Western Apache groups and those Chiracahua Apache living in southern Arizona are even more uncertain. Forbes believes that the Apache in Arizona "probably acquired mounts gradually after 1630–1640."[33] I think it quite probable that they procured some horses from raids on Spanish ranches of New Mexico and northern Chihuahua, as well as from other Indians of this area, before they began to acquire them from the mission-ranches, which were established by Father Eusebio Kino in southern Arizona and northern Sonora at the turn of the seventeenth century. However, almost nothing is certain here except that none of the Apache raided Sonora regularly until sometime around 1688. A Spanish record by an unknown Jesuit padre, entitled *Rudo Ensayo,* assures us of this.[34]

Transmission into Navajo and Apache Folklore

In summary, from the limited research I have done on the spread of the horse in the Southwest in order to date its transmission into the realm of Navajo and Apache folklore, I would prefer to date the New Mexican Apache's acquisition of the horse sometime between 1600 and 1638, because from 1638 on, historical documents concerning New Mexico and northern Mexico contain much material about Apache raids for horses.[35] With the Navajo, I prefer to assign no date before 1680 because they are seldom designated "Navajo" in earlier raid documents, even though it is likely that the Navajo, going under the name "Apache," were involved in some of the heavy raids on the Spaniards' ranches, which began in the late 1630s. It is considerably later in history—around the time of the Pueblo Revolt of 1680—that the name Navajo appears frequently in historical writings. Other scholars agree, however, that the Navajo acquired horses sometime after 1630 and were an established horse people at the time of the reconquest of New Mexico by de Vargas in 1692.[36]

With the Eastern Apachean groups such as the Lipan and Kiowa-Apache, I think it safer to date their adoption of the horse in the 1680s because of the specific references to the Texas Lipan as horsemen in 1691 by Father de Massanet and to the Kiowa-Apache as horse traders in 1682 by La Salle. With regard to the Western Apache and the Chiricahua Apache in Arizona, I prefer to hold the line at 1688 because of the concentrated raiding that began on Sonora and continued from that time until these Apache were subdued by United States forces. Thus, for a period of roughly three hundred and fifty years—in some instances around three hundred and eighty years—the horse has been at work on traditional forms of Navajo and Apache folklore.

The Importance of the Horse

The acquiring of horses by the Southern Athapascans was of major importance to their lifeways. It brought greater mobility and freedom of movement to those semi-nomadic people who had previously known only the tedious foot journeys of a few miles a day with all their possessions carried on their backs or loaded on slow pack dogs. Neither man

A conical-shaped tepee like this one at Mescalero was widely used by some of the buffalo-hunting Apaches after the acquisition of the horse because it could then be easily transported on a travois.

nor dog was a match for the wonderful new animal that could carry so much more at a pace twice as fast. In their pre-equestrian days, the people could not possess much property or make very long marches when they moved. In Navajo and Apache societies, continual movements within de-fined territories were essential for their mode of subsistence. With horses, they could make their seasonal rounds, carrying all their goods on pack horses while the entire family rode to the new camp in previously un-known comfort.

Widening the territory over which the Navajo and Apache ranged, the horse also increased contact with other peoples. They could trade and barter their goods more easily. New trade ties meant more trade, for as with trade in any other society, new possessions and property increased the need for more possessions and property.

Horses could be butchered for food, and the Navajo and Apache, more than other Southwestern Indians, depended upon the horse as one of the basic sources of subsistence. The horse also enabled those Apache groups with the buffalo complex to hunt buffalo more easily when it was sought after by many other Indian tribes and the white man as well, and became increasingly difficult to find. What was true of hunting buffalo was of course true as well of hunting other game.

The very ownership of horses brought the individual Navajo and Apache added prestige and a place in society as warriors and wealthy men. A man who owned a horse could hold his head high. A poor man was a man who possessed no horses. A coward was a man afraid to go on raids to get them for himself and his relatives.

With such a great need for horses in their societies, it is no wonder that the amazing body of folklore, which we are about to explore, surrounds the horse of the Navajo and Apache today, or that their ceremonies, and the myths and symbols behind them, record an unusual story—the story of how they sang for horses.

Notes

1. Herbert E. Bolton, *Coronado on the Turquoise Trail: Knight of Pueblos and Plains* (Albuquerque: University of New Mexico Press, 1949), pp. 245–247.
2. Frederick Webb Hodge, George P. Hammond, and Agapito Rey, eds. and trans., *Fray Alonso de Benavides' Revised Memorial of 1634,* annotated by F. W. Hodge, Coronado Cuatro Centennial Publications, 1540–1940, IV (Albuquerque: University of New Mexico Press, 1945), p. 303.
3. Bolton, *Coronado on the Turquoise Trail,* p. 246.
4. Hodge, Hammond, and Rey, *Fray Alonso de Benavides' Revised Memorial of 1634,* p. 303.
5. Pedro de Castañeda, "History of the Expedition," in *Narratives of the Coronado Expedition of 1540–1542,* ed. and trans. George P. Hammond and Agapito Rey, Coronado Cuatro Centennial Publications, 1540–1940, II (Albuquerque: University of New Mexico Press, 1940), p. 214.
6. Ibid., p. 218.
7. Hartley B. Alexander, "The Horse in American Indian Culture," in *So Live the Works of Men,* ed. Donald D. Brand and Fred E. Harvey (Albuquerque: University of New Mexico Press, 1939), p. 67.
8. Castañeda, "History of the Expedition," p. 235.
9. Bolton, *Coronado on the Turquoise Trail,* pp. 261–262.
10. "Letter of Francisco Vázquez de Coronado to His Majesty, Giving an Account of the Discovery of the Province of Tiguex, October 20, 1541," in Hammond

and Rey, *Narratives of the Coronado Expedition of 1540–1542,* p. 186. See also Bolton, *Coronado on the Turquoise Trail,* pp. 253, 256, 262. The "Teyas" Indians are commonly identified as a Caddoan group who had foregone a settled, farming life to become buffalo hunters; however, other evidence suggests that they also may have been members of an Eastern Apache group. See John R. Swanton, *Source Material on the History and Ethnology of the Caddo Indians,* Bureau of American Ethnology Bulletin, No. 132 (Washington, D.C.: Government Printing Office, 1942), p. 35; John P. Harrington, "Southern Peripheral Athapaskawan Origins, Divisions, and Migrations," in *Essays in Historical Anthropology of North America,* Smithsonian Miscellaneous Collections, Vol. 100 (Washington, D.C., 1940), p. 512.

11. Castañeda, "History of the Expedition," p. 262.

12. See Clark Wissler, "The Influence of the Horse in the Development of Plains Culture," *American Anthropologist,* new series, XVI, No. 1 (January–March 1914), pp. 1–25. Wissler (p. 2) also noted that the Apache were among the first Indians to get horses. See also Francis Haines, "Where Did the Plains Indians Get Their Horses?" *American Anthropologist,* new series, XL, No. 1 (January–March 1938), pp. 112–117; Bernard Miskin, *Rank and Warfare Among the Plains Indians,* Monograph of the American Ethnological Society, III (New York: J. J. Augustin, 1940), p. 5, n. 2; D. E. Worcester, "Spanish Horses Among the Plains Tribes," *The Pacific Historical Review,* XIV, No. 4 (December 1945), pp. 409–417.

13. Haines, "Where Did the Plains Indians Get Their Horses?" p. 117; Wissler, "The Influence of the Horse in the Development of Plains Culture," pp. 9–10.

14. D. E. Worcester, "The Spread of Spanish Horses in the Southwest," *New Mexico Historical Review,* XIX, No. 3 (July 1944), pp. 225–226.

15. Fray Gerónimo de Zárate-Salmerón, "Relaciones de Todas Las Cosas Que En El Nuevo México Se Han Visto y Sabido, Así Por Mar, Como Por Tierra Desde El Año 1538 Hasta El de 1626," *Obras Inéditas de José Fernando Ramírez,* ed. Vargas Rea, Biblioteca Aportación Histórica, Segunda Serie (México, D. F., 1949), p. 36.

16. Fray Alonso de Benavides was the author of two memorials on New Mexico. The first, published in Spanish in 1630, appears in English in a translation made by Peter P. Forrestal. See Fray Alonso de Benavides's *Memorial of 1630* (Washington, D.C.: The Academy of American Franciscan History, 1954), p. 42. The second memorial, though basically a revision of his first, differs in some respects from it. Benavides rewrote parts of it, incorporating some new material, after he had returned to Spain. The second, which was written in 1634, was not published in English until 1945 when the translation of Hodge, Hammond, and Rey appeared. See their *Fray Alonso de Benavides' Revised Memorial of 1634,* pp. 85–89, 308.

17. Jack D. Forbes, "The Appearance of the Mounted Indian in Northern Mexico and the Southwest, to 1680," *Southwestern Journal of Anthropology,* XV, No. 2 (Summer 1959), p. 208.

18. Ibid., p. 200.

19. Ibid., p. 202.

20. Jack D. Forbes, *Apache, Navaho and Spaniard* (Norman: University of Oklahoma Press, 1960), p. 108. See also John P. Harrington, "The Ethnogeography of the

Tewa Indians," in *Annual Report of the Bureau of American Ethnology, XXIX* (Washington, D.C.: Government Printing Office, 1916), p. 575.

21. Forbes, *Apache, Navaho and Spaniard,* pp. 108–109.

22. France V. Scholes, "Juan Martínez de Montoya, Settler and Conquistador of New Mexico," *New Mexico Historical Review,* XIX, No. 4 (October 1944), p. 340.

23. Forbes, "The Appearance of the Mounted Indian in Northern Mexico and the Southwest, to 1680," pp. 200, 202.

24. Ibid., pp. 204–205.

25. Ibid., p. 204.

26. William Edward Dunn, "Apache Relations in Texas, 1718–1750," *The Quarterly of the Texas State Historical Association,* XIV, No. 3 (January 1911), p. 203.

27. For detailed research concerning the complexities surrounding the proper identification of the Jumano Indians and the various groups called Jumano, see W. W. Newcomb, Jr., *The Indians of Texas from Prehistoric to Modern Times* (Austin: University of Texas Press, 1961), pp. 225–245.

28. Dunn, "Apache Relations in Texas, 1718–1750," pp. 268–269.

29. Forbes, "The Appearance of the Mounted Indian in Northern Mexico and the Southwest, to 1680," p. 205.

30. Herbert E. Bolton, ed., *Spanish Exploration in the Southwest, 1542–1706: Original Narratives of Early American History* (New York: Charles Scribner's Sons, 1916), pp. 291–309, 335.

31. Dunn, "Apache Relations in Texas, 1718–1750," p. 203, cites as his source, "Diario de los Padres Misioneros, 1691" in an unpublished manuscript entitled "Memorias de Nueva España," XXVII, f. 100.

32. Translated from "Rivières et Peuplades: Feuille détachée, sans commencement ni fin, de la main de La Salle," in Pierre Margry, *Découvertes et éstablissements des Français dans l'Ouest et dans le sud de l'Amérique Septentrionale (1614–1754), Mémoires et documents originaux,* Vol. II (Paris: Imprimerie Jouaust et Sigaux, 1876–1886), pp. 201–202.

33. Forbes, "The Appearance of the Mounted Indian in Northern Mexico and the Southwest, to 1680," p. 202.

34. Anonymous (1763), *Rudo Ensayo,* trans. in 1894 by Eusebio Guitéras (Tucson: Arizona Silhouettes, 1951), p. 139.

35. For example, see Father Juan de Prada, "Petition of September 26, 1638," in *Historical Documents Relating to New Mexico, Nueva Vizcaya, and Approaches Thereto, to 1773,* recorded by Adolph F. Bandelier and Fanny R. Bandelier, ed. and trans. Charles Wilson Hackett, Vol. III (Washington, D.C.: Carnegie Institution, 1923–1927), p. 110.

36. See Richard Van Valkenburg and John C. McPhee, *A Short History of the Navajo People* (Window Rock, Ariz.: Department of the Interior, Navajo Service, 1938), p. 4.

The Horse of the Gods

T HE HORSE OF NAVAJO AND APACHE MYTHOLOGY IS A GLORIOUS HORSE—
a supernatural steed, springing from the fertile imagination of
the Southwestern Indians who produced it. To its creators it came
to be as much of a reality as the deities born in like manner from the
roots of their native religions.

The Concept of the Supernatural Horse

The Navajo and Apache express their concept of the horse their gods
rode in songs, myths, tales, and medicine rites. When they relate the story
of its splendid creation, they seem to step into the shoes of their deities
and culture heroes, turning themselves into supernatural horse breeders.
They tell of how they used the most precious gifts given them—sacred
jewels, potent feathers, fetishes, and plants—as well as nature's supercharged elements and forces to bring forth the mightiest horse of all. And
as the creature evolves, they stand before their own earthly models, and
by the magic they believe contained in a spoken wish, they try to sing
into these lowly creatures the powers of the one above.

Though the Navajo have sung many songs of the holy horses since
they first saw the white man's possession some time in the seventeenth
century, these words of a song belonging to one of their medicine men
named Tall Kia aȟ ni are characteristic of a common type of good luck
song the people sing when they wish their horses to be "beautiful horses—
slim like a weasel"—horses such as those they believe belonged to one of
their Twin War Gods.

A White Mountain horseman rides a palomino of the coloration of the lead mare in Sun's cardinal herd.

My horse has a hoof like striped agate;
His fetlock is like a fine eagle-plume;
His legs are like quick lightning.
My horse's body is like an eagle-plumed arrow;
My horse has a tail like a trailing black cloud.

His mane is made of short rainbows.
My horse's ears are made of round corn.
My horse's eyes are made of big stars.
My horse's head is made of mixed waters
(From the holy springs—he never knows thirst).
My horse's teeth are made of white shell.
The long rainbow is in his mouth for a bridle,
And with it I guide him.[1]

The Apache tribes, cousins of the Navajo in the Southern Athapascan linguistic family, echo the Navajo's sentiments. For, although the Southern Athapascans are broken up into seven separate linguistic families— Navajo, Chiricahua Apache, Jicarilla Apache, Kiowa–Apache, Lipan Apache, Mescalero Apache, and the Western Apache groups (Cibecue, Northern Tonto, Southern Tonto, San Carlos, and White Mountain)—they have all believed at one time or another in a related kind of supernatural creation of the horse. While it is true that none of the Eastern or Western Apache tribes saw horses before 1541 or acquired them in any numbers until around 1638, the horse is as deeply ensconced in their mythologies as if it had always been there. The almost extinct Lipan Apache possess a myth that relates that when their culture hero, Killer-of-Enemies, formed the first horse, he dwelt in what the Lipan call "the upper world, above the clouds." Shaping the animal with his hands, he used a dazzling array of nature's forces and elements, of plants and artifacts. First, he started to work on the animal's inner anatomy. He took a sturdy cornstalk and used it for the spine and legs, and according to the Lipan, from that time on the skeleton of the horse has been jointed like the stalk of corn. Then he found a substance that forms on the ground after a heavy rain and resembles soapsuds, and formed the lungs from it. He found some hailstones and put them together to mold the kidneys and the liver, and he used more hail to make the teeth. He got a bolt of lightning and fastened it on the inside of the nostrils to give his creation a fiery breath.

After he finished the inside, he started to work on the outer parts. He collected rain to form the mane and tail, and he also used rain, along with the rainbow, to form the hoofs. The Lipan say that today we can still see the results of his using the rainbow: it makes the hoofs of some horses—especially white and gray ones—look as though they are tinted. From dew Killer-of-Enemies formed the fetlocks, and unfortunately for mankind, under the hoofs he fixed an arrow, which makes a horse's kick very dangerous.

For the completion of his work of art, the culture hero had saved some of his finest resources. For a short while, he borrowed the crescent moon to form the ear, and he took the evening star down from the heavens long enough to make the horse's eye from a piece of it. From these luminaries his horse received the power to see and hear both day and night. Last of all, he gave his creation life. To do this, he drew in a whirlwind from each of the four directions and put them in four different places—one entered the flank, another went under the shoulders, and the remaining two penetrated the hips on either side. When the winds entered its body, the Lipan Apache's first mythical horse began to breathe and move, and Killer-of-Enemies had himself a fine stallion to ride from that time on.[2]

As late as 1928 when the ethnologist Aileen O'Bryan was collecting material in Mesa Verde National Park, a Navajo chief called Sandoval by his English-speaking friends, and Hastin Tló tsi hee (Old Man Buffalo Grass) by the Navajo, discussed with her in a similar way a myth of the creation of horses. Explaining the names of certain parts of the horse in the Navajo language, Sandoval recited those that a goddess named White Bead Woman gave his people to call these parts in the medicine rites for producing a horse. The names that the goddess gave are the ones that the Navajo have used ever since in their ceremonies and good luck formulas for bringing fine colts into the world. These are Sandoval's words:

> The horses' hoofs are *hadá huniye* [agate], the banded male stone. The hair of the mane and tail is called *nltsá najin,* little streaks of rain. The mane is called *é alinth chene.* Horses' ears are the heat lightning, that which flashes in the night. The big stars that sparkle are their eyes. The different growing plants are their faces. The big bead, *yó tso,* is their lips. The white bead is the teeth. *Tliene delné dil hilth,* a black fluid, was put inside horses to make the whinny.[3]

This account of Sandoval's is in basic agreement with a horse creation myth he had recounted some five years earlier to Dr. Pliny Earle Goddard, lifetime student of the Southern Athapascan languages and collector of Navajo and Western Apache folklore. However, he elaborated further for Goddard about the parts belonging to the horse's body. It should also be noted that part of this latter myth taught him by his maternal grandfather is similar to "The War God's Horse Song" of Tall Kia ah ni. This is not an unusual occurrence, since the Navajo get their inspiration for both secular and sacred songs from myths. Sandoval told Goddard that the horse's hoofs have stripes because they were made of mirage (variegated stones) and because the rainbow went into the making of its very gait. Its mane came from a small rain cloud, and its tail from black rain, while its intestines came from water of all kinds. Some of nature's most majestic forces and elements went into the composition of its head. Sandoval related that "distant lightning composed its ears. A big spreading twinkling star formed its eye and striped its face." The face itself was formed of living plants, and the growing vegetation that made up its face illuminated it at night. Large sacred beads composed its lips, and its teeth would not "wear out quickly" because they were formed of the Navajo's treasured white shell. Sandoval's mythical horse was indeed a forceful and beautiful creature—when it

Apaches believed in supernatural powers bestowed upon them by guardian horses who also gave them ceremonies to conduct. See *infra* pp. 130–133; p. 179.

neighed, the sound really came from a black flute inside its mouth. More-over, Sandoval supplied Goddard with some additional information about the horse's body, which is not included in the O'Bryan recording. It seems that red stone was used to produce the horse's heart, sunrays its bridle, and that even the dawn played a role in making up its belly, thus dividing it into two parts—one black and one white, which meant that it belonged to both day and night.[4]

These notions about the creation of the horse's body are found to be common when one further explores Southern Athapascan mythologies. A Chiricahua Apache shaman extended the association a step further in one of the ceremonial songs he sang. He used the names of the elements composing the horse to identify various parts of a saddle in ceremonial use. He called the saddle itself "strap lightning," the back of it the evening star, the sides the clouds, and the saddle blanket a cirrus cloud. The saddle horn was the sun, while the buckle was the moon, and the cinch the rainbow. He called the forehead of the horse abalone, and the ears whirlwind.[5]

Apache folk tales show us that certain organs of horses were thought to have magical powers, which could aid culture heroes in their perilous exploits with the monsters that troubled the Apache peoples before the culture heroes destroyed them. For instance, there is the Lipan Apache hero tale in which Killer-of-Enemies goes to slay the monster eagle, who lives in an inaccessible home atop a treacherous mountain. Needing some supernormal mode of transportation to carry him to the eagle's nest, he stopped a worthless-looking old horse that he chanced to meet along the roadside. Antonio Apache, the Lipan who recorded this tale for Opler in 1935, related that the culture hero asked the horse what he was good for. The animal replied that he was "good for many things"—in fact, he said he could help him in just about any way he wanted. Losing no time in enlisting the animal's aid, the protagonist immediately asked him for his entrails, and the old horse generously complied. The narrator said he "took out his entrails and gave them to Killer-of-Enemies," who "took them and wrapped them all around his body."[6]

Antonio Apache's version of this widely distributed type of Southwestern Indian tale concerning the culture hero's slaying of the eagle is interesting because it employs the motif of the horse's entrails to protect the culture hero in his encounter with the giant bird. While one version of a Chiricahua Apache tale does report that a culture hero "killed a horse or a cow" before his encounter with the huge eagle, and "wrapped" the animal's intestines "around himself," after he had filled them with its blood, other Southern Athapascan tales usually record that the hero either donned a war coat or depended upon the power of a "life feather" for safety under similar circumstances.[7]

Antonio tells us of how Eagle swooped down on Killer-of-Enemies, stuffed him under one of his huge wings and carried him up to his house where two eaglets anxiously awaited their father's return with the evening meal. Before leaving his children with their dinner, however, the big eagle decided to make certain he had killed the Lipan culture hero. According to Antonio Apache, "the eagle put his talons in and squeezed where he thought the heart was. But he did not penetrate more than his entrails. He thought he had killed Killer-of-Enemies and said to his children,

'Now eat. I'm going out to hunt.'"[8] Thus Eagle was tricked and met his death later at the hands of the mighty war god, who never missed a chance to kill a monster and who on this occasion was made invulnerable by the protective entrails of an old horse, who had certainly proved he was "good for many things."

The motif of the scrawny, worthless-looking old horse appears again in a hero tale told by the San Carlos Apache. This particular horse, "through which one could see grass," offers his hidden powers, in the form of his potent blood, to a folk hero in peril of being boiled alive in lead.[9] Though thin and ungainly appearing, the old sawbuck just happened to have the power to resuscitate himself; therefore he could graciously offer his neck to the hero in the moment of crisis. He told the hero to cut off his head, fill four buckets with his blood, bury his remains to the east, and then to do the following: "Wash himself with one of these pails of blood, drink one, and pour the remaining two into the pot of lead before he jumped in."[10]

The San Carlos Apache say that the hero did as the old horse told him to do, and the next morning when the people pulled the cover off the pot in which the hero had been boiled, they found him still very much alive. Furthermore, they add: "He got up and came out. He returned to his home and continued to live there happily."[11]

In summary, then, when we examine closely the information given us by the Navajo and Apache in their songs, myths, medicine rites, and tales, we are assured that these people conceived of their mythical horses—the worthless-looking horses of their tales as well as the glorious steeds of their myths—as possessing bodies composed of supernatural elements that gave them the necessary powers to perform wonderful feats.

With this concept of the supernatural horse in mind, it seems no wonder that the mythologies of all the Southern Athapascan peoples endorse the belief that their deities possessed horses before they allowed the people to have them. Their traditions say that the deities had had them since the beginning of time. While the Navajo and all the Apache groups have a horse creation myth relating the various ways in which the horse was created for humans by a culture hero or given by some benevolent deity in a ceremony, the mythological records are not very clear on how the deities themselves got their steeds.

The Deities' Creation of Horses

When the myths refer to such technicalities, most often the story is that the sun deity created horses for use in the heavenly world and that it was a very long time before earth people possessed them. Of course, this is not always the case. Sometimes other deities are instrumental in creating horses for the exclusive use of the gods in their world. Among the Navajo creation myths that tackle the problem of how the deities acquired horses for themselves, there is one recorded by Washington Matthews at the turn of this century from a Navajo medicine man named Hatáli Natlói (Smiling Chanter). In Hatáli Natlói's version, a god with many unusual and conflicting characteristics called Békotsidi seats himself at the northern end of a room across from his father, Tsínihanoai (Sun Bearer), at the southern end. In this position, he begins the arduous job of molding the very first horses, singing these words as he shapes them: "Horses of all kinds now increase. For them I make [sic]." Hatáli Natlói explained to Matthews that the reason the antelope is so much like the horse is that the father Tsínihanoai was involved in shaping it while the son Békotsidi labored with the horse. Nevertheless, later in the same recitation, Hatáli Natlói switched the roles played by the deities in creating horses and said: "While Day Bearer was making the horse and domestic sheep, Békotsidi was making antelope and bighorn."[12] Since neither Matthews nor Goddard, who edited his manuscript for publication after his death, explained this peculiar reversal of creation roles, I am at a loss to account for it here.

Trying to solve the extent of Békotsidi's creative labors, Matthews on another occasion wrote: "Some say that Békotsidi made all the animals whose creation is not otherwise accounted for in the myths. Others say that he and the Sun made the animals together. Others, again, limit his creation work to the larger game animals and the modern domestic animals."[13]

On the other hand, a modern student of Navajo folklore, Stanley A. Fishler, records that in the beginning of time, when the Navajo were living in the first of their four worlds, the gods assembled in hogans and "talked of making the various animals." He informs us that the hogans where the gods assembled are said to have been located atop Crown Point (Gobernador) and Reversible (Huerfano) Mountain—mountains located in the present state of New Mexico.[14] In a version of a Navajo creation myth he collected in 1950 from a Navajo medicine man named Frank Goldtooth, four gods called Begochiddy (Békotsidi) of black, blue, yellow, and white colors are said to have created the game animals at this time. Goldtooth told Fishler that "the four Begos [Begochiddys] took various colored clays and earths and molded them into the shapes of the various animals. After each was formed, one of the Begos would say to the figure, 'You will be a _____,'" telling the animal its name. Goldtooth explained that all the animals except the domestic animals "were created in this way," adding that "while the Begos made all the game, the other gods were making the sheep, horses, goats. . . ." Since Goldtooth placed the creation of the sun deity after the creation of the game and domestic animals in his version, he does not include Sun among the gods who molded the horses for their own use in the other world.[15] However, according to Goldtooth, one of the four Begochiddy deities—the one named Black Begochiddy—did show the unnamed gods creating horses how to bring life to their creations. Goldtooth said: "They were having a hard time making the animals come alive so Black Begochiddy went over and said, 'What is the matter here? Why don't you make the animals come alive?' He then said, 'Bego' and they became alive and stood up. After Bego did this, all the gods could make the animals come alive themselves."[16]

In Goldtooth's version of the Navajo creation myth, Black Begochiddy does an amusing thing. He finds so attractive the jackasses created by the gods who formed the domestic animals that he selects one of them for his own special mount. Perhaps the reason he fancied the jackass was that the appearance of the animal is said to have been rather different from what it is today—"very big with large hoofs, a long mane and tail." Nevertheless, his preference for the jackass made all of the other animals jealous. To restore peace and make the other animals happy with him again, the deity proposed that the animals race around the horizon, and Goldtooth said they consented to do so when Black Begochiddy said that he would give the winner a "special name."

Secretly, Black Begochiddy favored the two jackasses running in the race, so he took particular pains to groom them before they ran. In grooming them to be winners, he changed their appearance considerably, which accounts for their present form. Goldtooth explained that he

> laid rainbow people under the feet of the two jackasses . . . then made
> their feet very narrow and said, "I have to do something about you.
> This will bother you while you run the race." So he pulled out part of
> their tails and left a little one. Then he began to take the hair from
> the mane. Each time he did this he said, "Some of this hair will be in
> your way, so I will tear it off." The jackasses' ears were still long, but
> the race was ready to start.[17]

When the race started, it seemed for a while that Black Begochiddy had made a mistake in favoring the jackasses. They ignored the race until it was halfway finished, meandering around, "smelling the ground," while the other animals raced with all their might. But during the last lap, the jackasses got busy, made a record-breaking dash for the finish line, and came through as victors, "running with their noses in the air." Goldtooth related that Black Begochiddy rejoiced because his favorites won, but he confided that they won because the deity had put "rainbow spectrum underneath their feet."[18]

The late Gladys Reichard, longtime friend and interpreter of the Navajo, described *be'yotcidí* (the spelling she preferred) as the youngest son of Sun, "spoiled by his father, who put him in control of many things, such as game and domesticated animals." But she said the young god's job was to create antelope, mountain sheep, elk, cows, donkeys, jackrabbits, cottontails, prairie dogs, and wood rats. Horses, mules, goats, sheep, and deer were left to Father Sun.[19]

The most common belief among the Apache about the way the deities acquired horses for themselves is that Sun, sometimes called Yusn, and at other times Giver-of-Life, created the horse as well as many other things for use in the gods' world. Later, Sun let the Twin War Gods, Killer-of-Enemies and Child-of-the-Water, choose which of the animals and plants would be given to the white man, which to the Indian. One White Mountain tradition records that the creation took place at Sun's home and that "on one side, horses were being made and on the other deer," the latter by a deity identified only as *Iltca'nailt'ohn*.[20] Clearly, this particular myth echoes the Navajo myth collected by Matthews in which game and domestic animals are created simultaneously, but on opposite sides of a room.

The Deities' Use of Horses

The belief that the sun or the moon could be described as riding a horse does not appear incongruous to the Navajo or Apache. Perhaps they equate the motion and rapid changes of these heavenly bodies with the rapid, changing motion of a horse. One Navajo, who had apparently been unable to settle in his own mind the question of whether the moon rode a horse or not, suggested something of the sort when he commented to a fellow moon watcher: "The moon is a funny thing. It is always changing its size and moving around. I wonder if it rides a horse."[21] In fact the idea of the movement of heavenly bodies seems to be so closely associated with the movement of the horse that one Navajo myth explains that there was no way to move the sun deity until the Holy People who created him decided to put him on horseback.[22]

Sun probably possessed more horses than any of the other deities; that is, if we can calculate these statistics from his horseback rides through Navajo and Apache mythology as compared to those by other deities. All over the heavens, Sun rides about on his horses, appearing to humans

Frank Mitchell, 1881–1967, Blessing Way singer of Chinle, Arizona, recorded much lore about the deities' horses, including the creation myth of the Navajo, which contains the story of the origin of horses. *Infra*, p. 285. (Courtesy David P. McAllester)

from time to time and then just as magically disappearing. One Navajo myth describes the sky "dip[ping] down and touch[ing] the earth to let the [Sun's] horse ascend," but a White Mountain Apache myth relates the opposite—the earth going down and the sky coming up as Sun's stallion climbs the heights.[23] At noon the deity's steed stands still above the ground with no hoof touching it.[24] Navajo traditions say that this is the time when the animal and his master stop to eat at the hole that opens into the center of the sky—a place the people locate directly above Mount Taylor in

New Mexico. Sometimes they called this sky opening Nitsi yá hatsis, a term meaning literally "the place where the Sun Man has his lunch and his horse eats out of a basket."[25]

White Mountain Apache mythology records that Sun owned some trappings for his horses that had the power to fasten themselves on without any assistance from him. A wise fly who knew about the hidden power of the equipment explained it to the twin culture heroes in this way: "Everything is alive; the rope on the horse moves about of itself. The saddle will jump on of itself."[26] It was said that when the saddles, the blankets, and the bridles fastened themselves onto the horses under their own power, they made a "sound 'gij' of moving leather and 'tsil' as they came to rest." In this myth, we also see how well-disciplined Sun's horses are. The deity is pictured as driving two of them up to a post in front of his dwelling, "where they stood without being tied."[27]

The Sun's Cardinal Horses

Sun possessed entire herds of horses in each of the colors of the cardinal directions, the Navajo and Apache believe. In Navajo mythology his horses were lovingly cared for in the other world by a guardian who was formed of mirage and thus called Mirage Man. A peek inside Sun's heavenly corral was not an everyday occasion, but once, according to a Navajo myth that was recorded movingly by Edward Sapir and Harry Hoijer, Mirage Man opened the gates of this huge enclosure and showed the cardinal horses to a culture hero named Turquoise Boy. When this youth, who was at that time searching for horses to give to the people, looked behind the gates, he was overwhelmed by what he saw. And small wonder—most of us are astounded too when we share with him the fabulous view of the Sun's corral. As the account from this myth opens—an account phrased in a typically Navajo way—we find Mirage Man conducting his inquisitive earth visitor on a tour of the eastern wing of the stables and commenting about the holy white horses inside:

> "Here they are, those with which in time to come (people) will live," he said. . . . He opened a door toward the east, they say. The place was so large that it extended as far as one could see. . . . At the entrance, white shell was prancing about, they say, white shell in the likeness of a horse. . . . Gracefully doing like this, lifting its foot continually, it was prancing about, they say. All of different kinds, white shell horses extended off in great numbers. . . . A great amount of mist-like rain falling on them continuously, they extended off in great numbers. . . . Blue birds fluttered over their heads, they say.[28]

This myth tells us that after showing Turquoise Boy these holy white horses in the first enclosure, Mirage Man continued his tour with a visit to another wing of the place, built just like the eastern one, but facing the south this time. In this place, a great turquoise horse tied with a handsome turquoise-blue rope was prancing about at the entrance, and from him had sprung the many blue horses that stood behind as far as the culture hero could see. The youth could also see that rainbows formed an arch over the sky around the blue horses while blue swallows fluttered over them, doubtless empowering the horses with the speed and endurance they contained in their blue feathers. The birds also symbolized the happiness and the immortality surrounding Sun's herd.[29] Again, the horses were enveloped by a mist, which only intensified their beauty.

Now, there remained only two other enclosures—a western one and a northern one—and as before, Mirage Man showed the youth these places too. Basically, they resembled the other two, except that the horses, ropes, and birds inside each one differed entirely in coloration. The western horses and the things surrounding them were yellow, while the northern horses and the things surrounding them were spotted.[30]

The horses of the cardinal directions, which Mirage Man showed to Turquoise Boy, are sacred to the Navajo. Like the Navajo, the various Apache peoples also have sacred horses and station them, according to their colors, at cardinal points relevant to the particular color patterns employed in their myths. In the above myth, it will be noted that the Navajo color circuit employed for the quadrants is white—east; turquoise (blue)—south; yellow—west; and spotted—north. It must be stated at this point that neither the Navajo nor the Apache have any one fixed color circuit that they can always be depended upon to employ for the cardinal points. Instead, they use a number of different cardinal color patterns to suit particular ceremonial needs. For instance, black and red occur frequently at cardinal points. However, when a particular color circuit is employed it does run either clockwise—east, south, west, and north—or in paired groups, such as east—west; south—north. Likewise, within a particular color circuit, there is a fixed sequence of colors at certain cardinal points.[31]

The Navajo and Apache also have directional color associations for certain stones and shells, which, because of the religious significance attached to them, play important roles in their mythologies, ceremonies, customs, and beliefs. These stones and shells are also commonly associated with the cardinal horses, as the above myth illustrates in its references to the horses of white shell and of turquoise. A fine example of this association is supplied in some information that the Navajo named Hatáli Natlói gave Matthews. Hatáli Natlói said that the first white horse was made of white shell, the first iron-gray horse of turquoise, the first black horse of cannel coal (jet), the first piebald horse of haliotis shell, and the first red (sorrel) horse of red stone (carnelian).[32] Thus, horses, according to their colors, are called after the different substances of which the Navajo believe the cardinal horses were made. For that reason, the Navajo speak of turquoise or gray horses as *dolízi lin,* red stone or sorrel horses as *bástsili lin,* cannel coal or black horses as *bászĭni lin,* and haliotis or spotted horses as *yolkaí lin.*[33]

The best way to throw light on the symbolism of the different colored horses associated with the cardinal points is to focus our attention on each type of horse and examine it as it is found represented in the myths, tales, ceremonies, beliefs, and paintings of the Navajo and Apache.

The White Shell Horse

First of all, in the preceding myth concerning Turquoise Boy's tour of the sun's corral, there is the white shell horse, which the culture hero saw "prancing about" at the eastern wing of the enclosure. The white horse of the cardinal directions is also sometimes called "white bead" horse in Navajo and Apache myths, with reference to the small, flat, white beads the Navajo and Apache often use in ceremonies to replace the white seashell, since the latter is more difficult to obtain. These white beads are often called wampum by the white man.

The earthly model for this cardinal horse is an albino, or any horse of solid white coloration—an animal that in the language of horse lovers has always been a mount fit for a king. Navajo mythology expresses this same regard for the white horse and often describes the sun and moon deities riding about on their elegant, milk-white steeds. In the foregoing myth, it will be noted that the white horse occupies the east, his most common cardinal position in Navajo mythology, for the Navajo frequently associate white with the color of dawn or early morning light, which banishes the shadows and mysteries of night.[34] Because of this association, it is said that a Navajo who owns a white horse feels himself fortunate and believes he will have no bad luck when he rides it.[35]

Sun's dawn horse plays a prominent role in a version of the myth concerning the Twin War Gods' visit to their father's house, which Maud Oakes recorded from a famous Navajo scout and medicine man named Jeff King.[36] King told Oakes that at the beginning of time the Navajo's first holy beings chose this white horse for the young sun deity to mount each morning as̆ he carried his burden of light into the sky. He told too of how the Twins, at a much later time, saw this horse at the deity's home in the other world and of how they met their previously unknown sister—Sun's daughter—who helped their father catch his horse every day. "Each morning," she would shake "a rattle to call the white horse for Sun to ride," he explained. Implying a change of its color with a change of its cardinal position, King also said that Sun's horse "moves around as it faces the four directions."[37]

The white horse the Twins saw appears in a sandpainting that King made for Oakes to copy and reproduce with her recording of the text of his myth. In this sandpainting, the white horse resembles one of the small stone horse fetishes the Navajo use ceremonially. It is depicted as standing between the colors of darkness and of light—in other words at dawn—above the eastern wing of Sun's house. At some distance away, outside the opposite end of this house of four directions, Sun's daughter is shown standing below the yellow and turquoise colors of earth and skylight, ready, it appears, to summon the deity's horse.[38] King informed Oakes that this sandpainting was used in Navajo ceremonies "when a person wants something plenty: weapons, seeds, good crops, horses, beads."[39]

Most versions of the Navajo myth concerning Sun's courtship of Changing Woman (a goddess sometimes referred to as White Shell Woman) say that when Sun first appeared to woo her, he was dressed in white and chose to ride his splendid white horse, which sported a bridle and a saddle of the same color.[40] The deity's choice of the white horse for this occasion signifies something else this time. First of all, Sun and his horse are attired in white to complement the theme of whiteness surrounding White Shell Woman. But more important is the purpose of Sun's visit to the goddess, who was then but a girl out gathering seeds. He wishes to instruct her as to how she might accomplish conception. The fact that Sun insisted on white dress for both himself and his white steed at this particular time "apparently differentiates," as Reichard says, "the naturally sacred from the profane."[41] Newcomb lends support to such an interpretation by identifying white as "the color of purity and of the spirit"—qualities commonly associated with the goddess whom the Navajo picture as being almost entirely above reproach.[42]

White horses also appear at the third station in another of the color circuits the Navajo employ, and here they symbolize the moon deity's horse. This particular circuit employs the paired groups of colors I mentioned earlier; for instance, blue in the east is paired with white in the west. Newcomb calls the law governing this kind of circuit, "the law of

opposites," or of "twin powers," and illustrates it in this way: "For example, when the blue sun is painted in the east, the white moon is always
in the west. . . ."[43]

Moon's horse is addressed third in a prayer to the holy horses in the
Navajo ceremony known as Flint Way; it is called "horse of the moon,
who puffs along the surface of the earth."[44] The third zone of the west is
also frequently regarded by the Navajo, and by the Apache too, as being
the home of the goddess White Shell Woman, who sometimes represents
the moon. Though Moon often appears as a female goddess in Navajo
and Apache mythology, this deity can also be masculine.[45] In one Navajo
myth, the elder of the Twin War Gods encounters the male moon deity
mounted on his white shell horse and riding behind Sun. Moon and
some of the other heavenly deities have come out early to accompany
Sun in a late afternoon ride toward the west. [46]

White horses in the mythology of the Apache do not seem to be
esteemed as much as they do with the Navajo. When Apache myths mention a white horse, it is usually placed at northern or southern positions,
apparently with little more significance than that of just being another
one of the cardinal steeds, necessary to complete a certain color sequence.
In fact, apparently the only important relationship of the white horse
with an Apache deity occurs in White Mountain mythology where this
horse is described as being the mount for Tobatc'istcini (Child-of-the-
Water), the younger of the Twin War Gods. The very fact that this horse
belongs to the younger brother—the weaker twin whose subordinate
role appears in sharp contrast to the forceful one played by the elder
brother in the majority of Southern Athapascan myths—only stresses the
white cardinal horse's lack of prestige among the Apache. A case in point
is that a White Mountain myth makes an issue of having the Twins' mother
order her younger son to stay off the mount belonging to her one day
when she sees him riding it. She tells him to ride instead the "white
gelding," which represents his color in the myth.[47] This incident implies
that Child-of-the-Water lacks the strength of his aggressive big brother
and is destined to tag along most of the time in his shadow. Since Child-
of-the-Water's cardinal colors are associated with those of his mother—
yellow and white—throughout this Apache myth, and since she is also
identified with the moon in the same account, this may explain why he is
made to ride the emasculated white horse.[48]

Further, the white horse in Apache tales is often presented as one of
the slower mounts. In fact, after reading through Apache lore, one gets the
feeling that the white horse was considered more of a dress horse than a

swift horse. Interesting glimpses of this attitude are shown throughout a long Jicarilla Apache tale, telling of the exploits of the folk hero Dirty Boy in horse raids and on the warpath. In one scene of this tale, an old Apache chief is presented with two horses—a white and a black—that his men have captured in a battle with the Sioux Indians. The tale recounts how the old man used the horses for separate purposes. On the white horse, he rode in stately fashion slowly around camp giving orders to his people. But when he got ready to go to war, he proudly donned his warbonnet and "mounted his black horse."[49] There are also humorous episodes in White Mountain, Lipan, and Chiricahua Apache tales when the sly trickster Coyote paints white horses, mules, and burros black and trades them to gullible buyers for better mounts.[50]

The Black Horse

Generally speaking, the Apache prefer the black mythical steeds because they associate them with the sun and other powerful forces—for example, White Mountain Apache myths often refer to the deity as Black Sun and to his swift mount as Black Wind Horse.[51] A San Carlos Apache myth verifies that Sun's favorite horse was a black one with "a small white spot on his forehead," emphasizing the point several times that this was "the horse Sun went everywhere with."[52] The white spot on the horse's forehead has special significance too, for the Apache share a belief, also common among the Navajo, that a horse with a white spot on its forehead, or with a bald face, signifies that it has particular characteristics of intelligence, speed, and power.[53] A Lipan Apache myth describes the herd of cardinal horses as being guarded by an intelligent "black stallion with a bald face."[54] Such a horse is also ridden by the elder of the Twins in a mythical race around the world—a story the Navajo also possess. The Apache myth differs in many ways from the Navajo one, but the basic elements are the same. Like the Navajo hero, the Apache hero needed desperately to borrow a swift mount from Father Sun to beat his opponent on the race track around the edge of the world. Unlike the Navajo hero, who wanted only Sun's blue horse, the San Carlos Apache's best jockey desired especially Sun's black horse with the white spot on its forehead. When he broached his problem to Sun, his father was reluctant to lend him a mount; Sun said evasively that "none of his horses looked good." However, after a little persuasion, he finally had a change of heart and offered to lend his son a number of different colored steeds. The young war god's invisible friend, Air Spirit, who sat behind his ear and advised him on matters, whispered for him to refuse each one and to hold out for "the horse his father used when he travelled." This was good advice, for the sun finally gave in and led out from the east "the black one that had a small white spot on its forehead." And with that particularly fiery black stallion to ride in the race that day at the border of the earth, the youth easily defeated his opponent.[55] On another occasion, when Naiyenezgani, the elder of the White Mountain Apache Twins, had to relinquish Father Sun's horse and choose his own mount to ride on earth, a myth informs us that he "caught a black stallion." This particular mount represented the culture hero's color, just as the white horse stood for the color associated with his younger brother. Later on, the same myth reveals that Naiyenezgani's black stallion also had a white spot on its forehead.[56] Then, again, a choice of the same kind of horse is made by Dirty Boy's chief in a war scene from the Jicarilla tale, because the chief knows that the black horse with the white spot on its forehead will not tire in battle and will make him a swift mount.[57]

Outside mythology's realm, there are also Apache stories that illustrate the extremes to which an Apache would go for a good black horse. One of these stories concerns the famous Eastern White Mountain Apache Chief Diablo, who favored black horses. Diablo's daughter Anna Price told Goodwin of the severe punishment of an Apache who made the mistake of stealing a favorite black horse, killing it, and eating the meat. She said that her cousin, "Angry-He-Offers-Something-Slender," and some of the subchiefs from her father's group took the culprit over to Chiricahua Butte, a landmark some twenty miles south of Whiteriver, Arizona, and "when they got him there, they burned a hole through each wrist between the two arm bones, stood him up facing a pine tree, drew his arms about it, and pegged them together. Then they tied him up and left him to die." Anna Price said her cousin was so angry about what this man had done to her father's horse that he thought the punishment a just one. According to her, he told the subchiefs who helped him carry out the terrible sentence: " 'That's what he had coming to him. . . . My cousin always used to keep a bell on that black horse when he rode him. Now the bell is without a horse. It is not much good that way. We will leave him tied up there to die slowly. It will be harder for him that way.' "[58]

Because they associate it with the sun, the majority of the Apache groups most often place black in the east where it occurs first in their color circuits. Represented in ceremonies by the jet-stone, it is the most sacred color to all the Apache with the exception of the Kiowa-Apache, and it is often used ceremonially to imply extreme holiness or power.[59] Because of its ceremonial significance, the Lipan Apache observed a custom that required that when a shaman was asked to relate the myth concerning the acquisition of the Lipan's first horses, he was to be given a black horse and a set of trappings prior to telling it.[60]

The Navajo, on the other hand, usually place their black horses at the north rather than at the east. This northern cardinal horse represents the night sky and is called Sun's "black jewel" horse in one Navajo myth.[61] Though darkness can be associated with dreaded forces and places of danger, night is not necessarily considered an evil time by the Navajo, unless, as Newcomb observes, it is "cloudy, windy and moonless. Then it is said to be filled with evil spirits."[62] This mythical sky horse was depicted with great imagination by the late Adee Dodge, a modern Navajo artist, in a painting called "Space Stallion."[63] One look at Dodge's mighty midnight horse, which stands in the center of the sky on what appears to be the upper circle of the rainbow, leaves little doubt that he belongs to Navajo mythology. Though Dodge omits the white spot on the stallion's forehead, he has given him white ears, flowing white mane and tail, and a strong, sturdy body—all characteristics that emphasize the animal's prowess and stamina. The vigorous mount possesses too the "white stockings," which are said to have special significance, for, according to the Navajo medicine man Sandoval, if a "horse has white stockings, he also sees by [means of] them."[64] The fact is that any white shown on an almost solid-colored horse represents valuable power to the Navajo, and Dodge's "Space Stallion" has even the "white eyelashes" that Mirage Man singled out as a treasured detail on one of the cardinal horses he showed Turquoise Boy.[65] Also, just as Turquoise Boy saw certain birds flying above the horses of their particular coloration in the Navajo myth, we see a blackbird flying rapidly and gracefully over the head of Dodge's handsome horse. A black feather tied to a front leg is a fetish further assuring speed to the black horse.

The Red Horse

Unlike the other Apache, the Kiowa-Apache prefer red, rather than black, at the east in their traditional color sequence. Their preference for red may point to an influence from the Kiowa Indians—a Plains group, under whose protection these Apache have traveled and functioned as a band for as long as they can remember. However, they do associate red with dawn; a Kiowa-Apache who was narrating a myth in which red-east occurred explained to the recorder that it symbolized "morning sky."[66] The earthly models for the mythical red steed are horses with red coloration—bays, red-roans, and reddish-brown duns and sorrels. Except in Kiowa-Apache myths, where the mythical red horse assumes importance as the traditional horse of the eastern station, this steed plays a minor role in Navajo and Apache mythology. Sometimes the Navajo use this horse as a substitute in their color circuits, pairing it with a black mount to indicate such dangerous things as dark skies.[67] Accordingly, a Navajo tradition says that Sun mounts either his red horse or his black horse "when the heavens are dark with storm."[68] When the red horse appears in such a Navajo ceremony as the Flint Way—a ceremony employed to heal a person who has suffered any injury from a horse—it, as well as black, blue, and yellow horse spirits, is addressed in prayer as Sun's horse. It is represented in the Flint Way by a stone of a red color, which may be any of three stones used ceremonially—native redstone, red coral, or carnelian.[69]

The Turquoise Horse

The cardinal horse that Navajo mythology values most is the turquoise or blue horse. Much of the association that the black cardinal horse has for the Apache, the turquoise has for the Navajo; for this is the mythical horse the Navajo think of as being Sun's favorite—the one he rode all day. Undoubtedly, that is why Mirage Man, as mentioned earlier in connection with the Navajo myth, kept Sun's turquoise horse behind the second door of the otherworld corral—the door that opened to the south. In the color circuit employed in this myth, the blue to the south "signifies"—to use Gladys Reichard's words—"the bright blue sky of day." Thus, it seems consistent to reason that the Navajo would extend the association a step further and think of the sun as a deity riding his blue horse across the sky all day. Reichard, who made quite a study of Navajo color patterns, wrote that blue's position at the southern quadrant is more prevalent than that of white at the east. She labeled the color circuit running east—white; south—blue; west—yellow; and north—black as the Day-Sky sequence, and interpreted the arrangement to mean the following: white—dawn; blue—day sky; yellow—evening light; and black—darkness. Citing the Day-Sky sequence as the most popular color pattern among the Navajo, she noted that it was the one that she felt might be called the "normal" order, appearing "when there seems to be no question" about the place of the colors in the quadrants.[70] In the myth concerning Turquoise Boy's look at the sun's cardinal horses, the color pattern follows the Day-Sky sequence, except that in some places spotted is substituted for the black at the north, which appears elsewhere in this same myth.[71]

The majority of the Apache groups also generally place the blue horse to the south in the color circuits they employ, but the symbolism behind this cardinal position for them is obscure, unless, as may be the case, they place them at the south for the same reasons the Navajo do. The most common color circuit I have found in use among the Apache groups is black—east; blue—south; yellow—west; and white—north. This color sequence is popular with the Chiricahua, Lipan, Mescalero, and White Mountain Apache.[72] It is the one most frequently used by the Jicarilla Apache too, except that they have a tradition of placing glittering, sparkling, or spotted colors at the northern station instead of the white the other groups use.[73] So far as I know, no study has been made on color symbolism among any of the Apache groups, but this sequence, which also occurs sometimes among the Navajo, has been examined by Reichard and Matthews.[74] However, in their analyses of its use by the Navajo, neither of these scholars was able to offer any satisfactory interpretation of the symbolism behind each of the colors in this particular sequence as each relates to its cardinal position. Therefore, until a more thorough examination of this sequence has been made, the true significance behind the Apache's placing of blue horses in the south must remain obscure.

The Navajo and Apache conception of the true shade of blue differs considerably from ours. Blue, they feel, is the shade of turquoise, a color in which our eyes see hues of green and aqua. In the Navajo language, the very name of the turquoise stone—the stone associated with the blue horses in myths and ceremonies—means "the-particular-one-which-is-blue."[75] Naturally, no one in a sober frame of mind—not even a Navajo or an Apache storyteller—ever saw a horse that was literally the shade of turquoise. However, now and then a yarn will drift in about a strikingly colored horse, and Walker D. Wyman records one of them in his fine book on the wild horse of the western United States. Wyman relates with caution that "a living ex-mustanger tells of a friend living in Fredonia, Arizona ('whose word I would take on the subject') who caught a respectable horse that 'was absolutely green.' "[76] Few of us have this man's experience, but many Southwestern horse lovers know well the kind of horse that the Navajo call *dolízi lin,* and the Apache call "Sun's blue horse." This horse is either the blue roan, or else the grullo, an animal whose colors can range from mouse-gray to salt and pepper shades, some of which have a definite blue or mauve tint. In Southwestern saddle slang, a horse with blue shades is often spoken of as a "steelduster"; Spanish-speaking people frequently call it a *rosillo azul.* Robert M. Denhardt, a foremost authority on Southwestern horses, defines the perfect grullo as having a straight color without spots. "The main part of the body," he says, "is almost slate colored, while the points are always black." According to Denhardt, the grullo has "the reputation of being an extremely tough and hardy" horse.[77] These are the qualities that the busy Navajo sun deity would find essential for his long daily journey across the sky.

Two Navajo songs for good luck with horses picture for us their idea of the mythical turquoise horse. One song says that as it moves along, it does not raise dust; only glittering grains of mineral, of the sort the Navajo use in religious ceremonies, fly behind its speedy hoofs. When it gallops, sacred pollen surrounds it as dust would an ordinary horse. Through the pollen, it seems enveloped by mist, and the Navajo speak poetically of mists. They say that "mist on the horizon is the pollen that has been offered to the gods."[78] The other song, which the elder of the Twins is said to have sung for good luck in the Navajo version of the horse race around the world, extols, in the youth's own words, the powers of the mighty blue stallion. Here is the way part of it goes:

> The turquoise horse prances with me.
> From where we start the turquoise horse is seen.
> The lightning flashes from the turquoise horse.
> The turquoise horse is terrifying.
> He stands on the upper circle of the rainbow.
> The sunbeam is in his mouth for a bridle.
> He circles around all the people of the earth
> With their goods. Today he is on my side
> And I shall win with him.[79]

Many intimate glimpses of the sun with his favorite horse are given in Navajo mythology. First of all, Sun was ever mindful of the needs of his powerful turquoise stallion, which was larger than an ordinary horse.[80] One of the deity's first remarks after he had been created and put in the sky concerned the care of his majestic blue horse. As he went on his initial trip across the heavens, Sun looked for a nice place to pasture his mount at the noon hour. Approaching the center of the sky, he discovered a likely spot and said: "The blue horse that I ride will eat there." Perhaps his preoccupation with the pasturage of his horse accounts for the fact that he, in the Navajo myth that reminds us of Phaeton driving the chariot of the sun, scorched the earth on his first four trips across the sky.[81] Apparently, though, the turquoise horse was well pleased with the unusual kind of pasture Sun chose for him. The first of the Navajo songs discussed above describes him "neighing joyously" as he stands on precious hides of all kinds that are spread out across the sky to symbolize clouds. There in that cloud pasture, he feeds on the tips of lovely new flowers and drinks of four mingled waters from a stream that connects with the four regions of the world.[82]

Other Navajo mythical incidents show "Sun returning home" from work "on his big turquoise horse." Sun's wife and mother could always recognize this horse by the "loud galloping noise" it made as it came up to the hogan late in the afternoon.[83] Once, this horse is even stolen from Sun's premises at night by some Navajo medicine men practicing the art of raiding for the first time.[84] Indeed, the association of the blue horse with the sun deity is so common in Navajo mythology that one version of the myth concerning his courtship of Changing Woman goes so far as to take him off the white shell horse more frequently associated with this theme and to put him on a turquoise horse, which he is described as riding right up to the door of the goddess's hogan.[85]

Rarely is Sun's favorite horse pictured as blue in Apache mythology. However, two myths—one from the San Carlos Apache and the other from the White Mountain Apache—do record such instances. Both myths associate the blue horse with the sun-in-the-sky motif. In the San Carlos myth, Sun takes the elder Twin for a ride with him on his best blue, which prances down "a trail of blue metal." The youth and his father ride the powerful steed until they reach "the center of the sky," where it is said that Sun "put the boy on a black cloud and shot him down [to earth] with lightning." This gives the San Carlos culture hero his fourth Apache name: "Shot down with lightning."[86] On the other hand, the White Mountain example identifies the blue horse with the sun-in-the-sky motif through-out the story. The White Mountain people say that when the Twins visited Sun, they saw the special saddle room in the deity's dwelling where he kept his and his wife's elaborate horse trappings. They learned that the beautiful blue saddle, blankets, halters, bridles, and ropes were special trappings of Sun's favorite mount while those of another color lying beside the blue equipment belonged to the mare owned by Sun's wife. Because the Twins were such smart boys and Sun and his wife were impressed with them, Sun decided to lend them his handsome blue stallion, as well as the pretty mare belonging to his wife and the splendid trappings for both horses, to ride to earth. As the boys got ready to leave Sun's house and start the trip back to earth, the deity instructed the youths about what to do on the hazardous journey ahead of them. He told them that his horse and his wife's would take care of them, since they knew "the dan-gerous places on the way back."[87] Implying that his blue (gray) stallion was familiar with the trail across the sky, the myth informs us that the deity said: "Children, this stallion will go well in the lead. Now mount the horses." According to the myth, Sun even explained to the Twins that this "horse should go in the lead because he knew the trail to the place midway between the earth and the sky," and he further emphasized his point by personally addressing the blue horse and commanding him to take charge until they reached that place. As they traveled, the Twins found that the blue horse knew the trail across the sky so well that he led them swiftly to the center of the sky and automatically changed places with the mare, who knew the way from there on.[88]

On earth, the elder brother rode his father's blue mount for a while until Sun decided it was time for him to take it back to the sky again. When Sun quietly retrieved the mount from his older son, one of the first clues Elder Brother had about what had happened to his mount was when he suddenly heard it "whinneying . . . from the top of the sky." Always ready to help the Twins in any crisis, Fly traveled up to the middle of the sky to spy on Sun, and returned to report to Elder Brother that Sun had indeed taken his blue horse back home. Fly said he saw this horse "standing behind him" at the center of the sky.[89] Since Sun's horse was lost from earth forever, Elder Brother rode another horse from that time on. His new mount was the one mentioned earlier—the black stallion with the small white spot on its forehead, which, as we have also seen, is the horse the Apache more commonly identify as Sun's favorite horse.[90]

Another switch in the colors of a deity's horse occurs in Navajo mythology when the moon deity takes over a blue horse, instead of a white one, so that Sun can be associated with the white dawn-steed. This particular Navajo myth employs a paired-color sequence. It stations a female Moon and her blue horse in the moon's western region to represent "Night Time Sun" and a masculine Sun and his white dawn-horse at the sun's eastern home to represent "Day Time Moon."[91]

The Navajo esteem for blue horses is often displayed in the paintings of four modern Navajo painters: Andy Tsinajinie, Adee Dodge, Quincy Tahoma, and Yel-Ha-Yah (Charlie Lee). Of these four, Andy Tsinajinie paints the only real turquoise-colored horse, and he does so with a sweeping vivacity. In his painting "Going to the Sing," Tsinajinie depicts a Navajo atop an ethereal turquoise steed, which moves along at an almost curving gait. The effect is one of violent motion and power defined in the winds, which seem to move the turquoise horse along. The faces of both the horse and rider are turned to the east; the streaming white mane of the horse and the dark hair of the rider fly forward in wild threads, giving a touch of fantasy to their movement. A series of mounds, resembling clouds, seems to float along the ground beneath the horse's hoofs. In fact, the whole scene looks like it happened in a Monument Valley of some other world.[92] Another Tsinajinie painting, "Young Navajo Riders," introduces a second turquoise horse with dilated nostrils and a spirited head bent down sideways. Tsinajinie perches a Navajo lad on top who rides along in true Navajo fashion. Following the lead of another youth mounted on a steed of another color, the boy seems as confident as one of the Twin brothers, as his horse gallops down a steep incline with little guidance and with only one hoof touching soil. In the background, distant eroded mesas and varicolored landmarks rise, which belong as much to mythology as they do to Navajoland.[93]

A better-proportioned blue sky-horse has been executed by Adee Dodge in the untitled work of his belonging to a museum in Spokane, Washington. As shown earlier in the discussion of his black "Space Stallion" painting, Dodge has once more revealed his dependability for executing compositions that are always in accord with Navajo beliefs. Again, we see the familiar motifs: the lone blue horse sporting a flying white mane and tail, its ears erect and outlined in white as it prances along a trail of precious stones. The fetishes displayed on its white-stockinged front legs further assure it the magical powers of speed and far-seeing that, as we have seen, such stockings promise.[94] In another painting, "So Proud the Blue Stallion," Dodge provides all these features to a spirited powder-blue mount, additionally furnishing it with a white spot on its forehead and a bald muzzle. These markings, along with the emphasized whites of the creature's alert eyes, convey that he wanted us to realize also that this stallion was made "by the big stars," to use the words of the Navajo medicine man Sandoval about such attributes. But instead of the precious stone fetishes for its forelegs, this time the artist has given his blue creation the same kind of eagle feather fetish that his black horse has to assure it speed and endurance of the same kind. Like his blue horse in the museum collection, however, the animal is additionally accompanied by a familiar companion: the bluebird. Dodge often included this bird in his paintings as a motif that in itself endorsed his close familiarity with the sacred horses of Navajo chants and lore. In addition to providing the protection, happiness, and health noted before, the bluebird, as Dodge frequently pointed out, appeared with the blackwing swallow in ancient migration legends to symbolize the division of the Navajo into two groups. One followed the bluebird of the daytime-sky toward the sea of the East. The other identified with the swallow and traveled with it toward the darkening skies of the West and the setting sun.[95]

The other two Navajo painters, the late Quincy Tahoma and Yel-Ha-Yah, favor dappled blue-gray horses in their works. Tahoma, who died in 1956, left fine close-ups of such horses in "The Winner Takes All" and

"Going to the Navajo Chant."[96] In the former painting, Tahoma gives his wild, dappled, steeldust stallion a bald face and white-stockinged legs, presenting him as he is caught preparing to fight a black stallion of similar markings over the drinking rights to a water hole. Two groups of mares stand calmly behind their stallions at a respectable distance. In "Going to the Navajo Chant," a very dignified Navajo husband, dressed in ceremonial costume, handles, with much poise and assurance, the reins of a spirited blue horse with handsome trappings and a dancing gait.[97] Equally as fine, but more serene, is the part-mauve, part-gray dappled colt, which is about to nuzzle a young fawn in Yel-Ha-Yah's "Friendship." Very much a part of this world, Yel-Ha-Yah's wide-eyed colt is a splendid example of the degree to which the blue tones of a horse can be carried.[98]

The Yellow Horse

Now, let us turn our attention to another mythical horse—the yellow horse. The Navajo and all the Apache groups usually place the yellow mare at the western cardinal station, since they commonly associate its coloration with the various hues of yellow seen in a sunset or in early evening light. The "abalone shell in the likeness of a horse," which the Navajo Mirage Man is said to have kept behind the third door of the sun's corral, is the sacred shell associated with this horse in myths and ceremonies by all the Southern Athapascan people.[99] Sometimes called ear shell, abalone is spiral-shaped, lined with mother-of-pearl, and perforated along its outer edges. The Navajo expression for abalone is "the-particular-one-that-is-iridescent, the-one-whose-various-colors-scintillate."[100] Oyster shell is also a common substitute for this shell.

The earthly models for this mythological horse are a yellowish-brown sorrel, a coyote dun, or a palomino. In White Mountain Apache mythology there is a tradition that the lead mare in Sun's herd of cardinal horses was a sorrel of a yellow-hued coloration. This sorrel mare is often paired with Sun's black stallion in color circuits, but in at least one instance its partner is Sun's handsome blue-gray horse. The mare is said by the Apache to have belonged to Sun's wife. Sun himself attested to his wife's ownership of this mare in a scene from a White Mountain myth, though he implied that the yellow trappings the animal wore belonged to him.[101] We get a good look at the yellow mare inside Sun's Apache corral in this same myth. She is pictured as standing quietly in the center of the herd of animals milling around in the enclosure, which differs completely from Sun's Navajo corral. She is a gentle, graceful animal with a white spot on her forehead and a beautiful long mane reaching the ground. Her handsome companion, Sun's favorite stallion, is running around outside the herd, guarding the deity's animals. When the Twins visited this corral with their father, he told them they could borrow some horses from him, if they could select the best two in his herd and rope them. The Twins listened to the counsel of their invisible companion, the all-wise Fly, and roped the stately yellow mare and her impressive companion—on this occasion, the blue stallion.[102] In another White Mountain myth, which will be examined in more detail in the next chapter, the yellow mare appears with her more traditional companion, Sun's black stallion, and the elder of the Twins discovers that the two animals are inseparable.[103]

It is logical enough that the White Mountain Apache associate this mare of yellowish coloration with Sun's wife, since the yellow horse is the one Navajo and Apache mythologies usually fix in the west. According to Southern Athapascan traditions, the goddess married to the sun deity lived in the west, and Sun retired to her home each evening to spend the night. In Apache, as in Navajo mythology, there are sometimes two goddesses who call themselves sisters and who are both wives of Sun. Both are goddesses of fertility. One is named White Shell or White Painted Woman, and she is frequently identified with the female moon deity. The other is called Changing Woman, and she is commonly endowed with supreme rule over the earth, which is always considered to be female. However, just as often the Navajo and Apache think of these two wives of Sun as being the same goddess—that is, one deity whose two names are used interchangeably and who is identified with the same things the separate goddesses are.[104]

Thus, it is also harmonious with their reasoning that the White Mountain Apache associate the yellow mare with both the female moon and the earth. The moon has important fertility attributes, and the early evening moon is most often yellow. Yellow is also a symbol of fertility on earth, for it is the color of the ripened harvest and of the yellow pollen, which has prime religious significance and which brings numerous blessings to the people.[105]

One of the White Mountain myths mentioned above clearly establishes the Apache's association of the yellow mare with the goddess of the earth. In the myth, Sun told the Twins to let his stallion guide them to the center of the sky, but when they had reached that point, he said "the sorrel horse was to lead because that one knew the way from there on." In this way Sun implied that his wife's yellow mare was the mount better acquainted with the earth-trail. When the boys reached the center of the sky where the trail toward earth began, the myth relates that "before they knew it the horses had changed places, and the sorrel was leading." It adds that "they thought the earth was far off but they soon found the horses were trotting along on the earth."[106]

In the same myth, the Twins' mother, White Shell Woman, who at that time lived on earth and was Sun's earthly wife, also represents Changing Woman, the goddess of the earth who lived in the world of the gods. In fact, in this particular version, Changing Woman (Sun's wife in the other world) forgave Sun for his infidelity to her and made White Shell Woman (his earthly wife) her sister-goddess, putting her in control of the same things. Later, Sun's earthly wife joined her sister in the gods' world where she is more commonly identified as the female moon deity.[107]

When the Twins discovered that the horses, which they had borrowed from Sun, had disappeared, their mother reminded them that the blue-gray stallion and the sorrel mare "were made for them." The White Shell Woman meant that these horses belonged to Sun and to her sister-goddess Changing Woman and to herself also, by way of her relationship with the earth goddess. No sooner had their mother said this than the Twins realized they could never recover their borrowed mounts, for they began to understand the full meaning of her words when they heard the distant whinneying of the missing horses. The White Mountain Apache say that "it sounded like the voice of the gray [blue] stallion that used to be his [Elder Brother's] horse. Another horse whinneyed in this direction [that is, the direction nearest earth] and the voice was like that of the sorrel mare [the mount Younger Brother rode for a time]. They knew their horses when they whinneyed and one said to the other, 'Brother, those are our horses whinneying but we cannot do anything about it.' " The Twins' mother also told her sons not to use Sun's yellow saddles anymore, and her instructions remind us again of Sun's own identification with this color too.[108]

After he had lost possession of the yellow mare, Younger Brother (Child-of-the-Water) rode two different mounts—the white gelding mentioned earlier and a sorrel gelding with a "white spot on its shoulder." This was appropriate too, for as I have also mentioned before, the younger twin is associated throughout this White Mountain myth with the white and yellow cardinal colors of the moon and earth goddesses. His sorrel gelding also became the steady companion of Elder Brother's black stallion.[109]

In numerous passages of *Dirty Boy: A Jicarilla Tale of Raid and War,* the merits of yellow horses are praised. First of all, there is the scene where Dirty Boy mounts a yellow horse he has taken from the enemy in preference to a white one. The tale offers the explanation that its hero "knew it was a good runner . . . he galloped off, leaving the enemies behind." Later on, when the raiders are resting, Dirty Boy's rival uncle lays claim to a yellow horse "with a necklace of antelope horns." In this way, he was making sure he had a good warhorse for the next attack; the necklace of antelope horns was as powerful as some eagle or hawk feathers, for any of these fetishes made a horse speedy.[110] At still another time, a Jicarilla Apache war chief who owned "a good sorrel pony, one with a long mane," decided to prove his prowess over a Jicarilla rival by showing his abilities at warfare in front of his men. He mounted his yellow horse, and the tale relates that he rode out "in front of the enemy. There was a leader on the other side wearing a big war bonnet and mounted on a white horse. The Jicarilla chief shot him with his arrow and the enemy pitched forward over the neck of his horse." The chief's Jicarilla rival, who was mounted on a gray horse, tried to match his chief's deed. He rode his gray horse out in front of the enemy too, and although he killed two of them, two others caught up with him just before he reached safety and killed him.[111]

The palomino, the sorrel, the buckskin, and the "coyote dun" have been the favorite subjects of various Navajo and Apache artists. A Jicarilla Apache painter named Frank Vigil has produced a number of studies of yellow horses, but my favorite from all of them is an untitled study of a palomino mare. Displaying white stockings, a flowing white mane and tail, and complete with a blaze on her face, Vigil's palomino mare prances across the desert like a circus horse on a holiday. The artist might well have intended his yellow horse for an Apache goddess, for his mare possesses all the features that would make her a mount befitting one.

Beautiful palomino mares have also been painted by such Navajo artists as Ed Lee Natay and Quincy Tahoma. In "The Desert Rider," Natay exhibits the sun god beaming his golden rays on a high-stepping palomino dressed up with a silver bridle and ridden by a stately Navajo woman. Although Natay's burnished-orange mare wears white stockings and possesses a bald muzzle, her mane is of a silvery-orange hue.[112] Of similar coloration and markings, but with a creamy-colored mane containing spun-silver threads, is the splendid palomino mare that serves as a mount for the wife carrying her baby in a cradleboard in Quincy Tahoma's "Going to the Navajo Chant." This mare serves as a companion to the blue stallion, which is ridden by the husband and which I have already described in connection with the paintings of blue horses. As the title of the painting implies, the Navajo family depicted is heading for a ceremony, and they are traveling across the desert at sunset. Companion birds fly over each horse and rider and toward one another from the eastern and western regions of the heavens.[113] Another Tahoma work, "Navajo Sing," shows the fondness this artist had for all kinds of yellow horses. While this painting is a large panoramic production containing tall horsemen seated on horses of every color, it displays an abundance of "coyote duns," buckskins, sorrels, and palominos.[114]

Yellow stallions are featured by other Navajo artists. Yel-Ha-Yah's "Startled Horse" has a body of a true yellow coloration that is handsomely set off by a black mane, black tail, and gray legs. With mane, tail, and legs of a similar color, the alert "Golden Stallion" of Beatien Yazz (Little No Shirt, Jimmy Toddy) commands his place on a hill covered with rocks and yucca somewhere in Navajoland.[115]

The Horse of Two Colors

The last kind of horse found among the Navajo and Apache cardinal herds is the horse of two colors—the dappled, the spotted, or the pinto. Such animals frequently appear at the north in color circuits of the Jicarilla, Lipan, and Navajo; for, as I noted earlier, the Jicarilla have a tradition of placing spotted colors at the fourth cardinal station, and the Lipan and Navajo sometimes vary their more traditional black or white with color combinations in this quadrant.[116] The haliotis shell of many-colored flecks, which resembles the abalone in texture, is often used in myths and ceremonies to signify spotted horses. So is agate. Sometimes the word "spotted" is substituted by the words "sparkling," "glittering," or "variegated" in Navajo and Apache myths and tales about this horse. In ceremonies when such a color impression is intended, either mixed jewels—tiny fragments from all the sacred stones—are used, or else a type of stone called "mirage stone." Mirage stones are white, gray, yellowish-striped stones, which are shiny when polished, causing a magnified reflection of a number of colors. For instance, the Navajo refer to certain types of quartz as "mirage rocks," and in one Navajo myth, some small stone horse fetishes of different colors, called "Mirage Quartz Rock Horses," are shown the Twins by a supernatural being named Frog Man.[117]

Star symbolism is frequently associated with spotted colors, or, for that matter, with spotted horses, appearing at the northern sphere, since the fourth station often represents the night. In fact, spots so commonly signify stars or fiery elements to these Indians that the Chiricahua Apache have come to consider a pinto horse a dangerous thing to have around during a thunderstorm. They seem to feel that its spots can draw lightning.[118] Besides star symbolism, another important function of spotted colors in

The pinto was the most favored mount of the Navajo and Apache. Like the Twin War Gods—their counterparts in myths and tales—Western Apache youths like these modern-day boys still gravitate to horses and horse-related activities when given the opportunity.

the northern quadrant is to summarize.[119] Thus, spotted horses can also be mentioned fourth in a series of mythical events involving the cardinal herd in order to emphasize the climactic nature of the fourth time. Mythologically and ritualistically, it is the fourth time a thing occurs that an act is considered fully culminated.

Much has been written in this chapter about the popularity of the white, black, blue, and yellow horses among the Navajo and Apache deities, but little has been mentioned about the favorite horse of the folk heroes and the guardian beings—the more common folk of the myths and tales—who, like their living Navajo and Apache counterparts, again and again prefer the pinto or piebald. Perhaps their preference for this horse is simply that they feel its colors combine in one the best characteristics of all horses. Assuming that the pinto is the Indian's "best horse," it might logically be considered the summary of them all. The Apache feeling for the pinto is best expressed by the Jicarilla's legendary horse raider, Dirty Boy, who requested that his Grandmother (whose dreams and prayers always came true) pray last for a "spotted" horse in her prayers for him while he was away on a raid. In this way he indicated to her his preference for a pinto on a raid where he might have obtained any color mount he desired.[120] The Navajo Mirage Man, who was himself a combination of colors, expressed the same sort of regard to Turquoise Boy when he was showing him around the sun's corral.[121] Implying the climactic nature of the fourth time, the Navajo myth states that the old man showed Turquoise Boy the horses he valued most when he opened the last door of the corral—the door that led to the "spotted horses" with "the white eyelashes."[122] In a similar way, Frog Man, who in another Navajo myth was acknowledged by Sun as knowing as much about the breeding of fine horses as anyone in the gods' world, treasured the "Mirage Quartz Rock Horses" he kept in a ceremonial basket. It was said that Frog Man "raised all kinds and colors of horses, sheep and goats," and that he, like the sun's corral keeper in the other myth, was formed also from a mirage substance—quartz rock, in this case.[123]

However, Navajo traditions say that their horse-loving sun deity prized his paints, his dappled and his spotted horses too—so much, in fact, that he kept an entire cardinal herd of them. Those who saw these beautiful horses must have had a rich experience, for one glimpse at them in a Navajo myth is enough to convince us that they combined all the colors Sun most enjoyed on the many good horses he rode in each of the quadrants. According to the myth, "to the east were ones with white bodies with all kinds of blue designs and spots. To the south was a blue one with white spots and all kinds of designs. There were also horses with white fingermarks with a blue background. To the west was a yellow one with black and white spots, while to the north was a black one with a yellow-reddish nose and white spots all over it."[124] Some of these horses in Sun's multicolored herd sound more like Appaloosas than any other kind of spotted horse, and doubtless some of them were, for Sun could certainly possess any kind of mount he desired. Nevertheless, while the Navajo and Apache undoubtedly possessed some of the fine spotted horses the Spaniards brought to the New World, not all horses with unusual combinations of spots are Appaloosas. Although the foremost scholar of the

Appaloosa horse, Francis Haines, writes that these horses "appeared from time to time in various parts of the American west," and though the Navajo and Apache may have possessed a few of them, the true breed as we know it today was a mount scarce among these people until sometime in this century.[125]

A painting of some lively pinto ponies by the Navajo artist Beatien Yazz reminds us of how a young Navajo might visualize Sun's herd of multicolored horses, except that the featured ponies possess tan, gray, red, and even pink bodies with white spots, dark manes, and dark tails instead of the colorations recorded in the above myth. Yazz's frolicky ponies caper through white space as though freshly seen from the old world of mythology by new eyes. The artist produced the appealing ponies when he was still a lad called Little No-Shirt. At that time he lived near the trading post at Wide Ruins, where the friendly traders named the Lippincotts encouraged him to develop his style as a painter by interpreting and expressing the traditions of his people in his own way.[126]

In an adult composition of his entitled "Going to Market," Yazz has recorded a scene that belongs to this world, though the horse he has given special prominence would be just as much at home among the richly spotted animals owned by Sun. A sedate young Navajo woman sits on her sprightly mount, which is peach-colored all over except for its white and peach-spotted hindquarters. But while the horse in the painting may be of unusual coloration, the principle behind it expresses a fundamental truth about the Navajo, for in this work Yazz reveals the pride that his people take in showing off colorful horses and the sense of prestige they feel in owning handsome trappings for them. Owning a good horse and outfitting it in becoming dress is one of the best ways they have of displaying their social position and good taste to their friends. Undoubtedly Yazz meant to tell us that much of the attractive equipment we see on his prancing horse was made by skilled Navajo craftsmen. On closer inspection, we see an elaborate silver-mounted bridle and headstall, a sturdy solid leather saddle, and a Navajo saddleblanket, designed with perfection and with the tasseled ends befitting a lady rider. The reins of the bridle are probably made of braided rawhide or buckskin—perhaps of twisted horsehair. The roll behind the saddle is a finely wrought hide blanket—possibly a deerskin, for among the many riding customs the Navajo borrowed from the Mexicans is that of embellishing the mount with a rolled blanket behind the saddle.[127]

Concerning a similar theme, but varying greatly in the execution of subjects and details, is Gerald Nailor's "Navajo Woman on a Horse." Like

Yazz's rider, the self-assured woman seated on Nailor's piebald knows well how to sit and handle her horse, which steps to a spirited gait. Unlike Yazz's well-bred mount, Nailor's reddish-brown-bodied horse with white and red circle-shaped patches is an uncombed, half-broken mustang—but noble in his own way. In further contrast to the complete set of fashionable trappings owned by the woman riding Yazz's horse, Nailor's maiden—just as much a lady—is seated on a Navajo blanket rather than a saddle, and her bridle is homespun. It is simply a rope tied in a loop around the horse's lower jaw, and it represents the most common type of bridle found among the Navajo of the past century. This painting by Nailor (Toh-Yah or "Walking-by-the-River") is one of the many fine paintings that he produced before his death in 1952.[128]

Spotted horses have also been strikingly painted by Harrison Begay, a Navajo artist known to almost everyone interested in Indian art. Begay has painted horses of all colors and has probably influenced more Navajo horse painters, with his delicately detailed animals, than any other painter. Among his most ethereal steeds are his palomino paints and spotted grays; there is no denying that they were made for the gods' world. Handsome Appaloosas also frequently come from his brush. The clean swift rhythm one feels in watching a smooth horse race is the emotion evoked by his "Navajo Horse Race." It catches the motion of two horses—a fan-tailed, silver-gray Appaloosa and a bright copper-colored palomino paint—as they float across the canvas. With bald faces and happy countenances, they actually seem to soar along with the two young women they carry. Another Begay painting, "Wild Horse Family," makes credible the unusual and infinite color formations many mustangs are known to have exhibited. A dappled pinto stallion, whose large yellow spots stand out like blocks of sunshine on his reddish hide, poses beside his unpastured mare and colt. His liquid brown eyes look at the world from a radiant face. His tail is calmly alerted for possible sudden flight. Standing under a sun symbol and rainbow clouds, he and his rain-drop-dappled silver-gray mare and their spry mouse-colored offspring seem as believable as any ordinary horses do. Serenity fills the spacious desert they inhabit, and the sun god actually seems to beam approval on them—the "Wild Horse Family" of Harrison Begay.[129]

"The Emergence"

Emerging out of a four-covered layer of fire, water, winds, and waves of zigzagged precious stones and shells swirled across the floor of the other world, Adee Dodge's majestic lemon mare leads the cardinal horses to earth from "The Emergence" canvas, which is now featured on the cover of this revised edition. One of the finest horse paintings done by any Indian, Dodge's work reflects the elements of which the Navajo say their first horses were composed. Symmetry is carried out in the line of motion and the anticipation of the horses as they gallop toward earth from the elements of their composition. Their white-stockinged feet, by means of which the people say they see, never quite touch the earth below. The bird feathers tied on the foreleg of each horse assure them continued swiftness. The lightning streaks of which their bodies are composed flash patterns across the earth, moving layers of abalone, jet, carnelian, turquoise, and haliotis, while a sheet of heavy raindrops, which nourished them, beats upon the blue and black waters of the background. The wind buoys their tossing white manes and their flying tails; it whips life into them. Fire flames at the very back at the pit of emergence and heat lightning sparks their wild eyes. Trailing at the back, the last horse, a new black stallion, races through a mirage, following the lead of a blackbird flying overhead.

Notes

1. Dane Coolidge and Mary Roberts Coolidge, *The Navajo Indians* (Boston and New York: Houghton Mifflin Co., 1930), p. 2.

2. Morris Edward Opler, *Myths and Legends of the Lipan Apache Indians,* Memoirs of the American Folklore Society, XXXVI (New York: J. J. Augustin, 1940), pp. 30, 32—hereafter cited as *Myths and Legends* of *the Lipan*. Opler has recorded the same motif of the horse creation in the sky for the Mescalero Apache.

3. Aileen O'Bryan, *The Diné: Origin Myths* of *the Navaho Indians,* Bureau of American Ethnology Bulletin, No. 163 (Washington, D.C.: Government Printing Office, 1956), p. 178.

4. Pliny Earle Goddard, *Navajo Texts,* Anthropological Papers of the American Museum of Natural History, XXXIV, Part I (New York: The American Museum of Natural History, 1934), p. 164.

5. Morris Edward Opler, *An Apache Life-Way: The Economic, Social, and Religious Institutions of the Chiricahua Indians* (Chicago: University of Chicago Press, 1941), p. 296—hereafter cited as *An Apache Life-Way*.

6. Opler, *Myths and Legends of the Lipan,* p. 19.

7. For the Chiricahua Apache tale, see Morris Edward Opler, *Myths and Tales of the Chiricahua Apache Indians,* with an appendix of Apache and Navaho comparative references by David French, Memoirs of the American Folklore Society, XXXVII (New York: The American Folklore Society, 1942), p. 12—hereafter cited as *Myths and Tales of the Chiricahua*. For the more traditional examples of this familiar type of tale among the Southern Athapascans, see Washington Matthews, *Navaho Legends,* Memoirs of the American Folklore Society, V (New York: G. E. Stechert and Co., 1897), p. 119; Pliny Earle Goddard, *Myths and Tales from the San*

Carlos Apache, Anthropological Papers of the American Museum of Natural History, XXIV, Part I (New York: The American Museum of Natural History, 1918), pp. 17, 40–41—hereafter cited as *Myths and Tales from the San Carlos;* and Pliny Earle Goddard, *Myths and Tales from the White Mountain Apache,* Anthropological Papers of the American Museum of Natural History, XXIV, Part II (New York: The American Museum of Natural History, 1919), pp. 132–135—hereafter cited as *Myths and Tales from the White Mountain.*

8. Opler, *Myths and Legends of the Lipan,* p. 20.

9. Goddard, *Myths and Tales from the San Carlos,* p. 80.

10. Ibid., p. 78.

11. Ibid.

12. Washington Matthews, "Navaho Myths, Prayers and Songs," ed. P. E. Goddard, in *The University of California Publications in American Archaeology and Ethnology,* V, No. 2 (Berkeley: University of California Press, 1907–1910), pp. 58–59. Hatáli Natlói added that he thought Békotsidi dwelt either in the sky or in Changing Woman's house in the western ocean (p. 59). In another myth collected by Matthews, Békotsidi is identified as "the god who carries the moon." Matthews observes that in other instances Kléhanoai is said to be the moon bearer, explaining that perhaps the "two names are for one character." See Matthews, *Navaho Legends,* p. 226, n. 78.

13. Matthews, *Navaho Legends,* p. 226.

14. Stanley A. Fishler, "Navaho Picture Writing," in Franc Johnson Newcomb, Stanley A. Fishler, and Mary C. Wheelwright, *A Study of Navajo Symbolism,* Papers of the Peabody Museum of Archaeology and Ethnology at Harvard University, XXXII, No. 3 (Cambridge, Mass.: Peabody Museum, 1956), p. 71. It should also be noted that the Navajo often call Reversible Mountain, Mountain-Around-Which-Moving-Was-Done.

15. Stanley A. Fishler, *In the Beginning, a Navaho Creation Myth,* Anthropological Papers of the University of Utah, No. 13 (Salt Lake City: University of Utah Press, 1953), pp. 16–17, 19—hereafter cited as *In the Beginning.*

16. Ibid., p. 17.

17. Ibid.

18. Ibid.

19. Gladys A. Reichard, *Navaho Religion: A Study of Symbolism,* Vol. II, Bollingen Series, XVIII (New York: Pantheon Books, 1950), pp. 387, 388–389—hereafter cited as *Navaho Religion.* See also pp. 386–387 where Reichard throws more light on the many shadows surrounding the role of *be'yotcidí* in Navajo mythology. She notes that the translation of his name from Navajo means "One-who-grabs-breasts." He was conceived after Sun who had "intercourse with everything in the world" was "put away off so that monsters could not be conceived again." She explains that when Sun rose to go into exile, he "touched a flower, which became pregnant and gave birth to *be'yotcidí.* " On the other hand, Fishler's informant told him that of the four Begochiddy deities of different colors, it was the yellow one who "went around holding women's breasts," and that "they named him Begochiddy because of this." He does not explain why the

three deities of other colors were also called Begochiddy. See Fishler, *In the Beginning,* p. 11.

20. Goddard, *Myths and Tales from the White Mountain,* p. 118.

21. Willard W. Hill, *The Agricultural and Hunting Methods of the Navaho Indians,* Yale University Publications in Anthropology, No. 18 (New Haven, Conn.: Yale University Press, 1938), p. 71.

22. Maud Oakes and Joseph Campbell, *Where the Two Came to Their Father: A Navaho War Ceremonial,* Bollingen Series, I (New York: Pantheon Books, 1943), p. 14.

23. Matthews, *Navaho Legends,* p. 233, n. 118; Grenville Goodwin, *Myths and Tales of the White Mountain Apache,* Memoirs of the American Folklore Society, XXXIII (New York: J. J. Augustin, 1939), p. 37—hereafter cited as *Myths and Tales of the White Mountain.*

24. Goddard, *Navajo Texts,* p. 153.

25. O'Bryan, p. 21.

26. Goddard, *Myths and Tales from the White Mountain,* p. 100. An all-wise fly often acts as a guardian companion or friendly counselor to the twin culture heroes. At other times they depend on the services of Air Spirit or the Little Breeze.

27. Ibid.

28. Edward Sapir and Harry Hoijer, *Navaho Texts,* ed. Harry Hoijer, William Dwight Whitney Linguistic Series (Iowa City: University of Iowa, 1942), pp. 119, 121.

29. The Navajo commonly associate the bluebird with the same things they associate the sun with—turquoise, happiness, and immortality. For a song that makes this symbolism apparent, see Fishler, *In the Beginning,* p. 13. It is interesting to contrast the position of the bluebird in Navajo mythology with that of the yellow bird in White Mountain Apache mythology. These Apache consider the yellow warbler, as well as the oriole, to be of chief importance and often mention them as Sun's birds. See Goodwin, *Myths and Tales of the White Mountain,* p. 19, n. 1.

30. Sapir and Hoijer, p. 121.

31. Here again there are exceptions. As Franc Newcomb has aptly observed: "There are occasions when the color arrangement does not follow any established rule. A symbol of great power, such as that of the sun, will take precedence over all other symbols and will occupy the position of honor, no matter what its color may be." See her "Navajo Symbols in Sand Paintings and Ritual Objects," in Newcomb et al., *A Study of Navajo Symbolism,* pp. 13–14.

32. Five stones and colors are included here instead of four because one of the colors represents the zenith. Often, a sixth is included for the nadir. My arrangement of the colors of these stones in the preceding sentence is an arbitrary one, not meant to follow a definite color sequence.

33. Matthews, "Navaho Myths, Prayers and Songs," p. 59. Matthews does not include the Navajo name for white shell horses.

34. Reichard, *Navaho Religion,* I, pp. 217, 220. Newcomb offers a similar interpretation of the meaning behind white placed in the east of a Navajo color sequence. See her "Navajo Symbols in Sand Paintings and Ritual Objects," in Newcomb et al., *A Study of Navajo Symbolism,* p. 24.

35. Franc Johnson Newcomb, *Navajo Omens and Taboos* (Santa Fe: The Rydal Press, 1940), pp. 18, 50.

36. Jeff King enlisted as a scout with the U. S. Army in 1891 and served until 1911 with the troops that were engaged in the long-drawn-out conflicts with the Apache groups, notably the Chiricahua. He was 117 years old when he died in January 1964, and because of the service he performed for his country, he was buried with military honors in Arlington National Cemetery.

37. Oakes and Campbell, pp. 14, 39.

38. See ibid., Plate V of the separate sandpainting series accompanying this work.

39. Ibid., p. 39.

40. For representative versions of this myth, see Goddard, *Navajo Texts,* p. 153; O'Bryan, p. 76.

41. Reichard, *Navaho Religion,* I, p. 187.

42. Newcomb, "Navajo Symbols in Sand Paintings and Ritual Objects," in Newcomb et al., *A Study of Navajo Symbolism,* p. 14.

43. Ibid.

44. Father Berard Haile, *Origin Legend of the Navaho Flintway,* University of Chicago Publications in Anthropology, Linguistic Series (Chicago: University of Chicago Press, 1943), p. 287—hereafter cited as *Navaho Flintway.* Scholars vary in their spellings of the name of this ceremony. Although Fr. Haile spells the name as one word, I shall observe the two-word system of Flint Way used by most Navajo scholars.

45. Reichard, *Navaho Religion,* II, p. 451; Oakes and Campbell, p. 15; Goddard, *Myths and Tales from the White Mountain,* p. 101, n. 1.

46. Sapir and Hoijer, p. 117.

47. Goddard, *Myths and Tales from the White Mountain,* p. 106.

48. Ibid., pp. 99, 100–101, 103, 106.

49. Morris Edward Opler, *Dirty Boy: A Jicarilla Tale of Raid and War,* Memoirs of the American Anthropological Association, No. 52 (Menasha, Wis.: American Anthropological Association, 1938), p. 52—hereafter cited as *Dirty Boy.* For similar treatment of the white horse, cf. ibid., pp. 18, 45.

50. See Opler, *Myths and Tales of the Chiricahua,* p. 57, n. 2; Opler, *Myths and Legends of the Lipan,* p. 167; Goodwin, *Myths and Tales of the White Mountain,* pp. 194–195.

51. Goodwin, *Myths and Tales of the White Mountain,* pp. 19, 37.

52. Goddard, *Myths and Tales from the San Carlos,* pp. 24–25.

53. See Opler, *Myths and Tales of the Chiricahua,* p. 57, n. 2; O'Bryan, p. 178.

54. Opler, *Myths and Legends of the Lipan,* p. 75.

55. Goddard, *Myths and Tales from the San Carlos,* pp. 25–26.

56. Goddard, *Myths and Tales from the White Mountain,* pp. 106, 112.

57. Opler, *Dirty Boy,* p. 30.

58. Grenville Goodwin, *The Social Organization of the Western Apache,* University of Chicago Publications in Anthropology, Ethnological Series (Chicago: University of Chicago Press, 1942), p. 386.

59. Goodwin, *Myths and Tales of the White Mountain,* p. 4, n. 3.

60. Opler, *Myths and Legends of the Lipan,* p. 30.

61. Sapir and Hoijer, p. 127. As mentioned earlier, the moon deity's horse is usually pictured as white rather than black and is placed in the west.

62. Newcomb, "Navajo Symbols in Sand Paintings and Ritual Objects," in Newcomb et al., *A Study of Navajo Symbolism,* p. 16.

63. The original painting was owned by the late Byrd H. Granger, accomplished Southwestern folklorist.

64. O'Bryan, p. 178.

65. Sapir and Hoijer, p. 121.

66. J. Gilbert McAllister, "Kiowa-Apache Tales," in *The Sky Is My Tipi,* ed. Mody C. Boatright, Publication of the Texas Folklore Society, No. 22 (Dallas: University Press, 1949), p. 34. Cf. p. 35 for the use of red in the sequence pattern.

67. However, the Navajo seldom place a red color at the east—the Red Ant Chant seems to be one of the few exceptions where this color occurs there. Perhaps, their general feeling about red-east is best explained by Fishler's Navajo informant who said: "In the morning, if there is a red or gold color in the east, it foretells fevers, coughs or epidemics to come." Fishler, *In the Beginning,* p. 11.

68. Reichard, *Navaho Religion,* I, p. 197; Natalie Curtis, *The Indians' Book* (New York and London: Harper and Brothers, 1907), p. 360. Adee Dodge has also painted a powerful black Navajo storm horse against a gray background, which he calls "Jet Cloud." His forceful stallion has white markings similar to his black "Space Stallion" examined above.

69. Haile, *Navaho Flintway,* p. 287.

70. Reichard, *Navaho Religion,* I, pp. 190, 217, 220.

71. Sapir and Hoijer, pp. 121, 127.

72. For representative color circuits among these Apache groups, see Goodwin, *Myths and Tales of the White Mountain,* p. 1, n. 2, p. 86; Harry Hoijer, *Chiricahua and Mescalero Apache Texts,* with ethnological notes by Morris E. Opler, University of Chicago Publications in Anthropology, Linguistic Series (Chicago: University of Chicago Press, 1938), p. 188; Morris Edward Opler and Harry Hoijer, "The Raid and Warpath Language of the Chiricahua Apache," *American Anthropologist,* new series, XLII, No. 4 (October–December 1940), p. 622, n. 9; Opler, *Myths and Legends of the Lipan,* p. 78.

73. It should be noted, however, that the Jicarilla sometimes substitute white for spotted or glittering colors at the north, and that the Lipan, on the other hand, vary their most common spot for white at the north with a spotted substitute. See Morris Edward Opler, *Myths and Tales of the Jicarilla Apache Indians,* Memoirs of the American Folklore Society, XXXI (New York: G. E. Stechert and Co., 1938), p. 10, n. 1—hereafter cited as *Myths and Tales of the Jicarilla.* See also Opler, *Myths and Legends of the Lipan,* p. 18, n. 3.

74. See Reichard, *Navaho Religion,* I, pp. 221–223; Matthews, *Navaho Legends,* pp. 215–216, n. 18.

75. Reichard, *Navaho Religion,* I, pp. 190, 209. Newcomb observes that the Navajo consider blue and green the same color. See her "Navajo Symbols in Sand Paintings and Ritual Objects," in Newcomb et al., *A Study of Navajo Symbolism,* p. 16.

76. Walker D. Wyman, *The Wild Horse of the West* (Caldwell, Idaho: The Caxton Printers, Ltd., 1945), p. 308.

77. Robert Moorman Denhardt, *The Horse of the Americas* (Norman: University of Oklahoma Press, 1948), p. 200.

78. Curtis, pp. 361–362.

79. O'Bryan, pp. 179–180.

80. Matthews, *Navaho Legends,* p. 233, n. 118. Another Navajo myth mentions Sun showing the Twins a huge horse that he kept under "a trap door in the center of the floor" of his house. Though the color of this horse was not given, he was described as being "like a team horse with hoofs about a foot in diameter." See Fishler, *In the Beginning,* p. 71.

81. Goddard, *Navajo Texts,* pp. 136–137. The Phaeton myth is well known. Phaeton, son of Phoebus, was carried away by the horses of the chariot of the sun when he lost control of the reins. The sky, scorched by the runaway chariot, still shows traces of the damage in the Milky Way. Cf. Dante's reference to this incident in *Inferno,* pp. xvii, 11, 101–102 (John Ciardi's translation):

> Phaeton let loose the reins and burned
> the sky
> along the great scar of the Milky Way.

82. Curtis, pp. 360–362.

83. O'Bryan, p. 79. See also Sapir and Hoijer, p. 117; Mary C. Wheelwright, *Hail Chant and Water Chant,* Navajo Religion Series, II (Santa Fe: Museum of Navajo Ceremonial Art, 1946), p. 58.

84. See Father Berard Haile, *Origin Legend of the Navaho Enemy Way,* Yale University Publications in Anthropology, No. 17 (New Haven, Conn.: Yale University Press, 1938), p. 205—hereafter cited as *Navaho Enemy Way.*

85. Wheelwright, *Hail Chant and Water Chant,* p. 56.

86. Goddard, *Myths and Tales from the San Carlos,* p. 37.

87. Goddard, *Myths and Tales from the White Mountain,* pp. 99–101.

88. Ibid., pp. 102–103. It should also be noted that the Apache, and the Navajo too, use the colors of blue and gray interchangeably.

89. Ibid., pp. 107; 107, n. 1.

90. Ibid., pp. 106, 112.

91. Oakes and Campbell, p. 15.

92. See Andy Tsinajinie, "Going to the Sing," illus. f. centerfold in *Arizona Highways* (December 1958).

93. Andy Tsinajinie [Tsihnahjinnie], "Young Navajo Riders," illus. f. p. 144 in Clara Lee Tanner, *Southwest Indian Painting* (Tucson: University of Arizona Press and Arizona Silhouettes, 1957).

94. O'Bryan, p. 178.

95. See Adee Dodge, "So Proud the Blue Stallion," cover, *Arizona Highways* (July 1959). The untitled Dodge painting of the turquoise horse is found in the American Indian Collection of the Northwest Museum of Arts and Culture in Spokane, Washington.

96. Tanner, p. 117.

97. Quincy Tahoma, "The Winner Takes All," illus. f. p. 112, and "Going to the Navajo Chant," illus. f. p. 144 in Tanner.

98. Yel-Ha-Yah (Charlie Lee), "Friendship," illus. f. p. 112 in Tanner.

99. Sapir and Hoijer, p. 121.

100. Reichard, *Navaho Religion,* I, p. 210.

101. Goddard, *Myths and Tales from the White Mountain,* pp. 100–101.

102. Ibid., p. 99.

103. Goodwin, *Myths and Tales of the White Mountain,* p. 37.

104. Goddard, *Myths and Tales from the White Mountain,* p. 101, n. 1; Reichard, *Navaho Religion,* II, pp. 406–414, 494–497.

105. Newcomb, "Navajo Symbols in Sand Paintings and Ritual Objects," in Newcomb et al., *A Study of Navajo Symbolism,* p. 15.

106. Goddard, *Myths and Tales from the White Mountain,* pp. 102–103.

107 Ibid., p. 101.

108. Ibid., pp. 106–107.

109. Ibid., pp. 106, 112.

110. Opler, *Dirty Boy,* pp. 18, 30.

111. Ibid., p. 45.

112. Ed Lee Natay, "The Desert Rider," illus. f. p. 112 in Tanner.

113. Quincy Tahoma, "Going to the Navajo Chant," illus. f. p. 144 in Tanner.

114. Quincy Tahoma, "Navajo Sing," illus. f. p. 112 in Tanner.

115. Beatien Yazz, "Golden Stallion," frontispiece illus. no. 4, p. 10 in Alberta Hannum, *Paint the Wind* (New York: The Viking Press, 1958).

116. See Opler, *Myths and Tales of the Jicarilla,* p. 10, n. 1; Opler, *Myths and Legends of the Lipan,* p. 18, n. 3; Sapir and Hoijer, p. 121.

117. Fishler, *In the Beginning,* p. 74.

118. Opler, *An Apache Life-Way,* p. 241.

119. Reichard, *Navaho Religion,* I, p. 204.

120. Opler, *Dirty Boy,* p. 10.

121. Cf. Reichard, *Navaho Religion,* I, p. 231. She states that a mirage-encircling guardian was described as "black with white, blue, yellow and red" colors.

122. Sapir and Hoijer, p. 121.

123. Fishler, *In the Beginning,* pp. 71, 73–74, 83.

124. Ibid., p. 71. Note the reddish nose on the fourth and last horse mentioned. This probably signified the life principle in this animal and summarized its presence among its companions in the other cardinal directions. Newcomb notes that in Navajo sandpaintings, red "represents the life principle of animals and humans as well as immortals. . . . Many animals are drawn with a red and blue line from the mouth to the heart, which represents the breath and circulation." See her "Navajo Symbols in Sand Paintings and Ritual Objects," in Newcomb et al., *A Study of Navajo Symbolism,* pp. 16–17.

125. Francis Haines, *Appaloosa: The Spotted Horse in Art and History,* Publication of the Amon Carter Museum of Western Art at Fort Worth (Austin: University of Texas Press, 1963), p. 63. See also p. 3, where Haines observes that "although the

spotted strain has been known to man for two hundred centuries or more, this name Appaloosa is less than a century old and was coined during the 1870s." The name refers to the breed of spotted horses developed by the Nez Perce Indians who lived inside the Columbia Basin and along the Palouse River in Idaho. See also pp. 5 and 77–95, where Haines defines the characteristics marking the breed and gives an excellent history of its modern development in North America among the Nez Perce.

126. Beatien Yazz (Little No-Shirt), Untitled Painting, illus. f. p. 132 in Alberta Hannum, *Spin a Silver Dollar: The Story of a Desert Trading Post* (New York: The Viking Press, 1946).

127. See Beatien Yazz, "Going to Market," illus. f. centerfold, *Arizona Highways* (December 1958).

128. Gerald Nailor (Toh-Yah), "Navajo Woman on a Horse," illus. f. p. 144 in Tanner.

129. See Harrison Begay, "Navajo Horse Race" and "Wild Horse Family," illus. f. centerfold in *Arizona Highways* (December 1958).

The Gift of the Gods

T HE GODS POSSESSED THE HORSE, but the Navajo and the Apache traveled over the earth with their possessions on their backs or on teams of pack dogs. At first it did not matter, for all the Indian people had to manage with the aid of those animals that nature had provided them. Then the white man appeared on Southwestern soil riding this animal that belonged to the gods. The Indians were puzzled: why had the white man and not they been given that "something, by means of which to live?"

The Wrong Choice of Gifts by the Twins

The old men of the Navajo and the Apache, who knew the stories of their people, knew the reasons. They told of how their culture heroes had made the wrong choice in selecting things for the Indians in the beginning.

Back in the days when time was new, the Twin War Gods went to Father Sun and asked for gifts for their people. What they sought specifically, on this occasion, was weapons to use against the monsters that were devouring the things of the earth, the "Lonely Traveling Big Ye-i." But the Navajo legend of this visit relates that Sun offered the Twins horses, and they refused them. The Navajo recite this story when telling of the origin of their Enemy Way ceremony. They say that after Sun offered the Twins much white bead and many imitations of plants, he offered them great numbers of horse figures of white bead and turquoise to take back to earth. These little horse fetishes are the necessary equipment for any Navajo medicine man wishing to produce horses. But the Twins were far too

Two White Mountain Apache youths mounted on fine horses with lariats in hand call to mind the visit of the Twin culture heroes to Father Sun to get horses for their people. See *infra,* pp. 85–86.

interested in lightning, sun ray, and rainbow arrows, which could be used against the monsters, to see any advantages in horses.[1]

Numerous versions of the Twins' refusal on this the first visit to their father's house are in existence among the Navajo. Although they follow the basic form of the version given above, others vary in minor details from it and from one another. In a version O'Bryan recorded from Sandoval, the Twins were shown "all the different kinds of horses that [Sun] owned" and kept in the east. Sandoval said, "He asked his sons if they wanted the horses, but they said it was not their wish"; they had come for lightning "that strikes crooked" and lightning "that flashes straight."[2] Some other Navajo medicine men told O'Bryan that the Twins refused the following choices of gifts: "East, fields of finest corn; South, game; West, domestic animals; North, precious stones."[3] In Jeff King's variation of this myth as told to Maud Oakes, after the Twins had seen the south room of Sun's house, where all the game animals were kept, "they went to the west room, and when they looked in the door, they saw a vast country with all kinds of tame animals useful to man, all kinds of grain and growing things, and flowers." But while in King's version the Twins also refused horses and the other wonderful gifts in the west room, and took instead a medicine bundle to protect themselves against the monsters, they recognized the importance of the gifts they passed over. They told Sun: "We shall need this in the future, but not now."[4]

The mythological twins of the Southern Athapascans, with their versatile identities, often personify the struggles between Indian and white. The White Mountain Apache tradition upon the visit of the Twins to their father declares that Naiyenezgani (Killer-of-Enemies) chose for the Indian from the gifts that Sun offered, and Tobatc'istcini (Child-of-the-Water) chose for the white man. A Western White Mountain Apache named Palmer Valor told Goodwin that Sun offered a mountain with horses and domesticated animals on it first to the elder brother, Naiyenezgani, but the youth, after climbing a beautiful mountain in the west covered with "lots of ripe fruits and good things to eat," made the mistake of choosing it over the seemingly barren one he had climbed in the east. This left the eastern mountain to his younger brother, Tobatc'istcini, who took it for the white people.

Immediately, Sun warned Naiyenezgani that he had made the wrong choice for his people. The story goes that Sun turned to Naiyenezgani, saying: "All right, there is nothing fit to eat there, but you will have to eat it anyway. Those grasses are no good to eat, but you will have to eat them just the same." With these words Sun moved the eastern and western mountains aside, and "from the hill to the east came lots of horses, mules, burros, cattle, sheep, goats, all such animals. They were on that hill."[5]

In fact, this was but the last of three times when Naiyenezgani missed the chance to get the best things for his people. "The first," a White Mountain Apache tale explains, "was when he failed to choose . . . the rifle in the Sun's house."[6] The second occurred "when he threw the book away, and the third when he chose the wrong mountain."[7]

While other Apache groups—the San Carlos, Jicarilla, and Lipan—make Killer-of-Enemies the Indian protagonist, the Chiricahua and Mescalero Apache associate Child-of-the-Water with the Indian and

Killer-of-Enemies with the white man. Therefore, when the choice of possessions (gun or bow, domesticated animals or wild animals) is made, Child-of-the-Water chooses for the Chiricahua and Mescalero Apache and makes the same mistakes the protagonists of the other groups make.[8] The Chiricahua say that Killer-of-Enemies stands for the white man because of the word enemy in his name: enemy is the word they always called the white man in the old days.[9] The twin brothers of the Kiowa-Apache, Fire Boy and Water Boy, whose exploits we shall follow later, received their names when their mother hid one of them in ashes and the other in a pool of water. The brother named Fire Boy has characteristics much like those of the Lipan, Jicarilla, San Carlos, and White Mountain protagonist, Killer-of-Enemies.[10]

The ubiquitous Navajo god Békotsidi, as I earlier noted, is at times identified as the son of Sun and at other times as the moon deity. Another tradition places him as identical with the God of white men. Called Begochiddy or Bego Yellow by Fishler's Navajo informant, he is described as being a blue-eyed, yellow-haired god. In a Navajo myth collected by Matthews, it is recorded that he is "the god who carries the moon," and that "he is very old, and dwells in a long row of stone houses."[11] The Navajo say that "the moon was given to the whites . . . in the beginning of life on this earth." They reason that "it belongs to the white people" because it "has a nose and a mouth with a face of a white man"; also it "is like the white people's skin, transparent."[12]

Further, the moon-god attributes of Békotsidi also suggest that he may be identified sometimes with the younger of the Navajo Twins, Child-of-the-Water. Though these boys were born as twins, Naiyenezgani (He-Killed-All-The-Monsters), who was born first, and Tobatc'istcini (Born-of-Water), who came second, were conceived in different ways by their mother, White Shell Woman (Changing Woman).[13] The elder son is the protagonist of the Navajo and was fathered by Sun with sun rays. The younger Navajo Twin was conceived by the goddess from drops of water from a waterfall, following instructions Sun had given her.[14] The Navajo consider the moon the controller of waters, and they say that Sun appeared in white—a color often associated with the moon—when he instructed White Shell Woman upon the conception of her younger son—all of which relates Child-of-the-Water to the moon. These, among other associations, led to identification of the white man with the moon and the subordinate Twin. The Southern Athapascan liked to think of himself as a special charge of the principal Twin and the sun.

The Gambler's Horses and People

In Navajo mythology, there is a story that tells of a time when Békotsidi befriended a man named Nohoílpi. This young man, whose name means "The Gambler" in the Navajo language, had lost all his possessions in a game of chance and was shot into the sky on a "bow of darkness" by his rival, who was determined to keep his recently won possessions. Nohoílpi was shot so high in the sky that he came to the home of Békotsidi, "the God of the Americans."[15] He told all his troubles to the white man's god, who took compassion on him, saying: "You need be poor no longer. . . . I will provide for you." And according to the Navajo:

> he made for The Gambler pets or domestic animals of new kinds, different to those which he had . . . ; he made for him sheep, asses, horses, swine, goats and fowls. . . . He made, too, a new people, the Mexicans, for The Gambler to rule over, and then he sent him back to this world again, but he descended far to the south of his former abode, and reached the earth in Old Mexico.[16]

The story goes that Nohoílpi still lives in Mexico where he is called the "Nakaí Dígíni, or God of the Mexicans." However, the Navajo believe that on one occasion, he did return from Mexico to visit his former homeland. That was a time long ago when he brought with him some of his Mexican people and started them building towns along the Rio Grande in New Mexico. By that time his new people had "increased greatly" and needed additional territory in which to live. "Nohoílpi came with them," the Navajo say, and he stayed with them "until they arrived at a place north of Santa Fe. There they ceased building, and he returned to Old Mexico," where he has lived ever since.[17]

While we may assume that Nohoílpi had given his Mexican people some of his horses by the time they moved north to build their settlements along the Rio Grande, the above account, nevertheless, does not mention that they gave any of them to the Southern Athapascans. Another variant of this tale brings up this particular subject. It mentions that "the Pueblos and some Navajo believe they got the sheep and horses" from the Spanish descendants of The Gambler, who brought them to America from "the land to the east [Europe]." But the Navajo narrating the variant scoffed at the Indians who believed such a thing. He explained that only "the big mules, sheep with rough heavy wool and the chickens came from overseas," whereas "the horses and small mules" and the sheep with "long curly black, brown and white wool" were "over here" to begin with.[18]

And according to the traditions of the Southern Athapascans, this man was correct in his feeling that the white man had nothing to do with bringing horses to his people. It matters little to the mythological record that in reality the gift of the horse could not have come to the Navajo or Apache before the early part of the seventeenth century, for the mythological accounts that tell of the acquisition of the horse are so indelibly inscribed in the traditions of these people that on hearing or reading them, one could almost believe them to be as old as emergence or migration myths. And in becoming acquainted with them, one learns that they tell a different story from the one recorded by history: they disclose that a time came when the deities of all the Southern Athapascans decided to give horses to their Indian children too.

The Culture Hero's Search for the Gods' Horses

All the Southern Athapascan tribes have stories of how the gods made the gift to their people. The most beautiful myth, I think, is a Navajo version recorded by the great linguist Edward Sapir and edited after his death by his able student Harry Hoijer. It illustrates the Navajo storyteller's charm in telling a story and his ability to build suspense by continual repetition of certain words and phrases. It relates in great detail the exploits of Turquoise Boy (whom Hoijer identifies as Enemy Slayer, the elder of the Navajo Twins, using another of his many names) when he went searching for the necessary something "by means of which people live" well.[19]

When he began his arduous search for horses, Turquoise Boy decided to contact his mother, Changing Woman, first of all. This was a logical choice; obviously, the goddess of earth and fertility could help her son with his problem, for she possessed unlimited knowledge about the welfare of her earth children. Surely, he thought, she, more than anyone else, would know the answers to his questions and help him settle his problems without too much trouble.

But, like every good Navajo mother, Changing Woman knew how to make her son work for what he really wanted. When he broached his big question ("How will things be created, the things whereby the people will live?"), she answered him evasively: "I don't know. It is not known to me, my son. . . . Why don't you travel about for that purpose?"

Although Turquoise Boy did not yet know it, Changing Woman expected an offering of four baskets of sacred shells and stones before she would act upon his request. She now sent her son off on a wild-goosechase to the holy eastern mountain of the Navajo, Pelado Peak, with these few vague directions: "You may go to the holy places for your purpose, my son. . . . Go to the summit of Pelado Peak. There twelve of the Talking Gods live. It seems to be a place in which holy things take place. You may go there, that for which you travel about is known there, perhaps."[20]

When Turquoise Boy arrived at Pelado Peak, he was given audience by one of the twelve Talking Gods, standing near a holy ear of corn. "For what reason are you traveling about, my grandchild?" the Talking God inquired.

Being a little secretive about his true purpose, Turquoise Boy answered the Talking God, returning the courtesy of kinship: "In order that things be created I am traveling about, my great-uncle. . . . In order that that by means of which (people) live will be created I am traveling about."[21]

The Talking God did not understand in the least what the boy meant, but he was willing to be as helpful as possible. He offered him treasures that would delight any ordinary Navajo's heart. "Yes! All right, just look!" the Talking God replied. "What is it for which you travel about? Now, you see, there are all the soft goods. There are white shells. . . . There is turquoise. . . . There are buckskins. . . . mountain lion skins. . . . And there are quite all of the blankets."[22]

But Turquoise Boy would have none of the things a Navajo usually wanted from the gods. He told the Talking God in no uncertain terms: "That is not what I am traveling about for, my great uncle." He decided to make his true purpose known: "All right! I am traveling about for this. And now I shall tell you about it, that for which I travel about. In order that we may have a means of travel I go about."[23]

The Talking God was appalled at such an unorthodox request, and he lost no time in letting this troublesome youth know it.

> "That is not in existence here, my grandchild," he said, they say.
> "Had you said 'Hard goods, for that reason I travel about,' now that
> exists here," he said to him, they say. "Had you said 'I travel about
> for white shell and turquoise,' now, that exists here," he said to him,
> they say. "Had you said 'I travel about for soft goods,' now, that exists
> here. . . . So, my grandchild, that for which you travel about is
> lacking here . . . . The rainbow is our only means of travel," he said. . . .
> "The sun's rays are our only means of travel," he said. . . . "We travel
> about by those means alone," he said.[24]

Unable to help the boy, the Talking God suggested that he take his problem over to Mt. Taylor, another of the holy mountains of the Navajo, where the twelve Hogan Gods lived. "It seems to be a place in which holy things take place. . . . There, perhaps, it exists," the Talking God advised him.[25]

The Hogan Gods at the summit of Mt. Taylor, the holy mountain of the south, were not of much help either. They just repeated the same thing the Talking God had said. One of the Hogan Gods assured him the second time: "That for which you say you are traveling about, that is lacking, my grandchild. The sun's rays are our only means of travel. The rainbow is our only means of travel."[26] Then they sent him off to the western mountains of Navajoland, the San Francisco Peaks near Flagstaff, Arizona.

Twelve more Talking Gods lived at San Francisco Peaks, and while they received their visitor cordially and offered him the usual gifts, they assured him, likewise, that they did not possess the thing for which he so intently searched. As the other gods had done, they sent him off to another mountain. At this fourth mountain, the summit of the La Plata Range, he was received by another twelve Hogan Gods in the accustomed manner. However, since this was his fourth quest, the Hogan Gods on the holy northern mountain did have at least one suggestion to make. They marveled that the son of Changing Woman and Sun was indeed wearing himself down with such a search. They said as much, offering him the most valuable suggestion of all: "Surely your mother has it. White Shell Woman, Changing Woman, surely she has it, my grandson. . . . That for which you say you are traveling, surely your father has it, the Sun. . . . Why are you traveling for (it)? Surely your father, the Sun, has it. . . . Go back to your mother, the White Shell Woman."[27]

So Turquoise Boy had to make the long toilsome journey back to Huerfano Mountain, where his mother lived near the spot the Navajo call "the center of the earth."[28] Understandably, he was disgruntled. He had traveled in vain to the four sacred borders of the four directions. He scolded his mother when he got to the summit of Huerfano Mountain. He made her admit that she knew the answers to his questions, though before she would give him any help at all, she demanded ceremonial offerings, such as those any Navajo must make before learning a ceremony. An invisible companion named Air Spirit now came to the youth's rescue, whispering from behind his ear for him to argue no further, but to tell his mother that the four baskets of white shell, turquoise, abalone shell, and black jewel existed indeed. Turquoise Boy had no sooner spoken as advised than the four baskets magically appeared. After counting them to make sure there were four, Changing Woman answered her son: " 'Well, they exist indeed, my son. Now these will be my offering.' . . . She spoke as if these were to be used as a payment for something here,"

Navajo sacred mountain Debentsa, or Big Sheep Mountain (Hesperus Peak), the summit of the La Plata Range, Colorado.

meaning that the things necessary for creation were present. Then she faced her son and said: "Although it is so, you shall now go to your father, my son."[29]

At this point in the Sapir and Hoijer version of the horse acquisition myth, anyone familiar with Navajo or Western Apache mythology would expect the famous incident of Enemy Slayer's (or the Twins') visit to Sun to occur. However, this familiar theme, which I have mentioned earlier, is barely touched upon. Charlie Mitchell, Sapir's informant, who told and translated this version with the help of another Navajo named Albert Sandoval in 1929 at Crystal, New Mexico, does not include the usual type of story. Mitchell makes short work of the war god's interview with his father, whom he met suddenly along a roadside, riding his turquoise horse. Sun was followed by Moon on his white shell horse and a company of Mirage folk on white, gray, yellowish, and striped horses. There were twelve persons and horses in all, Mitchell said, rounding out the multiple of four, which is a common Navajo counting motif.

It was quite a sight to Turquoise Boy, who had never before seen horses. The Air Spirit had told him to tell Changing Woman, "they exist, indeed." And she had echoed his words when he gave her the offering for them: "Well, they exist indeed, my son." And now through the compulsive power of these words, he saw the holy horses being ridden by his father and the other heavenly deities.

But Father Sun did not choose to offer the boy his horses. His major concern was that his son was out on the road scouting around so late in the afternoon. "'Where are you going, my son?' he said, they say. 'I am on my way over yonder,' (Enemy Slayer) said to him, they say."[30]

The evasive answer did not please Sun. He told the boy to lose no time in going back home: "We have started to go to the home of the White Shell Woman, we have started to go to the Changing Woman. So now we have started to go over there. From right here, you start to go back."[31] For when the sun went to the home of Changing Woman, it meant that the sun was beginning to set for the day, and with the sun ready to set and night soon to come, there really was no reason for a boy to be out on the road alone. In the wink of an eye Sun and his company disappeared, and with the failure of this his third attempt at securing horses, the youth had no choice but to return again to his mother on Huerfano Mountain.

"There is just one thing left (for you to do), my son," the goddess told the weary boy. She said that he must go this fourth time to a place called Sisna.te.l, and he did so.[32]

Sapir identified Sisna.te.l as a small mesa about fifteen miles southeast of Huerfano Mountain. Hoijer adds: "The Navajo term is probably composed of *sis*, an archaic word for 'mountain' and *-na.te.l,* a form of the verb 'to be wide.'"[33] Neither Sapir nor Hoijer had further information about this place name, but I am quite sure that it is the same place where, Sandoval told O'Bryan, the first fetishes for horses were laid. According to Sandoval, White Bead Woman had decided that the horse fetishes should be laid "in the center of the earth, in a place called Sis ná dzil, near, or beyond Haines on the road to Cuba, New Mexico."[34] If Sandoval's Sis ná dzil is identical with Sapir's Sisna.te.1, then Turquoise Boy's last quest took him to a spot known to the Navajo as Dinétah, which means Old Navajoland, the first Southwestern home of the Navajo. Today, much of the Dinétah territory is located in the area of the Jicarilla Apache Reservation, but the Jicarilla are newcomers to that region. From around 1550 until the end of the eighteenth century, when the Navajo moved westward to their second homeland between the four mountains of the present Navajo Reservation, they lived in Dinétah.[35] It was some time after the Pueblo Rebellion of 1680, while they still lived in Dinétah, that they acquired their first horses.

Upon arriving at Sisna.te.1, the first thing Turquoise Boy saw was a ladder "sticking out of the undisturbed soil." When the youth stooped over to look down the hole where the ladder was, the story goes that he saw "a certain person . . . sitting down below. . . . An old man, a very fat one, was sitting there." He also noticed an old woman, a young man, and a young woman—all three of whom were "likewise very fat"—sitting there with the old man. We are told that they were the old man's wife, son, and daughter.[36]

Though neither Sapir nor Hoijer make any observations concerning the similarity of the above scene on the mesa at Sisna.te.1 to that of Pueblo Indian life, the evidence given seems to me conclusive. There is the familiar ladder extending from the subterranean room, which one can easily associate with the kivas of the Puebloid peoples of northern New Mexico, who have lived in this particular vicinity since before the time of the Navajo. These fat, squat northern Rio Grande Pueblo Indians taught many ceremonies to the Navajo while they lived as neighbors for over two centuries. They were the first Southwestern Indians to be given horses by the Spaniards, acquiring them in the early part of the seventeenth century.

In this region of Dinétah, the Jemez Indians were among the close Pueblo neighbors of the Navajo. Constant communication came to exist between the two Indian groups. In 1696, when the Jemez pueblos revolted again from Spanish rule after De Vargas had made a successful reconquest of New Mexico, history records that practically all the Jemez people fled from their homes. Many of them went to Dinétah to live with their Navajo neighbors for a while.[37] The Jemez refugees founded a new Navajo clan called the Coyote Pass or the Jemez Clan, which still exists today because many married the Navajo and never returned to their homeland. Furthermore, the closest association of the Jemez people with the Navajo came at the very same time, when the Navajo were building up their first horse herds.

Charlie Mitchell's story takes on a colorful and charming note at this point. As Turquoise Boy peered down at the fat family in the room below,

Charlie Mitchell (left), 1884, Navajo head man, recorded a horse creation story for Sapir c. 1929. Wittick photographed him and his companion Atta-kai-bi-tzu-ih (right), probably doing it when both were serving as Army scouts at Fort Wingate, New Mexico. (Photo by Ben Wittick, courtesy Museum of New Mexico, neg. no. 15726)

the daughter of the group espied him and told her father four times that
"an earth man is standing up there."[38] The fat man finally arose, and upon
seeing his earth visitor, invited him to come down the ladder with the
twelve rungs.

After he had descended, Enemy Slayer (for he is now called this name
by the informant) happily saw that the fat man was also Mirage Man, the
mirage-encircled guardian of Sun's horses, who inquired: "What are you
traveling about for, my grandchild? . . . It must be your travels nearby we
have been hearing of." And Enemy Slayer replied: "It has indeed been I,
my great-uncle. . . . In order that that by means of which (people) live will
be created I travel about, my great-uncle. . . . That our means of travel be
created, I do so for this purpose, my great-uncle."[39]

And it was then that Mirage Man told the culture hero the words he
had traveled so long and so far to hear. " 'Yes, my grandchild, it really
exists here,' he said to him, they say. 'Now you will see it.' " And leading
him into the sun's corral, he showed him the herd of cardinal horses,
"those with which," he said, "in time to come people will live."[40]

The Holy Beings' Gifts

When Enemy Slayer had finished feasting his eyes on the cardinal steeds,
Mirage Man closed the doors to the four directions and gave the youth a
good lecture to the effect that humans are never able to keep sacred things
holy: "This now, of that which is like this, what is it that you who are earth
people can keep holy, my grandchild?" He then led the young man back
to where the white shell horse was tied at the entrance to the door of the
east and concluded wearily, "You who are earth people keep nothing
holy, I shall just shake (the pollen) off (the horses) for you."[41]

And this is what Mirage Man did. He went around to the four horses—
the white shell to the east, the turquoise to the south, the abalone to the
west, and the spotted to the north—and shook pollen off their bodies for
Enemy Slayer.[42] Next, he made the same circuit around those horses moving
a white bead, a turquoise bead, an abalone bead, and a black jewel bead
in and out of their mouths. He did this to get the horses' saliva. He put
the four types of pollen and the four precious beads with the saliva into a
bag and gave them to the boy, saying: "Now that is all, my grandchild. . . .
Now, you may start back to your mother."[43]

Thus Enemy Slayer, like many another Navajo who learned from his
Pueblo neighbors, took the ceremonial equipment home to Changing
Woman, to use in creating the people's first horses. Indeed, when she saw
the pollen and the beads the boy brought home, she knew the moment

had come for horses to appear on earth. Happily she received and acknowledged the ceremonial medicines: "That for which you have been
traveling; now, it has indeed been acquired, my son."[44]

In another version of this myth, Frog Man, rather than Mirage Man, is
the holy being who provides ceremonial objects to the Twins for use in
the creation of horses on earth. This version, which the Navajo medicine
man Frank Goldtooth recorded for Fishler near Tuba City, Arizona, in
1950, sends both brothers instead of only the elder one on the search for
horses for the people. Like the culture hero in the above version, the
brothers started their mission by asking for help from their mother. But
the goddess, called White Bead Woman in this account, only told them
that "their father had everything that was needed upon the earth." Actually, White Bead Woman had "everything" the Twins needed at that particular time. She had the knowledge as well as the ceremonial equipment
necessary to produce horses, but she did not enlighten the Twins about
her powers, because, as Goldtooth said, "they were not behaving and
obeying her." Since the youths had just "finished cleaning up all of the
evil on earth" and had plenty of spare time, with "little to do around the
hogan," they decided to pursue their mother's suggestion and pay their
father a second visit. They were now anxious to secure horses and felt that
Sun might agree to supply them.[45]

After arriving at their father's house, they discovered that Sun had
four horse fetishes of mirage stones and shells; he kept these sacred possessions in a beautiful ceremonial basket. The boys longed for the horse
fetishes so much that they passed up the live horses of the cardinal directions, which they saw in the deity's corral, and asked, instead, for his
horses of shell and stone. Now, this was not, as it might appear, a foolish
thing for them to do; their choice proved to Sun, just as it would prove to
any Navajo father, that his boys were bent upon acquiring the necessary
ceremonial objects to produce live horses on earth. Still, being a wise
father, Sun decided, as the boys' mother had, to make them first earn the
right to this valuable equipment. So instead of giving them the mirage
horse fetishes, he only gave them two eagle feathers. Goldtooth explained
why: "The boys were running around doing nothing, and they were given
the feathers in case they ever needed help." But Sun did give the boys
some valuable information. He told them: "The White Bead Woman has
these [stone and shell] horses and she knows the songs to go with them
to raise them correctly." Realizing that their mother would not be willing
to let them have her horse fetishes without their first acquiring the proper
ceremonial knowledge, Sun advised his boys to "go over to Wide Belt

Mountain, *sísnajíní*, and get them from your brother." Their brother's name, he informed them, was Frog Man.[46]

The boys returned home to their mother with the aid of the eagle feathers. Again they confronted her with their problem, and again they found that she was unwilling to give them horses. According to Goldtooth, she told the youths that her reason for not giving them "these things" was that "there was no place to raise stock." The Twins were "very disappointed," he said, but they knew they could not make their mother change her mind.[47] White Bead Woman was holding fast to her decision to make her sons work for what they wanted.

About this time, the boys began to have a number of supernatural experiences that led them to follow their father's suggestion and consult Frog Man at the holy eastern mountain. To reach his domain, they had to crawl down a hole in the mountainside, to a subterranean lake, where they found all kinds of horses—"palominos, pinks and others"—feeding on pollen on the eastern side of the lakeshore. And here they also found the unusual-looking holy being named Frog Man, the god of this particular body of water. Perhaps Frog Man's uncommon parentage had something to do with his odd appearance, for Goldtooth said that he was the son of a Mirage Quartz Rock woman, who was "one of the wives of the Sun, one of the thirty-three."[48] Because of his associations with mirage, he reminds us up to a point of the Mirage Man of Charlie Mitchell's version; like this holy being, he too was described as being "heavy set." But here the resemblance ends. Goldtooth said that although Frog Man "was like us in figure" and possessed "a face like us," he had "a big neck and throat like a frog," which made him look "like he had the mumps." He also "had clothes made out of frog skin," and obviously he took a great deal of pride in dressing gaudily, for he displayed all over his person the handsome jewelry he owned. According to Goldtooth's description, he "was loaded up with all kinds of turquoise, white bead, jet and oyster shell that were sewn onto his clothes and worn on his body as jewelry."[49]

When Frog Man saw he had visitors intruding on his privacy, he spoke gruffly: "What are you doing roaming around here? This is no place for Earth People to be." Nevertheless, as soon as he realized that his guests were involved in a serious mission to obtain something so dear to his heart as horses, he became most hospitable. Acknowledging that their quest had carried them to the right place, he announced proudly: "I have everything, just like White Bead Woman on the earth." Looking over at his horses and sheep that "were having fun running around in the dust," he asked the Twins if they wanted any of those animals. Since the Twins knew their brother possessed a valuable ceremonial basket full of rock horse fetishes and that he used his fetishes in ceremonies to produce the frisky horses surrounding his place, they said: "No, we did not want the live ones, but we wanted [the] Mirage Quartz Rock horses."[50]

The holy being was most obliging. He picked up a turquoise basket—it resembled the Navajo marriage basket in size and shape. Goldtooth noted: "He put four Mirage Quartz Rock horses of different colors, of white, blue, yellow and black inside the basket. He then put corn pollen on the top of the horses. Frog Man told them, 'Take the basket out and put it on top of the Wide Belt Mountain, but do not look. Go home and then come back later. Go and look at the basket in four days before the Sun comes up.' " In this way, Frog Man was preparing the Twins to receive their mother's unlimited ceremonial knowledge about the creation and care of horses. The basket he filled for them was to be their offering to her for the treasured fetishes she kept inside her basket, the ones that until now she had given to "no one—not even her sons."[51]

On the way home the boys did exactly as Frog Man had told them. Inside the basket that they placed on top of Wide Belt Mountain, a male rock horse lay to the east, a female to the south, another male to the west, and a second female to the north. They let the basket lie there for four days, and when they returned before the dawn of the next day, they found themselves to be the possessors of a wonderful new power. Goldtooth described it in this way: "Everytime the Twins blinked their eyes the Mirage Quartz Rock horses changed from rock into live horses. As they blinked again the horses changed back as they had been before."[52] By following Frog Man's instructions they had acquired valuable ceremonial knowledge, and this knowledge, along with their basket of rock horse fetishes, would be certain to impress their mother.

When the Twins finally got back to their mother's hogan, the goddess was as happy to receive them and their ceremonial offerings as we found her to be when Elder Brother returned home with his gift of a ceremonial bundle from Mirage Man in the Sapir and Hoijer account. As soon as she saw her sons arriving with their basket, White Bead Woman showed that she had changed her attitude completely. She greeted the Twins, saying: "It is a good thing for you to ask for these things and to take good care of them." After all, Goldtooth confided, the goddess had been wanting to give her sons horses for a long time; she had just been waiting until they "prove[d] themselves capable."[53] Now the goddess knew that her sons were properly prepared; at last she could share her basket of treasured horse fetishes with them and show them how to use it with ceremony and song to bring live horses to earth. Filled with pride in her sons, she now revealed to them, "I have everything here."[54]

A dominant theme in most Navajo myths about the gods' gift of horses is that Changing Woman (White Bead Woman or White Shell Woman) assumed the task of creating horses for the people. Navajo tradition has it that animal gifts for her earth children were on her mind from the beginning of time. Before she would agree to Sun's demands that she live as his wife at the home in the west, she made him promise to give her animals to take along for company. With animals around her, she would not be lonely in her new station. Sun obeyed her wishes, making elk, buffalo, deer, mountain sheep, jackrabbits, and prairie dogs to accompany her. But she and her people had to travel on foot, driving their animals along, since Sun did not supply horses.[55]

Now that the time had come to create horses for the people, messengers were sent out, according to Charlie Mitchell's account, inviting many distinguished guests to the ceremonial hogan. Among them were the very deities who had appeared to Enemy Slayer in his vision on the road when he went in search of horses: Sun, Moon, the Mirage People, the Mist People, the Sun People, the Moon People, and other holy ones. When they were all assembled, Changing Woman spread out a blanket made from "one of those which are not arrow marked," meaning a deerskin.[56] On the surface of this, she placed white beads, turquoise beads, abalone shell beads, and black beads in four spots along with four kinds of pollen. Then she put all kinds of treasures, or "hard goods," alongside the ceremonial beads and pollen. Finally, when she had spread "twelve of those which are not arrow marked" over the first blanket containing the treasures, the offering to the powers was ready.

The audience sat down and the ceremonial singing began. The ceremony would appear to be a Blessing Way, though very few details are furnished.[57] However, we are informed that the people sang the hogan songs first and following these, the horse songs. None of the horse songs is supplied by the Sapir and Hoijer text, but the narrator says: "When the singing was about half finished, those things which had been put down rose up to this (height), they say. That which had been shaken off the horses [the pollen] had begun to move, they say. It was just before dawn, they say. In this way, without interruption, the singing went on, they say. (Then) the dawn broke, they say, (and some of them) fell asleep, they say." And he repeats: "Some of the God People, they were sleeping, they say."[58]

And truly, the God People, those drowsy guests in that warm, earthen hut, must have been sleeping, for they lost the gift they had so long withheld from their Navajo children. At that very moment, the narrator exclaims: "Over the entrance (to the hogan), the neighing of horses was heard. . . . From the other side, the neighing was also heard up above."

The neighing awakened the God People. They blinked their eyes, amazed at what was taking place in the hogan. Looking around guardedly, they inquired, "What has happened?"

" 'Get up!' was said to those who were asleep. 'Here people have heard something extraordinary!' "[59]

Suspense surrounds those twelve deerskins "which are not arrow marked." The narrator repeats again: "While some of the God People were sleeping, they say, the others were asking questions, they say. 'What is it that they heard?' they said as they asked questions, they say. The neighing of horses sounded above again, from the opposite side also it sounded again, they say. And it happened four times, they say."[60]

Indeed, something extraordinary was happening. An entire herd of horses, it seems, was being born at that very moment through the efforts of Changing Woman. Mitchell's narration brings us to the birth scene: "Then those horses stirred more violently (they were not yet born; they were still under the twelve deerskins), they say. Those things which had been put down, those which had been put down with the hard goods, grew to this size, they say. Then the horses (that is, the pollen of the sacred horses which now were being created as horses for the earth people) which had been put there stirred more violently, they say."

The people sang as hard as they knew how. They sang the songs about the pollen and the jewels that the goddess had placed under the deerskins. They sang for horses as the dawn broke all around.

And with the new day, the horses came. Mitchell says:

They kicked the covering off themselves. . . . They began to get up. . . . Just as the singing was finished, they stood up. . . . These, the turquoise horse and the white shell horse, they called to each other, they say. On this side, the abalone shell horse and the black jewel horse, they called to each other, they say. This having happened, horses were created (and) the naming took place.[61]

The Navajo people rejoiced over their gift, but Charlie Mitchell ends his version of the creation story on a sad note:

These things took place at the place called Sisna.te.l.[62] The old men's stories began there. These (stories) have all disappeared with them. Now, their stories (telling of) the different things that exist, all of the things by means of which people live, (those) have disappeared with them. So this one was told to me by him who used to be called Wide Man, I having paid for it.[63]

Goddard, Reichard, and O'Bryan record other versions of the creation of the Navajo horses by Changing Woman (White Shell Woman) that are interesting to compare with the preceding myth at this particular point. Goddard's version records that once the goddess had settled herself in the elaborate new home at the "place called Black Water," where Sun had built her a western replica of his house in the east, "she thought horses should exist for people."[64] And she began to sing their creation song almost immediately:

I am yołgaiesdzan [White Shell Woman]. I am thinking of clothing [deerskin blanket] spread out on there. A white shell horse lies in a white shell basket. I am thinking about [it]. They [horse fetishes] lie in the pollen of flowers. Those who come to me will increase. Those that will not die lie in it [the basket].[65]

Reichard's version of the establishment of Changing Woman in the west—a myth she collected from a Navajo named Gray Eyes and recorded in her unpublished manuscript titled "The Story of the Male Shooting Chant Holy"—gives more concrete information on the kind of ceremonial equipment Sun supplied to Changing Woman. Fortunately, the things the goddess needed to create the first horses for people were already at the new residence. Inside this palatial hogan were four horses made of jewel substances, belonging to each of the directions, and in the center of these stood a stately jet horse "at the root of a perfect cornstalk. . . . On the cornstalk's top sat a black songbird."[66]

Like everything else in her western home, the goddess's cornstalk was modeled after the one Sun kept at his eastern home. A better idea of what it looked like and what purpose it served can be had by examining the one belonging to Sun. According to a description Goldtooth supplied Fishler, Sun's cornstalk grew in the center of a basket that he kept on a shelf in the center of his house. Inside the basket were also some pieces of turquoise, all types and colors of corn, and four horse fetishes facing the cardinal directions and surrounding the cornstalk, on which hung two ears of corn, most probably representing the male and female sexes, since this is what they ordinarily symbolize in Navajo myths. The sacred stone and shell horse fetishes "ate the corn pollen that fell from the corn tassels," Goldtooth said. They were tied to four posts that also stood inside the basket, facing the four directions. Sun and moon designs were carved on each post and attached to each were eagle feathers and rattles of precious stones and shells. "There were rattles made out of white bead on the pole to the east, turquoise rattles to the south, oyster shell rattles to the west, and jet rattles to the north.[67]

Perhaps the white rattles were the ones that Sun's daughter used each morning to summon Sun's white horse, a daily chore mentioned previously.[68] Goldtooth said that when Sun himself shook the rattles of white bead, the horse fetishes tied to the poles of the four directions "would also begin to rattle and move just as if they were alive." In fact, this was how the fetishes got their exercise, he noted, adding that Sun also shook the rattles "to give pep and energy to all animals, plants, bushes, trees and all things upon the earth."[69]

Doubtless the horse fetishes around White Bead Woman's cornstalk were also tied to elaborate poles with rattles attached. For Goldtooth said that when Sun showed his beautiful ceremonial equipment to the Twins, he informed them that their mother had the same things.[70]

The story of the goddess's creation of horses collected by O'Bryan is an interesting one to compare with the one collected by Goddard, because the same man—the Navajo named Sandoval—served as the informant for both. The sequence of events leading up to the creation of horses in the version he gave O'Bryan is arranged somewhat differently than in the one he gave Goddard, and perhaps this may be explained by the lapse of five years between the first telling and the second. Perhaps Goddard's untimely death also accounts for some of the differences, for he died before he was able to complete the task of editing and revising his work. But other differences aside, the two versions show how oral transmission is constantly at work reassembling myths and tales and the motifs associated with them. Contrasting the two versions demonstrates the part that memory plays in the process, and reveals better than any explanation, the tedious task a collector faces in drawing out all the information an informant has at his disposal and in making sure that the informant does not forget any details at the time of the recording.

In the O'Bryan account, Sandoval relates that two boys were living quietly among their people on earth. Though he does not mention their names, he implies that they were earth people who had a holy experience rather than the Twin War Gods. One day a certain Chief Bá neé sent them to gather corn in the fields with two girls. Only the girls returned with the corn, reporting that the boys had disappeared while they were playing hide-and-seek. The girls insisted that the boys' "tracks ended right out in the open where they had stood side by side." In his knowing way, Chief Bá neé told the people that he believed "the boys had returned to their Grandmother," implying in this way that they had gone to visit Changing Woman.[71] That he called the goddess "Grandmother" meant only that he employed the term of respect that the Navajo use for any older woman.

Chief Bá neé was correct, for several days later the boys reappeared as suddenly as they had disappeared. At an assembly of the people, the youths told their story. They said that the deities Hasjelti (Morning) and Hasjohon (Evening) had magically appeared before them in the form of old men, while they were playing, saying that the goddess wished to see them. They asked each boy to raise his right foot, and the moment the boys obeyed they were transported to the top of a mountain peak called Chush gaeye (White Spruce).[72] Then they took a second step and found themselves on the summit of another mountain. Here the old men gave each boy a ritualistic washing, exactly like the bath Navajo medicine men give patients in the brush shelter at curing ceremonials. This act prepared them for the holy experience they were about to have. From the second peak they went to a third one, and from there the fourth step brought them to the goddess's home. At first she appeared to them as an old woman seated in a chair; but within an instant she arose, and while they watched, she did a series of marvelous things. "With the help of her walking stick," they said, she "hobbled into the east room of her dwelling. She returned younger, and she went into the south room. From there she came back a young woman. She went into the west room, and she came back a maiden. She went into the north room, and she returned a young girl."[73] The boys were witnessing the goddess's power of perpetual rejuvenation, for Changing Woman, or White Bead Woman as she is called in this account, had the ability, as the former name implies, to change her age at will. The Navajo say she grows old and young again with the cycle of each year's seasons.

After this display of her powers, she told the boys that she wanted them to learn the Night Chant "and all the prayers that went with it. For it was by this ceremony that they should live." Called the Yeibitchai by the Navajo, the Night Chant is one of their most popular ceremonies, employed for many purposes. Though its major purpose is curing the sick, it also provides other benefits for the health and happiness of the people. Many of its prayers directly concern the increase of horses, cattle, and crops. After obeying the goddess's request and learning "all the chants and the prayers that they were to use in the spring when the plants and the flowers and the young animals come out," the boys received from her the happy news: "The Dîné [the Navajo people] shall have horses."[74]

Goddard recorded the above myth from Sandoval too, but in this account, the story of the visit of two children to the goddess appears in

Navajo Mountain Range: the Chuskas, often mentioned in myths, run along the Arizona–New Mexico border of the reservation. See *supra,* p. 77, n. 72, and also *infra,* p. 109, n. 72.

another myth cycle and is not combined with the story of how Changing Woman created horses. In Goddard's account, the children sent to visit the goddess are a boy and girl rather than two boys, and when they return to their people, they simply report without further explanation that horse songs were among the many songs they had been taught for the benefit of the people.[75]

While the sequence of events leading up to the goddess's creation of horses differs in the Goddard and O'Bryan accounts, Sandoval's description of the actual occurrence is much the same in both. He goes immediately into the ceremony in both, and does not, as Charlie Mitchell does in Sapir and Hoijer, tell us what guests, if any, assembled themselves. His account for Goddard merely begins:

Something was spread over it [meaning that a deerskin or some blanket was spread over a horse fetish.] It moved and became alive. It whimpered. Woman-Who-Changes began to sing:

Changing Woman I am, I hear.
In the center of my house behind the fire, I hear.
Sitting on jewels spread wide, I hear.
In a jet basket, in a jet house, there now it lies.[76]
Vegetation with its dew in it, it lies.
Over there,
It increases, not hurting the house now with it it lies,
inside it lies.[77]

A more complete creation scene appears in O'Bryan, where Sandoval has White Bead Woman singing two chants. The first verse of one is as follows:

From the East comes a big black mare.
Changed into a maiden
She comes to me.
From the South comes a blue mare.
Changed into a maiden
She comes to me.
From the West comes a sorrel mare.
Changed into a maiden
She comes to me.
From the North comes a white mare.
Changed into a maiden
She comes to me.[78]

Sandoval informed O'Bryan that the above chant was divided into two parts. He gave only the above and followed it with another of White Bead Woman's chants, which much resembles the preceding song he recorded for Goddard. He again attributed this chant to the goddess at the time of creation, but told O'Bryan that there are about twenty sections to this chant and that these sections change but slightly each time. His rendition follows:

This is my plan:
I am the White Bead Woman.
In the center of my home I planned it.
On top of the beautiful goods I planned it.
The white bead basket which contains the horse fetishes,
They lay before me as I planned it.

All the beautiful flowers with their pollens
And the horse fetishes,
They lay in each other,
They lay before me as I planned it.
To increase and to multiply, not to decrease.
They lay inside (the animals) as I planned it.[79]

Supplying an interesting belief about twin colts as well as the humorous reason for the mule's sterility, the Goddard text now brings us close to the ceremonial baskets. Notice that it also explains how the bird companions for horses of different colors, especially black birds, came into existence on earth.

A white shell basket stood there. In it was the water of a mare's afterbirth. A turquoise basket stood there. It contained the water of the afterbirth. An abalone basket full of the eggs of various birds stood there. A jet basket with eggs stood there. The baskets stand for quadrupeds, the eggs for birds. Now as Changing Woman began to sing the animals came up to taste. The horse tasted twice; hence mares sometimes give birth to twins. One ran back without tasting. Four times, he ran up and back again. The last time he said, "Sh!" and did not taste. "She will not give birth. Long-ears (Mule) she will be called," said Changing Woman. The others tasted the eggs from the different places. Hence there are many feathered people. Because they tasted the eggs in the abalone and jet baskets many are black.[80]

O'Bryan's text, again more detailed and much clearer, supplies the missing links of the Goddard version:

After the White Bead Woman's chanting, the four horses began to move, the white-bead horse fetish, the turquoise horse fetish, the white-shell horse fetish and the banded stone horse fetish. These four stone fetishes were made into living horses.
    Life came into them and they whinnied. Then the White Bead Woman took the horses from her home. She placed them on the white bead plain, on the turquoise plain, on the white bead hill, and on the turquoise hill. Returning, she laid out four baskets—the white bead basket, the turquoise basket, the white shell basket, and the black jet basket. In these she placed the medicine which would make the horses drop their colts. The White Bead Woman then went outside and chanted, and down came the horses from the hills; but instead of four there came a herd. They circled the home, and they came to the baskets and licked up the medicine with one lick. Now

Forked stick (four-forked-beams) hogan behind the once-popular buckboard wagon. A home like this on Gobernador Knob (a sacred rise in Dinétah crested by a rock outcropping of a similar shape) served the Navajo goddess as an earthly home.

some of the horses licked twice around the baskets; so once in a long while there are twin colts. But the horses that licked out of the black jet basket licked more than once, and they have many colts. Then out of the herd there came one with long ears. She snorted and jumped away; and the second time she approached the basket she snorted and ran away. So she was not to have young, either male or female.

It was planned that the fetishes of the horses were to be laid in the center of the earth, in a place called Sis ná dzil. . . .[81]

At this point O'Bryan's account differs completely from that of Sapir and Hoijer on the subject of how the gift of horses was made to the people. However, it supplies information omitted from the Goddard account. According to O'Bryan, Sandoval said that after White Bead Woman created the horses, she did not give them to the people immediately, as she did in the Sapir and Hoijer myth. Instead she caused the horse fetishes to be buried at the center of the earth at Sis ná dzil and promised the two boys that in time "they were to have horses in their country."[82] Thus it remained for another Navajo man—really the first horse medicine man—to learn the necessary chants and ceremonial rites to bring to life on earth horses from the buried fetishes.

The Franciscan Fathers allude to this same theme, noting that at the time of their creation by the goddess, "the animals, such as horses, burros, sheep, and cows, which she made for them, were not given to the Navaho."[83] On the other hand, the account Fishler recorded from Goldtooth is more in agreement with the Sapir and Hoijer version supplied by Charlie Mitchell. It informs us that after the Twins returned home with the horse fetishes Frog Man had given them, White Bead Woman gave her sons her fetishes too and taught them the ceremonies and songs to produce and care for horses on earth. After teaching them these things, she said they could begin raising horses, because they had learned how to care for them, and horses began to live on earth from that time on.[84]

A dominant theme in White Mountain Apache mythology concerning the gift of horses to the people is that Sun lent either the culture hero or both Twins two of his sacred horses and also supplied the ceremonial knowledge as to how these animals could be used to create others on earth. We have already examined the Navajo and Apache traditions that the protagonist brother chose the wrong gifts for his people the first time Sun offered him horses, and we have seen how he left these animals for his Twin, who took them for the white man. Now it is time to take a look at the White Mountain Apache myths that explain how the Indian people finally got horses. Though most White Mountain Apache myths of this type agree that their culture hero was given a second chance to acquire horses for them, some variations exist in the myths about the time when this opportunity came his way.

Bane Tithla, an Eastern White Mountain Apache, told of how Elder Brother made a second trip alone to his father's home to acquire some horses after he had killed all the monsters on earth and "was living well among the people." According to Tithla, when the culture hero "got to Sun's home, he said to him, 'My father, give me something good. The people on the earth do not have much. My father, give me a horse.'"

Sun was indignant; he answered, "I have no horse. Do not talk this way, because we have no horses here. Where could I get a horse for you? What horse would I give you?"[85]

But acting this way was merely a part of Sun's personality. To the Apache or Navajo mind, he was always a man with whom one had to stand one's ground. He had a horse, all right, for now, the narrator said, "Sun went off to the east where Black Wind Horse was. When Sun rode this horse the earth went down and the sky went up."

It was the youth's turn to be wily. When Sun offered him the Black Wind Horse, Naiyenezgani merely answered: "No, not that horse. I don't want him."

By this time, Sun was enough impressed with the lad to try to satisfy his wishes: "Then Sun went to the south where there was Lightning Horse, and he led this horse back with him." Again, the culture hero shook his head.

Sun was a little weary of the whole thing by now; he asked: "Then, what horse shall I give you? These are all the horses I have."

This did not discourage the boy at all: "Just the same he kept on asking. After a while Sun went off to the west and led back a black stallion.[86] This seemed like a good one, so he took it off home with him."

But the third horse proved to be a bad choice, and Naiyenezgani soon saw that he had been outwitted by his father. For when the boy had arrived home with the black stallion and tied him to a tree for the night, he ran in a circle all night, making a great noise and nearly pulling the tree down in his efforts to get away.

The next morning Naiyenezgani decided that he had better go back to see his father about this matter. Maybe Sun could explain what caused his problem with the horse.

Naturally Sun, who was an expert in the care and treatment of horses, knew exactly what the trouble was. Sun gave him a good tame yellow mare with these instructions: "Take this mare with you back to your home and put her with the black stallion. If you do this, the stallion won't want to get away any more."

Being also a White Mountain Apache father, Sun had a few horse ceremonial tips for the youth, who was beginning to learn what the Apache call "the ceremony of the horse." He gave Naiyenezgani "a saddle, bridle, rope and blanket, and told him, 'When you get back home put the bridle to the east the first night.'"[87] He also gave him other directional instructions.

As soon as he had returned home, with the yellow mare and the horse trappings, the boy followed his father's instructions to the letter. He put the mare with the stallion, and he also placed the bridle to the east for the first night. According to Tithla, "the black stallion stayed where the bridle was all night and kept neighing." Again obeying his father's wishes, on the second night, the boy put a saddle blanket at a place facing the south. All through that night, he could hear the neighing of horses coming in from a southerly direction. When morning came, he returned to where he had left the saddle blanket and found "horse tracks all around the place." On the third night, after he had put a saddle to the west, he heard horses neigh around it all night and found their tracks by it the next morning. But the fourth night, after he had placed a rope to the north, something quite different occurred: "All that night there were horses neighing, also colts, at that place to the north. When he went in the morning to where he had put the rope, there were lots of horses, all kinds, black ones, white ones, blue ones, and others." This was a very important occasion, for as the narrator informs us, "from that time on there were horses on the earth."[88]

Goddard collected another variant of this White Mountain Apache myth in 1910, and the two are similar in many respects. In the Goddard version, Sun gave the culture hero, on his first visit, a second chance to choose horses for the Indians, after, that is, he had reproached him several times for selecting the wrong gifts for his people in the first place. When he at last relented, Sun gave the hero a "chestnut stallion" to take to earth. Back home, however, the youth found this stallion "was not satisfactory"; it "kept nickering and pawing the earth all the time," and it would not graze either.[89] So the youth took it back to Sun's home, and his father rewarded him for his efforts with another stallion, as well as a mare, neither of whose colors are mentioned. Sun also gave the boy a rope, halter, saddle blanket, and a saddle, and endowed the youth, it seems, with intuitive powers about how he could use these trappings in the proper ceremonial way to cause the sacred stallion and mare to breed horses for the people.

The culture hero led the stallion and mare back to where a cottonwood tree stood at "the center of the earth"—a place the White Mountain Apache call "Cottonwood-branches-hang-down."[90] At this place, black cottonwood branches were hanging toward the east from the tree, while blue, yellow, and white branches hung to the south, west, and north respectively. To the east of this tree, in a dry stream bed, black, blue, yellow, and white burdocks also grew, facing the cardinal directions of their colors. The culture hero turned the stallion and mare out in this place, putting them in the eastern quarter; he let them stay there for four days. It is said that when he went back on the fourth day to where he had left them, he saw a colt's tracks. Moreover when he looked at the cottonwood tree that stood in the middle of this place at the center of the earth, he saw that "on the east side of it, a black stallion stood; on the south side, a blue stallion; on the west side, a yellow stallion; on the north side, a white stallion. Horses were walking around in the valleys to the east, south, west, and north." The myth concludes that "thus there came to be horses here on the earth."[91]

Yet another version of this myth gives no evidence that the protagonist ever had a previous opportunity when he missed the chance of acquiring horses for his people. In this version, collected by Goddard, also in 1910, from a White Mountain Apache chief named Noze, both Twins worked together on their first visit to their father's home to acquire the necessary ceremonial knowledge so that they could bring horses like their father's to the White Mountain people. Parts of this myth were examined in the previous section, but only with regard to the symbolism behind Sun's blue stallion as his sky-horse and his wife's yellow mare as the earth-horse. Now, however, a close look is in order to discover the details of how Sun lent the Twins his blue stallion and the goddess's yellow mare, and how they bred progeny for their people. These two horses are presented as the best mounts in Sun's cardinal herd, undoubtedly because of the sky and earth symbolism surrounding them, even though, as we have seen on a number of occasions, the black stallion rather than the blue is usually given the favored position by the Apache.

According to Noze, after Sun tested the Twins' abilities in choosing the most desirable horses from his herd, he said they could take the stallion and mare to earth with them for a time. We gather that the deity felt some nostalgia as he bade farewell to his favorite animals, for Noze relates that "the Sun felt the horses all over. He felt of their legs, their feet, their faces, their ears, their manes, their backs, petting them. 'Goodbye, my horses,' he said, 'travel well for my boys down to the earth. There is food for you on the earth the same as here.' "[92] And small wonder that he felt sad as he sent his horses off to earth to share them with people; he knew an era was ending and that never again would such animals live exclusively in the world of the gods.

After the boys were safely carried back to earth on Sun's horses, they were greeted joyfully by their mother, who, as noted earlier, lived among the people at that time. Noze said she "laughing[ly], ran her hands over the horses, saying, 'Your father gave you large horses.' "[93] He illustrated too the prestige element involved in the Apache's ownership of horses,

for he explained that the Twins' attitude toward their earth companions
had changed completely after their journey. They were now full of authority and acted as leaders of the people. The elder Twin addressed the
people in this manner: "When we were here before you used to laugh at
us because we were poor. We used to walk because we were poor. We
have visited our father where he lives. . . . Call me Naiyenezgani. That one
was given the name Tobatc'istcini. These will be our names and be careful
to call them correctly. Do not come near these horses. . . . You may go."[94]

On the fourth day after their return to earth, the Twins took the horses
to a place where four canyons came together from the four directions, just
as their father had instructed them to do. At this spot, the boys hung up
four saddle blankets their father had given them, one over the mouth of
each canyon. Noze explained that horses would not pass a blanket that
had been placed so as to block the entrance of a narrow canyon. Thus the
boys made an enclosure for their father's horses.[95] They left the four horses
here for four days, and when they returned, they found "the valleys in
four directions full of horses."[96] In fact, the valleys were so full of horses
that they could not tell their mounts, the blue stallion and the yellow
mare, from the others. In order to distinguish them, they put pollen on
their palms and held them out to the herd. Then "two horses trotted up to
them and licked the pollen" from the hands of their owners who "caught
them while they did it." According to Noze, the Twins led these two
horses back to camp, and all the others followed. Their all-wise fly companion "told them all about the two horses, what they had done, and that
they had made many horses for them." Fly prophesied that in four days
from that time "it would come about that the broad earth would be covered with horses."[97]

The Twins sent the fly back to their father for further instructions. Sun
told the fly that they should make a second enclosure out of some halters
and ropes he had also given them, and drive into it the offspring of the
mare and stallion. There was to be a halter on top of the eastern sacred
mountain, a rope on the southern one, another halter on the western
one, and again a rope on the northern one.[98] The Twins followed this
plan, and on the dawning of the fourth day when Elder Brother went to
look at how conditions were on the eastern "mountain top where the
halter lay," Sun appeared suddenly, and accompanied him on his rounds
to see whether or not he and his brother had carried out the instructions.
They found that the space between the mountains "was level full of horses."
This pleased Sun. He told Naiyenezgani: "Fine, my son, . . . with ropes
and halters you made a fence so the horses cannot get out. You have this

broad world for a corral."[99] Thus the fly's prophecy had come true, and horses had been supplied forever to the White Mountain Apache. But once the blue stallion and yellow mare had bred horses for the Apache, it is said that they disappeared from earth and returned to live again in the world of the gods.[100]

The Creation and Release of Horses by Culture Heroes and Holy Beings

A second major theme in Apache mythology concerning the gift of horses is that the culture hero or a holy being, working under his own power, undertook to create them for the people. This is the dominant theme in Jicarilla, Mescalero, and Lipan Apache myths. Sometimes, as in the case of the Lipan, the protagonist appointed assistants to help him in his work, but at no time in performing his task did he seek or need ceremonial help from Father Sun or from his mother, as we have seen that the Navajo and White Mountain Apache culture heroes did.

A Jicarilla Apache origin myth attributes the creation of horses to a holy being rather than a culture hero. The Jicarilla say that an anthropomorphic supernatural whom they call Black Hactcin performed this task in the underworld. The Jicarilla religion recognizes many Hactcin. There are Black, Blue, Yellow, and Variegated or White Hactcin, as well as others, and all of them personify the power of objects and natural forces to the Jicarilla. Black Hactcin, as well as the other divinities, is often said to be the offspring of Black Sky and Earth Woman. These Hactcin lived in the darkness of the underworld, in the womb of the earth mother, at the beginning of time before the people existed.[101] Black Hactcin was the most powerful of them and became leader in the world below. From clay images, he molded all the animals and birds, who asked him to make man for them as a companion.[102] In some respects his duties remind us of those of the Navajo's Black Begochiddy (Békotsidi), for as we have seen in the examination of the Fishler and Matthews accounts, the Navajo holy being was among the deities who in a similar way molded animals from clay for use in the gods' world. Again, as one of the holy beings belonging to the cardinal directions, Black Hactcin makes us think of Black Begochiddy, for it may be recalled that the Navajo also mention the latter in connection with the Blue, Yellow, and White Begochiddy deities.[103] The cardinal color associations of four of the Jicarilla Hactcin resemble too those of the Chiricahua Apache's four Great Black, Blue, Yellow, and White Gahe.[104] To the Chiricahua and some other Apache groups, the Gahe (Gan or Gans) personify the mountain spirits.

The Jicarilla origin myth relates that after Black Hactcin had formed all kinds of animals, including horses, the animals came up to him for instructions about what they should do with themselves. It says that in those days all of the animals could talk and that all of them "spoke the Jicarilla Apache language" as "they asked him many questions. Each asked him what he should eat and where he should go live, and questions of that order." And according to the myth, he spoke to each of them, dividing different foods among them. When he spoke to the horse, he gave to him, as well as to the sheep and the cow, some grass, saying: "That is what you shall eat." Then he proceeded to give brush to the next animal, pine needles to another, and "leaves but no grass" to still another. After finishing his individual conferences with the animals, he called them together in assembly and told them: "Now you can spread over the country. . . . Go to your appointed places and then come back and tell me where you want to stay all your lives." The myth informs us that once the assembly was over, some of the animals went to the mountains, some went to the desert, and some went to the plains. "That is why," it explains, "you find the animals in different places now. The animals went out and chose their places then." It records that Black Hactcin was pleased when he looked around and saw all the animals set apart in their new homes. He is said to have expressed his delight to them in this way: "It is well. It looks well to see you in the places you have chosen."[105]

At this point in the origin myth, it would seem that all the animals were settled on earth in their various habitats. But such is not the case. It must be remembered that all of this took place in the Jicarilla underworld and only mirrored the animals' existence on earth. The origin myth proceeds to tell us that considerable time elapsed before the animals and birds, following the lead of the ancestral people, emerged from the underworld by climbing up a mountain and through a hole into the earth above.[106] Fishler has collected a version of the Navajo emergence legend that records a story similar in a number of respects. The Navajo version relates that when the great flood wiped away the third of the four worlds in which the Navajo say they have existed, they emerged to the present one by climbing up to it through a hollow cane placed inside a mountain. They say their animals followed them up this cane and that after they were settled on earth, the gods lived on top of this mountain in the east—a mountain often identified as Pelado Peak—"while the people and animals lived in the middle of the world."[107]

The Jicarilla emergence account reveals that all animals were "gentle and tame" at the time of emergence, but explains that later incidents brought about by earth people, who were not respectful in their treatment of them, caused the animals to disperse across the face of the earth. And the Jicarilla had to go find them again.[108]

Another Jicarilla Apache myth attributes the gift of domestic animals to a ceremony performed by the culture hero. While not mentioning horses specifically, it relates that after Killer-of-Enemies had slain all the monsters inhabiting the world, he went to the top of a big mountain near the present Mescalero Apache Reservation to begin the creation of the white man and animals useful to humans. With the blood of the monsters still on his hands, he took a reed and threw it to the east, proclaiming: "This will be white people, Americans." Then he rubbed the blood of the monsters together with his hands and made a motion as though he were throwing something to the east. "Those white people will be strong in a life way. They will be like White Hactcin. They will help all peoples," he said. And then, he washed the blood of the monsters off his hands in a bowl of "holy water" his grandmother gave him, and he "raised his wet hands and shook them. As the drops fell he said, 'These will be sheep and cattle of all kinds.' "[109]

The Mescalero Apache story of the creation of the horse is a brief episode appearing in the long account of "Coyote and the Creation" collected by Hoijer; it tells us that the culture hero made the horse. As noted near the beginning of this chapter, the Mescalero protagonist is Child-of-the-Water rather than Killer-of-Enemies, whom they classify as the weaker brother and associate with the white man. Since the Mescalero have no emergence legend referring to the creation and origin of major ceremonies, as many Southern Athapascans do, they have turned to their Coyote cycle of tales to tell of the origin of things, and in doing so, they have extended the cycle so as to use Coyote for higher purposes than he generally fulfills in Indian lore. Hoijer's version has it that Coyote started the creation of many of the living things on the earth and had begun to form many of the wild game animals when his work was suddenly interrupted by Child-of-the-Water, who appeared on the scene and sent Coyote away because Coyote did not choose to be human.[110] It is said that the next act of Child-of-the-Water was to look around him and comment: "It seems that much is lacking. All that is lacking, you will be created."[111]

What was needed were human beings and horses and cattle, as well as some of the game animals that live in the mountains. As he brought the horses and other animals into existence, Child-of-the-Water spoke these words: "All varieties of cattle, all varieties of horses, all that live in the mountains, those that are bears, mountain lions, mountain sheep, elks, buffaloes, antelopes. All that I have named, you will be good to all kinds of Indians and white men on the surface of the earth. I have created you because they want to use you in some way."[112]

In Lipan Apache mythology the creation of earth's horses is a chore carried out by the more familiar Apache culture hero, Killer-of-Enemies. During the summer of 1935, an aged Lipan named Antonio Apache told Opler his version of the story of how Killer-of-Enemies accomplished this feat. Before he began his recitation, however, Antonio informed Opler that the actual telling of this myth was considered by his people to be the transfer of a horse ceremony from the teller to the listener. By this, he meant that in telling his story, the narrator could bestow some of his power with horses on the uninitiated. He explained this was the reason why the Lipan observed the custom requiring the listener to give ceremonial gifts to the person knowing the myth before he started telling it. In this case, the proper gifts would be a "bridle with bells on it," a bit, a horsehair rope, a black horse, and a cigarette.[113]

Creating horses was no new task for Killer-of-Enemies, for, according to Antonio, he had been the one who formed the first four horses for himself and the gods in the "world above the clouds." We are already acquainted with this theme, for the account of how he made horses up in the heavens from supercharged elements has been given in the preceding chapter. Antonio related that later, when the culture hero decided that the time had come for the Lipan to have horses, he brought these four steeds down to the earth and put them out on the plains, each facing in a different direction: a blue one to the east, a white to the south, a yellow to the west, and a black to the north. Leaving these cardinal horses on the plains, he went to his home in the Guadalupe Mountains—mountains located in southwestern New Mexico and western Texas.[114]

At this point, the Lipan story of Killer-of-Enemies' creation of horses on earth combines with another dominant theme found in the horse myths, a popular one among the Chiricahua and Kiowa-Apache as well as with the Lipan. This theme expresses one of two ideas—either that the culture hero called in certain birds or animals who sometimes helped and at other times hindered him in the creation or liberation of horses, or else that he had to outwit these birds or animals before he could release horses to the people.

The Lipan idea is that Killer-of-Enemies—in this respect unlike the Jicarilla and Mescalero protagonists—decided he could use some helpers in making horses for this world, and at the same time teach some of his earth companions how he had created these wonderful animals for the gods. Therefore, when he returned home after leaving the cardinal horses on the plains, he called together three of his bird friends and taught them the secrets involved in making four replicas of these horses.

Bat Boy, Cowbird Boy, and Crow Boy were the three birds Killer-of-Enemies chose as assistants. Since many Apache associate these three birds with horses and cattle, as well as with game animals, it is understandable that there exists a familiar motif in Lipan Apache mythology that these birds possess certain powers with horses that other creatures lack. The Lipan people came to know that the reason the cowbird followed the movements of horses was because it had "control" over them. They learned too, that the bat's ability to hang on precarious perches aided it in breaking wild horses and winning horse races. Knowing from hunting game animals that the crow was a scavenger, they always included this bird in their hunt rituals, so that he would take care of waste and undesirable parts that must be left behind.[115] Thus when the beliefs, ceremonies, and traditions connected earlier with game animals were shifted to the folklore surrounding the horse, it was only natural that the crow should be included.

Antonio's horse creation myth explains how the bird assistants learned their work. Killer-of-Enemies followed the same plan in forming the earth horses that he had in creating the sacred horses, working alone in making the first replica of the eastern horse on earth. "He was the one who was really doing it. The others, his partners, were only watching him," Antonio said.[116] However, when it came time to make the other three horses, Antonio implied that he allowed his bird assistants to help him.

The Lipan storyteller does not give a detailed description of how the culture hero and his helpers made the horse replicas. He simply turns our attention back to the sacred models for these earth horses by saying, "This form of the horse was already made, but it was out in the wilds," and explains that now the time had come for Killer-of-Enemies to show Bat, Cowbird, and Crow the cardinal horses he had previously brought down from the world above and put on the plains. Killer-of-Enemies told his companions that they were "going out in the plains after horses, going on a raid," and he led them to the flat territory east of his home in the Guadalupe Mountains. There they found the four horses—the blue one standing in the east, the white in the south, the sorrel in the west, and the black in the north. However, the cardinal horses "could not be approached because they were out on a flat place and were watching closely for someone to come near."[117]

After careful consideration, Killer-of-Enemies decided to call forth a heavy rain; Antonio describes it as follows:

> It rained so hard that one could see only a little way ahead. The wind blew too. The horses stood hunched up, trying to protect themselves from the rain. Then Killer-of-Enemies went around all four horses from the east clockwise four times. He came forward. He had no rope. He then made a blue rope from the sun's blue ray. He used that rope. He put it over the blue horse. It was raining while he got that horse and the horse did not move.[118]

Next, Killer-of-Enemies got a white rope from a ray of the sun and put it around the white horse of the south. Then he took a yellow rope from the sun and a black rope from the sun's shadow, and with these ropes he secured the sorrel of the west and the black of the north.

After he had roped all the cardinal horses, he stopped the rain. The sky cleared, and he called for his three partners to come over and mount three of the horses: Crow Boy, the black; Cowbird, the white; and Bat, the yellow. Killer-of-Enemies had saved the blue horse for himself.[119] Antonio admitted that the culture hero's choice of a blue horse was a personal fancy of his, handed down to him by his father. He explained that "black is usually considered the most sacred color, but in the case of the horse, according to my father, it is different. We always say that blue is most sacred."[120]

Realizing the innate abilities of his three companions in the handling of horses, Killer-of-Enemies decided to test them in a horse race. As he handed the sun-ray ropes to each bird, he made four motions each time with his hands to keep the horses still while the riders mounted. He watched them as they raced their horses in a clockwise course. "The horses didn't pitch."[121]

Having assured himself of the birds' affinities for horses and their powers to perform with them, Killer-of-Enemies was ready to complete his mission. He took Cowbird, Crow, and Bat with him on a journey to a mesa where "they found many horses." Though Antonio did not offer any explanation for how these horses got there, perhaps he meant to imply that they were the offspring of the horses Killer-of-Enemies and his assistants had created on earth and left behind when they went out to the plains to see the cardinal horses Killer-of-Enemies had brought down from the heavens. Possibly they were the progeny of the cardinal horses too. Whatever their origin may have been, Antonio said that wild horses came to exist from the ones they encountered at the mesa. Concluding the story of the first Lipan Apache horses, he related that Killer-of-Enemies and his bird helpers drove these horses "to the Guadalupe Mountains. At that place there was a lake. The horses stayed there and drank, and from there they went out in all directions. After that the Indians got the horses."[122]

Although, as we have seen before, the Mescalero do not credit the cowbird with helping their culture hero at the time of the creation of the horse, they do feel that it has supernatural horse powers. Like the Lipan, they have a tradition to the effect that Cowbird helped in bringing wild horses to their country, though the roles played by him in the two traditions differ at times. The similarities and differences are best illustrated by comparing a Mescalero tale with the preceding Lipan myth.

The Mescalero tale, explaining how wild horses came to exist in the White Mountains located on their reservation in southeastern New Mexico, was collected by Joe Storm from a white cattleman named Jim Jackson, who had lived among the Mescalero and learned the story from them. The "Cowbird" in Jackson's tale happens to be a legendary Indian warrior, who "hadn't an equal for riding pitching horses," and who proved he could handle any kind of horse—even an outlaw. However, with such a name and such "power" over horses, it soon becomes obvious that the Indian warrior is really the incarnation of the bird. As Jackson noted, "Cowbird was about the best rider the horseback Indians ever knew of. He had an instinct for knowing just what a horse was going to do next, no matter how fast he did it."[123]

The horse Cowbird had a special instinct for was one he had stolen from some Mexicans—a powerful black stallion named Diablo. Cowbird really fancied this horse, and the horse fancied him too. The only trouble was that Diablo was an outlaw at heart. One night when Diablo was angry, Cowbird decided to mount him and teach him a lesson. That, according to Jackson's description, was the night a great ride took place:

> The black [Diablo] does a sunfish to the moon, comes down on his
> back, rolls over and goes into some awful contortions. At times he
> flies sideways through the air, very much like a killdee; and at other
> times he turns over and over in the tall grass. But that Indian seems to
> he on like a wart. He's off on his feet at the fall and back on again
> before the horse can get to him. Diablo goes into a white-hot rage;
> and at times he gives the Indian some mean knocks. This keeps up
> most of the night, until Cowbird feels that he can last out no longer....

But Diablo is tiring steadily as morning draws near. Then he
stumbles and falls hard and knows he's whipped.[124]

Cowbird had proved he was master of the outlaw horse, but after the
ride was over, the horse wanted his freedom, and Cowbird allowed him
to go to the mountains. The motif of his releasing the horse to the mountains reminds us again of the incident in which the Lipan Cowbird helped
in driving horses to the mountains and releasing them there. Jackson said
that the fighting Mescalero stallion went off to his high retreat, taking
along as a mate what he called Cowbird's "best sorrel mare"—the "yellow mare" motif again. In the mountains, the black stallion and yellow mare
became the progenitors of the wild horses the Mescalero still see along
the slopes of "Old Baldy" in their country. That is the reason, Jackson said,
why the Mescalero sometimes call those mustangs "Sons of the Devil."[125]

The crow also has power over horses in Chiricahua as well as in Lipan
mythology. But instead of assisting the culture hero, Cowbird, and Bat in
bringing horses to the people, Crow here hinders the protagonist from
liberating animals for the people. Since the Chiricahua believe that crows
controlled not only horses but all the various kinds of animals from the
beginning of time, they feel that the animals had to be freed from these
birds before the people could have them. The Chiricahua say that the
animals were kept underground behind a door in the side of a mountain.[126] The jealous crow guardians watched for trespassers near a stump
placed at the door of their huge corral.

A Chiricahua version of the widely distributed type of Southern
Athapascan tale about the liberation of animals to the people concerns
the freeing of cattle.[127] Though only the liberation of cattle is specifically
mentioned, the tale includes numerous passages demonstrating the crows'
ownership of horses too, explaining that "the crows all had horses in those
days like cowboys," and that they herded their cattle daily on horseback.[128]

In this tale, Killer-of-Enemies is the one who accomplishes the miraculous feats of freeing animals from the crows, although he is considered the less important of the twin brothers in the main body of Chiricahua
mythology. Opler writes that the reason for his taking charge on this
occasion is that the Chiricahua, associating him with the white man, feel
it is only logical that he "be made responsible for the securing of cattle, an
economic good also connected with the white man." Opler also mentions that the Mescalero Apache have a cognate story to the Chiricahua
tale, but he says that in their version, Child-of-the-Water—their culture
hero—acts as protagonist instead.[129]

The Chiricahua tale tells of how Killer-of-Enemies disguised himself as a dog so that he could spy on the crows freely each day when they
let their cattle out to graze. Busy with their herding, the crow cowboys
paid no attention to the dog that trotted alongside the herd, watching
their every movement. The big buffalo bull, which the crows kept stationed by the stump at the entrance of the mountain corral to help them
guard their cattle, took no notice of him either.[130]

After observing the crows' daily comings and goings, Killer-of-Enemies
decided that the best opportunity for him to acquire the cattle would be
sometime when the crows were gone from home. That would mean,
however, that he would have to find a way to get to the cattle at a time
when they were penned up in the corral under the stump. This would be
no easy task, he knew, but he decided to bide his time until exactly the
right moment came. According to the Chiricahua, a good opportunity
soon arose: "One day the crows all got on their horses and went to the
mountains, in a direction which took them away from the stump. After all
the crow men had gone to the hills on their horses," Killer-of-Enemies,
still in the form of a dog, rushed to the stump and engaged in conversation the guardian buffalo, who warned him of the dangerous monsters
below.[131] But Killer-of-Enemies proceeded underground anyhow, after
changing back to his natural self and asking his friend Coyote to come
along with him.

Together, Killer-of-Enemies and Coyote made the journey to the
"holy home," past monster snakes, howling animals, lions with heads
facing each other, and hungry bears. Their journey symbolizes the experiences Chiricahua shamans claim to have when they obtain supernatural
powers. Finally, when they had passed all the monsters, they met another
big buffalo-guard, from whom they asked permission to see the cattle.
Killer-of-Enemies told him all about the earth: "Up there where we came
from there is a big prairie, fine grass, mountains, canyons, water everywhere. Why don't you turn these cattle out there and let them graze? You
have them all penned up here with no grass. Turn them loose up there
and let them get fat."[132]

It is said that the buffalo, after listening to Killer-of-Enemies' advice,
told him to take a pipe and a tobacco pouch over to a very old man in a
nearby dwelling. These were to serve as token gifts to the old man in
charge of the cattle, and they were to symbolize Killer-of-Enemies' request for supernatural power. The protagonist was told not to say a word;
this would make it hard for the old man to refuse him. In a way he, like
any novice shaman, was asking for a ceremony.

Killer-of-Enemies and Coyote followed the buffalo's advice, and with pipe and tobacco pouch in hand, they made their way through the herd of cattle standing everywhere in front of the old man's dwelling. The cattle must have sensed that something important was about to happen, for they fixed their eyes on the elder Twin and his assistant as they walked among them. Getting the permission they desired from the cattle's ancient caretaker was not a difficult problem. When the old man had had a smoke, he consented without further ado to let Killer-of-Enemies and Coyote take all the animals up to that beautiful country where they would thrive so well.

Now it was Coyote who proved to be the real problem. Quite suddenly, when Killer-of-Enemies had rounded up the entire herd and started to drive them out, Coyote changed from docile assistant to destroyer and began killing the cattle.[133] Nevertheless, Killer-of-Enemies managed to get most of the cattle out safely. Just as the last ones were emerging, Coyote slyly grabbed a buffalo by the neck and hid himself under the animal's chest, riding outside in that fashion. The Chiricahua believe that to this day one can still see evidence of where the coyote clung, in the fat lump on a buffalo's chest, which is "brown inside, just the color of a coyote."[134]

The Chiricahua say that since "the cattle belonged to the crows and these crows were trying to protect them in every way" against thievery, they were angry when they came back home late in the afternoon and found that Killer-of-Enemies was driving away their entire herd through the hole in the stump. The returning crows saw "dust coming out of that hole like fog," and made their horses gallop toward the place. They made noises—as real crows sometimes do—"like cowboys herding cattle. . . . They tried their best, but they couldn't drive them back; the cattle got away from them." And while the crows rode hard on the trail of their cattle, trying desperately to stop them, they also yelled out the names of all the bad food—the liver, eyes, entrails, and excrement—they had eaten that day. From that time on, they had to eat such things habitually, the Chiricahua note, adding that that is exactly the reason why "human beings get all the best part of the meat and the crows get what is left."[135] That is the story the Chiricahua tell about how they acquired their domesticated animals; before Killer-of-Enemies freed these animals from the crows, they were not to be found anywhere on earth.

The curious position of Coyote in the preceding Chiricahua tale is an interesting one to compare with his general role in Apache and Navajo myths and tales. In most Apache horse tales, Coyote appears as either a trickster or as a foolish cowboy; sometimes he has the personality traits of a human being, and at other times those of an animal. An exception to these roles occurs in Mescalero mythology, where, as we have already seen, he precedes Child-of-the-Water for a time as the creator of many of the things on earth. However, after the Mescalero culture hero appears on the scene, Coyote is transformed into the brute he is in tales from other Apache groups and plays a similar role. Generally speaking, Coyote's character in Apache tales epitomizes the less desirable characteristics of humans, since the main purpose of the Coyote cycle of tales is to teach moral principles to the young. The secondary purpose is to have a scapegoat around in mythology on whom such shortcomings as incest, adultery, perverse conduct, falsehood, theft, and laziness can be blamed.

Three basic types of Apache Coyote tales relate the trickster Coyote's exploits with horses. These are the ones in which (1) Coyote shows how he can lie and steal a horse, then pretends the horse balks because it wants handsome trappings; (2) Coyote paints a horse a color other than its natural color and sells it to a gullible buyer; (3) Coyote owns a horse that he makes a prospective buyer believe defecates money. There are versions and variants of the above three tale types in Chiricahua, Kiowa-Apache, Jicarilla, Lipan, and White Mountain Apache collections. Sometimes a mule or a burro is substituted for the horse, and quite often the tricked man is a white man. When he is not a white man, he is usually an Indian from an enemy tribe, but the pattern for all these tales is basically the same.[136]

In the type of tale in which he appears as a foolish cowboy, Coyote tries to lasso horses like some real Apache cowboys he happens to meet. Imitating their technique, he ties one end of a rope around his waist and goes to work. His trouble is that he does not know how to stop the horse once he has lassoed it. In a Chiricahua version of this type of tale, "the horse starts to run and drags Coyote, who bumps along with tail in air. The cowboys follow and find Coyote's bones and entrails along the trail." The Chiricahua cowboys decide that the foolish Coyote "must still be holding on to the horse with other parts of his body."[137]

In an episode from a Navajo myth, Coyote, as well as Crow, appear among five traditional horse thieves who attempt to steal a blue Mirage Quartz Rock mare that Frog Man has given the Twins. Their partners in this deed are Owl, Magpie, and Vulture. According to this Navajo myth, "these were looting people who stole from other people." When the Twins caught them "red handed" with their stolen horse, "they were angry. . . ." Each of them told the Twins: "We are your brothers, [but] you are the only ones on earth who were given the horse."[138] In their envy, the five thieves decided mutually that since this was the case, they would arrange at least for things to be different from that time on whenever a horse died. They vowed that then they would take charge. Plans were made for Coyote to have the "meat and bones," Crow the horses' eyes, and the others the various remaining parts. When Sun heard about what these five had planned, he said that they were his "naughty" children. He complained to the Twins about them, saying: "They never ask for animals or how to take care of them. That is why they never got any of them. You asked for animals and that is why you were given the horse."[139]

Another animal spirit—a guardian horse—appears in Kiowa-Apache mythology as a hindrance to the twin culture heroes in bringing horses to their people. In 1934, Alvin Shaman, a middle-aged Kiowa-Apache medicine man, who lived in Apache, Oklahoma, gave McAllister his version of the story about how the Kiowa-Apache got their horses. He recounted how twin brothers called Fire Boy and Water Boy released all the horses to the Kiowa-Apache from the guardianship of a wild, devilish horse while they were overcoming all the monsters and enemies of the people. During these trials, Thunderman told the boys: "Way out there is a wild horse. He looks at you and kills you with his eye.[140] You boys stay away from him."[141] But the boys talked it over among themselves and decided to overcome the wild horse just as the Chiricahua Apache's Killer-of-Enemies and Coyote had decided to free the animals belonging to Crow. Alvin continued: "They found the horse, spun their medicine, and then killed him. They told the old man [Thunderman], 'Now the Indians can get horses. They can get them and ride around on them.' "[142]

A completely different version of how his people acquired horses was told to McAllister the same year by a seventy-five-year-old Kiowa-Apache named Solomon Katchin, who also lived in Apache, Oklahoma. However, while the events preceding the release of horses to the people in Katchin's version follow a completely different pattern from those in the above account, the motif of the horses being controlled by another guardian horse is still present. This time the guardian is an "old mare" who—in Katchin's words—was "the leader of the horses." On the other hand, the animal spirit who releases the horses to the people is one not introduced here before—Mole. Unlike the animal spirits in the foregoing myths and tales, Mole does not aid or hinder a culture hero; instead he acts as an independent worker, performing this service in answer to a request from the people. They ask him to go over to a lake and get for them the horses that had come there to drink. At that time, Katchin explained, "the Apaches had no horses, only dogs," and according to him, this was the way the mission for horses was accomplished: "Mole went under the water across the lake. He . . . went after this mare [the leader]. When she stooped down to drink, Mole made ripples and these ripples became a rope and got around the mare's neck. Mole had a hold of the other end of the rope and led the mare to a tipi in the village. The other horses followed. That is how the Apaches got horses. They were the first to get them."[143]

Perhaps the belief that the first horses were captured around a lake has its origin in the fact that the Kiowa-Apache and the Kiowa Indians actually often captured their wild horses by surrounding them at water holes and driving them into corrals similar to those they built for hunting antelope.[144] Whatever the origin of the belief may be, the motif associating horses with bodies of water is a common one in Southern Athapascan mythology. When the preceding Kiowa-Apache acquisition tale mentions that the first horses were seen around a lake, it reminds us of the ending of the Lipan account given earlier in which Killer-of-Enemies and his assistants drove the first horses to a lake in the Guadalupe Mountains. The latter myth said that at that lake, the first horses stayed and drank, "and from there they went out in all directions" so the people could acquire them.[145] This motif points to only one of the similarities that exist between Kiowa-Apache and Lipan mythology and possibly is explained by the fact that these Apache groups belong to the same linguistic grouping—the Eastern Apachean division. The Jicarilla, who also belong to this linguistic grouping, likewise possess in their mythology the motif that associates horses with lakes. The Jicarilla tell of how a supernatural person who lived in a lake asked some Apache who were going out after enemy horses to bring him "the horse that is all black without a white spot." When the Apache got to their enemy's camp they found there "the black one with no white spots for which the supernatural one had asked." They caught the horse and took it back with them. On their return journey, as they came near to the place where the deity lived, "the black one ran immediately to the lake" and stayed there from then on.[146] It may also be remembered that another association between horses and lakes occurred in a Navajo myth examined earlier—this was when the Twins saw all of Frog Man's horses living around the subterranean lake where he kept them. Located underneath Wide Belt Mountain, the Navajo lake was said to have "a lot of weeds on the surface of the eastern side. There were water weeds, long reeds and pollen on the shore."[147]

In every society there are always skeptics, and not every Navajo or Apache was sure the gift of horses by the gods and other beneficent supernaturals was a real blessing to the Southern Athapascan people. Later, there were those who looked "the gift horse in the mouth," and decided that the animal the people had done so long without caused more trouble than it brought happiness. A Southern Tonto Apache named Henry Irving of Payson, Arizona, belonged to this set. He attributed the separation of the Apache groups from the Navajo and from one another to Sun's gift of the horse to Slayer-of-Monsters (Killer-of-Enemies). This gift also brought them trouble with the Hopi, he felt, expressing his idea to Goodwin in this way:

> Long ago, all our people were living at tálbà.ko.wà ("dance camp"). This place is right under a point of the mesa where the Hopi live. In those days, when we first came on this earth, there was nothing. We were living there with the Navaho and Hopi in that country. We were getting on all right, but Slayer of Monsters went to his father, Sun, and got a horse from him. From that time on trouble started, so our people moved south across the Little Colorado.[148]

If we can follow Irving's reasoning, even the automobile brought less trouble for the few remaining Southern Tonto Apache still living either at or around Camp Verde or down at the Fort McDowell or San Carlos reservations.

Though the separation of these people occurred long before horses arrived on the scene, the Navajo have a similar legend, which Sandoval related to O'Bryan. It tells of the separation of the Navajo from the Apache of the south—probably meaning the White Mountain Apache. Sandoval summarized the grievances that the horse brought among the people as follows:

> Now that the horses were given to the people, and there were a great many people in the land, they commenced to crowd each other. Some of the people wanted to go to war over the slightest thing. They taught their children to be quarrelsome; they were not raising them in the right way. They did not have peace in their hearts. At this time there appeared in the country many plants with thorns, in fact these were more numerous than any other kind of plant. Even the grass became sharp and spiked. It was because of the people's ill nature, and the plants and the grass, that another plan was formed.[149]

Besides the wars and separations that the folk tales and legends of the Navajo and Apache assure us the horse produced, it brought still another problem. Both the Navajo and Apache ate the first horses that fell into their hands, but before much time passed, they decided they had better learn how to ride them. Humorous Apache tales show us that this was not the easiest thing in the world to do.

Traditions say that the Foolish People, a not very bright Apache people found in Chiricahua and Mescalero folk tales, never learned to ride horses properly, much less to control them. The Jicarilla Apache call these same people either Foolish People or Traveling People, while to the Lipan Apache they are known as the Spotted Wood People.

These Foolish People, according to Opler, "are said by the Chiricahua and Mescalero Apache to have been an actual group, formerly living near or in Mescalero territory and speaking an Apache language."[150]

The Lipan named Antonio Apache extended this idea a step further. In his estimation they were the ancient people, who "didn't have much sense. They lived on mescal and stayed out in the flats. The other people, the Mescalero, the Chiricahua, the Lipan, and so on, started from the Spotted Wood People."[151]

Whether these statements contain elements of truth or not, such stories have now come to be purely traditional Apache folk tales. On the other hand, it might not be stretching the point too far to make a few conjectures. Could these tales, now considered merely as Apache humor tales, told only for amusement or to warn children against foolishness and misbehavior, possibly recount some of the experiences the early Apache suffered in learning to ride? Considering the fact that the Apache and the Navajo acquired horses from three hundred and fifty to three hundred and eighty years ago, this would give truth over three and a half centuries to work its way into the form of traditional tales.

Throughout these tales, the Foolish People are known only as fast runners, and the only thing that they ever accomplish that their chroniclers can cite with any pride is that they can outrun the horses of the Comanche or any pursuing cavalryman. No matter what the heart of the tale may center upon, the story seldom omits one fact that further emphasizes the extent to which fine horsemanship came to be admired by the Southern Athapascan cultures. This fact is—these people were so foolish, "they didn't even know how to get on a horse."[152]

When the Foolish People see their first horses, they hold councils to discuss what to call the horse, what to feed it, just what to do to make this unknown animal happy and comfortable. When they start to ride it, they usually mount it backwards; some even go so far as to smear pitch on their buttocks to assure success.

One of the best examples of the Foolish People's endeavors at learning to ride is found in a long Jicarilla Apache tale concerning these simple-minded people's acquisition of horses from an enemy Plains band. They camped with the enemy, being so dumb as not even to understand that they were enemies. Their antics delighted the Plains Indians so much that they took compassion on them and gave them some saddles and gentle horses when they started to move, so that they would not have to continue walking everywhere. According to the Jicarilla tale, "these people didn't know what the horses were for or what the saddles were for." The patient hosts, who spoke another tongue, explained in sign language that the horses were to be ridden and that the saddles were to be put on them for that purpose. "So," it is said, "these people put the saddle on, but put it on in reverse fashion. They didn't tie the cinch. They knew nothing about saddling horses."[153]

This amused the enemy people, who had never before experienced anything quite like it, and they decided to get the most out of the situation. In sign language, they told the foolish Apache people to sit on the saddles. When one of the group "tried to put his foot in the stirrup and mount," the Jicarilla say, "the saddle fell on him," and "the enemy people laughed and laughed. 'These are funny people,' they thought."[154]

The Plains Indians showed their guests how to saddle a horse properly and asked one of the men visitors to try sitting on it. This request, the Jicarilla note, set off a chain of humorous incidents, because "the man who tried it did not sit the right way. He sat on backward, facing the tail. He didn't put his feet in the stirrups, but let them hang down. Then he started off, but his face was turned the wrong way. He couldn't stop the horse. The horse just carried him around." Some of the Foolish People tried a number of different ways to help him bring his mount to a halt. One thought that if he pulled the horse's tail, this might stop the animal—so he tried that. When this did not work, the others ran around in front of the horse and put sticks in its path, only to find that the creature knew how to step over them and keep right on going. Finally, one of the men saw that the horse's reins were dragging; he caught the rope and stopped the runaway, but in stopping the horse he did not end the Foolish People's problems. The Jicarilla say that now the trouble was that they "didn't know how to make it go the right way. Every time the horse moved they pulled the rope, but they didn't know how to turn it around. So they waited till some of the enemy came and led the horse back."[155]

Back at camp one of the men from the Plains group rode a horse in front of the Foolish People, trying to teach them how to control it. One of the Foolish People mounted a horse and tried to follow his instructions. He kicked the horse to start it, but he forgot to place his feet in the stirrups, so he came tumbling off as soon as the horse began to move. His experience discouraged the rest from practicing riding with the Plains' teacher after that.

Among themselves, however, the men from the group of Foolish People conjectured about how the Plains Indians managed to stay on their horses. They decided the reason must be that the enemy had put "pitch on their buttocks." They said, "This is plains country without trees and pitch. Let's lead those horses back to our country and get pitch and put it on ourselves. Then we'll all ride." So they decided to leave their hosts and return home. Not knowing how to ride, they led their horses all the way back to their country.[156]

As soon as they got home, all the men headed straight for the woods to gather pitch. They took their horses with them, since they envisioned themselves returning to camp, seated in grand style on their horses, before the admiring eyes of their wives. Out in the woods, they smeared their buttocks generously with the pitch they gathered. When they decided to mount, it is said that they "helped each other and pushed each other up on the horses. They were not using saddles. Some men sat facing the horses' heads, and some sat facing the horses' tails. Some were sitting up on the horses' manes, and some were far back near the horses' tails."[157]

Their horses, which had just been standing around in all different kinds of positions while they waited for the men to gather the pitch, moved off in whatever direction they happened to be facing when the men mounted them. Since the men did not know how to guide the horses, and the horses certainly did not know where the men wanted them to go, they went first one way and then another. They carried the men around all over the country that night and the next day too, and the men, glued securely to their mounts, could not do a thing about it.

The men might have ridden around forever, but fortunately the women back at camp, wondering what had happened to their husbands, started searching for them when they did not come home. Most of the women had to walk long distances before they found their husbands. One man would be found away off in some place, and the next man would appear in an entirely different locality. Usually when the women found their husbands, the horses would be complacently grazing while the men just sat there, hopelessly stuck to the backs of their mounts. Each of the wives had to pick up the rope of her husband's horse, and lead it and its hapless rider back to camp.

The women could not imagine what the trouble was, and the men were so embarrassed that they would not tell their wives what had happened.

A San Carlos puberty maiden (left) dances with a girl companion to enact the role of White Painted Woman, the goddess who created horses for the Apache. Before her is a ceremonial deerskin similar to what the goddess used along with other objects like the four coiled baskets and containers that have been placed in front of the hide to serve as the ceremonial offerings.

When they arrived home, the women tried their best to persuade their husbands to get down from their horses, but the men would not budge. It especially annoyed the women that their husbands would not even dismount long enough to eat. They grew tired of trying to coax the men down; so they tried, unsuccessfully, to pull them off their mounts while the men protested: "Don't! That hurts!"[158]

Since all else had failed, the women talked it over among themselves, and, according to the Jicarilla, came to the conclusion that their husbands "must have defecated on the horses' backs" and became stuck there in that way. The tale recounts that "the women led the horses to the river to see if they could clean off the horses and get the men down. They filled the water bags with water and then threw it underneath the men's buttocks. . . . It took a long time to clean it up and get the men off. But finally they were off. The men were afraid then. They didn't want to get on the horses. They said it was dangerous."[159]

At this point, the long Jicarilla tale concerning the Foolish People's acquisition of horses turns away from the amusing incidents dealing with these people's complete lack of any kind of riding ability and combines with several other types of these horse tales. These types are humorous stories that relate how the people mistake the horse for another animal, how they try to find uses for horses, and how they learn what to feed a horse.[160]

A better example of the last type, however, comes from a Lipan Apache tale told by Antonio Apache. His version tells of how these people attempted unsuccessfully to go on a raid and how they suddenly came upon a horse on their return trip home. Antonio recounted that they tried to feed the animal some gravy first. When the horse refused to eat it, Antonio said: "They kept giving him food that humans eat. The horse would not touch it. While they were discussing what to do the horse walked off by himself and began to graze. 'Oh, that's what he eats,' they said. And they began to pull grass for him. Then, after the horse was fed, they let it go."[161] Thus, it seems that while the Foolish People learned what to feed horses, they did not learn what a raid was all about.

Nevertheless, the day came when even the "dumbest" Navajo or Apache knew the meaning of the raid for horses. The time came too when most of the Navajo and Apache people could fly along through the desert or up a trail into the mountains, their horses and themselves seeming as one. And there was also a time when all the enemies—Indian or white man—could attest that when these people made camp, they always tried to find the most succulent pastures for their best friends.

Those skeptical of the horse among the Navajo and Apache were to be outnumbered too, for by and large the Southern Athapascans agreed with the sleepy God People that "something extraordinary" had been happening to them. The Navajo, the Western Apache, the Chiricahua, the Mescalero, the Jicarilla, the Lipan, and the Kiowa-Apache realized they had acquired that "something, by means of which men live." And from the four corners of the Southwest, from Arizona to Texas and Oklahoma, from southern Colorado and northern New Mexico to down along the Mexican border, "These, the turquoise horse and the white shell horse, they called to each other. . . . On this side, the abalone shell horse and the black jewel horse, they called to each other."[162]

This was the story of the gift of the gods . . .

So they say.

Notes

1. Haile, *Navaho Enemy Way,* p. 107.
2. O'Bryan, pp. 81, 82.
3. Ibid., p. 81, n. 66.
4. Oakes and Campbell, pp. 27–28.
5. Goodwin, *Myths and Tales of the White Mountain,* p. 9. Note that Goodwin employs the spellings of Na.ye'nezyane for Naiyenezgani and T'uba'tc'istcine for Tobatc'istcini. For the sake of consistency, the latter spellings of these names, which occurred in the preceding chapter and which follow Goddard, will be employed throughout this work, except in quoted passages.
6. The Jicarilla Apache have a tradition about the Twins receiving some guns from their grandfather, Thunder, whom they had stopped by to see on their way back to earth after their visit with Sun. The Jicarilla relate that Grandfather Thunder gave the boys guns, "but they were just children and didn't know how to handle them. They began to shoot at everything in sight and soon were destroying many valuable possessions, such as horses." So Thunder made his grandsons give back the guns and "gave them arrows instead"! See Opler, *Myths and Tales of the Jicarilla,* p. 55.
7. Goodwin, *Myths and Tales of the White Mountain,* p. 38, n. 1. The book in this passage refers to the book of knowledge that the White Mountain Apache believe Sun gave Naiyenezgani instead of a horse on another occasion. It is said that Naiyenezgani threw the book away, but his younger brother picked it up, read it, produced white people, and "went off with them." See ibid.
8. See Hoijer, *Chiricahua and Mescalero Apache Texts,* pp. 13–14.
9. Opler, *Myths and Tales of the Chiricahua,* pp. 15–16, n. 6. A Chiricahua informant further elaborated to Opler about Killer-of-Enemies' relationship to the white man in this way: "Killer-of-Enemies represents the white people. They live on corn. All their possessions came from the corn. They became wealthy. When the Creator saw Child-of-the-Water again, he said: 'You have nothing and just run around. Your drinking water is the green water among the rocks.' And the Indians are that way. The Creator gave Killer-of-Enemies everything, so Child-of-the-Water had to steal. . . ." See ibid., pp. 14–15, n. 1.
10. See McAllister, "Kiowa-Apache Tales," p. 35 ff.
11. Matthews, *Navaho Legends,* p. 86; Fishler, *In the Beginning,* p. 11. Cf. *supra,* pp. 22–24; 50, nn. 12, 19.
12. Fishler, *In the Beginning,* p. 22.
13. Note Goddard's spellings of Naiye'nezyani and Tobadj'ictcini for the Navajo names of the Twins are practically the same as the Western Apache (White Mountain and San Carlos) names he recorded, thus the Apache spelling is employed here.

14. Goddard, *Navajo Texts,* pp. 153–156. It should also be noted that in some versions of this myth, when White Shell Woman and Changing Woman appear as separate sister goddesses rather than as the same goddess, the culture heroes do not have the same mother. In such versions, Naiyenezgani is usually the son of Changing Woman, while Tobatc'istcini belongs to White Shell Woman. See Matthews, *Navaho Legends,* pp. 105–106; p. 231, n. 101.

15. In a version of a Navajo creation myth recorded by Wheelwright, Békotsidi (Begochiddy) is further identified with the Christian God. See Hasteen Klah, *Navajo Creation Myth,* recorded by Mary C. Wheelwright (Santa Fe: Museum of Navajo Ceremonial Art, 1942), pp. 39, 69.

16. Matthews, *Navaho Legends,* pp. 86–87. The Jicarilla Apache have a tale about a hoop and pole game played between Killer-of-Enemies and a gambler called One-Who-Wins. The gambler had previously won everything on earth by which the people subsisted. Killer-of-Enemies defeated him twenty-four times and restored to the people all the animals and good things of the earth and sky. See Opler, *Myths and Tales of the Jicarilla,* pp. 131–133.

17. Matthews, *Navaho Legends,* p. 87.

18. Fishler, *In the Beginning,* p. 106.

19. Sapir and Hoijer, pp. 109, 111, 495, n. 13:2.

20. Ibid., pp. 109, 111. Pelado Peak is located in the Jemez Mountain Range of New Mexico, north of the Jemez Indian Pueblo.

21. Ibid., p. 111.

22. Ibid.

23. Ibid.

24. Ibid., pp. 111, 113. "Hard goods" are beads and jewelry; "soft goods" are skins and blankets.

25. Ibid., p. 113. Mt. Taylor is located northeast of Grants, New Mexico.

26. Ibid.

27. Ibid., pp. 115, 117. Debentsa, or Big Sheep, is the summit of the La Plata Range of Colorado.

28. Huerfano Peak is located outside El Huerfano, New Mexico, on State Highway No. 44, about twenty-three miles south of Farmington, New Mexico. The Navajo often refer to this mountain as "Mountain-Around-Which-Moving-Was-Done," or Reversible Mountain. The Navajo call it the latter name because they reason that "you can look at the mountain from all sides and it still looks that same way from any direction." See Fishler, "Navaho Picture Writing," p. 71.

29. Sapir and Hoijer, p. 117.

30. Ibid.

31. Ibid.

32. Ibid., p. 119.

33. Ibid., p. 496, n. 13:20.

34. O'Bryan, p. 178.

35. The first proof of Navajo presence in the Southwest is found in wood taken from a hut located in the Gobernador Canyon, forty miles north of Gallina, New Mexico. The wood dates around 1550. See Edward Twitchell Hall, Jr.,

Early Stockaded Settlements in the Governador, New Mexico, Columbia University Studies in Archaeology and Ethnology, II, Part I (New York: Columbia University Press, 1944), p. 6, n. 7; p. 7, n. 9.

36. Sapir and Hoijer, p. 119.
37. Lansing B. Bloom and Lynn B. Mitchell, "The Chapter Elections in 1672," *New Mexico Historical Review*, XIII, No. 1 (January 1938), p. 107.
38. Sapir and Hoijer, p. 119.
39. Ibid.
40. Ibid.
41. Ibid., pp. 121, 123.
42. Ibid., p. 123. Either pollen—the symbol of life and renewal—or a ritual substitute, is omnipresent on ceremonial occasions. The common substitute is cornmeal. Pollens used are those from piñon, pine, oak, tule, sunflower, flag, larkspur, harebell, or sumac. "Other preparations may also be regarded as pollen," the Franciscan Fathers observe; e.g. powdered dust from the bodies of certain animals as well as the hardened spittle of these animals. See Franciscan Fathers, *An Ethnologic Dictionary of the Navaho Language* (Saint Michaels, Ariz.: Navajo Indian Mission, 1910), p. 400.
43. Sapir and Hoijer, p. 123.
44. Ibid.
45. Fishler, *In the Beginning*, pp. 70–71.
46. Ibid. When the informant refers to *Sísnajíni* as Wide Belt Mountain, he is using one of the many descriptive names the Navajo have for the holy mountain of the east. Fishler and other Navajo scholars often identify *Sísnajíni* as Pelado Peak. See Fishler, "Navaho Picture Writing," p. 68; also Franciscan Fathers, *An Ethnologic Dictionary of the Navaho Language*, pp. 56, 136.
47. Fishler, *In the Beginning*, p. 72.
48. Ibid., pp. 73, 83.
49. Ibid., p. 73.
50. Ibid.
51. Ibid., pp. 73, 74.
52. Ibid., p. 74.
53. Ibid., pp. 75, 77.
54. Ibid., p. 75.
55. Matthews, *Navaho Legends*, pp. 133–134.
56. Sapir and Hoijer, p. 125. According to Mitchell, "one of those which are not arrow marked" refers to the skin of something that has been killed by a not too sharp object. "A deerskin is so called," he explained. See ibid., p. 123.
57. Cf. Franciscan Fathers, *An Ethnologic Dictionary of the Navaho Language*, p. 363; also *infra*, pp. 174–176.
58. Sapir and Hoijer, p. 125.
59. Ibid.
60. Ibid.
61. Ibid., p. 127; p. 497, n. 13:32, n. 13:33, n. 13:34.
62. For the location of Sisna.te.l, see *supra*, p. 66.

63. Sapir and Hoijer, p. 127. By paying for the ceremony, Mitchell means that he obtained this story from Wide Man, paying for it according to Navajo ceremonial order with ceremonial gifts.

64. Goddard, *Navaho Texts,* p. 157.

65. Ibid. These very words are a Navajo prayer formula for horses. As we shall see later the Navajo still use such prayers. For a deity to pray by formula was the next thing to producing the desired end, since the Navajo consider the words of prayer to be compulsive.

66. Reichard, *Navaho Religion,* II, pp. 412–413.

67. Fishler, *In the Beginning,* p. 70.

68. See Oakes and Campbell, p. 39; also *supra,* p. 29.

69. Fishler, *In the Beginning,* p. 71.

70. Ibid., pp. 71, 77.

71. O'Bryan, pp. 175–176.

72. The Franciscan Fathers identify this mountain as *Ch'oshgai* and locate it at the southeastern end of the Chuska Range, which runs across a northern section of the Arizona–New Mexico border. See their *An Ethnologic Dictionary of the Navaho Language,* p. 31.

73. O'Bryan, p. 176.

74. Ibid., pp. 176–77.

75. See Goddard, *Navajo Texts,* pp. 174–175. Cf. also Fishler, *In the Beginning,* pp. 89–91, 100. He has recorded a similar myth concerning White Bead Woman's instructing a boy and a girl in rites beneficial to the people, which she wished them to teach the Navajo after she left the earth.

76. It may be recalled that an account given earlier mentions that a jet horse stood at the center of the new house of Changing Woman in the west. See Reichard, *Navaho Religion,* pp. II, 412, or *supra,* p. 75.

77. Goddard, *Navajo Texts,* p. 164.

78. O'Bryan, p. 177. Note the color sequence, popular with the Navajo, but more so with the Apache.

79. Ibid. The last two lines are the blessing part of the chant. A blessing part is traditional in all Navajo chants.

80. Goddard, *Navajo Texts,* p. 164.

81. O'Bryan, pp. 177–178.

82. Ibid., p. 178.

83. Franciscan Fathers, *An Ethnologic Dictionary of the Navaho Language,* p. 356.

84. Fishler, *In the Beginning,* pp. 76–77. Another myth Fishler collected from Goldtooth tells how White Bead Woman gave cattle and other animals besides horses to earth people. It records that the goddess left them in various places throughout the country as she journeyed overland on her departure to the western home Sun had built for her in the world of the gods. See ibid., pp. 86–88.

85. Goodwin, *Myths and Tales of the White Mountain,* p. 37. Tithla lived in Bylas, Arizona, on the San Carlos Apache Reservation and gave Goodwin his version in 1932.

86. Ibid. In this particular mythical episode, the White Mountain Apache color sequence pairs black in the west with black in the east.

87. Ibid. The ceremony of the horse comes from the supernatural experience in which anyone receives the power of horses. The Apache believe that such power is necessary in producing and controlling horses or in treating an illness incurred in some way by them.

88. Ibid., pp. 37–38.

89. Goddard, *Myths and Tales from the White Mountain,* p. 119.

90. Ibid. While I have not been able to find any information regarding the present geographical location for the White Mountain Apache's cottonwood tree, which their traditions say stood at the center of the earth, I have found that the cottonwood tree also has an important position in Navajo mythology. See Goddard, *Navajo Texts,* p. 174, for mention of a place called "Cottonwood-tree-stands," as well as the tradition that the Navajo stopped on their migrations and planted corn beneath the tree where "water flows much spread out." O'Bryan, p. 168, also records a similar mythical episode, saying that after White Bead Woman created the Navajo, she sent them on their migrations to the country between the four mountains and told them to plant their corn at a place called Tseast tsó sá kade (Big Cottonwood Tree), which was located on a plain. Also see Fishler, *In the Beginning,* p. 100. His informant located two important cotton-wood trees that stand, he related, at a spring on the east side of Tohatchi, New Mexico. He said that the two children who were taken to the west to learn a ceremony from White Bead Woman were found in a cornfield at this place. Note further that the O'Bryan account also includes the motif of two boys being taken magically from the cornfield to learn the goddess's ceremony. For the incident, see *supra,* pp. 76.

91. Goddard, *Myths and Tales from the White Mountain,* p. 119. Cf. Goodwin, *Myths and Tales of the White Mountain,* p. 86, where a version of a myth concerning how the first Apache horse shaman acquired his powers and ceremony is given. The shaman discovers cardinal stallions of the same directional colors as the above, and they also surround a cottonwood tree. Note too that cockleburs of the same directional colors as the burdocks in the above account also figure in this myth.

92. Goddard, *Myths and Tales from the White Mountain,* p. 103.

93. Ibid.

94. Ibid.

95. Ibid., p. 102, n. 2; pp. 103–104.

96. Ibid., p. 104.

97. Ibid.

98. Ibid.

99. Ibid., p. 105.

100. Ibid., p. 107.

101. Opler, *Myths and Tales of the Jicarilla,* pp. 1, 141, 147–148, 185–186. Cf. Pliny Earle Goddard, *Jicarilla Apache Texts,* Anthropological Papers of the American Museum of Natural History, VIII (New York: The American Museum of Natural History, 1911), p. 265. Here the Jicarilla gods of the four directions are further identified, though associated with different cardinal colors, as sunrise or east—

Xastcīnyalkīdn, "the talking god"; south—Xastcīnyalgayī, "the white god"; sunset or west—Xastcīnīltsōyī, "the yellow god"; and north—Xastcīndīsōsī, "the variegated god."

102. Opler, *Myths and Tales of the Jicarilla*, pp. 1–2, 4. The origin myth says that after the animals and birds met at a council with Black Hactcin and told him they needed man as a companion, "he traced an outline of a figure on the ground, making it just like his own body, for the Hactcin were shaped just as we are today." Black Hactcin brought this tracing to life after his own image and named his creation, Ancestral Man. Next, he proceeded to form a female partner for the man; she was called Ancestral Woman. See ibid., pp. 5–6.

103. See Fishler, *In the Beginning*, pp. 11, 16–17; Matthews, "Navaho Myths, Prayers and Songs," pp. 58–59.

104. See Opler, *Myths and Tales of the Chiricahua*, p. 77, n. 1.

105. Opler, *Myths and Tales of the Jicarilla*, p. 2.

106. Ibid., p. 26. Jicarilla traditions vary about the identification of the emergence mountain. Some say it is a peak in the San Juan Mountains north of Durango, Colorado; others, a big mountain near Alamosa, Colorado. Still others place it at the "heart of the earth" near Taos, New Mexico. See ibid., pp. 26, n. 2; 57, n. 1; 163–164.

107. Fishler, *In the Beginning*, pp. 27–29, 34.

108. Opler, *Myths and Tales of the Jicarilla*, pp. 26, 215, 260.

109. Ibid., p. 77. Cf. Goddard, *Jicarilla Apache Texts*, p. 205, for a similar version of this myth concerning the origin of sheep and cattle.

110. See the ethnological notes by Opler in Hoijer, *Chiricahua and Mescalero Apache Texts*, p. 216. Coyote's role as a creator-transformer-trickster-dupe is a frequent theme in folklore from many other Indian tribes. Raven also appears in this role.

111. Hoijer, *Chiricahua and Mescalero Apache Texts*, p. 177.

112. Ibid., p. 181.

113. Opler, *Myths and Legends of the Lipan*, pp. 29–30.

114. Ibid., p. 32; *supra*, p. 17. As noted earlier, the most common Lipan color circuit is black—east, blue—south, yellow—west, and white—north. Regarding the color sequence employed here, Opler wrote: "This is a personal note. Another individual who knew the ceremony of the horse utilized the ordinary set of colors." See *Myths and Legends of the Lipan*, p. 30, n. 1.

115. Opler, *Myths and Legends of the Lipan*, p. 31, n. 1.

116. Ibid., p. 30.

117. Ibid., pp. 30; 32, n. 2.

118. Ibid., p. 30.

119. Ibid., pp. 30–31.

120. Ibid., p. 30.

121. Ibid., p. 31.

122. Ibid., p. 32.

123. Joe Storm, "Sons of the Devil," in *Puro Mexicano*, ed. J. Frank Dobie, Publication of the Texas Folklore Society, No. 12 (Austin: Texas Folklore Society, 1935), pp. 191, 192.

124. Ibid., pp. 192–193.

125. Ibid., p. 193.

126. The motif of animals being kept behind a door in the side of a mountain is a common one in Navajo and Apache mythology. For examples from the Navajo and from other Apache groups, see Fishler, *In the Beginning,* pp. 73, 126; Goddard, *Myths and Tales from the White Mountain,* p. 118; and Wheelwright, *Hail Chant and Water Chant,* p. 90.

127. For examples from other Apache groups of this type of Southern Athapascan tale, which contain many similar motifs about the release of buffalo and deer from the crow, or on some occasion from the raven, see the following: Goddard, *Jicarilla Apache Texts,* pp. 212–214; Goddard, *Myths and Tales from the White Mountain,* pp. 126–127; Opler, *Myths and Tales of the Jicarilla,* pp. 256–260; and Opler, *Myths and Legends of the Lipan,* pp. 122–125.

128. Opler, *Myths and Tales of the Chiricahua,* p. 16.

129. Ibid., p. 16, n. The Mescalero cognate tale appears in an unpublished manuscript by Opler entitled "Myths and Tales of the Mescalero Apache Indians," which I have not seen.

130. Opler, *Myths and Tales of the Chiricahua,* pp. 16–17.

131. Ibid., p. 17.

132. Ibid.

133. Ibid., pp. 17–18. The motif of Coyote killing animals while he herds them is common in Apache mythology. See Goddard, *Myths and Tales from the White Mountain,* p. 138, for the incident of his killing mules; Opler, *Myths and Legends of the Lipan,* p. 166, for the incident of his killing sheep.

134. Opler, *Myths and Tales of the Chiricahua,* p. 18.

135. Ibid.

136. For examples of these types of Coyote tales, see Opler, *Myths and Tales of the Chiricahua,* pp. 56–57; McAllister, "Kiowa-Apache Tales," pp. 78–80; Opler, *Myths and Tales of the Jicarilla,* pp. 316–317; Opler, *Myths and Legends of the Lipan,* pp. 163, 166–167; Goodwin, *Myths and Tales of the White Mountain,* pp. 194–196.

137. Opler, *Myths and Tales of the Chiricahua,* p. 72. This motif also appears in the "Foolish People" cycle of tales from other Apache groups. This tale cycle is examined later in this chapter.

138. Fishler, *In the Beginning,* pp. 74–75. The horse thieves meant that they were the Twins' half-brothers, for it is explained that each of them "had a mother who was the wife of Sun." See ibid., p. 75.

139. Ibid., p. 75.

140. The motif of the killing of eye-killer animals and birds is a very common one in Navajo and Apache mythology.

141. McAllister, "Kiowa-Apache Tales," p. 39. In this version, Thunderman appears as the Twins' father, and their mother is an earth woman. Reference is also made to a later marriage between Thunderman and a female Sun. See ibid., pp. 34–35. The Kiowa-Apache's culture heroes bear many resemblances to the twin hero-gods of the Kiowa Indians, who are called Sun-Boy and Water-Boy and who are said to be the sons of a male Sun or of Sun's son. Undoubtedly the resem-

blances between these culture heroes come about through the centuries of association the Kiowa-Apache have had with the Kiowa. For information on the Kiowa culture heroes, see Wilbur Sturtevant Nye, *Bad Medicine and Good: Tales of the Kiowas* (Norman: University of Oklahoma Press, 1962), pp. vii, n. 1; 49–50; and Newcomb, *The Indians of Texas,* p. 220.

142. McAllister, "Kiowa-Apache Tales," p. 39.

143. Ibid., pp. 51–52.

144. Newcomb, *The Indians of Texas,* p. 197. The author also describes here the manner in which these Indians captured antelope.

145. Opler, *Myths and Legends of the Lipan,* p. 32.

146. Goddard, *Jicarilla Apache Texts,* p. 221. This account also tells of how the Jicarilla built corrals near bodies of water to capture antelope. Cf. also the Jicarilla's supernatural being with the Kiowa-Apache and Kiowa water heroes, who disappeared into bodies of water and lived there. See Nye, *Bad Medicine and Good: Tales of the Kiowas,* p. 50; McAllister, "Kiowa-Apache Tales," pp. 35–38.

147. Fishler, *In the Beginning,* p. 73.

148. Goodwin, *The Social Organization of the Western Apache,* p. 620, n. 47.

149. O'Bryan, p. 181.

150. Note by Opler in Hoijer, *Chiricahua and Mescalero Apache Texts,* p. 146, n. 24:1.

151. Opler, *Myths and Legends of the Lipan,* p. 205.

152. Opler, *Myths and Tales of the Chiricahua,* p. 84.

153. Opler, *Myths and Tales of the Jicarilla,* p. 357.

154. Ibid.

155. Ibid., pp. 357–358.

156. Ibid., p. 358.

157. Ibid., pp. 358–359.

158. Ibid., p. 359.

159. Ibid.

160. Ibid., pp. 359–361.

161. Opler, *Myths and Legends of the Lipan,* pp. 205–206.

162. Sapir and Hoijer, p. 127.

The Magic and Ritual of the Raid for Horses

O NCE THE GOD PEOPLE HAD PUT HORSES ON EARTH, the Navajo and Apache sought them in the four directions. As their culture heroes had sought the horses of the gods, now the people trailed the earthly models down with ceremony and song. Through every coulee and over every divide, they went on holy missions to capture and bring home horses.

"Over there they sneaked off now and then, in groups of two or three they sneaked back and forth. The Mexicans' horses they stole from them, it is true. From over there to here they brought the horses, and mules too. It was just that which made them go wild." Such was the reminiscence of the Navajo named Charlie Mitchell about the heyday of Navajo horse raiding.[1]

Reasons for Horse Raids

The myths and tales of the Navajo and Apache record the mythical and economic reasons for the cycle of steady horse raids that began as soon as the people had acquired their first mounts. They remind us that while it was true that the Indian's culture hero had finally been given some horses for his people, the white man's benefactor had nevertheless received the marvelous gift first. Having this advantage, the white people now possessed horses in great numbers, while the Indians did not have enough to meet their barest needs. A Chiricahua Apache tale says that this was why "Child-of-the-Water had to steal from his own uncle."[2] A San Carlos Apache story echoed these sentiments:

Around 1932, John Rope, a former White Mountain Apache scout, is shown beside his wickiup. Rope gave a lengthy account of Apache procedures on raids and told of how leaders were expected to know supernatural powers to locate, control, and even attract horses. Photo by Grenville Goodwin. (Courtesy Arizona State Museum, photo #18257)

The Indians were living without anything. They were poor.

⌐══

Then they found out there were white men living somewhere. They
also discovered that [the] white people had something to live on. The
Indians then began to live by stealing. They stole burros, horses and
cattle and brought them home.

⌐══

Before this they were poor but now they lived well. . . . They were
happy.
   They said that stealing from those who lived on the earth was a
grand way to live.[3]

In legend and in life, they stole the horses of the Mexicans and the
Anglos. They stole from their Indian enemies too. But the records show
that the raid for horses was more than just a grand horse theft. Because
the raids grew from the economic necessities of the people, the Navajo
and Apache came to look on them as sacred missions to bring home "the
things by which men lived"—missions they believed they could accomplish successfully only by using the proper magic and ritual.

Use of Magical Powers on Raids

The Navajo and Apache boasted of the magical powers they took along
on every raid, and their Indian enemies agreed they had been subjected
to these powers when they reflected on how they had lost their horses.
Two tales collected by Elsie Clews Parsons from Tewa Indians at the San
Juan Pueblo in New Mexico assure us that the Tewa believed the Navajo
had employed magical powers on them to effect miraculous escapes after
horse raids on that pueblo. Though the tales tell about different forays the
Navajo made on San Juan, both of Parsons's Tewa informants were in
agreement that on each occasion the Navajo used plenty of *"pinang,"* a
term by which the Tewa identify magical powers of any kind.
   The first Tewa tale concerns the Navajo's use of magical powers to
hide their horse tracks:

One year Navaho stole some horses in the mountains. The snow was
so high (indicating half foot). They stole lots of horses, and the Tewa
started after them. They went into the big mountains where there
were lots of big trees. There they lost the tracks. They searched for
them, they said, "Wonder where they took the horses, underground

or up into the sky flying?" The Navaho had driven the horses on top of the fallen trees, jumping them from one fallen tree to another, so on the ground there were no tracks. . . . After they stole horses, Navaho would make wind and snow, through their *pinang*.[4] They had arrowpoints, large ones, and they made Wind by waving these arrowpoints around this way (sunwise circuit). That is the way they did, long ago, the old men said.[5]

In the other Tewa tale, three Navajo raiders were the first paratroopers of the region, escaping from a high mesa with parachutes made from their blankets:

The Navaho used to steal cattle and horses and boys out herding. The Navaho had lots of *pinang*. One time after a raid San Juan men went in pursuit of the Navaho. They saw their tracks. The chief chose three good strong boys to go up on the mesa to hunt the Navaho. The boys went up in the single place they could go up. They saw fresh tracks. Except the place they went up all the other sides were sheer. The Navaho were on top, the Tewa behind them at the only place of ascent or descent. There were three Navaho and three Tewa. The Navaho were running, and after them the Tewa. The Tewa said, "If they go to the edge of the mesa, they will have to fall off." The Navaho had blankets, tied around their middle. At the edge of the mesa, each man spread out his blanket, his arms stretched out like wings, and they went down the side of the mesa very slowly and softly, and got away. They had lots of *pinang,* but the wind buoyed them up, too.[6]

Sometimes the Indian enemies of the Navajo and Apache attempted to retaliate with magical powers they knew, in an effort to keep them from making off with their horses. When this happened the Navajo and Apache tried to counteract the enemies' efforts by using an even more potent magic. A Chiricahua Apache reported that such a thing happened when his father and other Chiricahua raiders took some horses away from the Yaqui Indians in Mexico. His father had told him of how the Yaqui started to work their powers, and of how the Chiricahua escaped:

The enemies used to know many ways to stop you, to make your legs ache so you couldn't get away with horses. My father was down in Mexico with a band. They drove away a good herd of cattle, burros, and horses from the Yaqui.

The Yaqui came on the trail. One of the men of the Yaqui knew a ceremony and was working against the Chiricahua. The Chiricahua had seen cacti thrown on their trail, and now they knew what it was

for. They got cramps, their legs hurt, and they couldn't go fast. They
were in danger, for the Yaqui were catching up.

For his raiding work my father mixed Wolf and Cactus (a small
variety of hedgehog cactus type) together. They asked him to sing
and he did. He found out what had been done against them.[7] He saw
that the enemy had used cactus with a spider's web. This makes the
toes twist (gives cramps) and makes the men fall off their horses. My
father found it out and let them have the worst of it. He went to the
edge of camp and "shot" four cactus plants on the back trail. They
had no trouble after that.[8]

Myths about the Introduction and Rules of Raiding

Undoubtedly those who had their horses taken from them wondered
why the raiders were so successful and how they had acquired such potent magical powers. Navajo and Apache myths supply the answers: the
magic and the rituals for raiding had their beginnings in the instructions
left the Indians by their culture heroes. As a matter of fact, the myths say
the culture heroes originated the art of raiding as a way of life for the
Southern Athapascans. A Lipan, Antonio Apache, elaborated at length to
Opler about the role that Killer-of-Enemies played in teaching his people
how to get more horses, saying: "Killer-of-Enemies is the one who started
all the work that the people had to do. . . . All the arrow making, the
raiding, the war. . . .

". . . Killer-of-Enemies was the one who started all the things that the
Lipan did later. That's why the Lipan went out raiding after horses and
fought their enemies when they met them."[9] Antonio explained that before the culture hero departed from the earth forever, he "started to make
rules for the human beings," and one of the first he made was that the
Lipan would be raiders. In order to establish this rule,

> He went out on a raid. His home was at the Guadalupe Mountains.
> From there he went out to the south. He went raiding for horses. He
> came back with many horses. He turned them out at the Guadalupe
> Mountains at a place they called "Blue Stem Grass Whitens."[10] There
> were many of them. At that place there are many black weeds and
> bushes. They cover the whole place. Those are the horses of Killer-of-
> Enemies which have turned to these bushes.

> Killer-of-Enemies did all that. He went out and gathered horses.

When he had finished the raid and had a good many horses he
finished all the fighting.

⟋⟍

Then Killer-of-Enemies started back to his home. He told his mother
what he had done. He told her his work was finished. He told her,
"The new generation of people is coming. They must do all that I
have done. They must follow my way and my rules."[11]

The story of how the Navajo culture hero established some of the
raid rituals his people followed is recorded in the origin myth of the
Enemy Way, a war ceremony from which, as we shall see later, Navajo raid
rituals borrowed heavily. In a version of the Enemy Way myth that Slim
Curly, a Navajo medicine man from Crystal, New Mexico, dictated to
Haile in 1930, Monster Slayer (Enemy Slayer) chose to teach the art of
raiding first to a Navajo medicine man and his assistant, so that they could
later instruct the people. Curly told of how the culture hero caused Father Sun's fine blue horse to appear suddenly before the medicine man
and his assistant one day when they were out learning warfare rituals. The
two Navajo captured the blue horse and led it home with them. After
they had arrived, they heard an owl hoot at twilight from "what seemed a
great distance." Then they heard it a second and a third time, each time
from a closer range. The fourth time "its call was heard very close by. That
was all that happened, it seems, and they went to sleep."[12] But the next
morning when they awoke, they were surprised to find the horse gone.
When they began to search for it, they discovered that its tracks led in a
"straight line towards the east." The medicine man left his assistant behind
and followed the tracks alone to a place called "Waters Flow Together,"
where Monster Slayer magically appeared before him. According to Curly,
the medicine man addressed the culture hero, saying: "To this place the
tracks of the horse lead which I had captured over there, to here my
horse's tracks lead. . . ." And the war god was said to have replied: "Yes,
when I found you had captured it . . . I sent the owl over there after it, but
when my father [Sun] said it was his, it was led away to him. It is now
standing (somewhere) in the sun's house. . . ."[13] The war god also revealed
his reason for taking away Sun's fine blue horse, and in this way gave the
medicine man one of the ceremonial rules that he intended for the Navajo to follow on their raids from that time on. He told him: ". . . while
any of you are engaged in war, the very first person that sees you with
booty and asks you for this or that, you must not refuse to part with it. To
refuse would be to refuse to part with the enemy."[14] Thus, it was decided

that henceforth whenever Navajo raiders chanced to meet someone who requested a gift as they journeyed home with the booty they had captured successfully through the ritual of the Enemy Way, they had to follow Monster Slayer's rule and give the person they encountered one of the horses or something else from their spoils. If they ignored this rule, they believed they were risking a serious illness—one brought on by contact with the enemy or with the things belonging to him.[15]

Raid and War Expeditions—Comparisons

Though Navajo and Apache raid expeditions shared many similarities with war excursions, important differences existed also. On raids, for instance, the men made every effort to avoid direct encounters, their sole purpose being to lay hands on the enemy's possessions, although, of course, they were often overtaken by the enemy as they fled with their plunder, and then a fight was unavoidable.

One Indian did not simply go off alone and steal a few horses. For since the ritual necessary to protect raiders from harm and the people from revenge could only be properly carried out by a number of men working together, a man who raided alone committed a serious offense against his own society in that he risked not only his own life but also put his people in danger of a retaliatory excursion from the enemy at a time when they might not be prepared for it. Individual thievery within a man's own society was also considered a serious offense. Often the punishment for it was more severe than that imposed on horse thieves by white pioneers. An example of such thievery and its severe punishment has already been given in an earlier chapter in the incident where a White Mountain Apache was suspended and left to die for stealing and killing Chief Diablo's black horse.[16]

Navajo and Apache raiding parties were small but highly organized affairs. A Navajo party was usually composed of at least three or four men, but no more than ten, in contrast with the thirty to two hundred warriors comprising Navajo war excursions.[17] Apache raiding parties ordinarily contained no more than ten, though they could have as many as forty; but, like Navajo raiding parties, they were smaller than war parties.[18]

While the band was the largest unit of Apache warfare, it was seldom that a band went on a raid.[19] Both Navajo and Apache raiding parties were formed from the local group—that is, from the smallest unit of social organization in Southern Athapascan societies and the basis of the whole tribal arrangement. Opler defined the Apache local group as "composed of families whose members are related by affinity, or who, though not related," had "elected to live together because of the chance to make a powerful economic alliance." The members of the local group, he says, usually camped "within easy reach of the same natural landmark," adding that "their residence in one general locality" made possible "co-operation for raid or warpath."[20] In general what he has to say about the Apache local group is applicable to the Navajo as well.[21]

However, as we keep in mind the differences between Navajo and Apache raid and war expeditions, it is also important to note that the magic and ritual used on a raid were often quite similar—in many instances, identical—to those used on the warpath, and that they were likewise deeply influenced by the hunting practices. In the case of the horse raid, it is especially apparent that the Navajo and Apache tried to capture the animals of the enemy by employing rituals similar to those they had always used in hunting wild game, both being missions in pursuit of sacred quarry.

Raiding Ceremonies

The Navajo and Apache possessed a number of different kinds of raiding ceremonies, each controlled by a certain supernatural power. They required the men who led their forays to know at least one of these raiding ceremonies, so that through its magical powers they might outwit the enemy. Properly conducted, these ceremonies assured success and protection to the entire party while they were in alien territory.

Let us first examine the raiding ceremonies of the Navajo. According to Hill, these were Bear Way, Big Snake Way, Turtle Way, Frog Way, and Blessing Way, all of them related to the great Navajo war ceremonies: Enemy Way, Monster Slayer Way, and Yei Hastin Way, which, as Hill notes, the Navajo "used almost entirely in the reprisal type of offensive warfare." The primary difference between the war ceremonies and the raid ceremonies patterned after them, "aside from the size of the parties . . . lay in the songs and prayers which the party sang and said," and the raiding rituals were also "similar in pattern to those used in hunting. . . ."[22] For instance, the Big Snake Way of raiding probably resembled the Big Snake Way of hunting deer, which Hill mentioned in another work. The Navajo who described it to him told of how the hunters attacked the deer "like snakes from ambush."[23] From this brief description, we can see how easy it would be for the Navajo to adapt such a hunting ritual into a Way of capturing horses.

That a Blessing Way is included among Hill's list of Navajo raiding ceremonies is logical enough when we look closely at the many uses the

Navajo have for their rites of blessing. The main purpose of these rituals in any of the many forms they may take is for good luck, good health, and general blessing.[24] For this reason, a Blessing Way rite was combined with the war ceremony of the Enemy Way to give warriors, as Jeff King explained to Oakes, "a personal blessing which has nothing to do with war."[25] But since Blessing Ways can be sung for animals as well as people, they are often sung for the protection of horse herds and other livestock too.[26] And there are still other special functions for certain songs from Blessing Way ceremonies. For instance, the "Traveling Songs" from the Blessing Way are believed to "give good luck in traveling," as well as to "favorably affect conditions for the increase of cattle, horses, and other livestock."[27] All of these applications of the Blessing Way, or of certain of its rites or songs, make apparent the reasons why Navajo raiders included it in their raiding Ways.

However, there is still another reason remaining to be examined. We have already seen how Blessing Way can be combined as a part of the Enemy Way to give a blessing to warriors, but we have not seen how it can be combined with other ceremonies to insure their effectiveness. Fr. Berard Haile, the foremost authority on Blessing Way, describes this latter function of it as follows:

> In matter of fact, no chantway ceremonial can be effective without it [Blessing Way]. Unostentatious in its own ceremonials, which cannot exceed a period of a single night this Blessingway rite, or parts of it, must be added to any chantway ceremonial, regardless of its eclat or duration, in order to render all functions effective and to correct possible mistakes and omissions. Though the rule is general that all chantway ceremonials must add portions of Blessingway to secure their effectiveness, no definite rule appears to be established for the time when this must be done.[28]

Thus, the inclusion of Blessing Way with the other four Ways of raiding in Hill's list indicates, it seems to me, that it served either as the blessing part to these other four ceremonies or else as one complete short ceremony to bring the raiders good fortune, insuring their personal safety in enemy territory as well as protecting the horses they drove home.

Unfortunately, Hill included almost no information about the Bear Way, Big Snake Way, Turtle Way, and Frog Way in his *Navaho Warfare*. In their work on the classification of Navajo song ceremonies, Wyman and Kluckhohn also listed the names of these four Ways, adding that Hill's work contained "almost all the printed data available on these ceremonials."

However, they classified them under war ceremonies rather than sepa-
rately as raiding ceremonies.[29] Another scholar who did not make the
distinctions that Hill made between Navajo ceremonies for raiding and
those for war was Haile. In his examination of the Enemy Way ceremony—
one of the Navajo war ceremonies on which Hill said the raid ceremonies were patterned—Haile discussed raid and war synonymously, and
said that the Enemy Way ceremony was applicable to both.[30]

Regardless of the differences of opinion among scholars about the
possible distinctions between raid and war ceremonies, we can still be
certain that Navajo raiders as well as warriors sought the powers of Bear,
Big Snake, Turtle, and Frog on their expeditions. We have only to look
closely into the traditions concerning these supernatural creatures to find
the reasons why the Navajo would think of their powers as being particularly beneficial to raiders.

In Navajo myths, we find that Bear and Big Snake, and Turtle and
Frog as well, often appear together as partners. Bear and Big Snake frequently represent evil, and sometimes Frog and Turtle also. On the other
hand, all these creatures can exercise their powers for the good of the
people or perform brave deeds for those whom they protect. An example
of such a thing occurs in a version of the origin legend of the Enemy Way
where they are paired as war companions. Haile collected the version
from the Navajo named Slim Curly, who also served a few years later as
one of Hill's informants. Curly reported that on different occasions Bear
and Big Snake, along with Turtle and Frog, lent their powers to Enemy
Slayer and taught him important rules of ritual to follow when he was
leading the first group of Navajo warriors on the warpath to Taos.[31]

By examining in particular the mythical attributes of Bear and Big
Snake, as partners and as individual creatures, we get an even better idea
of the importance of their powers to the raiders. A version of the origin
myth of the Navajo recorded by Matthews relates that Changing Woman
gave the people Bear and Snake to take along with them for protection
on their journeys, when they left to go and live in a world divided among
many *"gentes"* (people), and that as she did so, she told them: "It is a long
and dangerous journey to where you are going. It is well that you should
be cared for and protected on the way." She promised the Navajo that her
"pets" would "watch over" and "not desert" them, but she warned them
to "speak of no evil deeds in the presence of the bear or the snake, for
they may do the evil they hear you speak of. . . ."[32]

This is just one example among many of the guardian roles of these
creatures in Navajo mythology. According to other myths, Bear and Big

Snake—along with Thunder and Wind—are the traditional guardians of Sun's house and sometimes of the domiciles of other deities too.[33] They possessed the powers of allowing or refusing entrance to the dwellings of Sun and other holy beings where beautiful horses and other wonderful gifts abounded. Doubtless Navajo raiders felt that if they traveled under the protection of such powerful guardians, who controlled the doors of plenty, they would certainly be led to valuable booty.

Another mythical attribute that Bear and Big Snake possessed was the ability to travel about invisibly—a talent that would certainly be welcomed by raiders. A myth of the Mountain Chant collected from a Navajo named Hasteen Klah informs us that Bear and Snake proved their prowess as mighty war companions by traveling invisibly to the underground homes of two gods of some enemy cave dwellers. After killing the troublesome deities, they returned home victorious—this time traveling on their horses, which apparently could traverse enemy territory as invisibly as they, for this myth reports that Bear rode a "wind" horse while Snake traveled on one of "sunlight."[34]

Bear, it seems, was doubly blessed, for not only was he able to make himself invisible, but he also had the ability to become anything he chose to be, and therefore one of the Navajo words for bear means "turning into anything."[35]

As war companions in the myth of the Enemy Way, Bear and Big Snake introduced two medicines that, when used with proper ritual, had properties of dual importance to warriors and raiders: they could make the men invulnerable to attack, or, if that failed, could restore life. That is why "the medicine which the bear had and the medicine which the snake had, both remained in the Enemy Way. . . ."[36] That Bear's medicine was endowed with life-giving properties is verified by its name, which Halle translates as a "live one's plume" and Reichard as a "life feather." The Big Snake's medicine Haile describes as "the pulp of flag, the kind that is round in shape," and Reichard identifies it as the "pulp of the iris."[37] Today, whenever the Navajo perform the Enemy Way, they still use these medicines.

Other abilities of Bear and Snake would further enhance their powers to raiders. A Navajo informant of Fishler's told him of Big Snake's unique method of capturing whatever he desires. He has only to stay "inside his hole," where he "sucks" his captives to him. "Animals may be a long way off," but "Big Snake will draw them closer and closer until they go faster and finally run" to him.[38] In fact, Big Snake's powers at hunting and capturing animals are so frequently associated with him that when he is depicted in Navajo sandpaintings, he is often shown with designs that represent these powers. Fishler's informant drew a picture of Big Snake with "inverted V's" on his back, symbolizing, he said, "the tracks of the deer and antelope."[39] While Big Snake has the power to draw his captives to him, Bear is endowed with the ability to locate creatures or things. In one myth, he reveals his power by trailing down Secondborn, who is lost in the mountains.[40]

One of the raiders' greatest fears was that the enemy might work witchcraft against them. If properly entreated, Bear would exercise his power of dispelling this danger. The appropriate way of invoking Bear's aid was for a medicine man to offer the following prayer and ceremonial gifts to Big Black Bear, who guarded the eastern part of Sun's house:

> Big Black Bear, at the eastward, with the bear pollen, lying over
> there, I will give you this gift for my protection (turquoise and rust, a
> specular iron ore). Here is my gift to you for your power. . . . Black
> Bear, get up before me for my protection. Black Bear, get up before
> me with your black flint shoes. Black Bear, get up before me with
> your black flint stockings. Black Bear, get up before me with your
> black flint clothing. Black Bear, get up before me with your black
> flint cap.[41]

The Black Bear was invoked because he is chief among the bears of the four directions, who surround Sun's house. Black Bear stands to the east, the most powerful of the cardinal zones, followed in order by Blue, Yellow, and White Bears in the south, west, and north. Except for color, these cardinal bear spirits all have the same appearance. One Navajo's description has it that each is like "the ordinary bear" except that he "has been changed," because he "is now a god." This Navajo noted also that a bear spirit "has a red mouth," and that when "he gets angry," he displays his wrath by opening his mouth before any available spectators.[42] Undoubtedly, such an exhibition of his anger was one of Bear's best ways of frightening an enemy into helplessness, for the Navajo believe that Bear is a creature with the power to plunge an individual into a trance or a state of shock. However, it should also be pointed out that they also feel that he can lend his ceremonial aid to restore anyone suffering from the effects of such a state.[43] He could, for instance, bring back to normal a Navajo who had been scared out of his wits by the enemy.

Big Black Bear's powers are sought by the Navajo in songs as well as prayers. On war excursions, Navajo singers—as medicine men are often called—sang songs to Bear to give strength to the men in their parties, and they also used his songs with their war medicines to weaken the enemy.[44] A version of the origin legend concerning the wanderings of the Navajo, collected by Goddard from Sandoval in 1923 and 1924, includes the type of Bear songs that Wyman and Kluckhohn believe the Navajo may have employed in their war ceremonies.[45] Perhaps, too, these songs belonged to the particular kind of raiding ceremony that Hill called Bear Way. Certainly the following song, which Big Black Bear sang as he taught Navajo warriors the power of becoming unassailable in enemy territory, would be equally advantageous to a party of raiders. With the power of Bear's words to protect him, and girded also by the snake powers within the song, a Navajo capturing horses could imagine himself transformed into the fearless Bear:

Big black bear.
My moccasins are black obsidian.
My leggings are black obsidian.
My shirt is black obsidian.
I am girded with a gray arrowsnake.
Black snakes project from my head.
With zigzag lightning protecting from the ends of my feet I step.
With zigzag lightning streaming out from my knees I step.
With zigzag lightning streaming out from the tips of my fingers I
    work my hands.
With zigzag lightning streaming out from the tip of my tongue I
    speak.
Now a disc of pollen rests on the crown of my head.
Gray arrowsnakes and rattlesnakes eat it.
Black obsidian and zigzag lightning streams out from me in four
    ways.
Where they strike the earth, bad things bad talk [sic] does not like it.
It causes the missiles to spread out.
Long life, something frightful I am.
Now I am.[46]

Among their Navajo informants, Kluckhohn and Wyman found a man who had heard of a form of Blessing Way known as Bear Way Blessing Way. Unfortunately, this man could supply no further details about this particular kind of Blessing Way, and the authors state that their other informants had never heard of it.[47] One can not help wondering whether the informant was referring to a Blessing Way rite combined with a Bear Way ceremony, for as we have seen earlier, war ceremonies—or, for that matter, ceremonies longer than Blessing Way—included rites from Blessing

Way to provide a personal blessing to the participants of the ceremony, as well as to render effective that ceremony itself. An example of how a Blessing Way song is included with a cycle of war songs to properly complete the cycle appears in the final song that Sandoval recorded first for Goddard, and then later for O'Bryan, from the group of Bear's war songs. It follows the pattern of songs borrowed from Blessing Way and incorporated into other ceremonies. The O'Bryan recording, which includes more details and offers a smoother verse translation than the one by Goddard, follows below:

A Big Black Bear starts out.
Now he starts out with the black pollen for his moccasins.
Now he starts out with the black pollen for his leggings.
Now he starts out with the black pollen for his garment.
Now he starts out with the black pollen for his headdress.
He starts out for Black Mountain plains.
He starts out for the doorway of the two crossed spruce trees.
He starts out on the straight pollen trail.
He starts out for the top of the pollen foot prints.
He starts out for the top of the pollen seed prints.
He is like the Most High Power Whose Ways Are Beautiful.
   With beauty before him,
   With beauty behind him,
   With beauty above him,
   With beauty below him.
   All around him is beautiful,
   His spirit is beautiful.[48]

When Sandoval made his earlier recording of this song of blessing for Goddard, he told of how Bear taught the first Navajo warriors the ritual they should use, along with his songs, to insure protection from the dangers to which they were subjected. He said that Bear shook some pollen from his body and wet it by placing it in his mouth.[49] Though Sandoval did not say so, Bear had thus prepared, for ritual use, the type of pollen the Navajo refer to as "live pollen." This pollen was required for raiding ceremonies, and for certain others classified by Kluckhohn and Wyman as Evil Way chants.[50] While in this instance the dust from Bear's body served as "live pollen," such pollen could be any pollen or powdered dust shaken from or over the bodies of certain creatures. And often the saliva of the same creatures was mixed with the pollen to further heighten the power of life it was thought to acquire from the mixture.[51] Sandoval related that after Bear had taken the potent dust from his body and mixed it with saliva from his mouth, he put the ball of "live pollen" on top of his head. Then he proceeded to rub his hands with it and to sprinkle the remainder before and behind him. When he had finished doing these things, he went off to his home in Black Mountain singing his song of blessing.[52] By performing this ritual and by singing this song, Bear showed all future Navajo warriors how they could cleanse themselves of any contamination that they might suffer from contact with the enemy or merely from a journey into alien territory. Today, long after raids for horses have ceased, the people still sing these songs in ceremonies. As Sandoval explained it to O'Bryan, Bear gave his songs to be "used against anything that bothers the people, whether enemies or disease."[53]

The Navajo sang also to Turtle and Frog for their support on war excursions. Songs to these creatures were especially popular with the Navajo who lived on the west side of the Chuska Mountains, the Coolidges reported.[54] Although they did not include any of the Turtle and Frog songs, they did tell of the way a Navajo singer beseeched these supernaturals, as well as others, to "make their enemies' minds foolish, their eyes weak, their legs weak, their arms weak, and so on down to their feet." The formulation of such a song, downward from head to foot, followed the witchcraft pattern, the reverse of "good medicine," in which "the song goes from the feet to the head, driving the evil spirits out at the mouth."[55]

The Navajo seem to associate Frog more closely with horses than they do Turtle. While Turtle's only association with them appears to be as a successful warrior and raider, we have already been introduced to the Navajo tradition about how a Frog Man helped the Twins acquire the first horses for the people, how, when the culture heroes visited him at his domain in the subterranean lake under Wide Belt Mountain, they found that he knew the secrets of producing fine horses. Certainly this tradition would encourage Navajo raiders to invoke his powers and follow his way of raiding.[56]

Navajo myths assure us that Frog and Turtle were ready warriors and that they owned unique warpath equipment. Frog had a magic stone ax, designed to strike and kill anyone besides himself who tried wielding it, while Turtle possessed a tough shield—his shell—impenetrable by any weapon.[57]

But perhaps the greatest contribution of Frog and Turtle to the art of raiding was that they were the first to use the "altered, or sacred language"—a language the Navajo employed on all raids, as well as on all war excursions. This special language was one in which, as Reichard noted, "either the word symbol was slightly changed in the code, or a special meaning known only to fighters was given to the words."[58] It will be examined in more detail later in this chapter. One of the myths telling the story of how Frog and Turtle first used this "altered" language is Slim Curly's version of the origin legend of the Enemy Way. Here they are specifically referred to as Box Turtle and Green Frog. The story tells of how they, as war companions, accomplished a successful raid against Taos Pueblo without outside help, and of how this feat of theirs so impressed Monster Slayer that he sent Turtle Dove over to interview them and learn how they did it. Box Turtle and Green Frog, proud of their accomplishment, are reported to have willingly given Turtle Dove the information he sought: ". . . as we went along from here out of sight, over the ridge and on farther, we did not speak our own language. We spoke a language called 'altered-mention,' on our journey there and back." When Turtle Dove repeated what he had heard in detail to Monster Slayer, he mimicked the way "they acted when they spoke, and imitated them by jerking his neck back and forth." Since that time, the Navajo say, the turtle dove has had "the habit of doing that."[59] And from that time on, too, Navajo raiders and warriors also spoke only "in the 'altered-mention' language, after the manner of green frog and box turtle. . . ."[60]

Traditions relate also that Turtle and Frog possessed other powers valuable on raids. Like Bear, they could use their medicine to restore people who had been paralyzed by shock or fear, to cleanse the contamination brought on by contact with the enemy or other forces foreign or evil to them. A version of the myth of the Navajo Tohe, or Water Chant, tells us how Frog and Turtle performed a bathing ceremony to heal a hero who was suffering from enemy contamination and was paralyzed with shock to such an extent that he could not see. They "made the patient able to use his eyes" again.[61] From that time on, this ritual became one of the regular treatments for patients suffering from similar trouble.

Some of the Apache groups apparently possessed raiding ceremonies similar to those of the Navajo, though only vague traditions about them exist today. While almost no information is available about the methods of raiding that these ceremonies taught, scattered references to ceremonies from Bear, Snake, and Turtle in Apache mythology do tell us that at least three of the Apache groups invoked most of the same supernatural powers that the Navajo did to aid them on their missions for horses.

In the mythology of the San Carlos and White Mountain Apache groups, we find myths about the Apache possessing Snake ceremonies. A San Carlos Apache named Albert Evans told Goddard in 1914 about one that a snake-medicine man gave his people after some of them had returned from an unsuccessful raid. Goddard reported that Evans was "said to know" and to have practiced the ceremony that the snake-being taught his people, but he did not supply any further details.[62] He also collected an account from a White Mountain Apache in 1910 about a ceremony with restorative powers that a snake-being gave to Naiyenezgani after the culture hero had "danced on rawhide against white men" and had made successful war on them.[63]

A bear-ceremonial myth, which served as a basis for Apache hunting rituals, was also supplied Goddard by the same man. All of the "bear songs and medicinemen with bear power," he said, had their beginnings or received their powers from the ceremony that an Apache hunter was so fortunate as to secure from Bear.[64] Since the Bear ceremony provided Apache hunters with the necessary powers to protect and defend themselves during periods of danger, it is entirely possible that it contributed the same powers to Apache raiders and warriors.

Further, the Lipan Apache, like the Navajo, have tales about turtles going on raids together or alone. However, the Lipan tales do not mention frogs as being the turtles' raid companions, as those of the Navajo do. While most of the Lipan traditions about turtle-raiders appear in humorous tales for children and tell of their clumsiness and boastful lies, a tradition still exists that a spotted turtle taught some Lipan raiders a valuable song to use as they returned home from their excursions.[65]

While the Navajo spoke of the powers they used against their enemies as belonging to Evil Way chants, the Western Apache groups called all such powers employed "to gain from or disable others" by the term *gò'ndì*—a term perhaps best rendered as "holy powers." Though Goodwin gives little information about what these particular powers were, he does explain that the leaders of Apache forays put such powers to work against their foes for the same purposes as the Navajo—that is, "to weaken" them, "to confuse their minds," and to make the men in their own parties "impervious" to the weapons and powers possessed by the opponents. Like those of the Navajo, these sacred powers of the Apache shared some similarities with the ones used in witchcraft; however, as Goodwin emphasizes, they belonged to a separate category and should not be confused with the powers of "true witchcraft."[66]

Although the Apache employed some of the same ritual on raids as the Navajo, they also practiced an entirely different kind of ceremony, the one given an Apache in an encounter with a guardian horse spirit.

Apache society was full of men who knew "the power of the horse" and used it successfully on raids during the great Apache horse age. Since the basis in Apache society for receiving any kind of supernatural power was always the experience an individual shaman had with his own guardian being, no two Apache horse shamans would have exactly the same story to tell about how they first received their powers. One Lipan tale, however, furnishes a good example of how a horse could take a fancy to a person and bestow its magic potencies upon that individual. As we examine the tale, we find that the man in it has an experience with the cardinal horses, which resembles in some respects that of the Lipan's culture hero and his bird companions when they journeyed out to the plains east of the Guadalupe Mountains and roped the horses of the four directions.[67] We often find these similarities existing between myths and actual testimonies given by real Apache horse shamans; for although the reception of any power by an Apache was a private affair witnessed only by himself and his guardian spirit, we might reasonably expect a shaman's interpretation of a particular experience to be heavily influenced by a myth providing the details about a similar situation involving a culture hero. The tale recounted below was told to Opler by Antonio Apache, the same Lipan who recited the myth upon the acquisition of the first Lipan horses by Killer-of-Enemies and his companions, Cowbird, Bat, and Crow:

> There was a certain man who was going out after horses. He came out on the flats. There were four horses. The first was black, the second was blue (gray), the third was yellow (sorrel), and the last was white. These were standing in certain directions. This fellow was looking at these horses. He wanted to get them, but they were standing right in the open and were pretty hard to catch. Then the man asked for a heavy rain. The heavy rain came. The black horse shook his body then and the rain stopped.[68]

After this had occurred, the man again prayed on three different occasions for heavy rains, and each time he did so, the rains came. Each time, also, the next horse in the circuit of the four directions, following the order of gray (blue) to the south, yellow to the west, and white to the north, would stop the cloudburst by shaking its body in exactly the same way the black horse to the east had first done. When each of the four horses had proven that he possessed powers potent enough to stop at will even a violent downpour, the man responded by showing the horses that he did not intend to be outwitted. He called forth "a heavy rain for the fifth time," and "as soon as it came down," he walked over to the horses and stood in front of them. It was then that one of the horses addressed him, telling him the only terms under which he, as well as the other horses, could be captured: "I have been looking all over for people and could see nothing. But here you are and you are a man. If you know something about horses you can have us. If you don't know any power, we won't belong to you."[69]

Because the horse spoke in this way, the man knew he was being approached by a guardian who was willing to make a gift of his powers if he proved himself a worthy disciple. He proceeded to show this horse and his companions that they, indeed, had encountered someone who knew the proper way to deal with them:

> This man had ropes of four different colors made of horse hair. The first was black, the second was blue, the third was yellow and the fourth was white.
>   The black horse shook his body. A ball of white clay fell from his body and was scattered. Black-tipped eagle feathers fell from his body and blew about. The man shook himself then and white clay and eagle feathers fell from him. The man went to the black horse, using the black rope, and took him.[70]

Next the man roped the blue, yellow, and white horses by using exactly the same technique as for the others, except, of course, that he caught each horse with a rope matching the horse's color. His actions certainly impressed the horses. Antonio related that all four of them spoke in unison, saying: "Grandchild, you know our ways. We belong to you now."[71] So it was in this way that this Apache acquired the power of the horse. That the horses addressed him by a kinship term, "grandchild," also signified their recognition that from then on, their relationship with him would be intimate. Other accounts show that Apache shamans regarded their powers as relatives too, and that they observed the same kinship taboos with them that they did with their real relations. A case in point is the Jicarilla Apache, who practiced the custom of never slaying the source of their powers. They strictly adhered to this custom, for as a Jicarilla explained it to Opler, when the people spoke of their power-sources, they said: "We are all relatives now."[72]

A guardian horse could approach an Apache at any time to offer its power. Sometimes this took place when an individual and a horse had gone through some emotional crisis together. A Chiricahua Apache told of how such a thing happened to a man he knew when this man was out raiding for horses. After examining one tale concerning an Apache's reception of horse power, it is interesting to turn to the testimony of this Chiricahua and see how he reported the encounter as he had heard that it actually occurred. One day, he said, back at the turn of this century, the Chiricahua he knew was driving off some horses from "a town south of Tucson." This man and a friend were traveling along on foot until they decided to stop driving the horses long enough to rope some mounts for themselves. The friend caught a good horse, but unfortunately, the man with whom we are concerned lassoed a wild one, which pitched him off, seriously injuring him. His friend was now in great difficulty; there was no one around to ask for help, and he thought the man was near death, since he lay on the ground unconscious. But evidently the friend knew something about "the power of the horse," because he turned to an "old sorrel horse standing nearby," and after he marked its forehead with pollen, he "asked the horse to help him restore his companion."[73] Fortunately, the animal was a guardian horse, and it made no difficulty about lending its power to revive the man.[74] Afterwards, the sorrel horse grew interested in the man it had cured and decided to give him and his friend aid and counsel on their journey home. The Chiricahua who knew the details of this man's experience gave the following account of what transpired:

> Later this sorrel horse talked to the man it had cured. It told him where the two men should camp that night on the return journey. They followed this advice. The horse told him where to camp for the second night too. This was at an open place, but the horse said, "Do not be afraid even though it is out in the open." They camped in that place and were not disturbed. The third night the horse told him that they should camp at a place called Sand House. On the fourth night the horse told him that they should stop between two mountains.
>
> Then the horse spoke to the one it had cured. It told him, "I'm old and I'm no longer strong. I'd like to take you back to the place where you live, but I can't make it. A man who is thin can make it back to his home. But horses are different. We have to be fat and strong. So after you start out tomorrow you are going to miss me. But don't look for me. I am going back to my home. But I'll tell you now just how to continue your journey, where to stop each night, and where your relatives are now."[75]

But before the horse separated from the two men, he told the one he had restored: "I give these songs to you. You will be a shaman through the horse." And later the man did become a prominent horse shaman.[76]

The Apache considered a knowledge of horse power an essential part of any raid leader's background for many reasons. First of all, it was believed that if a leader possessed such powers, he would not only be successful in conducting his men on a safe journey, he would also be successful in helping them acquire horses. Remembering how he had employed his power advantageously on raids, an elderly Chiricahua Apache boasted to Opler that he could always depend on it, even after his raiding days were over: "[My] power told me that I was going to get something if I went out on the raid. If I go out and look for something, my power gives me the ability to get horses and mules. The power sends me out and tells me, 'You are going to get this.' "[77] He elaborated in detail too about how this same power of his had protected him from the enemy: "My power told me that the enemy was coming. It told me, 'If you want the enemy to see you, they are going to see you. If you want to see the enemy, you will see them. If you don't want to meet the enemy, they will swing around the other way.' "[78]

The Apache also felt that the power of the horse enabled a leader to protect and care for the horses he and his men captured on the raid.[79] Before leaving home, the Apache who had acquired such power usually sang and offered prayers to some "corralled horses, so the horses would give them good luck" with those they were setting out to capture.[80]

He likewise conducted a brief ceremony, previous to departure, for the benefit of the men going on the expedition. As one Chiricahua Apache explained it, the raiders needed his songs and prayers, so that "good horses [would] fall into their hands, so that their horses [would] be strong and carry them through, and so that all in the party [would] have good luck."[81]

If an Apache who wanted to lead a foray had not been so fortunate as to have his own supernatural experience with a horse, he could obtain a horse ceremony from a shaman who had been blessed with one. To obtain the shaman's knowledge and power, he usually had to pay four ceremonial gifts made up of horse trappings and sometimes including a horse itself.[82]

Divination Rites

Both the Apache and the Navajo used divination rites on their raids to ascertain the kind of luck that was in store for them, or to discern what kind of supernatural power the enemy might be working against them. The same rites could help them locate the enemy, or the enemy's horses, or any object or person whose whereabouts was unknown. The men who performed these rites employed many different types of divination practices.

Earlier we saw how a Chiricahua Apache shaman performed such a rite to discover what kind of power the Yaqui were using against his party as they were trying to escape after a successful horse raid. This man prayed and sang to his power, and the power complied by giving him a vision in which he saw exactly what kind of medicine the Yaqui were employing to bring harm to his party.[83] But the Apache felt that the power could also communicate with a shaman in other ways besides providing a vision. The power's method of responding to a shaman's pleas depended on the kind of help being sought. If, for instance, the object was to locate the enemy or enemy horses, the power would take possession of the shaman who was singing and praying to it and empower the shaman's arms to move in the direction of whatever was being searched for.[84]

The acquisition of power among the Apache being a private affair, the Apache did not always know exactly who in their society was so endowed. When a man received power (and usually the recipient was male rather than female), he ordinarily waited for a while before he told others about it. This was because, as Opler notes, his power would often forbid "him to inform others of it until the passage of a certain length of time." Generally he would "never openly" announce "the circumstances of his supernatural experience," he would continue waiting instead to be "'found out' by his fellows."[85] One disadvantage to this custom of the Apache was that it left the way open for a false shaman to appear on the scene and trick those who had dealings with him. Sam Kenoi, a Chiricahua Apache from Mescalero, New Mexico, recounted a story of how such a fellow outwitted a group of Chiricahua who asked him to perform a divination rite while they were out on an excursion toward enemy territory. They had stopped to camp for the night. Since "there was a moon," and "one could see well right there," they were feeling uneasy about what the enemy might do to them. Because of their anxiety, they asked one of their party to divine both what was "in store" for them and the whereabouts of the enemy. "The men with whom he went about did not like [that] man," Kenoi observed, but there was no one else available who could perform this rite. Somehow the word had circulated that he was the only person present who had the necessary power. At first, when they approached him about it, he refused, but "they asked him again and again."[86] Apparently his fellow warriors did not think there was anything unusual about his protesting. Perhaps they thought he possessed a newly acquired power and was following the normal procedure of being coaxed into displaying it. Or perhaps they thought he needed to be encouraged to hold the rite, because not all Apache who possessed ceremonial powers cared to make public use of them.[87] At any rate, after they had asked him to do it a number of times, he quit refusing and agreed to do as they requested. He

An Arizona Apache horseman mounting the kind of horse (a fast one—the fastest around) outfitted with the kind of trappings (a good saddle, blanket, and rope) that accounts affirm all raiders wanted.

told the rest: "All right! You people want it. Therefore, some distance over there to the westward, (tie up) a fast horse which is the fastest (you have), put a good saddle on him, tie a good blanket to him, tie a good rope on him, (and) a good gun (and) a belt filled all around with cartridges. You tie him up over there. Then, right away, it will be known. . . ."[88]

In this way he pretended that he was a horse shaman and was going to ask his power—the horse—to aid him in locating the enemy. The men did not question his instructions. For one reason, an Apache horse shaman often requested that the living source of his power be somewhere close by when he invoked its supernatural counterpart. It could help him establish contact with its power so as to work in unison with it in order to convey and interpret its message. For another reason, the Apache never questioned a shaman's demands, because if they did so, they were indicating, as Opler observes, a "lack of faith, which in itself is fatal to the success of the ceremony."[89] Therefore, the Apache did exactly what this man asked them to do. They rounded up a good fast horse and outfitted it with all the trappings and weapons he had requested. When they had everything set up in the proper way for his rite, he began to put on quite a performance for them. He started "to sing. He prayed. He knew nothing about it, but he . . . moved his arms about," Kenoi said. His procedure was exactly what his audience expected, and since they supposed his power was taking possession of him as he sang and prayed in this way, they sat there in good faith. Nor did they stir when, as Kenoi noted, "he ran outside" and "went over there" in the direction of "where the horse had been tied." They just "sat around waiting for him," thinking that he was under the influence of his power and expecting him to return at any moment with an important message for them about the location of the enemy and the details of what was in store for them. It never even occurred to them that he had "jumped on the horse" and ridden away.[90]

"A long time passed," Kenoi went on. Finally the Apache became disturbed about the missing shaman's whereabouts, so they sent a man out to search for him. When he returned, he could only say, "I looked where the horse had been tied up. The horse is not there. He has apparently gone off with the horse. . . ."[91]

Perhaps next time they made certain of the validity of a man's power before they insisted that he put it to use.

Navajo raiding parties employed hand-tremblers, star-gazers, and "listeners" to forecast forthcoming events or to interpret the unknown for them.[92] Just as most Navajo curing ceremonies of today require the services of someone who knows one of the gazing, trembling, or listening rites to arrive at the cause of an illness, so that the proper medicine person may be called in to perform an appropriate ceremony, so Navajo raiding parties had men who knew these rites employ them to ascertain what harm their enemies were devising against them. With such information at hand, they could counteract the evil with the proper movements or ritual.

The Navajo hand-trembler's rite had at least one similarity in common with the Apache's method of divining through arm movement, and that was motion—bodily motion. When the Navajo diviner had induced by ritual the proper state for a rite, then a hand, or the whole body of the practitioner, would be "seized," as Reichard explains, "with shaking, beginning usually with gentle tremors" and growing to violent agitation. In this state, lost to the surrounding world, the practitioner would "see" the answers to any questions and, if only the hands were affected, the shaman would obtain the answers by "reading" the quivering of the hands.[93]

Navajo star-gazers divined the unknown for raiding parties, according to Hill, by fixing "their eyes on a star until they received a vision."[94] Reichard reports that the rite of gazing could also be combined with the rite of trembling, meaning that a diviner who practiced trembling could induce this state by gazing in deep concentration at a heavenly body.[95] Another star-gazing method, described by the Coolidges, was for the seer to "hold a rock crystal in his palm with the point trained on a certain star, and as he gaz[ed] intently, in perfect silence, a vision [would] appear. The star [would] grow larger and come closer, revealing within its ball of light" a "black or white" symbol. If the symbol were white, it meant good fortune; but if it were black, bad.[96] To acquire the second sight needed for star-gazing, the Navajo caught "live eagles" and put "corn pollen . . . into their eyes." The pollen was "carefully removed" after it had become wet with the eagle's "eye water." It was then "mixed with finely ground rock crystal," and the resulting substance was the "medicine" that the Navajo "applied to the eyes" of the star-gazers to give them "the clearness of the crystal and the farseeing vision of the eagle." "When such medicine is used the vision appears as if thrown upon an inner screen, inside the head." Thus "it is a form of clairvoyancy. . . ."[97]

While the practiced star-gazer or hand-trembler performed the divination rite alone, the same was not true of the rite of "listening." Here two individuals were needed—individuals selected by the raid leaders, who were experienced in performing this rite and who knew the correct prayers to accompany it. The predictions achieved by "listeners" were also thought to be more reliable than the others. According to Hill, the rite was carried out in this way:

> The leader took wax from the ears of a coyote and badger and rubbed it on the ears of the "listeners" and under their eyes. This was thought to make their hearing acute and assist them in getting a vision. These men left the camp and went about a hundred yards toward the country of the enemy to "listen." If they heard the sound of horses or sheep, the trotting of animals, or got visions of horses or sheep, it was considered a good omen. Contrarily, if they heard the cry of a crow, screech owl, hoot owl, wolf, coyote, or any other "man

eating" bird or animal; heard the footsteps or conversation of the enemy, or heard someone shout as if he were hurt (this was believed to predict the death of one of the members of the party), these were considered bad omens and the party would turn back.[98]

Speaking of the assistance that the diviners in general gave raiders, a Navajo informant of Hill's had this comment to make: "Some of these men would say, 'There are a lot of horses at such and such a place.' Some of these predictions came true; others did not."[99]

The Raid—Its Pattern, Customs, and Taboos

The magical powers and ceremonies that we have examined were only a part, however, of the formal pattern the Navajo and Apache followed on their raids for horses. From start to finish, this pattern was shaped by the raider's performance of tedious ritualistic duties as he adhered to the formalized customs and taboos surrounding every organized expedition for horses.

That the raid came to be dominated by these customs and taboos is undoubtedly due to the fact that the Navajo and Apache looked on the raid as an endurance test where men were judged as courageous or cowardly. In Apache society, the training on four novice raids or war excursions, which began when a youth was about sixteen, was part of his initiation rites into manhood. Only when these were behind him was he accepted in society as a man.[100] In Navajo society, too, a boy became a man by joining a raid or war party sometime between his seventeenth and twentieth birthdays.[101] From the time when he was a young boy, he had been continually reminded of his future quest for horses, for instance by a line from a song he had grown up singing, the "War Exercise Song" White Bead Woman taught her sons before they went to visit their father. It was the song his people taught the young Navajo to sing at dawn when he and all the other little Navajo boys rose to greet the sun and run the races toward the east that would build them into strong men. "You were made for different kinds of horses, my son; run a race," the line from the song went, and the words of it were always there, standing before him.[102]

The formalized customs observed by the raider, as well as the taboos imposed upon him, had many similarities among the Southern Athapascan tribes, though they differed in minor respects. In the remainder of this chapter, we shall follow the pattern of the Navajo and Apache raid from beginning to end, investigating the customs and taboos so as to form a better idea of what these similarities and differences were.

In Opler's recording of the long tale praising the mighty deeds and daring exploits of Dirty Boy, the youth of supernatural prowess popular in Jicarilla Apache lore, we get interesting glimpses into the raid practices of the Jicarilla. The type of tale to which the Jicarilla story of Dirty Boy belongs has wide distribution in Southern Athapascan mythologies. Other Apache groups, and the Navajo as well, possess similar tales, though the featured heroes are often called Poor Boy, Lazy Boy, or by other names than Dirty Boy. This folk hero even appears once in the myth of the Navajo Water Chant under the name "Sleeps 'til Noon"![103] He is always a boy who is at first shunned or laughed at by the people, either because he is poor, and therefore wears dirty clothing; or because they mistakenly think him to be lazy, because he has no possessions. Yet, despite the obstacles, he still makes himself into a famous leader. His story belongs to a class known as the tale of instruction, told to children to encourage them to follow the fine example that the life of the folk hero provides for them, so that they will become as brave and as admirable as he was said to be. However, the long version of the Dirty Boy tale, which Opler collected from Alasco Tisnado—a Jicarilla man of about seventy-five years of age at the time of his recitation in 1938—furnishes something more than the ordinary story of how a poverty-stricken and ill-treated youth proved himself a model citizen and a mighty warrior. As Opler has observed, because Tisnado's version "is so entirely concerned with a description of Jicarilla Apache concepts of raid, war, relationship, and status, . . . it serves, in addition, as a reservoir of fact and exposition from which to build a picture of many important aspects of culture."[104]

Undoubtedly, the actual preparation the Jicarilla made for a raid differed little, if any, from those that Tisnado described as taking place in the tale. The following passage taken from his version contains part of the detailed account he gave of these preparations. It expresses to us, once again, the importance of the horse raid to Apache economy, and it also stresses the hardships the men were willing to withstand to get horses.

> . . . many people gathered and had a meeting. Many of the people were short of horses, So it was decided to go out and capture some enemy horses. Some of them did not wish to go. However, others were ready to do it, so a party was arranged for those who wanted to go.
> Two men said, "Why do some of you hesitate to go? You know we need some horses. Some of us, when we go out hunting, have to carry in the deer on our backs. When we move some of us who need more horses have to carry heavy loads on our backs, . . . If we had

enough horses we could hunt deer easily in the mountains, load the meat on the horses, and come home with it quickly."

Many agreed with what these two had said. "We will do it," a number of them agreed. "We'll get a group of forty strong men together for the expedition. We'll pick out forty men who can stand thirst and hunger well."

So those who wanted to go raised their hands and they were selected. The two men who spoke were going too. They brought together all who wanted to go. These forty men came together and lined up.[105]

Alasco Tisnado's recountal of the preparations made for the raid continues, demonstrating how the Jicarilla Apache chief observed the custom of asking his men the formalized questions a chief traditionally asked his raiders before they left camp:

The chief asked, "Are all of you of strong body, and mind, and are you prepared to stand thirst and hunger?"

All of them said, "Yes."

"Remember that you may not be able to get any sleep for four or five nights."

" We can stand it," they all said.

The chief told them, "We may have to be on the trail day and night. Are you strong enough for that?"

All of them said, "Yes."

"If we go to another country, you must not get lonesome and homesick. And will you be afraid if you see our enemies coming after us?"

They all said, "We are brave, we are not afraid."

"Now you must work and get all your friends to help you."[106]

In another scene of the tale, we find a young man installed as a new chief because of his luck in capturing enemy horses. Acknowledging the prestige he acquired from being a successful horse raider, the new chief told his people: "I have not been a chief long; I am a new chief. I became so recently through capturing enemy horses for you people."[107]

The formalized customs and taboos observed by the Navajo before they started on raids resembled those of the Apache in many respects, differing only in minor features. Both Navajo and Apache societies placed sexual restrictions on the raiders while they went through the preparations for the raid. If the men did not keep continence, it was felt that they would bring on an "encounter with the enemy."[108] Both the Apache and the Navajo purified themselves for four successive days in ceremonial sweat houses. The Navajo fired their sweat houses with "thunder-shattered wood" and stones turned over by bears, or else with stones on which "snake-like figures of moss" were found.[109] They sang the songs that Monster Slayer had taught them to the Wind and Sun People, and they offered traditional prayers to the same beings for protection and success. Like the Apache, the Navajo made shirts of several layers of buckskin to serve as armor.[110] One can not help comparing these buckskin shirts with the "medicine shirt" that John G. Bourke mentioned in the 1880s. It was owned by a prominent Tonto Apache medicine man named Na-a-cha, who told Bourke that his shirt possessed, among other things, the powers of Bear and Snake. Bourke saw several of these Apache "medicine shirts," which were made of buckskin and ornamented with decorations symbolizing "the sun, moon, stars, rainbow, lightning, snake, clouds, rain, hail, tarantula, centipede, and some one or more of the 'kan' [gan] gods." The shirts and the medicine sash of similar design, which secured it to the body, were "warranted," Bourke wrote, "among other virtues, to screen the wearer from the arrows, lances, or bullets of the enemy. In this they strongly resemble the salves and other means by which people in Europe sought to obtain 'magical impenetrability.' "[111]

The buckskin shields of the Navajo bore devices similar to those of the above medicine shirts. Hill describes these shields as having a black background with designs in white of "a pair of bear's feet, hands, the big snake, lion, the sun, the moon, the half moon, zigzag lightning, the rainbow, crescent, and Slayer of Monsters." Some of his Navajo informants told him that "these drawings represented the Way in which a man went to war. According to others they were put on the shields because 'they were powerful and feared, and because they strengthened the warrior.' " Their arrows too, they said, contained the power of lightning and the poison of snakes.[112]

When the Navajo and Apache began their journey into enemy territory, they began to use certain ceremonial objects and to observe other formal taboos and customs. The Apache had a taboo against scratching themselves with their fingernails while on the journey. The Jicarilla Apache used scratchers made of sticks shaped like a horse's hoof. When the Jicarilla raid leader distributed these, Alasco Tisnado said, he symbolically transferred his powers to the men to rub over their bodies "so the enemy would not see them."[113] Bourke had occasion to observe the importance of the scratch stick to the Chiricahua when he went on General Crook's expedition of 1883 to Geronimo's hideaway in the heart of the Sierra Madre in Mexico. He saw an "insignificant-looking" article of "personal

equipment," to which, he learned, "the Apache attached the greatest importance." He described this "scratch stick" as "a very small piece of hard
wood, cedar, or pine, about two and a half to three inches long and a half
a finger in thickness. . . ."[114]

Although I have found no definite information as to whether the
Navajo used scratchers on their raids, it seems likely that the crow bills
now used as head-scratchers by patients in the Enemy Way ceremony
served the same purpose for Navajo raiders and warriors.[115] Because the
crow eats carrion, having no fear of death or contamination from the
enemy, he offered in the origin legend of the Enemy Way to destroy
ghosts, saying, "You see I have no fear of enemy ghosts, therefore I myself
shall be [the] first to slay enemy ghosts."[116]

Navajo and Apache raiders even observed taboos in sleeping postures while on the trail. According to Tisnado, Dirty Boy's raid leader
cautioned his men not to stretch their legs out when they were sleeping,
no matter how tired they were, so that "the enemy would not come close
to them."[117] Furthermore, these Jicarilla raiders slept with their heads
toward the west, with arms and legs drawn in toward their bodies.[118]

Youths going on Navajo raids were forbidden to sleep on their backs
or stomachs. Though consigned to one uncomfortable sleeping posture
all night, the Navajo raider was not even allowed to indulge himself in a
good dream, unless he had one concerning horses, or cattle, for dreaming
of them was considered the next thing to capturing them. However, bad
dreams, such as those about being chased or defeated by the enemy, were
considered good signs, even though such dreams under everyday circumstances would be thought dangerous. If the raider dreamed, however,
of being killed, it was believed to be a good precaution to kill a horse or
any range animal he happened upon as soon afterwards as possible, so
that the horse or animal could take his place.[119]

During the day, Jicarilla Apache raiders had to control their thoughts,
for the Apache believed that "to fix" one's mind on unpleasant things
would encourage these things to take place. They directed their gaze to
the east, never to the sky above, lest they draw rain, and never to the side
or behind, lest they "draw the enemy."[120] If he had to look behind him, a
Chiricahua raider would glance over his shoulder first and then turn in a
clockwise manner in deference to the ceremonial circuit of the cardinal
directions.[121] Probably the White Mountain Apache had similar restrictions to protect their raiders from bad luck, for a myth of theirs records
that when the twin culture heroes left Sun's house to return home to
earth with horses, the deity told his boys "not to look at the horses' feet,

nor to look behind them, but to keep their eyes fixed on the tips of their [the horses'] ears."[122]

The Navajo had to keep his mind off problems at home. Joking was taboo because it would bring on trouble. The Navajo also trained their novice raiders not to look at things in the distance, only things nearby— to look far away was to risk their lives. Since the Navajo raid leader was not allowed to look about him, he gave his quiver, emblem of his authority, to a volunteer who was freed from gazing restrictions. This volunteer led the way, holding the leader's quiver and telling him all that was happening around them. This precaution was necessary because if the leader saw something unlucky, the result would be bad fortune for the whole party. The volunteer held the quiver until the attack began, and then he gave it back to the leader.[123]

Navajo women, as well as Apache women, had certain taboos and customs to observe at home while their men were away on a raid. A Navajo woman held a bundle in her hand in which was wrapped pollen mixed with her husband's saliva, and prayed continually for her husband's safe return and good fortune with booty.[124]

Remembering his experiences as a captive among the Lipan Apache, F. M. Buckelew wrote that when a group of Lipan raiders left on a foray, "the old squaws would go some distance from camp, to some kind of evergreen trees, often in the cedar brakes. There they would spend a whole night in a weird mournful chant. This was a solemn time for all, but only the older squaws took part in their chanting ceremony. I suppose they were imploring the Great Spirit for success for their braves."[125] Buckelew's conjecture seems to be correct, for undoubtedly the old women whom he observed were fulfilling their duties as Apache grandparents and offering traditional prayers for their grandsons' safety and success. Because grandparents oversee the ritual and secular training of their grandchildren in Apache societies, they are also expected to be more aware than other relatives of the adventures and the fate of their descendants, and better able to help them get divine aid in times of crisis.[126]

Tisnado's version of the tale of Dirty Boy offers fine examples of the way a grandmother performed the acts that Jicarilla society required of her while her grandson was away on a raid. She said traditional prayers for horses to come her grandson's way, while he looked for them. When he captured a certain number of horses, including a fine spotted steed, Dirty Boy was aware that his grandmother had kept her promise to pray for them, as he had requested her to do. Out of gratitude for her aid, he gave her a nice white horse.[127] On another occasion, when her grandson

sneaked quietly into camp ahead of the other raiders, he told his grandmother to spread the word around camp that the men were returning
safely with many of the enemy's horses. The aged woman went outside
her tepee and made a victory call before the raiding party came into sight.
When the rest of the Jicarilla in camp heard her call, they knew it meant
that the raiders had been successful, but they believed the grandmother
knew it by intuition. They said: "The old lady always knows. If a grandson has been raiding successfully a grandmother always knows it."[128] In
this way, they not only acknowledged her role as a seer of her grandson's
fortunes, but also her attention to duty in calling out to the people her
foreknowledge of the raiders' success.

Restrictions placed on a Jicarilla raider's wife, or on his nearest female relative, are summarized below by Opler:

> She could not bathe during the absence of the party. Her face was
> painted red, her hair hung loose and flowing, her shoulders were
> covered by a buckskin cape such as is worn by the adolescent girl
> during the puberty rites. She could not rid her hair or her person of
> lice [a restriction against scratching]. She could not eat anything
> sweet, anything tart, or any salt. Water she drank only sparingly out
> of a shallow clay bowl. She could not give away any food lest her
> husband or kinsman give away his spoils before reaching home. She
> did not tie her moccasin strings, but placed them loosely within the
> uppers of her moccasins, that her husband might not be harassed by
> the enemy. She could not smoke, for the men dared not smoke in
> enemy country for fear of detection. All her actions had to be
> exceptionally circumspect; the commonplaces of household work
> were governed by rules too numerous to list here and regulations
> extended to the most personal matters.[129]

Most of the restrictions placed on the Jicarilla women in this account
mirror other restrictions placed on the raiders themselves. The food and
water restrictions are a good example. The raiders ate sparingly too. They
carried a very few provisions in a small pouch and subsisted on them,
always on the verge of hunger.[130] The Navajo reasoned, "We will have
plenty to eat where we are going."[131] The Apache carried extra moccasins,
in case one pair wore out. He placed these at the pit of his stomach,
believing that in this position they would thwart hunger pangs.[132] When
Dirty Boy killed two antelopes to supply food for his raiding party, he
took only the kidneys, leaving the rest of the meat, and gave them to the
Jicarilla raiders to eat. Tisnado explained:

If the kidney is used this way the men never get tired. They always feel fresh. Their legs feel strong all the time. The liver is used the same way. They give strength if they are eaten raw. But only antelope liver or kidney is eaten for this purpose; not that of the deer or the buffalo or any other animals. The Jicarilla always did this. They did not put pollen on it first. They ate it just as it came from the animal.[133]

The Chiricahua, Mescalero, Jicarilla, and Western Apache groups considered the youths taken on raids—youths such as Dirty Boy, who were learning the art of raiding—sources of supernatural power. The Jicarilla folk hero demonstrates his superhuman powers throughout the tale, of course, and, as Goodwin notes, Apache novice raiders, in real life, were considered to have similar powers for achieving the goals of the raid.[134] The Chiricahua called the novices Child-of-the-Water for their culture hero who went to his father Sun to ask for horses.[135] If the raid was successful, one of the older men would give the novice a horse.

The Indians placed special food restrictions on these novices. The Navajo did not allow the youths to eat any warm food because it was said it would ruin their teeth.[136] The Chiricahua, too, required this warm-food taboo of the novice, but their reason for doing so was that "if he ate warm food at this time he would never be fortunate with horses."[137] He was also prohibited from eating various parts of an animal, such as the meat from the head and the insides, especially the entrails. Eating the entrails was thought to be the certain ruin of the youth's luck with horses. He was allowed to eat only meat considered undesirable, such as that from the neck region.[138]

Besides the "scratch stick," Bourke saw at Geronimo's Mexican encampment a drinking tube, which he described as another important Apache implement. It was a "small section of the cane indigenous to the Southwest" about three inches long and half an inch thick.[139] Opler describes the Chiricahua drinking tube as "a length of carrizo" and says that the Apache novices drank from it on their first four raids.[140] A raider had to learn to endure thirst because he was forced to travel through much waterless country in the course of his journey. Jicarilla and Chiricahua Apache traditions record that water drunk in other than this ceremonial way would cause hair to grow around the regions of the mouth. "Thus the people kept from getting mustaches and gained long life," Tisnado explained.[141] Though I have found no concrete evidence that the Navajo used the drinking tube on raids, it is possible that the large hollow reed, to which the previously mentioned head-scratcher made of a crow's bill is fastened, was formerly such an item of equipment. This reed figures in

The scratch stick and tube of cane around this San Carlos girl's neck (left) were used by her during her 1971 puberty rite. These items have known ceremonial use by Apachean people since at least their migration days through the Bering Straits. Pubescent boys once used both with ritual on raids serving as their initiation rites.

the ceremonial treatment of a patient suffering from enemy contamination.[142] Bourke observed among the Chiricahua Apache that "a long leather cord attached both stick and reed to the warrior's belt and to each other."[143]

The wearing of amulets in enemy territory was another method of protection and insurance of power. A Chiricahua Apache named Deguele showed his amulet to Bourke and revealed to him that "he prayed to it at all times when in trouble, that he could learn from it where his ponies were when stolen and which was the right direction to travel when lost. . . ." Bourke observed that the designs on it symbolized the rain "cloud and the serpent lightning, the rainbow, rain drops, and the cross of the four winds."[144]

According to Hill, Navajo raiders and warriors carried two different kinds of amulets on their journeys. The first type was a bracelet made of the claws taken from bears, mountain lions, eagles, and owls; in it resided power and strength. The second was a protective medicine bundle, containing five kinds of pollen, each bearing the powers of the being or force from which it had been shaken—a "live bear cub," or "the chief snake that lives in a den and never comes out," or "thunder" (how this was achieved is not explained), or "cyclone dirt" (that is "a pinch of mud formed by the melting hail which falls during a cyclone"), or a "plume taken from a live eagle."[145] Jeff King gave Oakes additional information concerning other medicines Navajo raiders included in their bundles: "They always carried . . . sand from the four sacred mountains," and "if their way passed any other sacred spot," they took samplings of sand from these holy places along with them too. A favorite spot to collect sand was Bear's Mouth, located near Mount Taylor, the Navajo's sacred southern mountain. In addition to the sacred sand, they kept a supply of "ground-up wood from a lightning-struck tree, and powdered bits of birds" in their bundles, using these along with the sand to rub "their bodies to make them strong" and protect them.[146]

On the dawn of the second morning of their journey into enemy territory, Apache raiding parties held a ceremony that signified that the most sacred stage of the raider's mission had begun. To make their men invisible in enemy territory, the raid leaders painted them in ritual fashion with white clay, a ceremony that occurs several times in the Dirty Boy tale. There the leader told his men: "If you are painted with white clay in the proper way the enemy will not see you, though you go on the level land."[147]

Jeff King said that when the Navajo "went to the flat country, they would put on feathers but never paint their bodies," implying that his people observed a restriction about painting their bodies when traveling in open country.[148] But traditions show that Navajo raiders and warriors did frequently paint their bodies, so it may be that they did so only when they were traversing through suitable terrain. Like the Apache, they used white clay but they also used other substances too. Hill mentions, in addition, red ochre, blue paint, and charcoal, for painting symbols of snakes, bear tracks, and human hands on their bodies. "The snakes were believed to give the man power and make him feared as the snake was feared, and the bear tracks to make him fierce and brave like the bear. The hands were thought to symbolize a five fingered being, namely 'a man.'"[149] White clay may have also protected the Navajo raider from becoming contaminated by the enemy or his possessions. The basis for such a belief can be found in the origin legend of the Enemy Way, which Slim Curly told Haile, where the magpie offered to daub any Navajo warrior "with white clay," in order to "drive enemy ghosts away from him."[150]

Once they had been treated with these substances, the men were under restriction to speak only when they had to, and then in the sacred or altered language mentioned earlier in this chapter. As Navajo raiders entered the enemy's territory, their leader reminded them that "the purpose of the party was to bring something back so all the talks were to be about such things." The Navajo, says Hill, never used the altered language in their own country because they felt that if they did so it would bring on an attack from their enemies.[151]

Slim Curly, a successful practitioner for many years of the ceremony of the Enemy Way, told Haile that when the Black Dancers today perform their rite in the Navajo ceremony, they speak this language, "whispering to one another." "Even if a horse has kicked or thrown a person [meaning the patient in the ceremony]" the beast must be called simply "a live one's plume."[152] Reichard, translating the term as "merely a life feather," explains that in the altered language it is "a circumlocution flattering to the horse and signifying its identification with supernatural speed and lightness." This is one of the few examples of altered language ever recorded, and in Reichard's opinion the scarcity indicates that Navajo informants were afraid of repeating such terms when they were not engaged in war or raid excursions and thus protected by the proper ritual from this potent language.[153]

The altered language of the Chiricahua Apache has been recorded and studied in much fuller detail than that of the Navajo has been. The prominent Southern Athapascan linguist Harry Hoijer has taken down and analyzed this language, and Morris Opler, a foremost Apachean ethnologist and scholar, has commented upon its place in raid and war excursions. The Chiricahua raiders referred to the horse as "nose to the ground," and a saddle as "that because of which the horse is not hurt." A mule was "he who drags his tail" or "he drags it about." A rope was "that by means of which would that it be tied," or "would that it be tied by means of it"—"an obvious reference to the hope that horses will be secured as booty."[154] A raider referred to his own eyes as "that by means of which would that I see," or "would that I see by means of it." Hoijer explains that the latter is in the optative mode, signifying, "in all probability . . . a means by which a prayer for the sight of horses and other booty may briefly be expressed."[155] The legendary raiders of the Dirty Boy tale spoke also in the sacred language. When they encountered the tracks of their enemies, the Sioux, they did not say, "These are the tracks of the enemy," but instead, "The enemy's horses have been here." The narrator, Tisnado, explained that they used this language because "if they spoke of the enemy in the usual terms it would mean that they would run into the enemy."[156] Opler writes that the total vocabulary of this speech was not a large one, that it took the Chiricahua from one to three days to master it.[157]

Altered language was not required for the whole journey. With the Jicarilla "as soon as the horses were obtained and the homeward spurt begun, all special forms of speech and most of the other restrictions were dropped."[158] The Navajo communicated in the special language while in enemy territory. As they prepared to leave the alien zone, the raiders "lined up in a row," facing it, and "the leader began a song in which the rest joined. At a certain part of the song all turned toward their own homes and the tabu against 'not talking plainly' was removed."[159]

When Navajo raiders neared the camp of the enemy, they had a certain established ritual to follow in paving the way for their attack:

> . . . the leader put on a pair of moccasins with the big snake painted
> on the soles, tied his good luck amulet to his cap, and went a short
> distance from the camp. Here he called the enemy by their secret
> names, sang songs, and said prayers. "The prayers are like this: he
> starts with the enemy's head and mentions all the different parts of
> his body right down to the ground, and ends his prayer in the
> ground. This is just the same as burying the man."[160]

After the prescribed ritual, the leader made his way back to his party and gave his men a report on how successful he felt he had been in carrying it out. If "he had hesitated or made mistakes in the songs or prayers" that he had offered, "the party would usually turn back," because they felt that the leader's failure in the ritual signified that circumstances were unfavorable for them to make an attack and that proceeding under such conditions would only result in disaster.[161]

Jicarilla Apache precautions on arrival at the enemy camp are illustrated in the tale of Dirty Boy. His feat of quietly slipping into the unnamed enemy's camp, catching them unawares, and driving a hundred and sixty horses out to the waiting ropes of the raiders demonstrates how a real raid leader was supposed to perform under such circumstances. In the ensuing excerpt from the tale, we get not only a picture of the folk hero's assumption of the role of leadership before the appointed older leader's jealous eyes, but also a glimpse of the method a Jicarilla raiding party actually used in capturing their enemy's horses:

> The boy went over to the enemy. He saw that they were having a round dance. But they did not see the boy. He went along the camps looking at each one. After a while he returned and met the party.
>
> He told them, "None of them saw me. They do not know we are around. Now soften your ropes. I'll get some of these horses for you."
>
> He went out again to locate the horses. He found them and drove together a big bunch of them, about a hundred and sixty horses. There were twenty-four men in the party.
>
> The boy said to the men when he came up with the horses, "Encircle these horses and catch the ones you like with your ropes."
>
> All of them were busy capturing horses.
>
> The leader said, "This time one is beating me."
>
> The men now brought together all the extra things which they could not take back and all the worn out moccasins. All these things were brought to one place, and those who had lances which could not be handled on the return trip, stuck them upright in the ground.
>
> The boy said to the men, "Take your time. Don't be afraid of the enemy. Don't frighten the horses or lose any of them."[162]

The tale goes on to tell us that Dirty Boy and his friends had an easy escape and a safe journey home, though they had to keep up a fast pace and be on constant lookout for pursuers. In fact, they had such an easy time of it that "the chief had sorrow in his heart because no enemies had come after them," and he could not regain the prestige he lost when Dirty Boy captured all the horses.[163]

Perhaps that Apache chief should have gone on a certain raid that some Navajo made on the Comanche about 1866. Hill heard the story from a man whose stepfather, along with some other Navajo men, decided to take absence without leave from Fort Sumner, while the Navajo were quartered there. Hill's informant recalled that when his stepfather's raiding party reached the Comanche encampment along a river bank one night, some of the Navajo sneaked into camp and found that the careful Comanche had stationed a watcher among their horses. Not to be outwitted, however, the Navajo raiders stole up near some tepees where the Comanche had tied a great many horses to a line, and waited there silently until dawn. When the sleepy Comanche sentry left his post, the Navajo swiftly cut the line tying the horses, roped one apiece, mounted, and rapidly drove the rest over to the other side of the river:

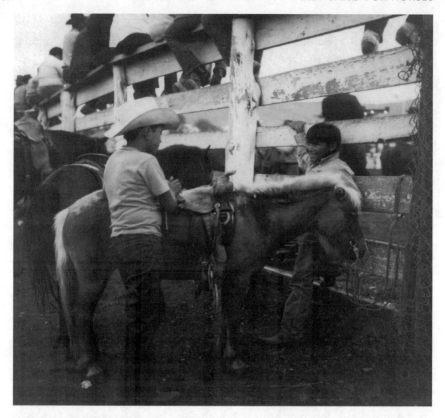

Youngsters like these at Whiteriver, Arizona, are as familiar with the cycle of Dirty Boy tales about that folk hero's exploits with horses as they are with ways of making their own ponies excel.

Just as everyone was mounted, the Comanche discovered the Navaho and gave a signal by tapping on a drum. You should have heard the noise in the Comanche's camp: coyotes, screech owls, and every other kind of noise was made! The Comanche chased the Navaho all that day and night. You could hear the bullets whistling overhead. One man rode ahead to lead the horses; the rest drove the horses after him. After a while half the horses turned back and the Navaho let them go. One man had roped a horse, around whose neck were tied eagle, mountain lion, bear, and owl claws. This horse had some bundles with plumes stuck in them tied in the hair of its tail. This horse must have been a warrior's horse. (They gave these bundles to some old warrior at home.) Finally the Comanche gave up the chase. . . .

Every so often, until after the third day, some one would be sent back to spy, and he would report that the enemy was still following. They rode and drove the horses for three days and two nights without food. The Navaho were so exhausted that they sent some of the party ahead to build a fire and when the herd arrived one of the horses was shot and eaten. By the fourth day some of the men were so sleepy that they fell off their horses; others slept on the saddle. By this time the enemy had given up the pursuit, so the Navaho slept in shifts; one section of the party driving the horses while the rest slept. On the fifth day they arrived at Fort Sumner. By that time only a few of the strongest horses were left. They took a zigzag route home. That is why it took so long.[164]

If the Chiricahua Apache were troubled by pursuing enemies, a shaman could make a ground drawing to hold back the foes. How they used one successfully against some American soldiers is revealed below in the words of an aged Chiricahua:

Once it was used when I was there. A regiment of cavalry and a regiment of infantry were after us. This shaman drew the picture in pollen on the ground and left it there. Then we retreated to a hill. Both regiments turned off the trail and went back by a roundabout way, though the trail was plain, and they could have kept going. That is the way the ground drawing works. When it is used like this, the enemy is unable to follow. Something happens to the enemy always. They give up before they get to the place of the ground drawing, or they cannot pass it.[165]

Sometimes the Navajo also made a protective ground drawing to stop enemies cold in their tracks. They made it after a successful raid had been staged, if time allowed, before they made their escape with the booty. It was drawn in the dirt by the leader, who used a flint arrow-point to draw four lines, representing zigzag lightning, straight lightning, sun ray, and rainbow. It was necessary for the zigzag lightning and the sun-ray designs in the drawing to have four angles depicted in each representation of them.[166] Probably the ground drawing served the added purpose of protecting the members of the party and the horses against the enemy's witchcraft and evil, for under other circumstances, the Navajo are known to have often employed ground drawings for such reasons. Maud Oakes informed Kluckhohn about ground paintings—three of them featuring the toad frogs of the four directions and one of them displaying the cardinal bears—which the Navajo used in this way.[167] One of Kluckhohn's Navajo informants also drew for him, with pollen, a ground drawing of "the sun and the sun's eyes, mouth and horns," and explained that the Navajo sometimes made the drawing to bring them good luck in gambling and to protect them from witchcraft.[168]

Bear boasted of his luck with a ground drawing in a war song he gave the Navajo. Tradition has it that he sang his song, after speaking first, as though he were Enemy Slayer. While he made four curved lines on the ground, he pretended to be the elder of the Twins, then assumed the role of Child-of-the-Water as he made four straight lines on the ground. Next he moved his hands across each other four times and stuck the red male and female arrowheads and some branches of plants he had been holding in his hands into the ground. With these preliminaries attended to, he proudly sang of his skill and power:

> I make a mark they won't cross it.
> *naye'nezyani* I am, they won't cross it
> Black obsidian my moccasins they won't cross it.
> Black obsidian my leggings they won't cross it
> Black obsidian my shirt they won't cross it
> Black obsidian four times my sides hang down
> Black obsidian my headdress.
> Black obsidian zigzag lightning darts four times from me stream out
> Where it goes dangerous missiles will be scattered
> I make a mark they won't cross
> I come back with lightning streaming out from me in four places.
> I come back, dangerous things and missiles being scattered.[169]

Obstacles encountered on the return trip could cause successful raiding parties to lose all that they had captured. They might become so frightened by something they saw that they would run off and abandon their herds. A Navajo explained that such a thing often happened when they were "driving livestock across big flats" and "saw mirages," which terrified them. Worst of all, "sometimes they saw mirages on both sides and did not know what to do."[170] But sometimes they crossed the prairies using the "darkness caused by heat mirage," associating themselves with it by singing Bear's song:

> I have become the heat mirage.
> Toward the east I have become the black mirage with points projecting upward.[171]

And sometimes, in moments of danger, they prayed to the Mirage God for help: "Black Mirage, rise before me so no enemy will see me. Can you see anything beyond me?"[172]

The journey back home could be equally as perilous as the journey into enemy territory; as a Navajo remarked when he summed up the dangers of the raid: "It was a very risky thing they practiced. They went on foot, only taking what food they could carry. Their food might have run out, and there they would have been—lost in a strange country. They did not even know where to find water and had to consult 'stargazers' and 'hand tremblers.' When they ran out of food they simply tightened their belts."[173]

But if none of the men had been killed or lost, the arrival home of the raiders with the horses was a joyous time for all. When a party of Jicarilla Apache raiders had been successful, their people always knew it from the way the men approached the camp, making a clockwise circuit before entering from the south side.[174] As the Lipan Apache raiders neared their camps, they sang the traditional song the spotted turtle had taught them, the "White Corn's Head" song, as a signal for the people to come out and greet them. Upon arrival, the raiders continued to sing, sitting down together in a circle, "slap[ping] their thighs" or a "sage-filled buckskin pillow" to keep time.[175] And on the night of this day when their grandsons had returned safely home, the old Lipan women "spent another night chanting their weird tunes," Buckelew recalled. But now the songs "were not so mournful" as the ones he had heard them sing when the men had gone out on the mission; in fact, they "seemed a little lively."[176]

The Navajo and Apache also observed formalized customs in distributing the horses and plunder taken on the raid to parents, friends, and relatives. Many descriptions of this procedure among the Apache are provided by the tale of Dirty Boy's adventures, but one of the best is given in this scene, narrated by Tisnado:

> All the people wanted to share in the distribution of the horses, but it was up to the chief to give away the horses.
>
> The boy took his share of the horses and drove them over to his grandmother's. The old woman danced and sang and all watched her. The boy gave the white horse to his grandmother. The old lady took it. The boy held it by the bit and another woman helped the old lady on it and the old lady rode it. At that time they had no bridles. They had only a rawhide rope fastened around the mouth of the horse. They tied it under the mouth.
>
> The old woman rode the horse, making the noise the women make, as she rode among the people.[177] That is the way this old woman obtained horses from the enemy so that she would not have hard times again.

All of the people who got horses gave at least one away to their poor relatives. It took nearly all day to dispose of the horses. Each of the men got four or five horses.[178]

As a payment for his services, if he so desired, a Navajo or Apache raid leader could keep a large share of the things taken on the raid, not just the things he had himself seized. Before the party went "into the fight, the leader was privileged to describe a particular piece of property or the color of a horse, etc., and if such an article or animal was found in the loot it belonged to the leader no matter who had captured it."[179]

Both the Navajo and the Apache held all-night victory dances. The Navajo, for instance, divided the booty among the people after a ceremony called "swaying singing," so designated because a group of singers formed a circle, and "swayed back and forth," as they sang before the hogan of each raider.[180] The hardships and dangers were past. It was time for unrestrained celebration. The bear and the snake, the frog and the turtle had been unstinting in their gift of magic aid to the Navajo. The guardian spirit of the horse itself had lent power to some Apache in a solitary vision, and that power in turn had brought victory to a whole party of raiders. The men had obeyed the rituals prescribed by the gods, had spoken the sacred language so that they could take home those creatures called "life feathers." Their women at home had sung and had participated through vicarious ceremony in the trials of their men. All joined in the dance of triumph. They had sung good songs for the horses, which now belonged to them.

Notes

1. Sapir and Hoijer, p. 341.
2. Opler, *Myths and Tales of the Chiricahua,* pp. 14–15, n. 1. A further extension of the interesting reversal of the protagonist role from Killer-of-Enemies to Child-of-the-Water among the Chiricahua Apache occurs in the above quotation. Note too that here Killer-of-Enemies is referred to as the uncle of Child-of-the-Water. This is only one of many such instances in Chiricahua folklore in which Killer-of-Enemies, usually the older brother of Child-of-the-Water, can also appear as a maternal uncle (a brother to White Painted Woman) or even as the husband of the goddess, becoming a stepfather to Child-of-the-Water.
3. Goddard, *Myths and Tales from the San Carlos,* pp. 47–48.
4. Many accounts testify that Navajo raiders traditionally prayed for snow and wind to erase their tracks into enemy country.
5. Elsie Clews Parsons, *Tewa Tales,* Memoirs of the American Folklore Society, XIX (New York: G. E. Stechert and Co., 1926), p. 166.

6. Ibid., pp. 166–167. See also n. 3, p. 166, where Parsons mentions that the Acoma Indians of New Mexico have a similar folk tale concerning "the parachutic escape of the Franciscan friars at the time of the Great Rebellion."

7. This means that the Chiricahua raid leader performed a divination rite. Divination rites are common to all Southern Athapascan peoples. Their use by raiding parties will be discussed later in this chapter. See *supra*, pp. 134–139.

8. Opler, *An Apache Life-Way*, pp. 284–285. The Navajo used cactus in their witchcraft practices, and also yucca. For accounts of this, see Fishler, *In the Beginning*, p. 125; Fishler, "Navaho Picture Writing," p. 60; and Clyde Kluckhohn, *Navaho Witchcraft* (Boston: Beacon Press, 1962), pp. 155–156.

9. Opler, *Myths and Legends of the Lipan*, pp. 36–37.

10. This myth concerning the origin of raiding is interesting to compare at this point with the version of the Lipan Apache myth concerning the acquisition of horses, which Antonio also recorded for Opler. It may be remembered from the discussion of the latter myth in the preceding chapter that Killer-of-Enemies and his three bird companions left on a raid for horses from the war god's home in the Guadalupe Mountains too, but the purpose of their mission at that time was to obtain the first horses for the Lipan. See *supra*, pp. 91–92. For the White Mountain Apache tradition that Killer-of-Enemies set up the rules and instructions for the raids on Mexico, see Goodwin, *Myths and Tales of the White Mountain*, p. 38.

11. Opler, *Myths and Legends of the Lipan*, p. 36.

12. Haile, *Navaho Enemy Way*, p. 205.

13. Ibid.

14. Ibid., p. 207.

15. See also ibid., p. 205, for an explanation of how this same rule is also the basis for the unraveling rite in the Enemy Way ceremony. This rite is performed today to release a patient from the evil influences believed to be "tied" within his or her body from alien contacts of various kinds.

16. For the account, see Goodwin, *The Social Organization of the Western Apache*, p. 386, or *supra*, p. 32.

17. W. W. Hill, *Navaho Warfare*, Yale University Publications in Anthropology, No. 5 (New Haven: Yale University Press, 1936), p. 7. Hill says at least four men composed a raiding party, but other accounts say the number could be as few as three.

18. Opler, *Dirty Boy*, p. 7; Morris E. Opler, "A Summary of Jicarilla Apache Culture," *American Anthropologist*, new series, XXXVIII, No. 2 (April–June 1936), p. 209.

19. Morris E. Opler, "An Outline of Chiricahua Apache Social Organization," in *Social Anthropology of the North American Tribes*, ed. Fred Eggan, The University of Chicago Publications in Anthropology, Social Anthropology Series (Chicago: University of Chicago Press, 1937), p. 177.

20. Ibid., pp. 180–181.

21. See Clyde Kluckhohn and Dorothea Leighton, *The Navaho* (Cambridge, Mass.: Harvard University Press, 1956), p. 73.

22. Hill, *Navaho Warfare*, p. 6.

23. Hill, *The Agricultural and Hunting Methods of the Navaho Indians,* p. 113.

24. Leland C. Wyman and Clyde Kluckhohn, *Navaho Classification of Their Song Ceremonials,* Memoirs of the American Anthropological Association, No. 50 (Menasha, Wis.: American Anthropological Association, 1938), p. 19.

25. Oakes and Campbell, p. 56.

26. For a more extended discussion of this ceremony and the way it is used to protect horses, see *infra,* pp. 174–176.

27. David R. McAllester, *Enemy Way Music: A Study of Social and Esthetic Values as Seen in Navaho Music,* Papers of the Peabody Museum of Archaeology and Ethnology, XLI, No. 3 (Cambridge, Mass.: Peabody Museum, 1954), p. 67—hereafter cited as *Enemy Way Music.*

28. Haile, *Navaho Flintway,* pp. 1–2.

29. *Navaho Classification of Their Song Ceremonials,* p. 34.

30. Haile, *Navaho Enemy Way,* p. 25.

31. Ibid., pp. 153–157, 173–175, 177.

32. Matthews, *Navaho Legends,* p. 149, n. 419.

33. See Reichard, *Navajo Religion,* II, p. 384; Fishler, "Navaho Picture Writing," p. 62.

34. Mary C. Wheelwright, *Myth of Mountain Chant, Told by Hasteen Klah,* and *Beauty Chant, Told by Hasteen Gahni,* Bulletin of the Museum of Navajo Ceremonial Art, No. 5 (Santa Fe, 1951), p. 3.

35. Hill, *The Agricultural and Hunting Methods of the Navaho Indians,* p. 158.

36. Haile, *Navaho Enemy Way,* p. 177. Cf. the Jicarilla Apache myth of emergence, where Bear and Snake introduce two curing ceremonies to the people. See Opler, *Myths and Tales of the Jicarilla,* pp. 27–39.

37. Haile, *Navajo Enemy Way,* p. 173; Reichard, *Navaho Religion,* II, p. 386.

38. Fishler, "Navaho Picture Writing," p. 62.

39. Ibid.

40. Reichard, *Navaho Religion,* II, p. 384.

41. Fishler, "Navajo Picture Writing," p. 62. It should be noted that Bear dressed himself in black flint garments whenever he was engaged in any kind of conflict.

42. Ibid. Concerning Bear's "red mouth," it may be recalled that the Navajo often use the color red to signify something dangerous. See *supra,* p. 34; also Newcomb, "Navajo Symbols in Sand Paintings and Ritual Objects," p. 16.

43. Reichard, *Navaho Religion,* II, p. 384. The Jicarilla Apache also enlist Bear's powers to introduce a shock or trance rite in a ceremony to restore a patient suffering from similar trouble. See Opler, *Myths and Tales of the Jicarilla,* p. 32.

44. Coolidge and Coolidge, p. 144.

45. *Navaho Classification of Their Song Ceremonials,* p. 34.

46. Goddard, *Navajo Texts,* p. 176. The song given here is similar in word and pattern to two songs that the Navajo say the War Twins used in going to war. For the Twins' songs, see Fishler, *In the Beginning,* pp. 51–53.

47. Clyde Kluckhohn and Leland C. Wyman, *An Introduction to Navaho Chant Practice,* Memoirs of the American Anthropological Association, No. 53 (Menasha, Wis.: American Anthropological Association, 1940), p. 187.

48. O'Bryan, pp. 174–175. Cf. Goddard, *Navajo Texts*, p. 179, for the earlier recording of this song.
49. Goddard, *Navajo Texts*, p. 178.
50. Kluckhohn and Wyman, p. 46.
51. See Franciscan Fathers, *An Ethnologic Dictionary of the Navaho Language*, p. 400. The Navajo considered the squirrel one of these creatures. Pollen brought alive by being shaken from its body was carried along on expeditions by raiders to make them invisible to the enemy. See Hill, *Navaho Warfare*, p. 11.
52. Goddard, *Navajo Texts*, p. 179.
53. O'Bryan, p. 173, n. 17.
54. Coolidge and Coolidge, p. 145.
55. Ibid. Jeff King also mentioned to Oakes some prayers that the Twin War gods gave to the Navajo. He refused to record these prayers, which were probably similar to "the witchcraft way" songs, because he said they were "not good" and were to be used only in enemy territory "against monsters, enemies and evil." See Oakes and Campbell, p. 57.
56. For the account concerning the Twins' visit to Frog Man and the story of how he befriended them with his gift of horse fetishes, see *supra*, pp. 71–72.
57. See Reichard, *Navaho Religion*, II, p. 440; Wheelwright, *Myth of Mountain Chant, Told by Hasteen Klah*, and *Beauty Chant, Told by Hasteen Gahni*, p. 2.
58. Reichard, *Navaho Religion*, I, p. 269.
59. Haile, *Navaho Enemy Way*, p. 153.
60. Ibid, p. 157.
61. Wheelwright, *Hail Chant and Water Chant*, p. 94.
62. See Goddard, *Myths and Tales from the San Carlos*, p. 64, n. 2; pp. 65–67.
63. Goddard, *Myths and Tales from the White Mountain*, p. 135.
64. Ibid., p. 137.
65. Opler, *Myths and Legends of the Lipan*, pp. 48, 200–201.
66. Goodwin, *The Social Organization of the Western Apache*, p. 175.
67. For the examination of the myth, see *supra*, pp. 90–93.
68. Opler, *Myths and Legends of the Lipan*, p. 78.
69. Ibid., pp. 78–79.
70. Ibid., p. 79.
71. Ibid.
72. Opler, "A Summary of Jicarilla Apache Culture," p. 214.
73. Opler, *An Apache Life-Way*, pp. 294–295.
74. For accounts of how horses have cured humans of injuries, see *infra*, pp. 232–238.
75. Opler, *An Apache Life-Way*, p. 295.
76. Ibid.
77. Ibid., p. 214.
78. Ibid.
79. Goodwin, *The Social Organization of the Western Apache*, p. 175. Raid leaders also had to know cattle power—a separate power from that of the horse. For an interesting account about cattle power and a White Mountain Apache's effective use of it, see ibid., pp. 667–668.

80. Opler, *An Apache Life-Way*, p. 298.
81. Ibid., pp. 298–299.
82. Ibid., p. 211; Opler, *Myths and Legends of the Lipan*, p. 29, n. 4; p. 30.
83. For the account of this divination rite and the story of the Chiricahua's successful escape from the Yaqui, see *supra*, pp. 117–118.
84. Hoijer, *Chiricahua and Mescalero Apache Texts*, p. 146, n. 34:1.
85. Morris E. Opler, "The Influence of Aboriginal Pattern and White Contact on a Recently Introduced Ceremony, the Mescalero Peyote Rite," *The Journal of American Folklore*, XLIX, Nos. 191–192 (January–June 1936), p. 145.
86. Hoijer, *Chiricahua and Mescalero Apache Texts*, pp. 1–2, 40; p. 146, n. 33:1.
87. Opler, "The Influence of Aboriginal Pattern and White Contact on a Recently Introduced Ceremony, the Mescalero Peyote Rite," p. 145.
88. Hoijer, *Chiricahua and Mescalero Apache Texts*, p. 40.
89. Note by Opler in ibid., p. 146, n. 33:2.
90. Hoijer, *Chiricahua and Mescalero Apache Texts*, p. 40.
91. Ibid.
92. Hill, *Navaho Warfare*, pp. 12–13.
93. Reichard, *Navaho Religion*, I, p. 99; Hill, *Navaho Warfare*, p. 13.
94. Hill, *Navaho Warfare*, p. 13.
95. Reichard, *Navaho Religion*, I, pp. 99–100.
96. Coolidge and Coolidge, p. 157.
97. Ibid., pp. 157–158.
98. Hill, *Navaho Warfare*, p. 13.
99. Ibid.
100. Opler and Hoijer, "The Raid and Warpath Language of the Chiricahua Apache," p. 620.
101. Hill, *Navaho Warfare*, p. 7.
102. Fishler, *In the Beginning*, p. 44.
103. See Wheelwright, *Hail Chant and Water Chant*, p. 80.
104. Opler, *Dirty Boy*, p. 3. Tisnado's version is similar to another shorter version of "Dirty Boy," which Opler collected from a much younger informant; however, the shorter version omits the raid material. For the shorter version, see Opler, *Myths and Tales of the Jicarilla*, pp. 384–387. Goddard also collected a shorter version of this type of tale in 1909, which also leaves out the raiding exploits of the hero. Dealing basically with the warfare and rivalry of two Jicarilla chiefs, Goddard's account tells the story of a hero who resembles the mature leader that Dirty Boy becomes in the long version that Tisnado gave Opler. Cf. Goddard, *Jicarilla Apache Texts*, pp. 15–18, 194–196.
105. Opler, *Dirty Boy*, pp. 7–8.
106. Ibid., p. 8.
107. Ibid., p. 50.
108. Opler, "A Summary of Jicarilla Apache Culture," p. 209; Hill, *Navaho Warfare*, p. 8.
109. Haile, *Navaho Enemy Way*, p. 203; Opler, *An Apache Life-Way*, pp. 218–220.
110. Hill, *Navaho Warfare*, pp. 8–9.

111. John G. Bourke, "The Medicine-Men of the Apache," in *Annual Report of the Bureau of American Ethnology*, IX (Washington, D.C.: Government Printing Office, 1892), pp. 592–593.

112. Hill, *Navaho Warfare*, pp. 10–11.

113. Opler, *Dirty Boy*, p. 10.

114. Bourke, "The Medicine-Men of the Apache," p. 490.

115. For a detailed account of the importance of these crow bills as head-scratchers in the Enemy Way ceremony, see Gladys A. Reichard, *Social Life of the Navajo Indians, with Some Attention to Minor Ceremonies*, Columbia University Contributions to Anthropology, VII (New York: Columbia University Press, 1928), p. 125—hereafter cited as *Social Life of the Navajo*. See also Franciscan Fathers, *An Ethnologic Dictionary of the Navaho Language*, p. 372:"The bill of a crow . . . is used in scratching the head, since the fingers are not to be used in this manner."

116. Haile, *Navaho Enemy Way*, p. 197.

117. Opler, *Dirty Boy*, p. 10.

118. Ibid., p. 38, n. 42.

119. Hill, *Navaho Warfare*, pp. 7, 13.

120. Opler, *Dirty Boy*, p. 27, n. 28; p. 38, n. 42; Opler, "A Summary of Jicarilla Apache Culture," p. 210.

121. Opler and Hoijer, "The Raid and Warpath Language of the Chiricahua Apache," p. 622.

122. Goddard, *Myths and Tales from the White Mountain*, p. 103.

123. Hill, *Navaho Warfare*, pp. 7, 12, 13.

124. Ibid., p. 12.

125. T. S. Dennis and Mrs. T. S. Dennis, eds., *Life of F. M. Buckelew, the Indian Captive as Related by Himself* (Bandera, Texas, 1925), p. 112.

126. See Opler, *Dirty Boy*, p. 35, n. 38.

127. Ibid., pp. 10, 20–21.

128. Ibid., p. 35.

129. Opler, "A Summary of Jicarilla Apache Culture," pp. 209–210. Note that the Jicarilla, like the Navajo, practiced the custom of sharing some of their booty with people whom they chanced to encounter on their homeward journey. For the discussion of the origin of the Navajo custom, see *supra*, pp. 119–120.

130. Opler and Hoijer, "The Raid and Warpath Language of the Chiricahua Apache," p. 621.

131. Hill, *Navaho Warfare*, p. 8.

132. Opler, "A Summary of Jicarilla Apache Culture," p. 210.

133. Opler, *Dirty Boy*, p. 41.

134. Goodwin, *Social Organization of the Western Apache*, p. 477.

135. Opler, *An Apache Life-Way*, p. 137.

136. Hill, *Navaho Warfare*, p. 7.

137. Opler and Hoijer, "The Raid and Warpath Language of the Chiricahua Apache," p. 621.

138. Ibid.; Opler, *An Apache Life-Way*, p. 137.

139. Bourke, "The Medicine-Men of the Apache," p. 490.

140. Opler and Hoijer,"The Raid and Warpath Language of the Chiricahua Apache," p. 622.

141. Ibid.; Opler, *Dirty Boy,* pp. 22–23; p. 23, n. 25.

142. See Reichard, *Social Life of the Navajo,* p. 125.

143. Bourke, "The Medicine-Men of the Apache," p. 490.

144. Ibid., p. 587.

145. Hill, *Navaho Warfare,* pp. 9–10.

146. Oakes and Campbell, p. 56.

147. Opler, *Dirty Boy,* p. 38.

148. Oakes and Campbell, p. 56.

149. Hill, *Navaho Warfare,* p. 14.

150. Haile, *Navaho Enemy Way,* p. 197.

151. Hill, *Navaho Warfare,* p. 12.

152. Haile, *Navaho Enemy Way,* p. 239.

153. Reichard, *Navaho Religion,* I, p. 269. Note too that earlier in Slim's version of the origin legend of the Enemy Way, the use of "the live one's plume" has been identified with the war medicine—a medicine with life-giving properties, which Bear gave to the ceremony. Bear's gift of this medicine has been discussed earlier in this chapter. See *supra,* p. 124.

154. Opler and Hoijer,"The Raid and Warpath Language of the Chiricahua Apache," pp. 629, 633–634.

155 Ibid., p. 629.

156. Opler, *Dirty Boy,* p. 42.

157. Opler and Hoijer,"The Raid and Warpath Language of the Chiricahua Apache," p. 625.

158. Opler, "A Summary of Jicarilla Apache Culture," p. 210.

159. Hill, *Navaho Warfare,* p. 12.

160. Ibid., p. 14.

161. Ibid.

162. Opler, *Dirty Boy,* p. 16. Also see n. 15, where Opler explains that "the cast-off articles were tied to the abandoned lances and left as a gesture of contempt for the enemy."

163. Ibid., p. 19.

164. Hill, *Navaho Warfare,* pp. 4–5.

165. Opler, *An Apache Life-Way,* p. 265.

166. Hill, *Navaho Warfare,* p. 16. See also Fig. 1.

167. See the letter of May 27, 1942, from Maud Oakes to Clyde Kluckhohn, in Kluckhohn, *Navaho Witchcraft,* p. 204.

168. Ibid., p. 187, and accompanying illustration.

169. Goddard, *Navajo Texts,* p. 177. Cf. Bear's mark in O'Bryan, pp. 173–174, especially Fig. 23, p. 174.

170. Hill, *Navaho Warfare,* p. 5.

171. Goddard, *Navajo Texts,* p. 176. Cf. O'Bryan, p. 173.

172. Fishler, "Navaho Picture Writing," p. 67.

173. Hill, *Navaho Warfare,* p. 5.

174. Opler, *Dirty Boy,* p. 36, n. 39.

175. Opler, *Myths and Legends of the Lipan,* pp. 48, 49; p. 49, n. 1; p. 201.

176. Dennis and Dennis, p. 112.

177. See Opler, *Dirty Boy,* p. 21, n. 22, where he observes that this is a traditional call made by the women to indicate "joy or applause."

178. Ibid., p. 21.

179. Hill, *Navaho Warfare,* p. 7.

180. Ibid., p. 17. Also see p. 16, n. 8, where Hill notes that "this swaying singing occurs today as a part of the War or Squaw Dance. It takes place just prior to and after the Squaw Dance proper."

The People's Ways for Keeping Horses Holy

L ONG AGO, THE NAVAJO REMEMBERED, Mirage Man had closed the door tightly on the sacred horses of the sun god. Turning to the eager Turquoise Boy who had come seeking horses for his people, he challenged him with a rhetorical question: "This now, of that which is like this, what is it that you who are earth people can keep holy?" Hesitant about entrusting the care of such precious things as horses to earth people, the ancient guardian of Sun's horses had added cautiously, "I shall just shake (the pollen) off (the horses) for you."[1]

The earth people did not forget his words. And once the culture hero had learned the secret of creating horses through the ceremony his mother Changing Woman performed with the sacred pollen and the beads saturated with saliva from the solar horses, the Navajo learned also the ways the God People meant them to keep horses holy. Following the teachings of their deities, they learned ceremonies, songs, and other ritual for the increase and protection of the animal, which the Turquoise Boy had always called "that by means of which people live."

The Apache learned too from the teachings of their culture heroes. Before departing forever from the world of humans, the heroes had laid down definite rules of animal husbandry that they intended earth people to observe explicitly from that time forward. From these practices, characterized like those of the Navajo by potent magic, the Apache accounted for most of their luck with horses.

Ceremonies and Songs of the Medicine People

The ceremonies and songs related to the care of horses were not known to every individual, for such knowledge was not easy to come by. An

Today more Navajo women are practicing rites, especially the hogan blessing and kinaaldá. Previously only older women, like the one above in the dress women of her age still wear, knew them. Traditionally women were restricted from practicing the longer ceremonials until after menopause. See also *infra,* p. 302.

Apache or Navajo had to go in search of it and obtain it through contact with a Holy Being, a horse, or its guardian agent.

The same type of horse ceremony an Apache raider used in locating horses could also be used to advantage in promoting their health and well-being, and like the ceremony a raider possessed, it was given to an Apache by a horse or by any of its guardian agents. A fine example of how an agent of the horse could bestow on a person the supernatural powers designed to take care of a horse's health is supplied in a tale recorded by the aged Lipan storyteller named Antonio Apache. In Antonio's tale, Cowbird gave a ceremony to a Lipan who liked horses so much that he spent most of his time out in the wilderness rounding up mustangs. The cow-bird, as it may be recalled, had received his power with horses directly from Killer-of-Enemies, who made him one of the three guardian spirits in control of horses on earth.[2] One day while Antonio's Lipan was out chasing down mustangs, he suddenly came to the edge of a hill, and saw down below a group of horses hunched together as though they were inside a corral. While he looked on, Cowbird—or "the little person" as Antonio insists on calling this bird throughout the tale—came out the side of a hill and walked straight over to the herd. He "was dressed in something that shone and he wore a hat" with "a little brim." When Cow-bird approached, "the horses didn't move." They permitted him to move around freely in their midst without seeming to be disturbed in the least. This certainly impressed the Lipan, and thinking over what he had seen, he reasoned to himself that if they allowed "the little person" these privi-leges, they might allow him the same. So he decided to make his pres-ence known. But the moment he did so, the entire herd protested. Antonio related that "they pricked up their ears and began to stamp." "The little person," jumped on "a big stallion, one which had never been ridden before," and hurriedly rode away. This sudden departure of Cowbird caused a general exodus by the entire herd, all of them fleeing after him.[3]

The Lipan's curiosity about this little fellow with such a forceful com-mand over horses was so aroused that he decided to take up the chase. He had to ride hard and heavy, trailing him for a long way before he even got close enough to get another good look at the tiny master of the mustangs, who was "carrying a stick for a whip," and applying it so earnestly that his stallion seemed literally to be flying across the land. Finally, when the exhausted stallion began to slow down, and the Lipan was able to see from a closer range, he saw "the little person" drop his whip-stick. The man noted that the whip fell to the ground near a rock, the location of which he took pains to remember. There was no time for him to stop then to inspect the stick, for Cowbird abandoned the tired stallion about that time and transferred "with ease to another one" trotting alongside. The Lipan continued in heated pursuit, but in vain, for Cowbird had vanished soon after he had settled himself on his fresh mount. Thus the man gave up the chase and took the only alternative left open to him. He went back to the spot where the switch was, found it lying there, still warm (or "fresh" as Antonio noted) from its use on the stallion's body, and recognizing its significance, he "picked it up" and carried it home with him.[4] He realized that with Cowbird's "live" stick he could bring about further encounters with its owner—encounters in which the guardian would teach him a ceremony of power over horses. And this, Antonio explained, is how he did it:

> After returning to his camp, the Lipan kept the switch and each night put it under his pillow. He finally had a dream about it. He learned something through the stick. The man who found this stick was named "Something Black." He kept on putting the stick under his pillow. Each night he learned more about it. He was becoming a horse ceremonial man.
>
> The Lipan learned much about his horse ceremony. The little man who had lost the stick kept thinking about that switch all the time. He didn't want to lose it. Through the switch he gave this man songs and a ceremony, a little more each night. Finally he himself came before the Lipan and stood before him. The Lipan saw him very clearly in his dream.[5]

After the Lipan had his dream of the face-to-face meeting with Cowbird, he "thought much about horses," and he started to practice the ceremony the guardian had bestowed upon him. "He began to raise horses"—many fat fine ones, and "when the seeds came on the grama-grass in the fall, he went out with his horses and collected grama-grass seeds. He chewed them and spit them out in front of his horses. In this way he kept them in good condition. He did that every fall." All of his success he owed, of course, to Cowbird.[6]

The Navajo tell a completely different kind of story about the way the first horse power was conveyed to their people. In telling this myth to O'Bryan, Sandoval combined it with that of the ceremonial creation of horses by White Bead Woman. As related previously, although White Bead Woman formed horses for the people in a ceremony, she withheld the real animals from them for a while, only causing some fetishes to be laid in "the center of the earth" at a place called Sis ná dzil (already located by Sandoval as "near, or beyond Haines on the road to Cuba, New Mexico"). It was the destiny of a certain man who lived near this place to learn the ceremony to bring these fetishes to life.[7] According to Sandoval, the man who lived in the vicinity of Sis ná dzil arrived on the scene not long after the two boys who had visited White Bead Woman had finished holding the first Night Chant performed on earth—the ceremony the goddess had instructed them to conduct for the people as soon as they returned home. The ceremony lasted all night, and at the end of it, they "chanted the chants of the horses" in accordance with the goddess's wishes. It was just after they had finished singing that "the man from near Sis ná dzil" experienced the first of a series of visions he was to have about horses.[8] He was out walking alone, and being near the center of the earth, was in one of the most sacred regions of Navajo mythology. It was here that Turquoise Boy, with his heart set on obtaining horses for the Navajo, had experienced the fourth of a series of encounters with Holy Beings—the one in which Mirage Man led him to Sun's cardinal steeds.[9]

In his first vision, the man walking around in the vicinity of Sis ná dzil "saw a horse standing in the distance, to the East." "He went over to it, but he found that it was only a plant called *gá tso dan,* jack-rabbit corn [grass]." On the three succeeding days he had three other visions of a horse to the south, to the west, and to the north. The one to the south turned out to be "only the grass" the Navajo call *"nit dit lede"* (mountain rice), while the one to the west "proved to be only *tlo nas tasse,* sheep-grass." The one to the north, which he saw on the fourth day, though not really a horse, was something different from the grasses of the other directions: but even that was "only the droppings of some animal."[10]

If we leave Sandoval's story at this point long enough to view it in relation to Frank Goldtooth's version of a Navajo myth concerning visions of horses the Twins had shortly before they obtained the potent fetishes from Frog Man, we find some marked resemblances between the two. In Goldtooth's description, what appears to be horses becomes in reality grass, and three of the same grasses Sandoval named—jackrabbit grass, mountain rice, and sheep (or grama) grass:

> In the distance they saw a horse near their brother's [Frog's] home at Wide Belt Mountain. They were just imagining they saw the horse for what they really saw was a plant. It was Jack Rabbit Brush, *gahzoh ḍá'*, which is gray. There was also another plant which was a salt plant called *dók'óží* [saltweed]. This plant they also saw in the distance. They also saw a grass called *ñdiʌídi'* [mountain rice] and one which was curly called *t'oh n'asťʲasí'* [sheep grass]. There was also a grass plant which had a bushy top and about two and one half feet high called *t'oh ćósi'* [rush grass]. In the distance the Twins saw these hunched together. All of these plants are those which horses feed on. The Twins went over to see these things. Four times they tried to find the horses, but found nothing.[11]

This is but another instance of how the same motifs persist in a tradition, although oral transmission may shift them into a completely different story. There are many more motifs in Sandoval's story recalling those of the Twins' visit to the sun deity.

After the man from Sis ná dzil had his visions, Dotso, the all-wise fly, who had counseled the Twins on many occasions, appeared to him out of nowhere and asked: "What are you doing here, my Grandchild?"

"I saw a horse four times; and each time it turned out to be a plant or something," the man replied.[12]

Dotso advised the man to visit the sun deity and tell him about his visions, and suddenly the man found that he had been transported to the home of Sun, whose only greeting was to ask him his reason for coming. Answering Sun's question in practically the same way he had answered Dotso's, the man said: "I have seen a horse four different times, and each time it turned out to be only some grass or plant." But as he answered, he could see horse fetishes standing around in every direction; there were "fetishes to the east, south, west and north."[13]

Sun acted swiftly. In what seemed an instant, he conducted the man to "the opening in the sky, to a place called Haya tsá tsis." This opening in the sky, as our narrator explained when telling another story, is a "square hole," which the Navajo say is located up in the center of the heavens at a point directly above Tso dzil (Mt. Taylor), their holy mountain of the south. The sky-opening is said to be "mirrored in a lake that lies between the two highest peaks of the mountain."[14] It was to this same place— "the opening in the sky"—that Sun had once taken the Twins to play a guessing game with him. As they peered through the opening at the world below, Sun tested the Twins' knowledge by pointing to certain mountains and rivers sacred to the Navajo and demanding whether they could identify them.[15] Now Sun seemed to have his heart set on playing the same game with his present visitor, for the moment they arrived at the opening, Sun asked him "to look back" and tell him: "From where did we start?" Before the man could answer, he heard the voice of the Little Breeze—another of the Twins' friendly counselors—whisper in his ear, warning him that if he failed to supply the right answer, "what he came for" would be denied him. So the man thought a while, then replied: "Way over where the two rivers come together, there is where we started."[16] Undoubtedly in giving such an answer, this man from "the center of the earth" was referring to a place the Navajo call "the crossing of the waters" —a place of extreme importance in Navajo mythology as the central point where waters traveling from the cardinal directions meet. As Sandoval once described it, it was a place where a great "Male River," traveling "from east to west," crossed a great "Female River," which flowed "from north to south." Though the "crossing of the waters" exists only in mythology, the Navajo do associate their "Male" and "Female" Rivers with two modern-day rivers sacred to their religion.[17] They say that the mighty "Male River" is the San Juan, which flows in a westerly direction across the northern part of their reservation and forms part of its northern boundary. They say that the placid Rio Grande, traveling in a southerly direction through some of the land in northern New Mexico, where they lived before they migrated west, is the gentle "Female River."[18]

But perhaps when the man followed Sun's orders and *looked back* to where they had *started* from, he also *looked back* in time to the genesis of life, for his answer that they had "started" from "where the two rivers come together," implies fertility symbolism, in accordance with the Navajo tradition that before humans were created, the very process of procreation came into existence because the waters met at the place called "crossing of the waters."[19] By such an answer the man demonstrated to Sun his worthiness to possess a horse creation ceremony.

Next, the man chanted for Sun the song the Elder Twin had composed for his race around the earth on Sun's turquoise stallion:

> I am the Sun's son.
> I sat on the turquoise horse.
> He went to the opening in the sky.
> He went with me to the opening.[20]

Like the Elder of the Twins, the man had also been transported with lightning speed to "the opening in the sky." However, as Sandoval explained, this song is one the Navajo still sing "to thank the Powers for horses."[21] No doubt the man was offering it as a prayer, entreating Sun to tell him how to acquire the horses he had seen in his visions. And Sun complied, saying that he must return to the place of his first vision and camp for the night. "He must offer a gift" to the jackrabbit grass "he had seen in the east," and also to the mountain rice plant in the south, to the grama (sheep) grass in the west, and to the animal "droppings" in the north, camping in turn at each of these places too. After that, Sun assured him, "he would see the horse."[22]

As soon as the man set foot on earth again, he faithfully carried out Sun's orders, and finally he sang "four sections of a chant," the story of how White Bead Woman had created the horses of the four directions.[23] Comparing this song with that of the goddess, given earlier, we find that many of the words are similar and some of the themes identical, an illustration of the intricate pattern by which one Navajo song is woven from another and the extent to which the Navajo coordinate ceremonial songs with mythical sequences.[24] By echoing the words and actions of the gods, a ceremonial singer strengthens his own. According to Sandoval, the novice medicine man sang as follows:

I came upon it.
I came upon it.
I came upon it.
I am the White Bead Woman,
I came upon it.
In the center of my home,
I came upon it.
Right where the white bead basket sits,
I came upon it.
The basket has four turquoise decorations,
I came upon it.
The white bead basket has a turquoise finishing around the edge,
I came upon it.
The white bead horses stand toward the basket from the four
    directions,
As I came upon it.
All the beautiful flowers are its pollen,
Black clouds are the water they [horses] have in their mouths,
As I came upon them.
White poles for its enclosure (corral)
As I came upon them.
Blue poles for its enclosure,
As I came upon them.
Yellow poles for its enclosure,
As I came upon them,
Iridescent poles for its enclosure, flashing,
As I came upon them.
The rainbow for its gate,
As I came upon it.
The sun closes its entrance (gate of corral)
As I came upon it.
The white bead horses pour out,
As I came upon them.
The turquoise horses pouring out,
As I came upon them.
The white shell horses pouring out,
As I came upon them.
The male banded stone horses pouring out,
As I came upon them.
All mixed horses, together with the sheep, pouring out,
As I came upon them.
As the horses pour out with the beautiful goods [man's possessions],
As I came upon them.

The earth's pollen (dust) rises as they pour out,
The shining dust of the earth covers their bodies,
As I came upon them.
To multiply and not to decrease,
As I came upon them.
Like the Most High Power Whose Ways Are Beautiful are my horses,
As I came upon them.
As I came upon them.
Before my horses all is beautiful,
Behind my horses all is beautiful.
As I came upon them.
As I came upon them.[25]

The singing of this song brought to life the horse fetishes that had been buried at the center of the earth, and from that time forward horses lived among the Navajo. But Sandoval believed the great gift was not without cost, for "the Holy Ones" took from the people's horse "the rainbow and all the supernatural powers."[26] The man from Sis ná dzil was now a full-fledged medicine man—the first man among the Navajo to learn the gods' secrets of bringing horses to life. Others would soon follow, because the gods now intended that horses should be bred and cared for on earth.

We have had a glimpse of how Apache horse ceremonies vary from those of their linguistic relatives, the Navajo. The main reason for the divergence of ceremonial patterns is the heavy influence that certain Pueblo Indian groups have exerted upon Navajo religion. Groups such as the Hopi, Zuñi, and Rio Grande Pueblo tribes, whose ceremonies are built upon elaborate blessing rites and prayer fetishes, taught the Navajo this emphasis after this tribe became their neighbors in the Southwest. Over a period of association with these Pueblo tribes, Navajo ceremonialism eventually superimposed many Pueblo borrowings upon its Southern Athapascan base, departing dramatically in many respects from earlier ceremonial patterns.

In order to gain a better understanding of the differences, let us compare the two preceding ceremonies, the Lipan Apache and the Navajo. The Lipan is representative of the Apache ceremonial pattern in that it depends heavily upon the solitary initiation of the shaman, whose power takes possession of him and leads him to knowledge through trial and vision. In the above account, the Apache shaman receives his power and teachings about medicine directly from the agent of the horse—in this case, the Cowbird. All that the Apache shaman is taught about power over

Bosnic Lupe, Cibecue Apache medicine man, with his horse. The medicine hat with the potent feathers and the medicine cord around his neck were to aid him with horses and supplement his power over them. Cf. also *infra,* pp. 299–300. (Courtesy Arizona Historical Society/Tucson, photo AHS#53771)

horses comes directly from his encounters with Cowbird, or through the Cowbird's switch, in which he keeps his knowledge stored. When Cowbird stands before him in a dream, the teachings are completed and the shaman is then ready to go out and practice his ceremony, performing it according to his own interpretation of the power bestowed upon him.

The Navajo medicine man, on the other hand, is not taught a ceremony whose pattern demands his own interpretation, but rather one whose pattern depends upon tradition. The foregoing vision of the Navajo occurs immediately after two important ceremonies: first, the one in which the goddess created the horses intended for the Navajo, and, second, the one that the youths who had visited her held on earth in behalf of the people. After the man experiences his vision, he sees plants and droppings, which symbolize horses, but these "power" symbols of the horses do not teach him a ceremony in the manner that Cowbird's switch revealed one to the Apache. Instead, the Navajo goes to the sun deity for an interpretation of his vision and both the experience he has and the ceremony he learns are patterned after the experiences of the gods and the ceremonies they have already held or prescribed. Like the

Twins, he journeys to the "opening in the sky" and is tested by Sun. He sings the song Elder Brother sang as he rode Sun's turquoise horse. He receives from Sun instructions about offering ritual gifts to the power symbols of the horse. To animate the buried horse fetishes, he imitates White Bead Woman's horse creation song. Thus, the Navajo's ceremony has already been shaped for him.

This brief summary of the contrasts between Navajo and Apache ceremonial patterns does not imply that the Apache do not practice some traditional ceremonies originating in tribal myths. When we move away from the horse creation ceremonies into others, we find many that are performed according to the established procedures of ceremonies held by the gods: for instance, the Apache puberty ceremonies. From this and others like it the horse shaman often draws inspiration when interpreting his power. Traditions having to do with culture heroes and mythical horse guardians will also influence him. The broad outlines of horse ceremonies, then, though shamanistic in character, are regulated to some extent by ceremonial patterns laid down by the deities.

The same distinctions prevail in curative and protective practices for humans and horses: the Apache shamans enjoys more freedom than the Navajo in executing their ceremonies. While the Navajo in horse rites may decide upon which songs and how many will be sung, they must follow the general pattern of the traditional ceremony called Blessing Way. On the other hand, the ceremony of one Apache shaman may differ completely from that performed by another, even if the purpose of both ceremonies is the same.

In the last chapter we saw how the Blessing Way entered into raiding.[27] Rites from this multipurpose ceremony are also held at frequent intervals in Navajo households to assure the increase, general health, and protection of horse herds. Any number of events may occur that will lead a Navajo to have a Blessing Way sung for the protection of horses, for instance, if there is reason to believe that someone has tried to bewitch one of them. Also if the owner should dream of the death of horses, sheep, or cattle, and see it as a prediction of sickness threatening the animals, a Blessing Way would be performed at once to counteract the danger.[28]

Although some Navajo ceremonies are elaborate ones lasting nine days, Blessing Way rites for horses are comparatively short affairs—short in the Navajo sense, in that while the rite may take anywhere from a few hours to a whole night to perform, it never lasts longer than one night. Gladys Reichard, who attended all sorts of these rites, once characterized them by saying that while each followed the established ceremonial pattern of Blessing Way, no two were exactly alike as to the number of songs offered or the time it took to deliver them. Selecting one of them that lasted all night as more or less typical, she noted that the medicine man began by singing for "about an hour and a quarter." "During this time," he sang without ceasing "a group of thirteen songs, another of ten, then one song, summarizing all the others. . . . After a short pause, the singing continued with short rest periods until dawn."[29] The final song of the man from Sis ná dzil belongs to the class of songs associated with Blessing Way rites of this sort. Sandoval told O'Bryan that he knew eighty-five such horse chants. All of them, he said, were sung for "the good of horses," and to insure their continuance he had taught many of them to his son and his nephew.[30]

The medicine man who knows Blessing Way songs can sing them three times during one month, but he is obliged to refuse if he is asked a fourth time, lest he endanger his power; he should, in fact, renew it after the third time by having a Blessing Way sung over himself.[31]

The little horse fetishes that the Holy Beings taught the Navajo to revere are important items of the medicine person's ceremonial paraphernalia when a Blessing Way of this kind is sung. Singers keep these tiny images of horses, usually carved from stone, in the medicine pouches that they hold while singing. A certain Navajo who was adept at a Blessing Way rite believed to be six hundred years old used mirage-rock horse fetishes in executing the ceremony and counted them among the pouch's most precious possessions. In the pouch with them, he carried "mountain soil" medicine collected from the sacred mountains and passed down to him by the singer who taught him the Blessing Way. His was a potent medicine bag because "it had been owned by powerful singers." Of its powers, he once avowed: "it helps [you] to hold onto it . . . and helps you gain everything you want."[32]

The contents of this medicine pouch are reminiscent of the "horses of stone" and the "black shining dirt" and the "many other things" that White Bead Woman left for medicine people on top of the mountain where she held her last earthly ceremony before she departed to the world of the gods. A medicine person in need of these things has only to make a trip to this mountain top, for it is said that they can still be found there.[33]

Medicine people are not the only ones who possess horse fetishes. Practically all Navajos who own horses have buckskin pouches in their hogans in which they keep their "sacred horses," usually among pollen, herbs, and pieces of sacred stones and shells, such as turquoise and white shell. These pouches keep their real horses safe from witchcraft and other dangers.[34] If the owners accidentally drop their pouches, or break anything in them, that is a very bad omen. According to one informant, that person must have a Blessing Way sung immediately so that everything will be "all right" again; otherwise evil will strike "in a few days."[35] Frances Gillmor, distinguished Southwestern folklorist and author, witnessed a Blessing Rite held for just such reasons when she was doing research on the Navajo Reservation in 1931. She told me that some Navajo friends of hers sang one whole night, beginning late, because the wife in the household had broken a little horse fetish she kept in her bag of pollen.

So important have these fetishes become that they are looked upon as a symbol of the Navajo way of life, explaining even the origin of the tribe. The Navajo and the Hopi, said Frank Goldtooth, were formerly one people. They emerged here from the underworld through the same length of cane, but once they reached the upper earth, two gods came forth and divided the people by a choice of pottery. One of the pots offered to the gods was "plain," while the other was "beautifully decorated." Talking God reached for the plain one without hesitating, for as Goldtooth explained it: "He knew this pot had the stone horse . . . and many other things inside. Calling God . . . reached for the decorated one."[36] The people of Calling God became the Hopi, who went away to their own place, and never raised many horses but instead made handsome pottery; while the Navajo stayed at the place of emergence to become the people with the little stone horses that brought them many fine real ones and always protected their herds.

Whether the purpose was to increase their number of horses, to protect those they already had by prevention and curing of disease and injury, to break them, to race them, or even to geld them, all of the Apache of the past generation felt that their horse shamans possessed the ceremonies to achieve the desired goal. Considering the nature of Apache horse rites, it would be difficult if not impossible to cover the wide range of practices that occur in them. The best we can do is examine some variations of detail within the characteristic structure on which these ceremonies are built. Usually a shaman's power will reveal the effective songs and prayers to be used. For instance, a Lipan shaman who had received power from Cowbird might be expected to possess songs and prayers beneficial in the breaking of horses, a specialty of Cowbird's. Killer-of-Enemies is responsible for that, for upon assigning Cowbird his duties on earth, he told him that if the Lipan wanted "to break a horse and make him gentle, they must mention your name [in prayers and songs] and then you must help them. But if they go ahead without mentioning your name, then you need not help and the horse will do anything it wants to."[37] This does not mean, of course, that only shamans with Cowbird power would know songs or prayers for breaking horses ceremonially; sometimes other sources were highly efficient too. The Chiricahua Apache tell about a woman shaman—a rarity, to be sure—who had power from a horse. She was renowned for breaking broncs with a ceremony in which she used "songs for the bridle and for every part of the horse." They say that even the wildest of mustangs was "always gentle to her."[38]

If a male Chiricahua horse shaman was performing a ceremony over a horse to give it power to win a race, in his songs he might make special reference to the swiftness of such animals and elements as "the coyote, the fox, the wind, or clouds," so that their powers of speed could be transferred to the horse.[39] In order to make both the horse and rider invulnerable to the sorcerers whose presence is always anticipated and feared at horse races, a Jicarilla shaman might also address prayers to Killer-of-Enemies, making reference to the way the culture hero had once overcome the attempted sorcery of Owl.[40] A shaman who was practiced at working with race horses had frequently gained his control over them from Bat, a special power that Killer-of-Enemies had awarded this bird in the distribution of duties, saying, ". . . You will have charge only while the horse is running, in horse races or when they are chasing horses. Before these things start, if they mention your name [in songs and prayersl, do not let the horse fall with them."[41] Bat's racing power extended as well to the rider, for Bat could transfer to the latter the ability to cling to an object. An aged Chiricahua Apache told Opler that when he was a boy ("before Geronimo's last war, about 1884 or 1885"), shamans with Bat power often trained and performed ceremonies for boys to insure their competence in horsemanship. He remembered seeing a boy who had been so trained ride an unsaddled bronco full tilt down a hill with only a rope to guide it: "That boy rode the horse down the hill just like nothing!" "The horse pitched all around with him but could not shake him off." In this particular case, Bat's power as conveyed by the shaman proved so effective that the boy could perform with ease any equestrian feat the shaman requested, "whether it was dangerous or not."[42]

Horse trappings were also significant ceremonial articles. Before performing his ceremony a shaman would ask the owner to give him four pieces of equipment that had been used on a horse. A Chiricahua Apache who had once enlisted the services of an elderly horse shaman recalled the following details about what the man had requested from him:

Trappings like the saddles, bridles, ropes, and blankets shown on sale at Fort Apache often serve in groups of fours as ceremonial offerings in the rituals of shamans with the power of the horse.

I had a man who specializes on mules and horses castrate my mules. The old man made a ceremony of it. . . . He said, "Give me a saddle blanket, a bridle, a little rope, and something else that is used for a horse. It doesn't have to be new. Give me something you don't want. I don't care how much it has been used. Just give me these to carry out the ceremony. Never mind other payment." He told me he usually gets paid besides, but he always gets these things to complete the ceremony. He made it pretty plain that his power wanted things that had already been in use on a horse.[43]

As the account implies, the requested items of equipment were to serve as ceremonial gifts to establish contact with the shaman's power and to assure its cooperation. Sometimes the kind of trappings shamans used would vary, but they were always four in number. This was in accord with general Apache ceremonial requirements, for whether the rite was elaborate or insignificant, and no matter for what purpose it was held, Apache shamans always needed four gifts to present to their powers.[44] By utilizing the trappings a horse had worn, the shaman could convey into each stage of the ceremony some of the power the trappings had absorbed from the animal's body and saliva.

Over and over again in Apache mythology, we find a power demanding that the trappings be offered to it as a condition of its granting support. Often the directions given seem to echo those from Sun to the Twins when they were learning ceremonies for horses. A White Mountain tale about a talking horse who taught a youth a ceremony to produce horses serves as a case in point. This horse demanded that the young man find a place where four mountain ridges came together from the four directions and put an offering of horse trappings on each side: "Put a halter on the east one and put a rope on the south side; put a saddle on the west side and on the north side put a saddle blanket."[45] The youth obeyed the horse, and after he had done these things and waited for four days, he found in the place of those trappings, the black, blue, yellow, and white stallions kicking up dust as they raced out to each of the four directions.

Besides songs and prayers and trappings, there remains one other procedure characteristic of Apache ceremonies for horses, and this is that the shaman often utilized certain medicines. These were commonly designed to cure a horse of illness or injury, to protect it from some imminent danger, or to provide it with some magical power. However, these medicines were not necessarily restricted to ceremonial application; often Apache horse owners administered them without the benefit of a shaman's ceremony. Before looking more closely at these medicines, however, it is interesting to note that an Apache horse shaman's power over another's horses was not always considered efficacious for his own. Opler discovered among the Chiricahua some differences of opinion concerning the extent to which a shaman could rely on his own power. One man observed: "Some persons have a ceremony from the horse and have fit horses all the time." Another had his doubts, illustrating them with this example: "I think that N. had power from the horse. His horses were poor. Some people say that a man with a horse ceremony has pretty poor horses. He can help others but not himself."[46] Opler found too that the

Chiricahua have come to think of the horse ceremony as useful in curing the illnesses of other domestic animals besides horses. Commenting on this trend, he wrote: "As various domestic animals have become more numerous, the horse shaman has seemed to be the logical person to cure them and is now thought of as the one who 'knows a lot about (domestic) animal sickness.'" He cited as example a Chiricahua's idea of a horse shaman's duties: "These are the ones who take care of the diseases of animals; they have a general knowledge of animals."[47]

Animal Husbandry Methods

Every Navajo or Apache horse owner has a wealth of folk medicines and remedies at his or her command with which to treat sick horses or to take care of healthy ones. Many of these can be applied as the occasion demands—either in a ceremony by a medicine person, or with or without ritual by the owner. The majority of the folk medicine practices of the Navajo and Apache can best be described as strange combinations of ingenious, though sometimes sound, methods of animal husbandry and big doses of magic. Often the magical elements play as prominent a role as the sounder aspects of the treatment do.

To assure strength and good health in their colts, the Navajo still prescribe the remedies that the Holy Beings taught the two sky-visiting boys:

> They were to run strings through a white bead for a female, and a turquoise bead for a male colt. And they were shown how to tie it in the mouth of a colt and run the string around the lower jaw. The colt must nurse with it for four days. The umbilical cord must be tied and left until it dries and drops off. The sacred earth from the mountains must be used for the female, and for the male colt, the crystal. Four turquoise beads must be placed in the medicine bag for the male colt. The same is done for the female, but white beads replace the turquoise.[48]

To treat the horse for various illnesses, injuries, and imperfections, the Navajo and Apache of the past generation depended upon medicines made from plants, as well as upon the magic provided by sacred stones or ritualistic formulas. One of the most important of such plants is antelope-sage (*Eriogonum Jamesii*), which belongs to the Buckwheat Family (*Polygonaceae*). The Navajo and Apache ascribe many medicinal properties to it. Besides giving it directly as a medicine to sick animals, the Chiricahua Apache also chew it themselves for luck with horses.[49] Wyman and Harris note that the Navajo call this plant either "twisted medicine" or "rotten medicine" and that they too use it as a chewing gum. According to these authors, the plant has a reputation among the Navajo as a cure-all and usually only the roots go into the making of the medicine. "It is administered internally as a cold (occasionally warm) infusion or as a dry powder; it is applied to injured parts as a hot or cold poultice (occasionally as a lotion), and sometimes the roots are chewed."[50] The Franciscan Fathers observe that another translation of its name from the Navajo means literally "that which is mixed with the tobacco."[51]

Another medicine prescribed by the Navajo as a cure-all for "horse's sickness," as well as the "inside pain" of human beings is called "shudtak" or "sea-foam" (coral?). Dr. Joseph G. Lee, who investigated the use of this "solidified sea-foam" among the Navajo, wrote that it is secured from the Gulf of California and that it looks "like a piece of porous skull bone."[52]

Animals suffering from "lightning infection," brought on either directly or indirectly from the effects of lightning, can be treated with an emetic, which one of Wheelwright's Navajo informants said was made from a sweet-smelling, gray plant with yellow flowers. This Navajo told Wheelwright that when a human being or an animal is suffering from "Ik-hoh-doklizh" ("lightning infection"), "he is supposed to have absorbed a powder which goes into his body and becomes part of him and makes him swell up." The informant valued his knowledge for treating this disease very much; he had paid a big buckskin to another Navajo for teaching him how to prepare the medicine.[53] Wheelwright does not identify this plant, but Wyman and Harris state that the decoction administered to cure "lightning infection" in the Shooting Way ceremony is made from "thunder plants," members of the species known as *Petalostemum oligophyllum* (white prairie-clover) and *Sphaeralcea marginata* (globe-mallow).[54]

The night-blooming cereus (*Peniocereus Greggii*) yields a Navajo medicine for diarrhea and bladder trouble.[55] A Chiricahua Apache, while not a horse shaman himself, told Opler about some of the elements of ceremonialism he practiced in caring for a horse that couldn't "pass water." The formula he prescribed was to "take a rope, hit the horse on the back with it, and tie a knot in the rope. Do this four times. Say prayers meanwhile. Don't hit the horse hard enough to hurt it. Then trot the horse a few hundred yards and bring it back to the same position."[56]

The Navajo concoct a laxative from creosote leaves. The Chiricahua Apache treat sluggish horses by giving them doses of a ground-up root called "black medicine." They get a horse to take this unidentified substance by mixing it with "oats or mescal or something the horse likes."

However, if a horse happens to be just lazy in general, rather than only sluggish, they practice "bloodletting" on it and treat the cut with turquoise. The Navajo employ "bloodletting" to some extent too.[57]

The Chiricahua also open a blood vein on a horse that is going blind in one eye, an Apache reported, noting with confidence: "They cut the vein leading down from the eye that's getting bad. The horse gets well then. This is done to sheep now too. I have done it to both."[58]

Saddle sores were treated with a powder made by the Apache (probably Chiricahua or Western Apache groups) from the unidentified *matadura* (saddle gall) herb, the German Jesuit priest Ignaz Pfefferkorn observed in the eighteenth century. The herb powder was "simply sprinkled on the injured part" of the horse and "complete recovery follow[ed] in a few days."[59] Wyman and Harris list such plants as *Orobanche fasciculata* (broom-rape, cancer-root), *Corallorhiza multiflora* (coral-root), *Pterospora andromedea* (pine-drops), as well as the root *of Rumex hymenosepalus* (wild-rhubarb, canaigre) as being among those that are dried and ground by the Navajo and made into dusting powders to treat sores of all kinds. They also use sheep grease and red ochre to make ointments for sores.[60] Lee informs us that the creosote bush (*Larrea tridentata*) also provides the Navajo with an antiseptic; they apply it "in powder form" to sore eyes and open wounds, or "as a salve (with animal fat)" on sores.[61] Still another way to treat horses with sores on their bodies was told to Kluckhohn by a Navajo informant of his. The leaves, the fruit, or the root of the "lucky plant, male" (*Datura Meteloides;* sacred datura, or Indian-apple) could be made into a concoction to heal the sores. This Navajo held that while *Datura,* which is a poisonous plant, made "very good medicine," it is dangerous and should be used only by medicine people who know how to handle it.[62]

The Navajo remove saddle galls with a knife and cleanse the wounds with an occasional washing, the Franciscan Fathers write. According to them, lampers (lampas), an inflammatory disease of horses, characterized by sores on a swollen palate, is treated in much the same way. "The horse is thrown by winding a rope around its feet, fore and aft, and slipping them under it. The lampers are then cut out with a knife." They add that the Navajo employ a similar process to castrate horses.[63]

Since the Navajo and Apache had no equipment with which to make horseshoes when they acquired their first mounts, they customarily shod their horses with skin boots to prevent lameness, fashioning them from the hide of buffalo, cow, or deer, in the form of a pouch that they tied over the hoofs with a rawhide drawstring. Some of the Apache, such as those Pfefferkorn witnessed raiding Sonora in the middle of the eighteenth century, even used thick horsehide.[64] The Southern Athapascans had to depend largely upon these hide boots to protect their horses' hoofs until near the end of their pre-reservation days, when they learned to handle metal, and could then copy the horseshoes made by the white man. However, they were not the only people who made horse-moccasins; so did the Indians of Mexico and other tribes in the Southwest, as well as the Spanish *conquistadores* and American pioneers when on long overland expeditions and without nails and other equipment to shoe their horses in a more traditional way.[65]

Lame horses were handicaps, if not hazards, to Indians when they were traveling, and in spite of the hoof moccasins, the Navajo and Apache often had to contend with tender-footed mounts. The Kiowa-Apache still tell a story about the miseries some horses with ailing hoofs caused their ancestors on a journey to the Gulf of Mexico. They tell, too, of a number of folk remedies: "They would put grease on a horse's hoofs, rub gun-powder on it, and then take a live coal and blow fire on it. It would explode and after that it would heal quickly." They used a considerable amount of buffalo fat as medication for tender hoofs. Sometimes "they would scrape buckskin and mix these shavings with grease and put it in the cracks. . . ." At other times, when there was no other kind of grease available, they were forced to use that which had accumulated on the jackets they were wearing. "They would get a knife and scrape the grease out and put that grease in the horses' hoofs." When they could find streams, they would let their mounts "stand in water a long time" to take the swelling out of their feet. Even though these Kiowa-Apache were desperately afraid of being overtaken by enemies, they had to stop many times— often for a period of a few days, either to kill a buffalo and make new shoes for their lame-footed horses, or to allow the poor creatures' feet to recover sufficiently to proceed. So handicapped, the group was able to travel only about five miles a day.[66]

J. Frank Dobie observes that the Comanche "sometimes hardened tender feet by burning wild rosemary—*Artemisia*—and applying the smoke and heat to them."[67] According to Wyman and Harris, the Navajo use some of the *Artemisia* (sagebrush) plants in making preparations to treat wounds and burns of all kinds. Such sagebrushes as *Artemisia filifolia, A. frigida,* and *A. tridentata* are known to have been used medicinally by many Indian groups as well as by early white pioneers.[68]

From the first numerous acquisition of horses until the present day, racing has been one of the proudest and most popular sports among the Navajo and Apache. Many of their medicines and customs are especially designed to protect their horses and to assure them speed and good luck in a race.

Sacred datura (*Datura Meteloides*) is such a medicine, acting upon the horse as a narcotic. But since it is poisonous, and thus for safety requires the services of a medicine person, the Navajo most commonly have it administered ceremonially before a race. The root of the plant provides the medicine, which may be chewed, taken as an infusion, or thrown in the face.[69]

Dobie notes that the Comanche and other tribes, whose names he does not specify, used to make racers long-winded by having their horse doctors blow "the pulverized root or leaves of certain plants up a horse's nostrils."[70] It is quite possible that the Navajo and Apache were among the unidentified groups of Indians who practiced this custom.

The Mescalero and Chiricahua Apache sometimes rubbed their horses' feet with certain herbs before races, John Harrell, a cousin of mine who worked as a cattleman on the Mescalero Apache Reservation between 1919 and 1930, informed me. Though he could not remember the names of the herbs used, he said the Apache believed this medicine could magically cause their horses to run faster.[71] According to him, some of the Mescalero and Chiricahua also used to practice slitting their horses' nostrils to make them long-winded while running, a custom known to be popular among the Comanche and the Sioux, and possibly among some of the other Apache groups and the Navajo as well.[72]

Before entering their horses in a race, owners are likely to take elaborate precautions against witchcraft, a thing they greatly dread. For at events like horse races, where the betting can be heavy and where there is usually much at stake—either in money, possessions, or prestige—many Navajo and Apache expect to find those present who will actively engage in malevolent attempts to control the natural course of events. Witchcraft may be practiced by either men or women. In fact, most often when the Navajo and Apache speak of the machinations of "witches," they are referring to male sorcerers, making no distinctions such as we normally make between male and female practitioners.

A horse about to be raced, then, may be given a medicine especially compounded to protect it from a witch's harm. Coyote pollen is one of the medicines that serves such a purpose. The pollen, actually powdered dust from where a coyote has stood, is applied at the base of the horse's tail. According to a Navajo, when this medicine is put on a horse, it will work wonders, for "then if some witch-man will say something in his mind . . . he won't be able to do any harm, because in a long time nobody has hurt coyote."[73] Several plants yield medicines that protect both horses and humans against witchcraft. Leaves and roots are often chopped into tiny pieces and made into drinking concoctions by soaking in water. *Wulfenia plantaginea* is the most common of such plants, but spruce, ponderosa pine, and juniper also furnish the required ingredients. All of these medicines, besides thwarting witchcraft, protect horses and people from being struck by lightning or bitten by snakes, or from being badly injured in any way.[74] Another highly beneficial plant, for horses, is *Peteria scoparia,* sometimes called camote-de-monte. A solution of it sprinkled on a horse's body will prevent most known evils, and smoke from burning it will cure horses and other livestock of coughs.[75]

Though an adequate study of the witchcraft practices of the Apache groups yet remains undone, a good deal of information can be found about those of the Navajo. Since there are a number of methods and medicines that are generally known by the Navajo and believed by them to be common procedures for witching horses, it is very probable that many of the Apache groups are also aware of the same practices and consider them to be equally effective in producing the same results.

The Navajo believe that one of the most efficient ways to witch a horse into losing a race is to acquire something that has touched its body and then have a witch perform a bad sing over it. Dirt from a horse's track, foam or saliva from its mouth, hair, sweat or dust from its body, manure, urine, or something it has worn—any of these will serve for the witch to take away and bury in some lonely or "bad" spot, often where an evil thing has occurred, or where someone has died or been buried or maybe only in some mysterious cave or wall of a cliff or arroyo. Having interred symbolically a part of the horse, the practitioner sings for evil to come, endeavoring to "take away" from the real horse "by magic the 'living part' which is its strength and make it foolish and weak." This procedure, the Coolidges say, is called "steal[ing] its shadow," and the unfortunate animal thus deprived "will give out before the end of the race, while the horse that retains its shadow will win."[76]

Medicine rubbed on the legs or administered orally may also be the means of witchcraft—medicine brewed from poisonous plants like Jimsonweed (*Datura Stramonium*), *Datura Meteloides,* or poison ivy (*Toxicodendron radicans*).[77] The wizard who possessed such medicine might "rub it on his hands. Then he would go over to the horse that was a sure winner and rub this medicine on the horse. This would make him lose. The man would go over and pretend to feel the horse's legs. He would say, 'This horse will win all right.' All the time he would be rubbing on the medicine that would make the horse lose." Often it is felt that these malicious practices achieve more than the loss of a race, that they may also bring about serious illness, madness, or death.[78]

The rituals and the medicines of today's witchcraft frequently have their origin in those that the Navajo once called upon for aid in hunting and war. In fact, the Coolidges note that since the Navajo have ceased to go on the warpath, "war medicine is no longer used, except in gambling and horse racing."[79] A sorcerer who knows the witchcraft of the chase can turn it against a race horse, one Navajo observed, doing it in the following fashion: "If they start to race, a witch man will sit way away and say some sing and pray and [cause] bad spell and say what's going to happen. The same as for hunting deer. The same you use on a horse. Just the ones who know do that, and don't tell anybody." He recalled a man who "used to do that" many years ago, a highly successful sorcerer—in fact, so successful that "all stopped racing on account of that man. That man sure knew how. . . ."[80]

A horse that had been subjected to witchcraft often displayed sudden and pronounced symptoms. Here is a Navajo incident from about 1910 involving the casting of a spell and subsequent developments: "The witch . . . says something to the man's horse, and the man's horse sweat and lay down and roll [sic] . . . The horse was ready to die." But a man who "knew the plants for the horse" treated the animal, and it "got well." On the other hand, this witch, like others who fail in attempts to carry out evil designs on victims, had his own sorcery turn upon him. He "lost his horse because he didn't do a good job."[81]

When a Navajo is convinced that his or her horse has been witched, he or she has a number of alternatives for curing it. The owner may, like the man above, try some plant-medicines designed to restore any victim—human or animal—who is suffering from the ravages of witchcraft. Among the plants that supply remedies for witchcraft are those the Navajo call "Gila Monster plant, bear plant and mountain lion plant," all names that imply great power. Bear plant has been identified as *Pedicularis grayi,* a plant of much humbler status in the botany of common English—lousewort.[82]

Other cures include recovery of the things from the horse that the witch buried, and having smoke rites of either the Game Way or Blessing Way ceremonies performed.[83] The Blessing Way smoke rite for horses or other stock requires that a medicine person burn a special preparation in the corral where the sick animal is penned so that it can inhale the fumes, a preparation concocted from "juniper, pinyon pine, and Ponderosa pine needles, pinyon pitch, shavings from the horns of deer, elk, mountain

A typical Navajo corral of the kind in which singers administer Blessing Way rites with songs for the good of horses and other domestic animals. See also *infra,* pp. 292, 297.

sheep, and antelope, with ten other [unidentified] plants."[84] The smoke rite would usually be held as a part of or in conjunction with the all-night Blessing Way song-prayer ceremony that we have examined earlier.

Still, one may try cure after cure in vain, for witchcraft sickness may entirely defeat its victim in the end. There are Navajo who feel that a witched horse is a hopeless case. Like the Chiricahua Apache whom Opler interviewed, they are convinced that "if a horse has been witched, you can't cure it."[85]

Throughout the territorial ranges of the Navajo and Apache, jack-rabbit grass, mountain rice, grama grass, and to a lesser extent rush grass and saltweed became symbols of horses, not only to the Navajo Twins and the man from Sis ná dzil, but to all other Navajo and Apache horse proprietors as well. This came about chiefly because these grasses were among the most beneficial native forage plants available. Perhaps the most important are those belonging to the grama grass (*Bouteloua*) family. Numerous species thrive in large areas of the Southwest, and like the Lipan Apache who was taught through Cowbird's ceremony, the majority of the Navajo and Apache learned the value of this grass in fattening horses and keeping them in good condition.[86] Still abundant on the reservations today, grama grass was found in even greater quantities over the far-ranging territory of the Navajo and Apache during the past century. Its merits were especially praised by such nineteenth-century travelers in Indian country as John C. Cremony and Josiah Gregg. Cremony, commenting upon the presence of grama grass in Apache territory from Dragoon Pass in Arizona eastward through New Mexico's Mescalero and Chiricahua territory, attributed to it much of the Apache's success: "By its singularly strength-giving properties, [it] is capable of enabling their [Apache] ponies to perform extraordinary feats of endurance. . . . It is this plentiful distribution of the most strengthening grass in the world that enables the Apache to maintain his herds, make his extraordinary marches, and inflict wide-spread depredations."[87]

Next to grama grass, *Eurotia lanata,* called jackrabbit grass by the Navajo and commonly known in our society as "winter-fat" because of its use as a winter feed for livestock, was probably the most valuable forage plant, growing copiously on the dry plains and mesas of Texas, New Mexico, Arizona, and Mexico. Sometimes mistakenly called white sage, this plant not only fattens animals, but Southwestern Indians have also put it to important medicinal uses.[88]

Oryzopsis (rice grass), often identified as Indian rice grass or Indian-millet, flourishes in arid sandy plains in the present and past territories of the Navajo and Apache. Past generations cut the stalks to make hay for their horses, while they themselves consumed the seeds.[89]

Sporobolus cryptandrus (rush grass; sand drop-seed), as well as other species of the Drop-seed plant family, such as sacaton, alkali-sacaton, and black drop-seed, is of widespread growth but not so succulent as grama grass and the others mentioned. Nevertheless, the drop-seed furnishes sustenance for horses that can be depended on throughout much of the year. Another plant common to much of the alkaline soils of the mesas and plains of the Southwestern desert regions, *Atriplex confertifolia* (shad-scale, saltweed), is of limited importance for grazing, since it does not exist in large quantities. Wherever it is found, though, often crowding out other plants, it has proved valuable because it successfully resists overgrazing.[90]

Another much-esteemed horse food among some of the Apache groups is the tuber of the flat-sedge (*Cyperus fendlerianus*). The Chiricahua and Mescalero even call it "feed to horses" and seek it out in the pine forests where it grows. Castetter and Opler note that the plant acquired this Apache name because "the flowers and seeds were salted and fed to horses, and were said to be very fattening."[91]

Clovers of various types (*Melilotus; Trifolium*) and alfalfa (*Medicago sativa*) are of importance as subsistence wherever they grow, but much of the Southwest is too arid to produce them in dependable quantities. In regions where they are available, wild oats (*Avena*) have been used as fodder, though the long awns of the grain can injure a horse's mouth. Even so, the Navajo have sometimes made it a staple feed, as their name for it—"horse corn"—implies.[92]

Turning to injurious plants, we find them almost as numerous as the beneficial. Most deadly to horses are certain species belonging to the *Astragalus,* or Milk-Vetch, family (*Astragalus allochrous, A. lentiginosus, A. nothoxys, A. thurberi, A. wootoni,* and most probably *A. arizonicus* and *A. bigelovii*). These are the well-known locoweeds, or crazyweeds, that cause the dangerous, often fatal, loco disease in horses and other livestock. *Oxytropis lambertii (Aragallus knowltoni),* a plant belonging to a genus closely related to the *Astragalus* family, has the same effect, and often in fact is considered to be worse. The loco disease is a serious chronic nervous disorder. Fortunately, healthy horses will usually avoid locoweeds when better pasturage is at hand. But often these plants, characterized by dense clusters of small flowers reminiscent of sweet peas, will invade the prairies and thrive to such an extent that horses can hardly avoid eating them in places where good grass is scarce. If horses ever begin on locoweeds, they may acquire the habit of eating them, and then little can be done to save them.[93]

Locoweeds have proved to be such a serious threat to their horses that the Navajo have traditions explaining their existence. While relating the Twins' visit to Sun, Frank Goldtooth told of how the deity showed the boys a specimen of locoweed and explained to them how he intended to use it. "Later horses will die from this weed," he said. "The animals will die so that the number of animals will be lessened. When there are too many horses coming upon the earth, I will send locoweeds and the horses will die from this. That is how I will get my horses back." Goldtooth added, "Whenever a horse dies and the flesh is gone, the bones also go somewhere. Somehow they go back to Sun's house." Sun keeps his loco horses under a big trap door in his house, and he showed one of them to the Twins. It had "a curly mane, tail and hair on its body," but it "was crazy, lazy and not worth much." It was also completely absorbed in "eating locoweed."[94]

Burroweed *(Aplopappus tenuisectus)* and Jimsonweed *(Datura stramonium)* often infest desert grasslands, doing serious harm to all livestock. Burroweed encroaches upon depleted ranges and poisons animals in drought when better forage cannot be found. Jimsonweed, common all over the Southwest, is extremely dangerous because all parts of it are intensely poisonous, and horses that get too much of it often die.[95]

There are, of course, other plants that the Navajo and Apache have either utilized or avoided as food for their horses, but the ones discussed above are the most important over Southern Athapascan territory as a whole.

The Navajo and Apache desire many horses just as they welcome many children. For this reason, individual families have forms of ritual, in addition to those provided through the ceremonies and ceremonial songs of medicine people, which they themselves maintain to multiply and protect their horse herds.

Because the Navajo have a firm conviction that singing over animals will bestow upon them well-being and numerous offspring, there is ordinarily someone in every family who possesses a number of songs directed to these purposes. Like ceremonial knowledge and equipment, good luck songs are transmitted from father or maternal uncle to son or sister's son and are considered to be the personal property of the man who sings them.[96] Navajo women, too, may own songs, for while women seldom practice long ceremonial rites (though they may do so if they choose), they are frequently taught songs by their mothers, maternal aunts, and grandmothers. In fact, it is a common practice for unmarried girls in a family to know and sing songs that make horses multiply or dispel harmful effects that come to them through the bad dreams of their owners.[97]

Even though there is little, if any, real information readily available about good luck songs among the Apache, it seems likely that there are at least some individuals in Apache societies who, while not horse shamans, also possess such songs for the benefit of their horses. A Chiricahua Apache seems to have implied the existence of songs of this sort when he told Opler that some Apache, who did not possess ceremonies themselves, knew songs they sang to horses to help them win races.[98] Probably they would also know songs for other kinds of good fortune as well.

Most of the Navajo good luck songs closely resemble those that medicine people sing in ceremonies, serving as briefer rituals considered efficacious in themselves. Some of them are said to have been given directly by White Bead Woman. This is true of the following song—one she instructed the Navajo to sing over their stone horse fetishes when they wanted real horses to breed and produce:

> Standing sideways, standing sideways, standing sideways, standing
>   sideways, white bead (this follows between each verse).
> I am the Dawn Boy, white bead horse turned to a boy, I stand up for
>   my horse.
> Turquoise horse turned to a girl, I stand up for my horse.
> Oyster shell horse turned to a boy, I stand up for my horse.
> Jet horse turned to a girl, I stand up for my horse.
> All kinds of horses go along with these others.
> All kinds of sheep go along with these others.
> Flexible goods go along with me.
> Chips of all kinds go along with me.[99]

Still other songs for producing colts are fashioned after the ones the god Békotsidi sang when he took pity on the Gambler who had lost his possessions and created for him horses and domestic animals. One example goes this way:

> Now Békotsidi, that am I. For them I make.
> Now child of Day Bearer am I. For them I make.
> Now Day Bearer's beam of blue. For them I make.
> Shines on my feet and your feet too. For them I make.
> Horses of all kinds now increase. For them I make.
> At my finger's tips and yours. For them I make.
> Beasts of all kinds now increase. For them I make.
> The bluebirds now increase. For them I make.
> Soft goods of all kinds now increase. For them I make.
> Now with pollen they increase. For them I make.
> Increasing now, they will last forever. For them I make.
> In old age wandering on the trail of beauty. For them I make.
> To form them fair, for them I labor. For them I make.[100]

Hatáli Natlói, who recorded this song for Washington Matthews, told him that it and three others made up a complete set of the Békotsidi type of good luck songs. He did not sing the other songs, but gave some information about their refrains. The second song's refrain, he said, was "Kat hadzídila', now they are made." That of the third stated that the animals had begun to breed, while that of the fourth was "Keanádildzĭsi, which means, they are multiplying."[101]

Good fortune is also accessible through a song to Sun's mighty turquoise horse. The singing of this song not only invokes his guardianship, but through communion with that sacred horse, it assures to earthly horses his majesty and power. Natalie Curtis, the collector and translator of the following song, observes that the Navajo call it "Hlin Biyin," a term literally meaning "Song of the Horse." These are the words:

> How joyous his neigh!
> Lo, the Turquoise Horse of Johano-ai [Sun],
> How joyous his neigh,
> There on precious hides outspread standeth he;
> How joyous his neigh,
> There on tips of fair fresh flowers feedeth he;
> How joyous his neigh,
> There of mingled waters holy drinketh he;
> How joyous his neigh,
> There he spurneth dust of glittering grains;
> How joyous his neigh,
> There in midst of sacred pollen hidden, all hidden he;
> How joyous his neigh,
> There his offspring many grow and thrive for evermore;
> How joyous his neigh![102]

Much of the beauty and richness of Navajo song is due to the singer's belief in the compulsive power of words. Not only does the singer feel that song preserves order and makes coherent the symbols of myths and ceremonies, as we saw earlier when we examined the ceremonial song of "the man from Sis ná dzil," he or she is also convinced that song will shield the singer or whatever is being sung over from evils lurking in every corner of the outside world.[103] Perhaps this feeling of the Navajo toward song has been best expressed by Gladys Reichard: "Time and again song and a blanket or curtain are identified. A song moving out into the space immediately surrounding an individual . . . establishes a zone of protection that gives comfort, for within it is the person who dissipates the evils by the compulsion of sounds and words. . . ."[104] What is true of song in general is true of the good luck songs discussed above.

Navajo prayer, as the preceding paragraphs illustrate, is closely allied to song. Separate prayers for increasing and protecting horses do exist, however, in both Navajo and Apache lore. A common kind requests that a deity grant particular kinds of horses. For example, after the Navajo sing a good luck song of the Békotsidi group, they pause to say such a prayer so that their horses will propagate the type of colts they desire. According to Hatáli Natlói, they "specify the color and kind" of horses they want, and if their prayers are heard, then soon afterwards exactly the colts they requested are sent them "from the house of Day Bearer [Sun]."[105] When the Jicarilla Apache desire a certain color horse, they offer prayers for models of the cardinal horses, stating their order of preference in such a way as to mention fourth and last the color they desire most. This was the class of prayer Dirty Boy's grandmother uttered in his behalf every night while he was away on a raid. Because her grandson had his heart set on capturing a spotted steed, the old woman would pray "first for black ones, then for blue, then . . . yellow, and then spotted."[106]

Often the Navajo accompany their supplications with gift offerings to the gods. When praying for increase, they offer soil from the sacred mountains, besides a piece of agate. This "sacred earth" pollen and the chips from the rock known as the "banded male stone" are believed to charge prayers with much power.[107]

The Navajo have special prayers to support pack horses burdened by heavy loads. In former times, when they made ritual journeys to salt deposits, they prayed for the horses that carried the salt. It is possible that such groups as the Jicarilla and the Cibecue and White Mountain people among the Western Apache, who made similar kinds of salt pilgrimages, also possess such prayers, but if they do, information about them is not as readily accessible as it is about those of the Navajo. While the custom of making salt journeys is not as widely practiced today as it once was, it still exists in some areas, for although these Indians use commercial salt, many still feel that only ritually gathered salt is effective for ceremonial purposes.[108]

In earlier days, about four or five people made up a Navajo salt party, and they took along three or four pack horses to carry the salt home. Like the raiding expedition, the trip to the salt site called for highly formalized behavior, the observance of a strict set of special taboos, and regulations governing every phase of the journey. If any of the prescribed ritual was violated, then bad luck would befall the members of the party, or their pack horses, or they would not be able to find any salt.[109]

Every time the salt collectors ate, they had to say special prayers to Changing Woman, Father Sun, and the Mixed Winds, enlisting the help of these gods for a safe, successful journey and for strong horses that would not become lame under their loads.[110] But most of the special prayers they offered in behalf of their pack horses were directed to a deity named Salt Woman—one who is said to be living still at the various salt sites, for tradition has it that a long time ago she told her friend Changing Woman that she intended to settle down and "stay where she now is . . . so the people could get salt. Sheep, cows, and horses too."[111] On every evening of their journey, the Navajo beseeched the Salt Woman to bless their pack horses by offering pollen to her from their medicine bags, and then praying to her in this way:

> I have come a long way to visit you, my Grandmother,
> May my horses' backs be tough
> May my horses' hoofs be tough
> May my horses be fleet footed
> May my burden be light.[112]

As soon as the party reached a wash or a lake bed where the salt was deposited, the first thing they did was to press saltwater to their mouths four times and then to the mouths of their horses. Following this, they would rub saltwater on their bodies and then apply some to the joints and hoofs of the pack horses. As they did this, they chanted the prayer,

> Grandmother Salt, I have come to get some salt for my own use.
> May my horse be strong and stand the load.[113]

When the salt had been gathered and heavy sacks of it had been loaded onto the pack horses, Salt Woman was again invoked with a kinship term. She would cooperate if each person prayed, "Grandmother Salt, act light for the horses and do not fall off."[114] Once the journey back home was underway, it was forbidden to "look back or jiggle the load or try to adjust the pack," for it was said that to do any of these things would cause the load to become "heavier and heavier."[115] Out of sight of the water, near some big rock, each man stopped, put salt on the rock, and prayed for himself and his horse in this fashion:

> May it be pleasant with me
> My Grandmother, the Salt Woman
> May you be light in weight
> As I carry you back to my country.[116]

As they made for home they had to give salt to any travelers they met along the way. Like returning raiders, they believed that giving away part of the spoils would fend off bad luck from their horses and themselves.[117]

Navajo hunters, in their rituals for deer and elk, also have special prayers to protect their pack horses. This is one a hunter prays following each meal while out hunting, and as he says it, he rubs his legs:

May my horse be strong
May my horse be fleet-footed
May my horse's hoofs be tough
May my own shoes be tough
May I be fleet-footed.[118]

At the time of each animal's creation, Changing Woman gave it a "sacred name." In divulging these names to the Navajo, she warned that they must be strictly controlled. Properly managed, they could produce the correspondent animals, but it was possible to overwork them, creating, for instance, too many horses. Many Navajo families know the sacred name of the horse, though sometimes these differ completely from family to family.[119] The Navajo's explanation for the differences goes back to a mythical time when Changing Woman met with the Mirage and Rain People and asked them for suggestions on lucky names to give the domesticated animals. These deities put their minds to work and came up with a suggestion apiece. From these names Changing Woman chose a "real name," and now no one can remember that name exactly as she gave it. Hence the variations. On the other hand, it is said that the names are sometimes identical for families living a great distance apart.[120] Because these names exert power when they are uttered, the Navajo fortunate enough to possess them zealously guard their knowledge, speaking them in the greatest secrecy and revealing them only to those who have proved themselves capable of respecting their value. As is the case with the good luck songs, these magic names are thought of as important personal property, and though intangible, may be willed by their owners to a relative or worthy successor. Many Navajo women inherit these names from older women in their families.[121]

Since great secrecy surrounds these names, examples of them would be difficult, if not impossible, to provide here. However, that the Navajo set great store by them is clear from their importance in mythology. It is said, for instance, that Frog Man revealed a secret name for horses to the Twins when he gave them the mirage-rock horse fetishes, and that the Twins employed the name to their advantage when they started breeding horses with fetishes. Frank Goldtooth related a mythical episode of this sort, in which horses also know the secret names of their owners. Goldtooth reported that when male and female "Horse People" suddenly came into being from Frog Man's fetishes, they addressed the Elder Twin, asking him this intimate question, "Is that you, _____ (his secret name)?" and the Twins would answer by repeating the same kind of question: "Is that you people, _____ (their secret name)?" The Horse People and the

Elder Brother would keep up this repartee until they had asked one another the same questions "four times back and forth," and "after the fourth time," the culture hero would "sing a song" to the Horse People, at which point they would be transformed into real horses.[122]

The Navajo voice the "sacred names" of horses to help them recover from serious illnesses or injuries. An owner who has always loved and tried to take proper care of an animal can save it at a time of crisis by calling its "secret name."[123] On the other hand, the "secret name" of the owner, in the mouth of a witch, may bring evil to horses and other livestock. When a man's secret name is known and invoked against him, "right behind him [his] stock will be destroyed."[124]

Extended research has not brought to light any definite proof that the Apache now use or have ever used "sacred names" in animal husbandry. However, a White Mountain Apache myth upon the Twins' visit to the Sun does hint that these Apache either do possess or have at one time possessed such names. An incident in which the boys surprise their father by asking "by name" for a set of horse trappings before they acquire horses is treated as if the boys were revealing that they had valuable "secret name" knowledge about horses merely by knowing the exact name of the equipment used on them. It is said that when the boys asked Sun for horse trappings, the deity replied that "he did not know what they meant by horse trappings. The younger boy said, 'Well, if you do not know what horse trappings are, do not again put them on these horses in the corral.' The Sun asked who it was who made them as smart as he was himself. They replied that he, the Sun, had made them smart and had made them speak wisely. They then asked by name for bridle, halter, saddle blanket, and saddle."[125] This so impressed their father that he presented them with the fine trappings and horses they desired.

Although there is no evidence to indicate that any of the "sacred names" for horses now in use among the Navajo are names left over from the days when raiders, trying to assure success in obtaining horses on forays, referred to them by circumlocution, one can not help wondering whether the two types of "sacred names" are one and the same. It could be—now that raiding is a thing of the past and the language raiders used is falling farther and farther away into the realm of songs and tales—that raiders' names for horses have come to be the "sacred names" the Navajo say the gods gave them in mythical times. While this is only a conjecture, it would not be unusual if this is what has happened, for shifting and accommodation of old meanings to new situations have occurred before in Navajo beliefs, in far stranger fashion, as oral transmission has done its work.

The Navajo used to surround their hogans with four tie-posts for their horses, facing a post to each of the cardinal directions. When they returned home after a ride, they tied their saddle-horses to the post facing the direction from whence they had come. In explanation of this custom, Frank Goldtooth said that the posts were located "about fifty feet away from the hogan" and that before they "were first placed in their holes, turquoise was placed in the hole to the south, white bead in the one in the east and so on"; then white bead rattles were attached to each post. A Navajo with such an arrangement of posts was "assured" of "having more and better horses" than a man who was "without these things." The posts worked various magic on horses; not only did they promote health and increase, they also instilled discipline. Even a horse that had "broken his hobble" would "return by itself because of the post."[126] The tradition behind all this is one with which we are already acquainted, if we remember that the sun deity had his horse fetishes tied to exactly the same kind of directional posts, also enhanced by white bead rattles, and standing surrounded by the same sacred stones in a basket in the center of his house. It is also well to recall that the deity sends strength and energy to all the horses in the world by shaking the white bead rattles and that his daughter shakes them to summon the white bead horse for him to ride each morning.[127]

White Mountain Apache mythology suggests that these Apache have at one time or another arranged posts around their dwellings for similar purposes. Much fertility symbolism surrounds some posts belonging to Sun and others belonging to the Twins in one White Mountain myth, and throughout this myth, the posts play an important role in the ceremonies the Twins learn for the creation of both horses and horse trappings, an idea of increase resembling that of the Navajo. In this myth, we find Sun instructing the Twins to ride the horses he is sending to earth with them four times around a certain post that stands facing east near his house. Sun's post is said to have "white hair which reaches to the ground and turns up again," and it is implied that rain falls continuously on this post. Goddard, who collected this myth, thought that the "white hair" referred to moss with rain falling on it. Perhaps this is the meaning; however, it could also be that the Apache Sun's post with white hair and the rain falling upon it is related in an obscure way to the tall stately cornstalk that sprang from the center of the basket containing the Navajo Sun's horse fetishes—the cornstalk that was surrounded by the directional posts and by the cardinal horse fetishes, which were nourished by the pollen that fell from the tassels of its male and female ears of corn.[128]

In the same White Mountain myth, other references are made to two posts the Twins requested their mother, the goddess White Shell Woman, to put up for them when they returned to earth.[129] They asked her to put a "smooth pole" across the tops of the posts and to hang on it the horse trappings Sun had given them for their ceremony to create horses on earth. "She was asked to put the saddles on this pole with their horns toward the east. The bridles were to be hung on the saddle horns and the saddle blankets spread over the saddles. They asked her to think about the saddles, where they were lying during the night." The goddess did as her sons requested, and through the compulsion of the prayers she offered about the saddles for four nights, four mornings later the two saddles had multiplied into eight saddles.[130] Later ten saddles appeared on the pole. A disagreement arose between the Elder Brother and his mother over the size of the pole she had erected. The Elder Brother claimed he had asked her to "put up a long pole" and that she had "put up a short one" instead. Her reply referred only to the spots where he had instructed her to dig the holes for the uprights, for she answered: "You said dig one hole here and another there, my son." Possibly the culture hero meant that if his mother had put up a longer pole, they would have received more saddles, for he looked at the ten saddles hanging on the pole and said: "Just these may well be our saddles," seeming to imply that no more saddles would be coming their way through the ceremony they were learning from Sun. The Twins later used the horse trappings that had multiplied on this pole as offerings in the ceremony they performed to make horses multiply on earth.[131]

Going beyond these forms of ritual some Navajo resort to "lucky medicines" to gain more horses. These potions are the weapons of gambling and dishonest horse trading, the same ones that witchcraft relies on. For example, an individual who has skill with "the lucky plant, male" (*Datura meteloides*), may chew a small piece of the dried root of this plant before he goes out to buy horses, in the belief that the medicine will help him "get them cheaper." Or he may put a little of the pollen on the rope of a horse he wants, or in some spot where the horse's owner is likely to touch it. Touching the medicine "makes his mind wrong," and prepares him almost to give the animal away.[132]

Four other witchcraft medicines that also serve in the trickery of bartering are: "laughing medicine" (from either *Eriogonum microthecum* or *Erisium neo-mexicanus*); "turns-toward-the-Sun medicine" (from either white prairie-clover, *Petalostemum oligophyllum,* or an unidentified variety of sunflower); "cone-towards-water medicine" (*Pericome caudata*); and "mind medicine" (from an unidentified plant that bears a close resemblance to *Datura meteloides*). These major witchcraft substances are often assisted by the following four plant medicines, which are said to "work under" them: "irritating medicine" (*Phacelia crenulata*); "gray irritating medicine" (unidentified); "my thumb medicine" (from either deer-vetch, *Lotus wrightii*, or *Hackelia floribunda*); and "smashed-down-sumac medicine" (from golden-eye or resin-weed, *Viguiera multiflora,* or poison-ivy, poison-oak, *Rhus toxicodendron*).[133]

According to one Navajo, if a person really knows how to use these witchcraft plants "in the right way, it is the very easiest way to get rich. You don't have to work hard for it." You can use it on a rich person and "get a lot of his money or sheep or horses or cattle."[134] For this reason, a person who becomes wealthy and possesses what seems to be an incredible number of horses, sheep, and cattle may arouse suspicion among neighbors, for they may secretly feel that this is a witch who has amassed a fortune by means of sorcery.[135]

Many taboos and other customs stemming from various beliefs are practiced by the Navajo and Apache in caring for their horses. Some have their foundations in religion, the result of indoctrination by holy beings. Others have evolved from customs formerly relied on for protection in other endeavors besides those having to do with horses. Still others—not widely practiced, but often well-known in certain localities—have their origins in the decisions some one person made in coping with an unpleasant problem. Though, on first sight, many such taboos and beliefs seem bewildering, if not absurd, to those outside Navajo and Apache societies, they usually are more reasonable when viewed with regard to their origins and the values of the people who practice them. And regardless of how impractical they may now appear to non-believers, in order to have survived, all have had practical values at one time or another to the people who have observed them.

The fear of witchcraft upon animals remains strong today. A taboo still kept by the Navajo is that the subject is never mentioned when horses or sheep are nearby, for mere reference to such potent powers may arouse their evil. In like manner, a Navajo who wants to learn something about witchcraft, for instance some practice to use in trading or gambling, would be most cautious about the place in which he or she learned it, selecting one away from home. For he or she would not wish to bring harm to his or her own people and animals while learning how to handle the dangerous power to his or her own advantage.[136] Many Navajo fear animals deformed at birth, because they consider them products of witchcraft.

In their attention to watering their mounts and caring for them, these White Mountain Apache horsemen are reminiscent of the way in which Geronimo's nephew Ace Daklugie once characterized Apaches: "We are just naturally a livestock people."

And to prevent bad luck to themselves or to their normal animals, they kill the deformed ones as soon as possible.[137] In previous times mares must frequently have given birth to deformed animals, because it was observed that some of the Southern Athapascans were slow in learning the importance of caring for the gravid mare. Writing of the "Padouca" (Plains) Apache in 1724, a French chronicler on the de Bourgmont expedition noted that these Apache—probably the Kiowa-Apache—never raised any colts, because their mares miscarried while the owners kept them chasing buffalo.[138]

Colts did not have to be born deformed, however, to cause the Navajo of past generations to suspect that witchcraft had influenced their birth.

They had only to make the mistake of coming into the world as twins. They brought their mother bad luck too, for as the Franciscan Fathers record, the Navajo in the early part of this century did not rejoice, as one might expect, in having two new animals rather than only one. Instead, they killed both the colts and the mare.[139] Underlying this heavy penalty was the belief that witches often catch horses at night and ride them around to perform evil deeds. As Franc Newcomb has noted: "The birth of twin colts is a sign that the mare has been ridden by a witch and all three are unlucky property for a Navajo to keep."[140] A Navajo once rationalized upon the tradition in this way: "Some say twin colts are bad luck and kill both as well as the mare. Others do not care. However if they are killed the owners will become rich anyway for it is better luck."[141] Newcomb says that this taboo is observed less and less among the younger generation of the Navajo, and Kluckhohn was not able to find any evidence of it among informants he worked with between 1930 and 1940.[142]

The witchcraft related to game animals came at length to relate to horses. The Navajo who adhere to certain rituals in hunting game are thought to be particularly vulnerable to witchcraft practices designed to make them lose not only their hunting powers, but all their horses and livestock as well. According to one Navajo, if some witch "gets you that way, the only thing to do is to keep giving Deer Raiser [the deity in charge of game] turquoise. Then, finally, if you kill a deer, the bad luck will go back to the man who did disease witchcraft to you. That's the only way to get rid of it. . . . Doesn't make any difference what kind of deer you kill—small and weak, old, just any kind."[143]

Because lightning is a very real danger in Navajo country where it kills people and horses every year, it is one of nature's most dreaded forces. It is understandable then that the Navajo have taboos to protect their horses from lightning or from anything that it has touched. If lightning strikes and kills a horse or any other domestic animal, a shaman must be summoned at once to perform a ceremony over surviving animals before their owners dare to go near them or to proceed with their ordinary care of them. The owner never ventures near the body of the dead animal. It is simply left where it fell for coyotes, buzzards, and crows, to whom it is said to belong. Horses that have been killed by cyclones or by drowning, or in any way by wind or water, are not touched either. The reason the Navajo avoid contact with horses killed in such ways is twofold. For one thing, they fear that they may attract lightning, wind, or water to themselves and their living animals. For another, their natural fear of being contaminated by ghosts makes them reluctant to handle dead bodies of any kind. There is a Navajo saying: "Never step across the body of a dead animal, bird, or snake," for to do so "would bring bad luck, . . . it would indicate that the person who did this was contemptuous of death. The punishment might be an accident in which that person was fatally injured."[144]

It is natural that a number of taboos confined to a single family group or to a few families in one locality would surround a force so feared as lightning. Newcomb found this to be true of some of her Navajo friends who had once had a horse killed by lightning. This family's grandmother believed she had angered the spirits and caused her pony's death merely by spinning yarn for a blanket she was making during the storm that killed her pony. From that time on, the old lady treated storms with the utmost respect; she would not allow any of her people "to card the wool, spin or weave" when the elements were all astir outdoors.[145]

Fear of storms and other bad weather makes it extremely dangerous for a Navajo to build a dwelling for himself or his animals facing any direction except east, the quadrant of good luck, for the sun rises there, and the Navajo reason that winds, hail, and storms seldom come from that quarter. To build facing east is also to follow the exact teachings of the gods on that score. The Navajo are cautious about the kind of lumber they use in building corrals and fences too. Care is taken that none of it comes from a hogan where a death has occurred, lest bad fortune befall the stock enclosed therein.[146]

Other taboos restrained certain people from riding horses. A Chiricahua Apache would never ride a horse again after he was bitten by a bat, which means that his people, like the Lipan Apache, believed that their culture hero gave Bat special powers to control horses. An acquaintance of the bitten man spoke as follows:

> If a bat bites you, you had better never ride a horse any more. All the Chiricahua say that. If you do ride a horse after being bitten, you are just as good as dead.
> B. never rode, because if a bat bites you, you shouldn't ride a horse. He never got into a buggy or an auto either. He would walk for miles.[147]

Riding taboos restrict Chiricahua girls who are menstruating. Because menstrual fluid is believed to have a paralyzing or deforming effect on any male, these girls are not allowed to ride stallions. They can ride mares, however, without bringing harm to them.[148]

Further, many Navajo believe that a woman should never help make a saddle or harness. Newcomb learned that "a woman who attempted leather work would be in danger of becoming crippled in her wrists or ankles, while a man suffers no ill consequences." She traces this belief back to the days of war, raiding, and ritual hunting when equipment was prepared only by men, since Navajo women were restricted from helping with the preparations for any of these activities.[149]

The superhuman inhabitants of lakes and streams, the serpent-like or anthropomorphic Water Monsters of Southern Athapascan lore, have a penchant for doing harm to domestic animals and human beings. When man or beast drowns, they are often held responsible for having grabbed or sucked their victims into the water and then swallowed them. It was said that one of the creatures lived in some springs near Whitetail, New Mexico, on the Mescalero Apache Reservation and horses that went near these springs would disappear into the water and "never come out."[150]

Since the Navajo believed that a Water Monster inhabits the same lakes the beneficent Salt Woman lives in, they observed a special taboo on their salt pilgrimages that probably was designed to protect their pack horses and themselves from its evil; this was a taboo about not looking closely into the water while gathering the salt, a custom they practiced to avoid bringing misfortune to the party and the horses.[151] Perhaps they feared attracting the monster's attention if they peered into the water.

Well-groomed horses were not common among the pre-reservation Navajo and Apache horses, nor are they found to any great extent today. Nevertheless, numerous owners did take particular pains in grooming their favorite mounts. The Chiricahua and Mescalero Apache of pre-reservation days, for instance, made combs of mountain mahogany and brushes of folded and pounded mescal or sotol leaves for the special purpose of grooming their saddle-horses.[152] And the Navajo and Apaches of the old days were just as interested in impressing friends and neighbors with fine-looking horses and trappings as they are today. An example of the meticulous care some Apache took in grooming and outfitting their mounts before they visited the Zuñi Indians on an annual trading trip comes from the narrative of a Mexican named José Mendivil, who told of his experiences as an Apache captive for seven years during the mid-1800s. Though Mendivil did not identify the Apache he lived among, they possibly belonged to one of the Western Apache groups—perhaps to the White Mountain or the Cibecue Apache, for both of these groups were traditional friends of the Zuñi, carrying on extensive trade with them.[153] Here is Mendivil's description of the preparations the Apache made for their long-awaited excursion:

Their horses are fattened in advance until their coats are glossy and sleek, and they are trained daily, like racers for the racetrack, with the utmost care. Each Indian strives to make the greatest impression on his Zuñi friends, by the quality of his horse, his fleetness and strength, the splendor of his trappings, and the magnificence of his rider, as well as by the value and beauty of the presents he carries with him.

The trappings of a single horse sometimes have the value of hundreds of dollars. If they can obtain them, by theft or purchase, they have the richest Mexican saddles embossed with silver, and sometimes even set with gems, their bridles of the finest wrought leather, resplendent with silver ornaments, and all the adornments which the Mexican, in his luxurious taste, lavishes upon a favorite horse.

A half-dozen horses are sometimes killed in the training, before one is found of sufficient bottom and fleetness to satisfy the fastidious savage. The horse is shod with rawhide, and many extra pairs of shoes are carried along, lest the hoofs of the favorite should become tender before the home-journey. The Indian himself dresses in the best style that his circumstances will permit.[154]

The ride to Zuñiland was a "five or six days' journey." As they came near they paused to prepare for an impressive entry into the pueblos. They "fed and rubbed" their horses, and they painted their faces and bodies anew with a dazzling array of colors and designs. They saw to the packs on their horses, arranging them and the presents for their friends "in the most attractive manner." And after they had finished doing these things, it was then time for "the full-dress charge of this barbaric cavalcade" into the Zuñi towns. As "the crowds of Zuñis" watched the approach, they could see the Apache's "long, plaited hair streaming in the wind as they gallop[ed] in full career toward the entrance" of the village. They could see the Apache's "plumes and gay-colored *serapes,* jingling spurs, and the gaudy trappings of their glistening steeds," as they ran out to meet their old friends, "shouting their welcome after an absence of a year."[155]

Of course, the Apache, and the Navajo as well, did not always possess splendid trappings of the kind Mendivil described. Often they were homespun products, imitated—sometimes crudely, but very often with great skill too—from those of the Spaniards, Mexicans, Anglo-Americans, and other Indian peoples. The equipment they made was frequently combined too with that made by the people whom they raided or with whom they bartered. Great ingenuity was expended upon making the decoration as sumptuous as possible.[156]

The purpose of all this splendor was not entirely esthetic. Some items of regalia exercised magic powers. Previous illustrations in this study have shown that amulets, such as hawk feathers, or bear, mountain lion, owl, and eagle claws, or antelope horns could be hung around the neck of an Apache's or Navajo's horse to promote fleetness, and that hawk or eagle feathers tied to the foreleg promised the same results, as did eagle feathers tied to the horse at the spot "just where the tail bone leaves off." The feathers of the hummingbird, too, made horses swift, and eagle feathers, at least, when tied to the mane or bridle, would prevent a horse from being fractious.[157]

Frank Goldtooth affirmed that many of the Navajo of the present day still find eagle feathers advantageous in horse racing, though, unlike their Hopi neighbors who "show their feathers when they make use of them, . . . the Navajo hide them, for they know all about [the proper procedure to follow in employing] such things." "Nowadays an eagle feather is used as a whip. Some Navajo put the live eagle feathers inside their whips and then use them to whip the horse and win a race."[158] Others put these feathers "inside the tail of a horse," or "braid" them inside their bridles or into their horsehide ropes. The Navajo of today, Goldtooth observed, feel "the same way" about their feathers as the Twins felt about those Sun gave them to use whenever they "needed help." Modern Navajo who possess "such feathers will not let everyone use them"—particularly not their whips, which have "great power to make the horses go faster."[159] However, when Sun taught mortals the talismanic properties of eagle feathers, he imposed a restriction: the people were forbidden to put "live eagle feathers" on top of their horse tie-posts. Only the original posts at Sun's house were ever to display the powerful feathers, to remain there where they could transmit life and energy to all the animals, plants, and growing things on earth—a force that the deity understandably wanted to keep under control.[160]

Although neglecting to identify the tribes to which he is referring, J. Frank Dobie found other Southwestern Indian customs whose purpose was sometimes stylishness and sometimes magic power. That the Navajo and Apache followed these customs is probable:

> Tribesmen slit and trimmed in varying forms the ear-tips of favorite horses, for style and to aid identification by feeling in darkness. . . .
> Few tribesmen ever became sufficiently refined to cut off the tails of their horses. Tails and manes, beautiful in themselves, were often decorated . . . with ribbons. . . . The rider might display his scalps by hanging them in his horse's mane. . . . The painted imprint of human

hands on a horse's hips indicated scalps taken by the rider; painted
horse-tracks indicated significant horse-lifting. . . . Young men
especially devoted to themselves sometimes chewed the leaves of
aromatic plants and perfumed their mounts by blowing or spitting
the particles into mane and tail.[161]

The People's Regard for Their Horses

Although the Navajo and Apache counted their wealth in horses, and
myths and legends commonly assure us that their horses were glorious
animals with beautiful long manes flowing in the winds and tails lightly
touching the ground, it was seldom that the white men of the nineteenth
century, traveling through the Southwest between army posts or on hunting and trading expeditions, ever encountered this horse of myth and
legend among the many Indian ponies they saw.

Our best accounts of Navajo and Apache horses in those days come
from white observers who saw the offspring of the majestic Spanish horse
after several centuries on Southwestern soil had transformed it into the
rugged little mustang. John C. Cremony described Navajo horses he saw
at the Copper Mines encampment of the Chiricahua Apache near Santa
Rita in southwestern New Mexico in 1850. The Navajo who had come
to visit the Chiricahua were "all mounted on small, but strong, active and
wiry looking horses."[162] A more complete description of the type is furnished by Lt. Col. Richard I. Dodge, whose extensive travels over the
western plains made him a good judge of the Indian horse. He saw it as
"scarcely fourteen hands in height, . . . rather light than heavy in build,
with good legs, straight shoulders, short strong back, and full barrel. He
has no appearance of 'blood' except sharp, nervous ears, and bright intelligent eyes. . . ." While Dodge took a very unsympathetic attitude toward
Indians and anything related to them, even he was impressed by the
stamina of the Indian pony, of which he said: ". . . the amount of work he can
do, the distance he can pass over in a specified time (provided it be long
enough), put him (in Indian hands) fairly on a level with the Arabian."[163]

A good description of modern-day Western Apache mustangs was
provided in 1939 by L. E. Holloway, who was at that time Agricultural
Extension Agent of the Fort Apache Indian Agency in Arizona. In a letter
to Walker D. Wyman, scholar of the wild horse in the West, Holloway said
that the animal is

> sure-footed and often possesses a stamina and an ability to work on
> little feed that is quite remarkable, but they are small, averaging

about 650 to 700 pounds which is too light for a good cow horse although the Apaches do manage to do a lot of roping of heavy cattle on them. Many, while they may have been branded as colts or as yearlings, often have been handled only the one time. Some are condemned cow horses that, when they join a herd of wild horses, become almost as wild as though they had never been broken. Others are brood mares which are seldom broken to ride or to work although they are branded whenever possible.[164]

In spite of the numerous methods the Indians employed to protect and adorn their mounts, the regard they held for their animals was often a paradox to white journalists of the eighteenth, nineteenth, and early twentieth centuries. Many of these writers—Dodge furnishes a characteristic example—judged the Indians' treatment of their horses by white standards and continually criticized the Indians for what seemed to them disregard for their horses. Apparently not stopping to think of what the Indians fed themselves when they sat down to eat, men like Dodge were impatient with them for their inattention to proper pasturage. Their lean, wiry horses roamed the range starving through the winter and in the spring fattened up enough to endure. Looking at Indians riding horses with saddle sores on their backs, Dodge wrote that the Indians were not humane to their horses.[165] Few writers stopped to think that many Indians possessed only one horse, or to consider that putting the horse out to pasture while its back healed from saddle sores would mean that its owner would have to walk miles on foot carrying heavy loads on his or her own back. Nor did these writers mention that Indians cared for their horses' health in the very same way they cared for their own—with ceremonies given to them by certain powers or with a few magic-working folk remedies.

Now and then a Navajo or an Apache tale illustrates that some of the Indians agreed with their white critics about the humble appearance of some of their horses; that the Navajo and Apache felt they possessed a great number of "poor old horses" simply because Sun did nothing to prevent the Twins from choosing an inferior animal when he offered them a horse to take to earth. This is true of a White Mountain tale where instead of offering the Twins a beautiful horse to take home, Sun showed them one that "was just skin and bones" and allowed them to take it back with them. He let them select a rope that "also was poor." The deity cautioned the boys that "the horse could not travel far, but the boys said that [it] was the animal they wanted." Nevertheless the deity was ashamed of the horse he gave his sons, for as they were leaving, he told them not to let their mother, the earth goddess, see it, since "she would send them away with it, it looked so bad." When the Twins assured their father that his gift "would be all right," Sun's only reply was that their mother would certainly "be surprised" when she saw it.[166]

But whether a horse was a creature of beauty and grace, or merely a tired old nag, the Indian owner could never be honestly accused of not having an affection for it. The essential thing about the Indian's relationship with the horse that critics never seem to have realized was that Indians thought of their horses as they thought of themselves; that they had such an intimate relationship with their favorite horses that they often talked to them as if they were examining their own souls. For instance, when a Navajo warrior took a horse to war, he would whisper in its ear the message he really intended for himself. "Be lively; you and I are going into a dangerous business, my horse. Be brave when you go to war and nothing will happen; we will come back safely."[167]

If the Indians' attitudes toward their horses sometimes appeared unjust to the white man, it was only that the hardships of everyday life were like those that Indians and their horses endured together on the raid or on the warpath. As a warrior fended for himself with only the help of the powers and the instructions left by the God People, his horse had to do the same. A glossy coat and a well-filled form were fine when they could be managed, but what mattered most to Indians was that they have a great many ponies and ones that displayed endurance. If they had to push a race horse to the limit, exhausting it cruelly long before it reached the goal line, the main thing that gave owners pride was when their horses won races.

Without their fine horses or their poor ones, the Navajo and Apache were a lost and unhappy people. When the U.S. government—in an effort to halt Navajo raiding and warfare—forced the Navajo to give up their horses and their homeland, and confined them at Fort Sumner, the Navajo expressed their great need for horses in practically everything they did during their imprisonment. As an illustration, it is said that in their performance at the fort of a certain rite of the Enemy Way—a part of the ceremony that they had become accustomed to performing on horse-back—they missed their horses so much that they "decorated long sticks to represent horses of different colors," and "rode" these sticks. It is said that they did this not merely because they lacked the horses that were needed to carry out properly this rite of the ceremony, but also so that "when they were set free, their children would have all kinds of horses again."[168]

While some of the white men of former times wrote unsympathetically of the Indians' regard for their horses, there were, however, a good many others who voiced an entirely different kind of reaction when they put down their impressions of Navajo and Apache horsemen. John C. Cremony was one of these men. He lived at various army garrisons while the Navajo and Apache were being rounded up to be put on their first reservations, and he came to be an admirer of a number of the Indian ponies he saw. While he marveled most at the horses' ability to endure in any chase, just as often he was impressed with the Indians' knowledge of horses and their ways of handling them. The Navajo, he observed, rode their ponies "with remarkable ease and grace."[169] A man who had first-hand information regarding the way Indians treated their horses was F. M. Buckelew. During the eleven months between 1866 and 1867 that he lived as a captive among some Lipan Apache, he observed the care these people gave their horses, and in his report of his experience with them, he commented that the Lipan centered their lives upon their horse herds. Noting that his captors possessed large herds of horses and mules, Buckelew said they moved quite often for the sole purpose of finding good pasturage for these animals. As was the custom of all the Navajo and Apache, the young Lipan boys, often Lipan captives too, spent all their time tending the horses and taking them to different pastures every day. Buckelew also commented on the special care given a Lipan's favorite horse, which was usually a warhorse. It was staked near its master's tepee and particular attention was paid to the feeding and grooming of it.[170]

Other white men who kept records of their journeys into the land of the Apache and the Navajo commented upon the impressive figure the Indians cut on their horses. There was Captain John R. Bell, for instance. In the journal he kept of his experiences on Major Stephen Long's expedition up the Arkansas River, Bell provided, in 1820, a colorful description of a Kiowa-Apache couple whom he saw eloping, traveling on horseback with all their worldly possessions. He noted that the couple were "both mounted on tolerable good horses & saddles of the Indian fashion," and he traded them "a mule, some Indian trinkets and an old dragoon jacket" for a "beautiful bay horse" the bride was leading as an extra. On her horse, the bride carried "all their baggage & travelling utenicels [sic]," as well as her husband's "war implements, [consisting] of a gun, lance, shield, powder horn & bullet pouch." The groom rode along with only "his bow & arrows & riding whip." Since the groom was in mourning for a brother of his who had been killed in a Spanish engagement, he was "divested of all ornaments." But the bride, Bell informs us, was most superbly dressed & ornamented, her dress consists of a curious fashioned loose gown of dressed deer skins, it fits close about the neck, extend[s], down below the knees, has large sleves [sic], that reach below the elbow, moccosins [sic], & legings [sic] that come above the knees, wears a belt around her waist, the whole dress ornamented with beads of different colours, a heavy flaunce [sic] around the bottom of beads and an abundance of tin trinkets of tubular form, that make a jingling noise, not in the least disagreeable—several rings on her fingers—her hair parted on the fore head, but hanging loose on neck & shoulders, when riding she puts it from before her face, placing it behind her ears, & brings the ends up & holds them in the corner of her mouth—she has an agreeable countenance, rather high cheek bones & person short & thick.[171]

On his tour of the West as Commissioner for the United States Boundary Commission, John R. Bartlett paid tribute to some of the Chiricahua Apache warriors and their mounts, those he saw at their Copper Mines encampment in 1850. These Apache, who "wore nothing but a breech cloth and boots," possessed "manly forms" and had a kind of "savage beauty," Bartlett observed, adding that they were "mounted on fine animals, and armed with a lance or bow." Henry C. Pratt, the artist accompanying Bartlett on his journey through the West, sketched the Chiricahua Apache braves at the Copper Mines and seated them on the fine-looking horses Bartlett mentioned.[172]

In 1885, the famous Indian artist George Catlin also made handsome on-the-spot paintings of "Ghila" (Western or Chiricahua) Apache horsemen he saw while traveling in the country of the Gila River of Arizona and New Mexico. One of the finest paintings ever produced of the pre-reservation Apache is his work entitled "Archery of the Apachees," which depicts the mounted Apache's excellence in archery.[173] Catlin greatly admired the proficiency of the Apache's horses and the grace with which their riders handled them. He described, in this way, the outstanding skills of the mounted archers who inspired his painting:

Much like the Sioux and Comanches, this tribe are all mounted, and generally on good and fleet horses, and from their horses' backs, while at full speed, with their simple bows and arrows, they slay their animals for food, and contend with their enemies in mortal combat. With their short bows, . . . as they have but a few yards to throw their arrows (the rapidity of their horses overcoming space), their excellency in archery depends upon the rapidity with which they can get their arrows upon the string and off, and the accuracy with which they can throw them whilst their horses are at full speed. Their practice at this is frequent and very exciting, and certainly more picturesque than rifle-shooting of volunteers in the educated world.

For this . . . sport, . . . a ground is chosen on the prairie, level and good for running, and in a semi-circle are made ten successive circular targets in the ground by cutting away the turf, and making a sort of "bulls-eye" in the center, covered with pipe-clay, which is white. Prizes are shot for, and judges are appointed to award them. Each warrior, mounted, in his war costume and war paint, and shoulders naked, and shield upon his back, takes ten arrows in his left hand with his bow, as if going into battle, and all galloping their horses round in a circle or so, under full whip, to get them at the highest speed, thus pass in succession the ten targets, and give their arrows as they pass.

The rapidity with which their arrows are placed upon the string and sent is a mystery to the bystander, and must be seen to be believed. . . . I have seen "tirs-national" and "tirs-*inter*national," but amongst them all, nothing so picturesque and beautiful as this.[174]

A similar kind of esteem for the horses and horsemanship of the Navajo was expressed in the work of the German artist and adventurer H. Balduin Möllhausen, who made several expeditions through the Indian country of the western United States during the 1850s. His "Navaho-Indianer," a painting executed in 1853, presents a lean, but prancing and nicely proportioned warhorse whose intelligent readiness is complemented by the alert and well-armed warrior it confidently carries.[175]

If some of the white people were confused or puzzled about the regard of the Indians for their horses, they were no more so than were the Indians over the whites' attitudes toward "those things by which [people] lived." The Navajo and the Apache feeling for their horses and their dislike of the whites' treatment of them expressed itself very clearly not too many years ago. When the Bureau of Animal Industry around 1930 began a campaign to remove many of the San Carlos Apaches' horses, it met with much opposition from the Western Apache groups. Although their horses were diseased with the dourine and were considered by the white men rounding them up as "practically worthless" wild mustangs, the Apache living at San Carlos still greatly valued those skinny horses.[176] Again in 1933, when the U.S. government began an attempt to preserve the rangeland of the Navajo from soil erosion, white men had the thankless job of making the Navajo understand why it was imperative for them to reduce drastically their numbers of seemingly useless horses. Needless to say, when authorities took many horses from unwilling owners and disposed of them, few Navajo understood that it really was for the good of themselves and the rest of their herds. "Washington," as the Navajo call anything having to do with our government, met with much difficulty. It is said that when the horsemeat plant went up in Gallup, New Mexico, to take care of excess meat that came from the extermination of thousands of worn-out range horses, the old Navajo men looked at the new building uneasily and said: "Our Grandmother will not be pleased with this." When a season of drought set in and more of their horses died from lack of water, they attributed the disaster to the government extermination of horses. That, they said, was what really caused the God People's anger.[177] In fact, some of the Navajo feel that this action of the government has caused such drastic change in the cycle of weather in their country that things never will be the same again. As one Navajo who felt this way expressed it: "In the old days it used to rain frequently. When the government cut down the number of animals the Navaho were to have, there was no more rain. . . . In the early days the whites made no rules about the livestock and there was much snow in October and November in Utah. Now there is little snow until January."[178]

Some of the Navajo remembered what White Bead Woman had once said about how she planned to control the number of horses she would send to them. She had said that "when she believes it is for their good," the horses "will multiply," or "they will decrease." And those who remembered her words said that this was exactly the way the goddess had always handled such matters, for everyone knew that horses did "not always multiply." Some years, when the grass was poor and the snow was deep, many died.[179]

Others said that Begochiddy was the deity who had set up a "basic law" governing animal reproduction, and that he was the one who was supposed to carry out "the rules" concerning the number of horses and other animals.[180] But most of the Navajo agreed on one point, and that was that the number of horses should be decided only by the Holy Beings, certainly not by "Washington." Whites could not seem to understand that sacred things required the most delicate handling. As Sandoval once observed:

> The medicines and the chants have been used and learned by those
> who wished to learn and use them. Those who discredit them and do
> not wish to use the medicines or learn the chants will have a difficult
> life. It is the belief that those who learn and use and care for these

sacred things will not regret it. Their work will be made lighter for them.[181]

Only by practicing the ritual prescribed by the Holy Beings in the tending of horses could the Navajo and Apache prove themselves worthy of so great a gift; only in this way could they answer the gods that they had kept holy the horses entrusted to them.

Notes

1. See *supra*, pp. 69–70; Sapir and Hoijer, pp. 121, 123.
2. For the story, see *supra*, pp. 92–95, or Opler, *Myths and Legends of the Lipan*, p. 31.
3. Opler, *Myths and Legends of the Lipan*, p. 77.
4. Ibid.
5. Ibid., pp. 77–78.
6. Ibid., p. 78.
7. See *supra*, pp. 81–82; O'Bryan, pp. 178, 179.
8. O'Bryan, p. 179. The purposes of the Night Chant and the fact that many of its prayers directly concern the propagation of horses have been noted earlier. For more information concerning this subject, see *supra*, p. 77. Cf. also Matthews, "Navaho Myths, Prayers and Songs," p. 35, where Matthews has recorded one of Hatáli Natlói's versions of a prayer from the Night Chant. This prayer, which mentions horses, is one the Navajo say on the morning after the great nocturnal dance has been held. The pertinent lines from the prayer, offered for the purpose of increasing things of all kinds, are rendered by Matthews as follows: "Horses of all kinds, hanging above me, I say."
9. See *supra*, pp. 66–69, for the incident from the Sapir and Hoijer myth concerning Turquoise Boy's experience at Sisná.te.l and for the identification of this place name with that of the Sis ná dzil of Sandoval's story.
10. O'Bryan, p. 179. More information about these grasses is supplied later in this chapter. The scientific identifications of them are available in a number of sources. Washington Matthews identifies *gá tso dan* as *kaí-so-tha*—the type of grass known scientifically as *Eurotia lanata* Moquin and commonly called jackrabbit grass. See his "Navajo Names for Plants," *American Naturalist*, XX, No. 9 (September 1886), p. 775. The Franciscan Fathers identify *ndīdlíди* (*nit' dit lede*) as mountain rice; *Oryzopsis cuspidata*. See their *A Vocabulary of the Navaho Language* (Saint Michaels, Ariz.: Navajo Indian Mission, 1912), I, p. 130; II, p. 136. For the identification of *tl'ŏ' nastą́ si* (*tlo nas tasse*) as bent grass, or grama grass (*Bouteloua hirsuta*), see also ibid., I, p. 99; II, p. 171.
11. Fishler, *In the Beginning*, p. 72. See Franciscan Fathers, *An Ethnologic Dictionary of the Navaho Language*, p. 185, for the identification of *dók' óží* (*t'ák'ōzh*) as saltweed, or salt-bush (*Atriplex argentea; Atriplex expansa*), or as shad-scale (*Atriplex confertifolia*). See also ibid., p. 191, for the identification of *t'oh c'ósi'* (*tl'ŏ' tšŏsi*) as rush-grass (*Sporobolus cryptandrus*).

12. O'Bryan, p. 179.

13. Ibid.

14. Ibid., pp. 21, 179. Note also on p. 21 the other names that Sandoval says were given to "the hole in the sky": "The first is called Tsé an an hí habetine, the Place Where the Most High Power Came Up; the second is Sash yotá betine, the Bear's Upper Sky Path; and the third name is Hojon yotá betine, Whose Ways Are Beautiful's Path." Matthews, *Navaho Legends,* p. 113, calls the opening *Yágalioka.* For still another Navajo name and tradition concerning this place, see *supra,* pp. 25–26.

15. O'Bryan, p. 82, especially the information supplied by the interpreter in n. 68. Cf. Matthews, *Navaho Legends,* pp. 113–114.

16. O'Bryan, p. 179.

17. Ibid. p. 4. Cf. also Matthews, *Navaho Legends,* p. 63, n. 137.

18. See Matthews, *Navaho Legends,* p. 114; p. 211, n. 3; p. 235, n. 137; also O'Bryan, p. 82, n. 68. Other sacred rivers to the Navajo are the Colorado, the Little Colorado, and the Rio Puerco. Although there is no juncture between the San Juan and the Rio Grande, real junctures, such as those of the San Juan with the Colorado, or of the Big Colorado with the Little Colorado, are often the settings for other important mythical events. According to one Navajo myth, the Twins, after the departure of their mother from the earth, moved to To'yě' tli (Meeting Waters), a place where two rivers joined. Matthews, who collected the myth, located the juncture of the rivers as being "somewhere in the valley of the San Juan River, in Colorado, or Utah," but could not determine the exact location. See his *Navaho Legends,* p. 134; p. 238, n. 163.

19. See O'Bryan, p. 4, n. 15; p. 179.

20. Ibid, p. 179. Only the first stanza of this song is given here, since the remainder of it, describing the turquoise horse and its grandeur, has already been recorded in an earlier chapter in connection with the discussion of the Sun's blue horse. See *supra,* p. 36.

21. O'Bryan, p. 180.

22. Ibid.

23. Ibid.

24. For the goddess's song, see *supra,* pp. 79–80, or O'Bryan, p. 177.

25. O'Bryan, pp. 180–181.

26. Ibid., p. 181. Cf. this statement of Sandoval's with the discussion of the supernatural elements used to compose the bodies' of the gods' horses in *supra,* pp. 15–21.

27. For the discussion of the Blessing Way's relationship to raiding ceremonies, see *supra,* p. 121–124.

28. See Kluckhohn and Leighton, pp. 180–181; Reichard, *Social Life of the Navajo,* p. 145.

29. Reichard, *Navaho Religion,* II, pp. 734–735.

30. O'Bryan, p. 178, n. 22.

31. Reichard, *Social Life of the Navajo,* p. 148.

32. Fishler, "Navaho Picture Writing," p. 51; p. 68, especially n. 32.

33. Fishler, *In the Beginning,* p. 89. The Navajo who recorded this version of the story of White Bead Woman's departure from the earth said the goddess traveled far

to the west of the Navajo country before she left the earth. He identified the mountain where she held her last ceremony as Mount Whitney in California.

34. Kluckhohn and Leighton, p. 141.

35. Fishler, "Navaho Picture Writing," p. 68. Note also pp. 67, 69 where the same man told Fishler that "if a flat rock were used in a ceremony and it were broken, this ceremony would have to be used to repair it," and that "if a person has Mirage Rock in a medicine bag and it is broken, he or she must give a gift before it can be fixed." This implies that the person's "gift," or ceremonial offering, would be "white shell, turquoise, oyster shell, jet and red stone," for all the colors of these sacred stones and shells are found in the colors of a mirage stone.

36. Fishler, *In the Beginning*, p. 37.

37. Opler, *Myths and Legends of the Lipan*, p. 31.

38. Opler, *An Apache Life-Way*, pp. 296–297. For a discussion of the role of Apache women as shamans, and for the story of how this woman performed a ceremony to heal a man of an injury inflicted by a horse, see *infra*, pp. 235–238.

39. Opler, *An Apache Life-Way*, p. 299.

40. See Opler, *Myths and Tales of the Jicarilla*, p. 57.

41. Opler, *Myths and Legends of the Lipan*, p. 31.

42. Opler, *An Apache Life-Way*, p. 71.

43. Ibid., p. 259.

44. Ibid.; cf. also *supra*, p. 90. The gift of trappings and a horse—four in number— that a Lipan was required to give a man who told him the myth of Killer-of- Enemies' gift of horses served the same purpose. Because the person who knew this story was usually a shaman and believed he could transfer some of his power with horses to the uninitiated listener, he had to have these things to serve as ceremonial offerings to his power to assure its willingness that such a transfer be made.

45. Goodwin, *Myths and Tales of the White Mountain*, p. 85.

46. Opler, *An Apache Life-Way*, p. 300.

47. Ibid.

48. O'Bryan, p. 178.

49. Opler, *An Apache Life-Way*, p. 295, n. 30. Cf. Gertrude Hill, "Turquoise and the Zuñi Indian," *The Kiva*, XII, No. 4 (May 1947), p. 49. Hill writes of the use of the root of this plant by the Zuñi for curing people of sore tongues. She says the root medicine is kept in an individual's mouth for a day and a night and "when the substance has been removed, the medicine man places with it a fragment of turquoise and some white shell beads. The whole is then deposited in a shallow pit in the river bed, from whence it may go to the Abiding Place of the Council of the Gods."

50. Leland C. Wyman and Stuart K. Harris, *Navajo Indian Medical Ethnobotany*, Bulletin of the University of New Mexico, Anthropological Series, III, No. 5 (Albuquerque: University of New Mexico Press, 1941), pp. 19, 28, 38, 68.

51. Franciscan Fathers, *An Ethnologic Dictionary of the Navaho Language*, p. 196.

52. Joseph G. Lee, "Navajo Medicine Man," *Arizona Highways*, XXXVII (August 1961), p. 9.

53. Wheelwright, *Hail Chant and Water Chant*, p. 76.

54. Wyman and Harris, *Navajo Indian Medical Ethnobotany*, p. 72.

55. Lee, "Navajo Medicine Man," p. 5.

56. Opler, *An Apache Life-Way*, p. 299.

57. Ibid.; Lee, "Navajo Medicine Man," p. 5; Franciscan Fathers, *An Ethnologic Dictionary of the Navaho Language*, p. 154.

58. Opler, *An Apache Life-Way*, p. 299.

59. Ignaz Pfefferkorn, *Sonora: A Description of the Province*, trans. and annotated by Theodore E. Treutlein, Coronado Cuatro Centennial Publications, 1540–1940, XII (Albuquerque: University of New Mexico Press, 1949), p. 63.

60. Wyman and Harris, p. 63.

61. Lee, "Navajo Medicine Man," p. 5.

62. Kluckhohn, *Navaho Witchcraft*, p. 188.

63. Franciscan Fathers, *An Ethnologic Dictionary of the Navaho Language*, pp. 153–154. For an excellent description of how the Navajo castrate horses, see T. D. Allen, *Navahos Have Five Fingers* (Norman: University of Oklahoma Press, 1963), pp. 163–165. Notice too that in her report, Allen also mentions that a Navajo whom she observed castrating horses always completed the operation by "blood marking"—smearing the gelded horse with its own blood on the forehead, forelegs, and hind legs—and last, slapping it on the thigh. One of Allen's informants explained that if this ritual did not terminate the gelding of a horse, then the emasculated animal would not be able to "run fast" (p. 165).

64. Pfefferkorn, *Sonora: A Description of the Province*, p. 147.

65. For a more detailed account of the use of hide boots for horses by the Navajo and Apache, see my article, "Early Horse Trappings of the Navajo and Apache Indians," *Arizona and the West*, V, No. 3 (Autumn 1963), pp. 246–248.

66. McAllister, "Kiowa-Apache Tales," pp. 127–128.

67. J. Frank Dobie, "Indian Horses and Horsemanship," *Southwest Review*, XXXV, No. 4 (Autumn 1950), p. 269.

68. Wyman and Harris, pp. 63–64. See also Thomas H. Kearney, Robert H. Peebles, and collaborators, *Arizona Flora* (Berkeley: University of California Press, 1951), p. 938.

69. However, Edward F. Castetter and Morris E. Opler deny the use of this weed, or any other species of *Datura*, as a narcotic among the Mescalero and Chiricahua Apache. See their work, *The Ethnobiology of the Chiricahua and Mescalero Apache*, Bulletin of the University of New Mexico, Biological Series, IV, No. 5 (Albuquerque: University of New Mexico Press, 1936), p. 55. See also Wyman and Harris, p. 59.

70. Dobie, "Indian Horses and Horsemanship," p. 268.

71. J. Frank Dobie writes that the Sioux Indians also practiced this custom. See his *The Mustangs* (Boston: Little, Brown and Co., 1952), p. 46.

72. For this practice among the Comanche, Sioux, and other Indian tribes, see Dobie, "Indian Horses and Horsemanship," p. 268.

73. Kluckhohn, *Navaho Witchcraft*, p. 203.

74. Ibid., p. 199; p. 248, n. 6.

75. Ibid., p. 203.

76. Coolidge and Coolidge, p. 145.
77. Kluckhohn, *Navajo Witchcraft*, p. 187.
78. Ibid., pp. 183, 187.
79. Coolidge and Coolidge, p. 145.
80. Kluckhohn, *Navaho Witchcraft*, p. 214.
81. Ibid., p. 153.
82. Ibid., p. 193; p. 250, n. 5.
83. Ibid., p. 51.
84. Wyman and Harris, p. 71
85. Opler, *An Apache Life-Way*, p. 299.
86. The Chiricahua and Mescalero Apache have also made much use of grama grass in ceremonial contexts, other than those associated with horses. Traditions exist that their culture hero, Child-of-the-Water, successfully used this grass as his arrow when he slew an evil giant. See Castetter and Opler, p. 32.
87. John C. Cremony, *Life Among the Apaches* (Tucson: Arizona Silhouettes, 1951), pp. 182–183. For Gregg's description of this fine fall grass as he found it in New Mexico in 1831, see his *Commerce of the Prairies*, ed. Milo Milton Quaife, Lakeside Classics (Chicago: R. R. Donnelley and Sons, Co., 1926), pp. 153–154.
88. Kearney, Peebles et al., pp. 260–261.
89. Ibid., p. 115.
90. Ibid., pp. 112, 114, 255, 259; Lyman Benson and Robert A. Darrow, *The Trees and Shrubs of the Southwestern Deserts* (Tucson and Albuquerque: University of Arizona Press and University of New Mexico Press, 1954), pp. 122–123.
91. Castetter and Opler, p. 47; Kearney, Peebles et al., p. 150.
92. Kearney, Peebles et al., pp. 100, 420–422; Franciscan Fathers, *An Ethnologic Dictionary of the Navaho Language*, p. 190.
93. Kearney, Peebles et al., pp. 445, 463–465, 468–469, 470.
94. Fishler, *In the Beginning*, pp. 71, 72.
95. Benson and Darrow, p. 341; Kearney, Peebles et al., pp. 759, 862.
96. Kluckhohn and Leighton, p. 142; Reichard, *Social Life of the Navajo*, p. 95.
97. Reichard, *Social Life of the Navajo*, pp. 114, 146.
98. Opler, *An Apache Life-Way*, p. 445.
99. Fishler, *In the Beginning*, p. 76. The "flexible goods" mentioned in the song refer to such things as blankets, or hides of animals, which the Navajo sometimes call "soft goods." The "chips of all kinds" mentioned in the last line mean little pieces of different kinds of sacred stones and shells.
100. Matthews, "Navaho Myths, Prayers and Songs," p. 58.
101. Ibid., p. 59.
102. Curtis, p. 362.
103. For the examination of the ceremonial song, see *supra*, pp. 170–172.
104. Reichard, *Navaho Religion*, I, p. 288.
105. Matthews, "'Navaho Myths, Prayers and Songs," p. 59.
106. Opler, *Dirty Boy*, p. 10.
107. O'Bryan, p. 178.
108. W. W. Hill, "Navajo Salt Gathering," *The University of New Mexico Bulletin*, An-

thropological Series, III, No. 4 (February 1940), pp. 5, 8. Hill notes (p. 8) that "salt from the Zuñi Lake is believed to have homeopathic properties and when a small quantity is mixed with the present day commercial product, it permeates it with sanctified qualities inherent in that which was ritually secured."

109. Ibid., pp. 9–10.

110. Ibid., p. 10.

111. Ibid., p. 8. See also p. 7, where Hill identified the most popular Navajo salt sites as the following: Zuñi Lake, "Black Cottonwood near Black Mesa; Escavada Wash; Chee Dodge's Flat, near Crystal; Buell Park; Black Rock, near Fort Defiance; and Jacob's Well, near Sanders."

112. Ibid., pp. 10–11.

113. Ibid., p. 11.

114. Ibid., p. 14.

115. Fishler, *In the Beginning*, p. 88.

116. Hill, "Navajo Salt Gathering," p. 14.

117. Ibid.

118. Hill, *The Agricultural and Hunting Methods of the Navaho Indians*, p. 102.

119. Reichard, *Social Life of the Navajo*, p. 147.

120. Ibid., p. 91.

121. Ibid., pp. 53, 90.

122. Fishler, *In the Beginning*, pp. 75–76.

123. Ibid., p. 73.

124. Kluckhohn, *Navaho Witchcraft*, p. 189.

125. Goddard, *Myths and Tales from the White Mountain*, p. 99.

126. Fishler, *In the Beginning*, pp. 70–71.

127. See *supra*, pp. 29, 75–76.

128. Goddard, *Myths and Tales from the White Mountain*, p. 102, especially n. 1. Cf. *supra*, p. 75, for the account of the Navajo Sun's cornstalk.

129. In the division of labor in Western Apache societies, the women of a household were supposed to do work of this kind for the men. They also saddled and unsaddled the men's horses.

130. Goddard, *Myths and Tales from the White Mountain*, p. 105.

131. Ibid., p. 106.

132. Kluckhohn, *Navaho Witchcraft*, pp. 187, 188.

133. Ibid., pp. 180–181, 247–248.

134. Ibid., p. 181.

135. See Walter Dyk, *Son of Old Man Hat: A Navaho Autobiography* (New York: Harcourt, Brace and Co., 1938), p. 357.

136. Kluckhohn, *Navaho Witchcraft*, pp. 178, 179.

137. Kluckhohn and Leighton, pp. 179–181; Reichard, *Social Life of the Navaho*, p. 135.

138. "Relation Du Voyage Du Sieur De Bourgmont," in Margry, *Découvertes et établissements des français dans l'ouest et dans le sud de l'Amérique Septentrionale (1614–1754)*, VI, p. 445.

139. Franciscan Fathers, *An Ethnologic Dictionary of the Navaho Language*, p. 451.

140. Newcomb, *Navajo Omens and Taboos*, p. 52.

141. Reichard, *Social Life of the Navajo*, p. 135.

142. Newcomb, *Navajo Omens and Taboos*, p. 51; Kluckhohn, *Navaho Witchcraft*, p. 29.

143. Kluckhohn, *Navaho Witchcraft*, p. 190.

144. Newcomb, *Navajo Omens and Taboos*, pp. 48, 67, 79.

145. Ibid., p. 16.

146. Ibid., pp. 18, 26.

147. Opler, *An Apache Life-Way*, p. 237.

148. Ibid., p. 154.

149. Newcomb, *Navajo Omens and Taboos*, p. 39. It should be understood, however, that not all Southern Athapascan groups restricted their women from preparing for or engaging in such activities. Cremony described a Mescalero Apache woman who "was renowned as one of the most dexterous horse thieves and horse breakers in the tribe." According to him, the translation of her Apache name was "The Dexterous Horse Thief," and she "seldom permitted an expedition to go on a raid without her presence." See his *Life Among the Apaches*, p. 243. See also *infra*, pp. 302–303.

150. Opler, *An Apache Life-Way*, p. 200. A Big Snake, reported by a Navajo to be living near Fort Defiance, Arizona, was said to be "over three feet long" and to possess "the power to eat animals whole." "When he eats a deer, he gets big enough to swallow him," this man noted. See Fishler, "Navaho Picture Writing," p. 62.

151. Hill, "Navajo Salt Gathering," p. 13.

152. Castetter and Opler, p. 19.

153. David Wooster, ed. and trans., "A Ride with the Apaches: The Unpublished Narrative of José Mendivil," *Overland Monthly*, VI, No. 4 (April 1871), p. 342. See also Goodwin, *Social Organization of the Western Apache*, pp. 76–82, for information concerning trading relations between these Western Apache groups and the Zuñi Indians.

154. Wooster, "A Ride with the Apaches: The Unpublished Narrative of José Mendivil," p. 341.

155. Ibid., p. 343. The "jingling spurs" refer to spurs with little bells on them. Many of the Navajo and Apache also attached bells to their horses' manes or to their bridles, as had the Spaniards and Mexicans in the Southwest during the seventeenth and eighteenth centuries. Called hawk bells by the *conquistadores*, they were worn by the horses that Don Juan de Oñate and his first caravan of settlers took into New Mexico in 1598. The inspection report of Oñate's equipment listed "sixteen dozen hawk-bells, large and small," as being brought along in one of the carts. Centuries later when they began to work silver, the Navajo copied the examples of their Mexican neighbors and made silver bells out of coins. See George P. Hammond and Agapito Rey, eds. and trans., *Don Juan de Oñate: Colonizer of New Mexico, 1595–1628*, Vol. 1, Coronado Cuatro Centennial Publications, 1540–1940, V (Albuquerque: University of New Mexico Press, 1953), p. 135; John Adair, *The Navajo and Pueblo Silversmiths* (Norman: University of Oklahoma Press, 1946), p. 7. For a Jicarilla Apache legend concerning the gift some Spaniards made to a group of Pueblo Indians of "horses fitted out with bells," see Goddard, *Jicarilla Apache Texts*, p. 240.

156. For an account of the horse trappings used by the Navajo and Apache of pre-reservation days, see my article, "Early Horse Trappings of the Navajo and Apache Indians," pp. 233–248.

157. Opler, *An Apache Life-Way*, p. 299, and especially n. 32.

158. Fishler, *In the Beginning*, p. 72.

159. Ibid., pp. 71, 72, and 76.

160. Ibid., p. 71.

161. Dobie, "Indian Horses and Horsemanship," pp. 268–269.

162. Cremony, p. 49.

163. Richard Irving Dodge, *The Plains of the Great West and Their Inhabitants Being a Description of the Plains, Game, Indians, &c. of the Great North American Desert* (New York: Archer House, 1959), p. 424—hereafter cited *as The Plains of the Great West*.

164. See the letter by Holloway in Wyman, *The Wild Horse of the West*, p. 295.

165. For Dodge's views on this subject, see his *The Plains of the Great West*, pp. 424–426.

166. Goddard, *Myths and Tales from the White Mountain*, p. 123.

167. Hill, *Navaho Warfare*, p. 12.

168. McAllester, *Enemy Way Music*, p. 9.

169. Cremony, p. 49. See also pp. 75–78, 185, 222–223, 253–255.

170. Dennis and Dennis, p. 74.

171. John R. Bell, *The Journal of Captain John R. Bell, Official Journalist for the Stephen H. Long Expedition to the Rocky Mountains, 1820*, ed. Harlin M. Fuller and LeRoy R. Hafen, The Far West and the Rockies Historical Series, 1820–1875, VI (Glendale: Arthur H. Clark Co., 1957), pp. 180–182, 186. It will be noted that throughout his account, Bell refers to the Kiowa-Apache (Kaskaia) people by their French nickname—"Badhearts" (Kaskaias). For the story behind the elopement of the Kiowa-Apache couple, see Edwin James, ed., *Account of an Expedition from Pittsburgh to the Rocky Mountains, Performed in the Years, 1819, 1820, Under the Command of Major S. H. Long* (London: Longman, Hurst, Rees, Orme, and Brown, 1823), II, pp. 247–249.

172. John Russell Bartlett, *Personal Narrative of the Explorations and Incidents in Texas, New Mexico, California, Sonora and Chihuahua* (New York: D. Appleton and Co., 1854), I, p. 328. See p. 326 for the illustration by Pratt.

173. For a reproduction of this painting, see George Catlin, *Episodes from "Life Among the Indians" and "Last Rambles,"* ed. Marvin C. Ross (Norman: University of Oklahoma Press, 1959), p. [140].

174. Catlin, *Episodes from "Life Among the Indians" and "Last Rambles,"* pp. 167–168.

175. For a reproduction of Möllhausen's "Navaho-Indianer," see Horst Hartmann, *George Catlin und Balduin Möllhausen: Zwei Interpreten der Indianer und des Alten Westens* (Berlin: Dietrich Reimer Verlag, 1963), p. 114.

176. Wyman, *The Wild Horse of the West*, pp. 294–295.

177. O'Bryan, p. 181, n. 27.

178. Fishler, *In the Beginning*, p. 18.

179. O'Bryan, p. 178.

180. Fishler, *In the Beginning*, pp. 17–18.

181. O'Bryan, p. 181.

The Horse's Powers Over the People's Health

A S THE NAVAJO AND APACHE LEARNED TO TEND HORSES according to the traditions established by their ancestors, they also learned the ways in which horses could take care of them. Believing in an order of life where animals, birds, insects, and plants could help the deserving or thwart the impious, Southern Athapascan societies sought assistance from certain beings to meet crises such as illness. Whereas once they had possessed only the game animals—particularly the deer, the antelope, and the buffalo—whose aid they could enlist in curing the sick, after the acquisition of the horse, they found they could also depend upon the power of this new domestic animal.

The Horse as a Helper in Healing

Though the horse plays many roles in Navajo curing ceremonies, one of the most important is that of beneficent helper. Let us consider first the mythical water horse that the Navajo invoke as an assisting spirit in two curing ceremonies designed to restore patients suffering from illnesses brought on by snakes, or illnesses or injuries attributed to lightning or water. This creature, which figures occasionally in Navajo myths and sandpaintings, belonged to Water Monster, and its main responsibility was to guard the door of that deity's home.[1] Reichard translated the Navajo term for Water Horse as meaning literally "deep-water-pet" and implied that it was among the aquatic pets that Matthews called "Tielín" in his recording of the myth of the whirling logs.[2] On the other hand, Wheelwright gave the particular term for Water Horse in Navajo as "Káithklee" and said the literal translation of the term meant "many-water horse."[3]

Sam Yazzie of Chinle, Arizona, modern-day Navajo singer, 1972.

One Navajo myth describes a water horse as having "the hoofs and the horns of a cow," but in all other respects as being like a horse.[4] The details of this description are borne out by a drawing of a typical water horse reproduced by the Franciscan Fathers.[5] Other fine drawings of water horses in stylized form are to be found in *Sandpaintings of the Navajo Shooting Chant,* a beautiful book assembled from sandpaintings collected by Franc J. Newcomb and published with a text by Gladys A. Reichard. In two of the plates they appear as squat, bow-legged quadrupeds with cloud symbols for hoofs. Plate XXIX reveals Water Horse as a pink creature with lightning symbols on its forelegs and mane. In Plate XXXIII we see the four Water Horses, black, yellow, blue, and pink. They breathe lightning out of their mouths, their bodies and upper legs are clothed in rainbows, and they have horns made of rainbows. They may at times depart otherwise from equine standards and appear without their tails.[6] According to Newcomb, the horns shown on the Water Horse in sandpaintings "are indicative of its power to travel through space— even above the sphere of the thunderbird" or of those of clouds and storms.[7]

Like Water Monsters, Water Horses sometimes do harm rather than good, and in further imitation of their masters, they can appear in human form.[8] Frank Goldtooth related the incident of how a Water Horse, appearing as a "fine young man" called "Sea Horse," was the seducer in one of the rare instances in Navajo mythology when White Bead Woman's reputation suffers a blemish. He suddenly appeared from "out of the water" before the goddess, who was journeying west with all her animals, and as she was preparing to rest for the night in "the canyon where the water meets from the two great rivers"—in this case, the Big and Little Colorado rivers. She "spent the night with this man," and as a result of her infidelity to Sun, forfeited all "the animals outside of her [ceremonial] basket." She was further penalized by having to leave her "Sea Horse" suitor gifts of "salt, shell, turquoise, jet, white bead, oyster shell and red shell." "These things," which she left at the juncture of the Big and Little Colorado rivers, "are still there to this day."[9]

In Beauty Way, one of the Navajo curing ceremonies in which they appear, White Water Horses are addressed in five songs sung during the sweat and emetic rite. The whole ceremony, ordinarily covering either five or nine days, is held for the benefit of a patient whose misery has been traced directly or indirectly to snake infection.[10] Snake bites or bad dreams about snakes may be the cause, or bites or bad dreams about lizards and certain water creatures associated with snakes. In yet other ways, too, the patient may be contaminated by snake sickness. As Wyman observes in his commentaries introducing the myths Haile and Oakes collected of Beauty Way:

> There is no definite association of etiological factors with specific diseases or categories of diseases. Navaho theory is certainly not physiological. According to mythological references and the statements of informants, certain factors may be linked with a few given illnesses, but most factors are thought to be possible causes of almost any malady. Among the diseases sometimes traced to snake infection, for example, are rheumatism, sore throat, stomach trouble, kidney and bladder trouble, and skin diseases or sores.[11]

In the sweat and emetic rite of Beauty Way—the external and internal purification act—a big fire is kindled to cause the patient to sweat profusely. At the same time the singer washes the patient in a special preparation, and gives the patient some of the same to drink to enhance purging.[12] Simultaneously the singer and an assistant sing ten songs, the last five of which invoke the assistance of White Water Horse and such other water deities as Water Monster, Blue Thunder, and Otter. These songs were called the "underwater-side-strung songs" by Singer Man of Deer Spring, Arizona, who dictated his version of Beauty Way to Haile in 1932. Singer Man had failed to learn many of the meanings and "burdens" of the words of these songs when he was taught them, but like many other Navajo, he felt that a number of the words were foreign, borrowed by the Navajo from other Indian languages.[13] When such terms could not be translated, Haile left them in the text, but put them into a spelling intended to Anglicize their pronunciation. Because of numerous omissions, the appearance of such terms as "*yo we*" and "*go la ne,*" and the differences between Navajo and English phonemes, the resulting translation is in many respects unsatisfactory.[14] The following are the five songs of White Water Horse, set down exactly as Haile renders them:

Song 6

Over here *yo we* I am walking in their midst, among them I am
    walking *go la ne* now in the white corn home of White Water
    Horses I am walking in their midst . . . over here *yo we go la ne*. . . .
Now in the blue corn home of Blue Thunders I am walking in their
    midst over here *yo we go la ne*. . . .
Now in the dark corn home of Otters I am walking in their midst . . .
    over here *yo we na* among them I am walking . . . *go la ne*. . . .
Now in the mixed corn home of Water Monsters I am walking in their
    midst . . . over here *yo we* among them I am walking *go la ne*. . . .

Song 7

e ne ye in the midst of nice ones I usually go . . . in the midst of nice
    ones I usually walk . . . now in the white corn home of White
    Water Horse I usually walk in their midst . . . in the midst of nice
    ones I usually walk. . . .
Now in the blue corn home of Blue Thunder I usually walk in their
    midst. . . .
Now in the dark corn home of Otter (etc.). . . Now in the mixed
    corn home of Water Monster I usually walk in their midst (etc.). . .

Song 8

I came to a holy one *yo ei* . . . to Water Horse whose corn is white I
came . . . to a holy (thing) I came. . . .
To Blue Thunder whose corn is blue I came . . . It's holy I see, to
which I came. . . .
To Otter whose corn is dark (etc.), To Water Monster whose corn is
varicolored I came . . . it's holy, I see, to which I came. . . .

Song 9

It's holy I see, *wo wo* . . . *la yo ye* . . . White Water Horse, whose corn
is white, is holy I see. . . .
Blue Thunder, whose corn is blue, is holy I see . . . Otter, whose corn
is dark, is holy I see . . . Water Monster whose corn is mixed, is
holy I see. . . .

Song 10

Somewhere a peal of thunder is heard . . . now toward the white
corn home of White Water Horse a peal of thunder is heard . . .
somewhere a peal of thunder is heard. . . .
Now toward the blue corn home of Blue Thunder a peal of thunder
is heard (etc.) . . . now at the dark corn home of Otter (etc.) . . .
now at the varicolored corn home of Water Monster a peal of
thunder is heard . . . somewhere a peal of thunder is heard. . . .[15]

Singer Man also spoke of a Water Horse sandpainting that might be
incorporated into Beauty Way, but neither Haile nor his editor Wyman
had seen such a painting at the time when the study of this ceremony was
published.[16]

The other Navajo curing ceremony in which a water horse proves
helpful is the Tohe, or Water Chant, sometimes called Water Way. According
to Newcomb and Reichard, it belongs to a large ceremonial complex
known as the Shooting Chants.[17] Its uses are diverse, for illnesses or injuries
caused by lightning or water or wind; it is also effective against deafness,
fear, rheumatism, and snake bite.[18]

Describing the procedures of the Water Chant to Wheelwright in
1937, Klah Zhin of the Gray Hills Trading Post vicinity told of how a
fringe of horsehair is used in the ceremony as a substitute for the hair of
Káithklee, the mythical water horse. Just before the emetic is administered,
this fringe of horsehair, dyed red, is tied to the top of a medicine
wand that already supports the feathers of birds, bundles of holy plants,
and bits of precious stones. "Dressing the wand of power," the tying is

called; the hair must point upward with the trailing end wrapped about the wand all the way down. Then two young men take the wand and its ceremonial companion, a basket, and following the progress of the ceremonial songs, elevate them to the roof of the hogan and lower them to the earthen floor. The songs tell of how the wand and the basket "go up through and above the sky, and then return to the earth and to the water under the earth and [are] blessed."[19]

Instead of a water horse, the mythical turquoise horse belonging to the sun deity is invoked as a beneficent helper to restore sick patients in the Navajo's versatile Blessing Way, previously examined as it relates to ceremonies of raiding, protection, and increase.[20] When a Navajo is suffering from the general symptoms of feeling "'bad all over" and is undecided what animal or supernatural being is responsible for an illness, he or she may attribute the loss of vitality to being out of harmony with things.[21] Such a case calls for a Blessing Way designed to restore peace and order to mind and body.

In the final movement of this kind of ceremony, the Blessing Way singer reaches the song of invocation to Sun's turquoise horse. How this and surrounding songs addressed to other deities fit into the ceremonial pattern is described below by the Leightons:

> The Singer sings a verse of a song dealing with legends, things the Beings have done and the origin of the ceremonial, and the crowd takes it up with increasing volume. It is repeated and repeated that the patient is identified with the Beings. It is said that the Spirit of the Mountain belongs to the patient, his feet are the patient's feet, the patient walks in his tracks, and wears his moccasins. The Blue Horse spirit belongs to the patient, the turquoise horse with lightning feet, with a mane like distant rain, a black star for an eye and white shells for teeth, the horse spirit who feeds on the pollen of flowers. There are songs that take up the patient's health directly, saying, "His feet restore for him, his mind restore for him, his voice restore for him." There are also repetitions of thoughts that proclaim all is well; thus, "My feet are getting better, my head is feeling better, I am better all over." Finally, it is said over and over again that all is being made beautiful and harmonious. The songs come in groups that form patterned relationships with each other. The effect of repetition, rhythm, and the antiphonal chorus is very impressive.[22]

The Horse as Retaliator and Restorer

The horse in ceremony is capable of overcoming not only the detrimental powers of other creatures, but also its own. When a horse throws, kicks, bites, or knocks a person unconscious, the Navajo and Apache believe that it can supply the remedy for the injury it has caused.

Before the horse arrived, Navajo and Apache beliefs had always respected the retaliatory ability of creatures like snake, spider, ant, and bear, and that of god people like the Mountain People and the Thunder People with their lightning arrows. After the horse and the mule had taken their place in Southern Athapascan societies, these animals were added to those that would bring about prompt retaliation when crossed.[23]

If a man offends a horse in some way, the horse may retaliate by inflicting upon him some injury or sickness. And then, in reversal of roles, a horse, or a guardian horse spirit, may through ceremony effect the patient's recovery. Anyone who has incurred a horse's wrath may expect to fall victim to "horse sickness," an inclusive term attached to any of the injuries or diseases caused by horses, a list that includes even venereal diseases. A certain Navajo, convinced that a man could "not only get venereal diseases from a woman, but also from . . . horses," declared that a person could contract the dreaded diseases by urinating in "places" where horses had "laid down or urinated," because horses sometimes have "poison in their blood" that is highly communicable.[24]

No doubt one of the reasons behind beliefs in the horse's tendency to wreak vengeance was to discourage harsh treatment of the animal. A Chiricahua Apache issued the following warning and recommendation: "If you mistreat a horse, if you hit it on the head repeatedly, it may take revenge on you. It will cause you to get sick. Then you must go to a shaman who specializes in the ceremony of the horse. The mule is bad if you mistreat it; it will cause you to be sick, too. The man who knows the horse cures both kinds of sickness."[25]

Jicarilla Apache children were told the following tale about two talking horses to instruct them as to how a horse expected to be treated and to caution them as to how they might arouse the horse's ill will:

> One time a man was treating his horse badly. He hit the horse
> needlessly and threw around the horse's bridle and rope carelessly. He
> didn't care what he did. He would hit the horse with rocks too. That
> man was very mean to his own horse. When he rode his horse, he
> would always make it run. He never took care of it. And that horse
> got very thin. It was just bones.
>
> There was another man who took good care of his horse. He
> didn't throw rocks or sticks at it. He treated it well. And this horse
> was always fat and strong and helped him a great deal.
>
> One night these two horses met each other.

The one who was well cared for spoke to the thin one, "What's the matter? You look thin and hungry and unhappy."

The badly treated horse said, "It's because my father doesn't take good care of me. He always chases me and hits me with rocks and strikes me with big sticks. And he whips me with the bridle and ropes. When he puts the saddle blanket on me he never makes it soft first. When he puts the saddle on me he always throws it. Always he says harsh words to me. He never gives me a kind word. That is why I'm thin, miserable, and unhappy. That's why, when I'm taking him out riding, I am heavy-footed and slow."

The other horse said, "My father is always kind to me. He always takes good care of me and calls me his child. He takes care of me as he would of his own baby. He never hits me with rocks or sticks. When he puts the saddle blanket on me he always brushes it and softens it so that it will not make my back sore. That's why I'm happy. I eat all I want and I'm fat. I'm very proud of my father. That is why, when I take him out anywhere, I am always light and dancing in front of all the people. I make him proud of me too."[26]

In conclusion, the Jicarilla storyteller always cautioned the children that the man who misused his horse was in constant danger of "horse sickness."[27]

Solomon Katchin echoed the same sentiments towards horses from the Kiowa-Apache of the past generations: "They didn't abuse them. It was forbidden to hit a horse on the face or with a bridle or with a saddle blanket."[28] Writing of the Western Apache groups, Goodwin observed the same fear of retaliation reflected in their treatment of horses:

Occasionally a man will beat his horse, and I once saw a man do this when his horse hid from him, but it is uncommon and considered cruel and likely to bring horse sickness upon the individual. Animals trespassing on a corn field are sometimes mutilated or even killed as an exactment of a penalty on the animal's owner, but the Apache do not compare such treatment with the beating of a horse.[29]

Navajo ideas on injuries received from horses and the remedy for them are well in accord with the attitudes of the Apache peoples expressed in the above examples. When a Navajo is suffering from a misfortune directly attributed to a horse, he or she will have a Flint Way (or Life Way) ceremony sung, and will address prayers at different intervals during the ceremony to a guardian horse spirit, calling upon it to repair the damages the real horse has done. The injured person will also placate the real horse by making an offering of pollen to the part of the horse's body that has caused the harm. Slim Curly, the Flint Way singer from Crystal, New Mexico, who gave Haile one of his two versions of the ceremony in 1939, said: "There is an offering (of pollen) to the horse's track, if the person has been kicked by a horse, a pollen offering to the horse's body, if it has thrown a person, a pollen offering to its head, if the horse has injured the person with its head."[30]

While the Navajo and Apache agree on the cause behind the injuries received from horses and the remedy for them, the ceremonial procedures for restoring the patient are completely different. The Navajo Flint Way follows the basic outline of its origin myth, in which the hero offends White Thunder and is in return gravely injured. Afterwards White Thunder contributes to the hero's cure in a ceremony conducted by the singer Gila Monster.[31] The prayers of this ceremony invoke the recuperative powers of guardian horse spirits along with those of White Thunder. The Apache way is altogether dissimilar. As in ceremonies for the care and treatment of the horse itself, those held for the recovery of humans are founded upon the direct communication of individual shamans with spiritual potencies, not, like the Navajo, upon traditional mythical forms.[32]

The Navajo Flint Way, like the Beauty Way and the Water Chant, combats many incapacities besides those traceable to the horse. A general description of its utility will enable the reader to see something of the whole design of Navajo curative ceremonialism and the place of horse powers within it. According to Haile, the major authority on Flint Way, this ceremony is beneficial against injuries caused "by a rolling stone or log, a misstep causing a fall against a stone, a tree or the ground, a fall in water, an injury caused by sheep, injuries in childbirth, fractures or dislocation of bones, and similar injuries that are considered internal. . . ."[33] In each case the spirit addressed in prayer is the one responsible for the mishap.

Flint Way takes its name from the flints and arrowheads and flint-decorated paraphernalia of the ceremony. Haile noted that the Navajo do not think of these "as surgical implements, but feel that the arrowheads, originally prescribed at the home of flint for use in Flintway ceremonials, are symbolical of the restoration of fractured or dislocated bones, as well as of impaired vitality in general." The regenerative association is so strong, in fact, that in Flint Way the Navajo never use "flints and arrowheads as cutting, or even as lacerating implements."[34]

Since "life medicine" is administered throughout the ceremony, Flint Way is often popularly called Life Way. One of Gladys Reichard's Navajo informants, Jim Smith, told her that "Flint Way (*bé cé*) is a word of the Holy People; Life Way, a word by which the Earth People denote the same thing."[35] The name Life Way is appropriate, too, because everything in the ceremony pulls life together in an effort to recapture the original order of the life substances. How Flint Way accomplishes its difficult task is best described by Haile's summary of the ceremony's origin myth:

> To demonstrate his power over life the singer, Gila Monster, deliber-
> ately destroys himself and broadcasts his body parts. When reas-
> sembled, the living pouch [the chief medicine symbol of the cer-
> emony] is made to step across these body parts and thus impart life to
> them again. Living medicine people then furnish the pattern for the
> figure of the hero's body which is to be restored. The lines on this
> figure are followed in reassembling even the minutest particles of
> flesh, blood, bone and marrow of the man. The living medicines
> themselves sing, while the living pouch puts life into the reassembled
> body parts. Spiders spin the marrow and ligaments of the bones, the
> sun and moon carriers restore his eye sockets, nerves and sight, deer
> birds prepare a stretcher on which he is to be transported, the
> medicine people continue to sing at every angle of his surroundings.
> Thus everything breathes life in an effort to restore the original
> lifestuff.[36]

The duration of Flint Way ceremonies is not fixed by a time limit as other Navajo ceremonies usually are. Kluckhohn and Leighton state that a Flint Way ceremony "continues until relief occurs or until that particular form of treatment is given up as useless."[37] Reichard found that "the emer-gency character of the chant is doubtless the main reason for its flexibility and emphasis."[38] The Flint Way ceremony can last, then, for one day or one night only, or it can combine various medicinal rites and continue uninterrupted for five days.[39]

The manner in which Blessing Way can take the form of a separate ceremony or be combined with other ceremonies has been noted previ-ously.[40] According to Haile, Flint Way "borrows heavily" from Blessing Way, incorporating many of its songs and prayers. As in the separate Blessing Way ceremony, "singing and praying consume most of the time" allotted to the patient.[41]

When the individual being treated has been injured by a horse, the prayer to the horse spirit is similar to the song addressed to the turquoise horse of the sun in Blessing Way.[42] The singer seats himself in front of the patient while reciting the prayer, and the patient repeats it verbatim.[43] The horse spirit implored is always of the same color as the horse that caused

the accident. The following prayer to the turquoise (gray) horse, recorded
by Haile from Slim Curly, is typical:

> Horse of the sun, who puffs along the surface of the earth, turquoise
> horse, I have made a sacrifice to you![44]
> Coming from the home of turquoise, from the floor of turquoise,
> from the square rooms of turquoise, along the outtrail controlled by
> turquoise, along the trail at the tip of turquoise, you, who travel
> along by means of turquoise!
> When you have come upon me by means of your feet of turquoise,
> you have thereby perfectly restored my feet, you have thereby wholly
> restored my legs, you have thereby perfectly restored my body, you
> have thereby wholly restored my mind, you have thereby restored
> my voice![45]

If the guilty horse is a bay, or red-maned, then the red horse is substituted for the turquoise, and the stones changed likewise. A black horse
calls for the jet horse spirit and jet stone; a yellow horse (yellowish-brown
or chestnut roan) for the abalone horse spirit and abalone shell. All these
are the property of Sun. On the other hand, if a white or white-maned
horse caused the injury, the situation demands the "horse of the moon"
(white bead horse), and white bead as the stone.[46] After the above invocation comes the main blessing, the same for all Flint Way ceremonies,
regardless of the color of the horse spirit invoked:

> Let the power that enables you to inhale also enable me to inhale, let
> the power that enables you to exhale also enable me to exhale, let the
> power that enables you to utter a word also enable me to utter words,
> let the power that enables you to speak also enable me to speak!
> Let the means that keep your feet in health also keep my feet in
> health!
> Let the means that keep your legs in health also keep my legs in
> health!
> Let the means that keep your body in health also keep my body in
> health!
> Let the means that keep your mind in health also keep my mind in
> health!
> Let the means that keep your voice in health also keep my voice in
> health!
> With its aid you have nicely made me perfect again, you have wholly
> restored me! You have put me back into my former condition!
> May you nicely restore me! Nicely you have restored me! May
> you nicely raise me on my feet, do walk me out nicely!

Do cause me to walk about nicely! May it be pleasant wherever I
go!

May it always be pleasant in my rear wherever I go! May it
always be pleasant in my front wherever I go! Pleasant again it has
come to be, pleasant again it has come to be![47]

After this prayer is another, called "Its Blessing Part," addressed to
Pollen Boy and Cornbeetle Girl. This likewise "is identical for all Flintway
prayers," Slim Curly told Haile, and it cannot be omitted even though it is
almost the same as the above prayer, except for the invocation.[48] The patient may request that any of these prayers be said at any time in the
ceremony.

During the prayers, the patient holds two crane bills in his hands,
from either sandhill cranes or diving herons, prepared by the Flint Way
singers to serve as the chief medicine symbols of the ceremony and func-
tioning as the crow bills do in the curing rites of the Enemy Way.[49] These
prayers must be spoken with the shoes off, so that their powers will "not
be recited into the shoes."[50] They should never be repeated except when
a Flint Way ceremony is in progress. For this reason Haile had trouble
convincing his informants to dictate the prayers to him.[51] There is even a
proper season to recount the story, prayers, or songs of Flint Way, that
between November and February, because Thunder, who acts as the destroyer of life in the Flint Way myth, is highly active during the summer
months, and it is dangerous to mention his name at that time. This limita-
tion does not, however, pertain to performances of the Flint Way ceremony; it can be given whenever it is needed—summer or winter—to
meet a crisis. If the prayers should be spoken out of season, "a sacrifice, in
the shape of a jewel and pollens, should be made to a lightning-struck
tree, in order to lift the taboo or fear of thunder, wind and other
supernaturals."[52]

In a preceding chapter a Chiricahua Apache injured on a raid was
cured by a horse and granted simultaneously the power to restore other
victims of accidents.[53] The same account of this Apache's experiences also
provides a characteristic example of the way the Apache employ their
horse ceremonies to treat the ailments of human beings. The physician
horse gave the man ceremonial songs, saying: "If anyone falls off a horse
and is injured, you can heal him with these songs. These songs will cure
even if bones are broken. And here is some medicine to use for those
who are hurt inside. But if the large cords at the back of the neck are
broken, the ones that hold up the head, this ceremony will not be able to
restore the person."[54]

When the Chiricahua got back to camp, he started to practice his ceremony. How successful he was is evidenced by the following:

A leading man rode out with others to get horses that they had tied out somewhere. The rest came back, but this leading man was still missing. His family were worried. Then someone saw his horse standing on a ridge. It was saddled, but the man was not on it. A group went out to look for him. They found him in a gully, unconscious and badly hurt. He had started from one hill to go to another where he had a horse tied to a tree, when the horse he was riding stepped into a badger hole, stumbled, and threw him.

They put him in a blanket, and four men, one carrying each end, brought him home. They asked the man who had learned the ceremony from the horse if he would bring the leader back to life. He said he would do it.

He told the people to get four poles like those which are used for the ceremonial tepee of the girl's puberty rite.[55] The shaman had the people make a tepee, one big enough so that the horse could get in. He had them bring the injured man in there. The doorway was to the east, and for a covering to it the shaman hung up a big buckskin with the head downward and touching the ground. They brought the horse which had caused the accident around facing the door and took the rope off him.[56]

This last bit of preparation illustrates the Apache feeling that the responsible horse can be pacified and help to undo the damages it wrought in anger. It is common occurrence for the shaman to demand that the offended horse be brought near the tepee where the ceremony is being held, so that the shaman may seek its cooperation, addressing it in songs and prayers, begging it to forgive the patient and help repair the damage. As Opler once noted in commenting upon a horse ceremony similar to the one above, "The horse is usually led to the patient during the latter part of the rite and if it neighs or demonstrates any interest in the patient at this time, it is considered a fortunate sign and an indication that the animal is relenting and will permit the cure to take place."[57]

But to return to the preceding ceremony:

The shaman, who was in the tepee, sang one song. The horse did not move. The shaman went on to his second song. The horse just stood there and made no sound. The shaman sang his third song. The horse stood in the same place. The shaman grew angry now. He spoke to the horse and said, "Why don't you cure this poor man? You are the only one that can help him. You had better do it without delay." The son of the shaman came out of the tepee now. He was angry too. He said to the horse, "You have done enough harm. There is no use thinking more evil things. You'd better neigh and do what you are supposed to." He hit the horse in the mouth.[58]

Then the horse began to walk to the tepee by itself. The horse stopped at the door, put its nose under the buckskin, pushed it up, and walked in. Then the horse approached the man from each of the four directions in sunwise order and neighed each time. Then it left the tepee. The shaman sang his last song.[59]

And now the patient, who had not stirred previously, suddenly arose, inquired about what had taken place, and "was all right after that."[60]

Apache horse ceremonies for treating humans, like those for other purposes, vary considerably in detail, no two ever being exactly the same. An account describing one held at the scene of an accident exemplifies how another Chiricahua shaman followed a completely different procedure. This incident occurred, a Chiricahua Apache recalled, at a little settlement named Baharito when a group of Apache were rounding up some mustangs. A man called P. was riding a horse that caught its foot in a hole, stumbled, and fell with him. When the narrator and his companions rushed to P's side, they found him lying on the ground, mouth gaping, as though dead. The horse he had been riding was not hurt at all; in fact, "it got up and walked a little ways and stood there."[61] A horse shaman named T. happened to be present. He told the others not to touch P., and they obeyed him, for it is an Apache belief that a person injured by a horse can be restored quicker if no one touches him before a horse shaman begins to administer treatment.

T. started trying to revive P. immediately. "Praying softly to himself," he approached his patient from the east, "touched him, kicked him four times under the foot, put pollen in his mouth, and told him to get up. And P. did." Then T. walked over to the place where the accident had occurred, picked up some dirt from four of the horse's tracks, and "put it in P's mouth." He also obtained saliva from the horse's mouth and smeared it "all over P's clothes." From that time forward P. was never bothered anymore by his injury.[62]

Instances are reported, too, in which horse ceremonies administered to humans were very simple affairs, consisting of little more than a few wonder-working songs sung at a time of crisis by a person who possessed horse power. One such was reported from near Whitetail, New Mexico, on the Mescalero Apache Reservation. Some rebellious horses, not wishing to be roped for branding, knocked an Apache down. The man was "nearly dead," the observer reported, when the shaman started to sing over him, and it was "three or four hours" before he regained consciousness. Some herbs were administered, but the treatment was chiefly a matter of songs, one of which the observer remembered, commenting, "If you ever get hurt from a horse, it will fix you up":

> The sun's horse is a yellow stallion;
> His nose, the place above his nose, is of haze,
> His ears, of the small lightning, are moving back and forth;
> He has come to us.
> The sun's horse is a yellow stallion,
> A blue stallion, a black stallion;
> The sun's horse has come out to us.[63]

Various accounts illustrate that some Apache horse shamans borrowed ideas from traditional long-life ceremonies like the puberty ceremony, as when, for instance, the Apache shaman mentioned earlier insisted that a ceremonial tepee be constructed with four poles, like the ones used in the puberty ceremony, before he would conduct his horse ceremony. But his borrowings are minor compared to those of the female Chiricahua shaman whose success in breaking broncos has already been treated.[64] Everyone said that the "old woman who knew the ceremony of the horse" had such good fortune with horses, and owned so many that "were nice and fat," because "she knew songs for them." People came to her for aid in healing. "When anyone fell off a horse and got hurt, they went to her and she cured them."[65] The analogies between her horse ceremony and the girl's puberty ceremony are many and striking. A ceremony she once conducted over a man who had been dragged by a horse and seriously injured was widely talked about among her people as one of the most elaborate they had ever beheld. A fellow tribesman of hers remembered seeing her perform this ceremony when he was a small boy and hearing his family talk about it for years afterwards:

> One time a young man got a bunch of horses. With the others there were wild horses and mules which had never been saddled or roped. He tried to get one wild horse out of that bunch. He roped it and put the halter on it. He staked it out for a while. Then he turned it loose on a long rope. He watered it and tried to pull it back. It tried to get away. It circled him two or three times and then started to run. The rope caught on his legs and he was dragged over a rough place. Finally the rope broke and he lay there. His face, arms, and legs were skinned. He was unconscious.

They picked him up and carried him to his tepee. Then his people
went to this woman and asked her to sing over the man. She came
and looked at him. "He's pretty much bruised up," she said. She
didn't want to do it. But they begged her. At last she said she would.

She started to work. I was there, just a little fellow then. She said,
"I want a bridle, a saddle blanket, a saddle, and a whip." She asked
for those four things because her power told her to. They gave these
to her. She started to sing. First she told the father of the boy to rope
that same horse. He did.

"Tie him close to the tepee."

They tied the horse near by, under a big tree. She had them tie the
head so that the horse couldn't eat grass or drink water. "If that horse
eats or drinks during this ceremony, the boy will get worse," she said.
She sang over this young man for four nights. She sang from sunset
to sunrise for the four nights. The horse had nothing to eat or drink
for the four days and nights.

They were in a tepee like the one the Mescalero have. The last day
at sunrise she told them to take the cover off and leave nothing but
the poles standing. Then she told them to clean up the inside. The sick
man was lying there. She painted the sun on the palm of her hand
with red paint and pollen. She sang and rubbed it off on the man's
face.[66]

The reference to the Mescalero style of tepee, the woman shaman's
painting "the sun on the palm of her hand with red paint and pollen," and
then rubbing it off on the man's face while singing a ceremonial song, all
these are familiar motifs from the Chiricahua girl's puberty ceremony.
The Chiricahua, now living with the Mescalero, hold their puberty ceremony with the Mescalero in the Mescalero type of tepee. According to
Opler, in building their ceremonial tepees, the Mescalero "use four main
poles of spruce and eight others—twelve in all. . . . They also build the
tepee with a runway of eight smaller spruces, four on either side, stretching eastward from the doorway." He writes that before the Chiricahua
came to live with the Mescalero, there was probably "a great deal of local
variation" practiced among them in the building of their ceremonial tepees,
noting that "most Chiricahua informants claim that their tribe used a
four-pole tepee without runway. But a number of spokesmen have mentioned either the twelve-pole structure, the runway, or both, as aboriginal
Chiricahua features."[67] Also, the woman shaman's demands that the cover
of the tepee be taken off at dawn has puberty ceremony echoes. No
doubt her reason for demanding this was so that the sun's rays could
reach the injured man. At dawn on the last day of the puberty ceremony,

Like the Chiricahua and Mescalero, the Western Apache also construct a conical-shaped frame for their ceremonial tepees with four main evergreen poles, each of which is associated in song with the four sacred directional horses.

the final events take place on the eastern side of the ceremonial structure so that the sun's rays can reach the pubescent girl while she is being painted in a manner similar to the way the injured man in the above account was painted.[68]

The Chiricahua who told about the woman horse shaman's ceremony said that after she had rubbed the painting of the sun symbol on the patient's face, she went over to the tree nearby, where the horse that caused the injury had been tied, and released it. As soon as she did this,

> Everybody got away. The horse began to paw the ground and
> neighed four times. Then it started to walk toward the man. The

horse went in there. The woman said, "Take the blanket off that man," and they did so.

The horse licked the man all over and rubbed him all over with his nose. Everyone watched. The horse was on the east side and it pawed there. Then it went to the south side and pawed the ground. And it did this in turn to the west and north. Then it went around the man four times and out to the east. It looked around for other horses. It saw some and ran to them. Then this man's senses began to come back to him and he got well.[69]

The Chiricahua female horse shaman was not typical of her sex. In Western Apache groups—the White Mountain, San Carlos, Cibecue, Northern Tonto, and Southern Tonto—women were usually excluded from handling wild horses. They were also handicapped in religious activities, since they were considered weaker than men. Because of this belief about women's stamina, they were thought to be more vulnerable than men were to the dangers involved in controlling certain powers. "Only a few women have acquired power by direct supernatural experiences," Goodwin states.[70]

Powers can make very exacting demands upon the individuals who exercise them. A White Mountain Apache tale concerning a guardian horse's jealousy is a good example. Goodwin collected this tale from a White Mountain Apache named Francis Drake, of Bylas, Arizona. It tells of how an Apache lad, captured by enemies—apparently Mexican or Spanish— was given a horse to escape from captivity by one of the soldiers who befriended him. According to Drake, the youth had ridden only a short distance from the enemy camp on his fine horse when he discovered that the horse could talk. It began to give him detailed instructions on how to get safely back to his encampment. The youth followed these instructions, which led him safely past many black, blue, yellow, and white bears. Encounters with such dreaded creatures as these bears of the four directions symbolized the dangerous tests of the journey to the "holy home" of a power, which any Apache seeking superhuman power must take.[71] The talking horse and the youth became the best of friends, and just before they arrived safely at the boy's camp, the horse asked the youth if he were married. When the youth said he was not, the horse cautioned him: "Well, don't get married. If you do it will be the end of things between you and me."[72]

After the Apache had returned home safely, he began to fall into his old patterns of living. His family was frightened because the horse could talk. The horse also annoyed them because it would not drink water from the river as other horses did, but insisted on drinking out of a pan like a human being. Moreover, the horse refused to eat grass; he insisted on eating the same food the family ate, and they came to dislike him because he ate too much. When the Apache had been home a month, his old girlfriend came to see him one evening and they sat up all night talking.

The next morning after the girl had left, the Apache went out to water his horse, but the horse would have nothing to do with him. He said: "You stink too much."[73] The truth was, of course, that the horse was jealous because the Apache had visited with his girlfriend. For three days the downhearted Apache could not make his horse drink or eat with him, and on the fourth morning when he went out to where he had tied his horse, he found only a rope hanging there. The horse had disappeared, leaving no tracks behind him.

The Apache searched in vain for his horse over three mountain ranges facing different points of the four directions. Finally when he had completed the cardinal circuit by going to the fourth mountain range, he found the tracks of his horse leading off somewhere. Suddenly, his horse appeared magically before him. Drake tells us that the horse said: "Well, there is nothing to be done now. You can't take me back. I have been to my old home and eaten food there already. For this reason I can't go back with you. I told you not to have anything to do with a girl, but you stayed with a girl all night."[74]

The lad cried because he believed he had lost the companionship of his guardian horse forever. But the horse took pity on him, and although he denied him earthly companionship, he offered the youth a horse ceremony instead. And so, according to Drake, "it was this man who first acquired the horse power and ceremony and this was how he got it."[75]

Because of the exacting demands a power can make on an individual in their society, many Jicarilla Apache refuse ceremonies when offered them; but individuals who follow the guide of a power and accept its ceremony are believed to be in communication with it at all times. According to Opler, the Jicarilla often say of a shaman, "For his power he works."[76] On the other hand, individuals in Chiricahua and Mescalero societies often court the recognition and favor of a guardian power. They feel that the gift is "something to live by," something with which they can always communicate through the medium of song and prayer, and on which they can always depend for guidance.[77]

The payment of a horse or horses to an Apache horse shaman, or any other kind of shaman for that matter, used to be a standard way among all the Apache for reimbursing practitioners for their services. The Navajo also paid in horses singers who had performed at any curative ceremony, regardless of the animal or agent blamed for the illness. This tradition is doubtless changing now that dollars are replacing horses, though it has probably not disappeared completely. An agreement used to be reached in advance of the ceremony, and according to the son of a famous Apache shaman, this is the way a sick man often approached the shaman:

> This is the way I have seen my father do his ceremony. Let us say I am a pretty sick man. I ride up on my horse. I come in with my turquoise and an eagle feather through it. I have pollen in my hand in a buckskin bag. I take some of the pollen in my right hand. I hold it up to the east, then I turn to the south, then to the west, then to the north, sunwise. I say, "My father (whether the shaman is my father or not), I hope with what you know I can get relief." I say to him, "This is your power," and I place a cross of pollen on his right foot. The shaman is sitting with his fingers touching his knees. Then I take my pollen and bring it up to the knee, then to the fingertips, down the left leg again, to the left foot, where I again make the cross with pollen. I still have the turquoise and eagle feather in my right hand. I either tie it to the buckskin string on his right moccasin or else just put it on there and he will pick it up.
>
> Then I will be standing before him and say, "There is my horse standing just as I got off him, with my bridle, saddle, and blanket. I am a poor man. I want to live. I have given you all I have." Then I sit down.
>
> Maybe he will not say anything for a while. I look as sick as I can so he will take pity on me. I am waiting for his answer. Finally he says, "All right," if he wants to take the case. He knows I am sick and have to be attended to right away. He says, "Bring your blankets and stay here."[78]

No Apache shaman is under obligation to use his or her power to cure people, though it is true that this is the most general use made of it. Sometimes shamans will only use their power to treat their immediate families. Others, however, seek requests for their ceremonies and are recognized among their people for the cures that they are given credit for having achieved.[79] The accounts of shamans' ceremonies and their success at curing usually come from people who believe in them—their families or people whom they have successfully treated—or from the shamans themselves. But all shamans are open to sharp criticism by skeptics who doubt their claims to more than mortal powers. Opler noted that when a certain Chiricahua shaman became aware that he was surrounded by doubters at a ceremony he was performing over a man, he told them: "Many of you people don't believe in what I'm doing. You think I'm a fake. I tell you to your faces that many of you will be willing to be this man when you see how I restore him."[80]

Impiety, the Apache say, is always a sure way to offend a power whose ceremony is in progress. A Lipan Apache tale of Cowbird and his switch-stick demonstrates the dangers to which a skeptic subjects himself by scoffing at a ceremony in which his companions have faith. We are already acquainted with the Lipan tradition that Killer-of-Enemies gave Cowbird important responsibilities in controlling horses on earth, especially power over the breaking of mustangs.[81] But Lipan mythology informs us that Cowbird's ceremonial duties with horses did not end here. The culture hero also asked him to help Lipan shamans "cure troubles caused by the horse," specifically designating the injuries of which he wanted him to take charge: "If anything happens to anyone because of a horse, if someone gets stepped on or is thrown by a horse, the one who cures the sick one must mention your name in his prayers and songs . . . and then you must help them."[82]

In the Lipan tale, a group of Apache had made several unsuccessful attempts to steal a bunch of fine horses from Cowbird, whom they recognized as the owner. Then finally one day, after the sly bird had once again outwitted them by driving his horses into a pond of water and disappearing with them, the men had been fortunate enough to find his switch-stick lying on the bank of the pond. Percy Bigmouth, a man of Lipan-Mescalero ancestry, who narrated this story in 1935, said the stick was "covered with sweat and dust," and "looked as though it had been used on the horses."[83]

The Lipan took Cowbird's power-stick back to camp with them and called in a man who knew "the horse ceremonially" to give them advice on how to use the stick to get the handsome herd of horses, particularly a big black stallion with a bald face, away from their bird owner. The horse shaman put the Cowbird's stick in front of the men and had each one blow cigarette smoke on it four times and ask for a horse of a certain color he desired. Meanwhile the shaman prayed to "the power of the horse" to help the men obtain the herd.

All of the men had faith in what the horse shaman was doing except one. Percy Bigmouth said this man scoffed: "Why do we blow on a stick? It is nothing but a stick!" He grabbed the stick, "rubbed it between his legs and threw it away."[84]

The other men strongly disliked his doing that, for they respected the stick, and later their faith paid off. When they went out again seeking the choice herd, each man, except the skeptic, got without the slightest trouble the very color of horse he had asked for at the horse shaman's ceremony.

Percy Bigmouth told the fate of the skeptic:

> ... the man who had rubbed the stick between his legs got nothing. He fell off and hurt himself and was brought home unconscious.
>
> They asked the shaman who knew the horse [ceremony] to hold a ceremony over this man and he was cured. But the shaman told him he must never make fun when others were having a ceremony, that he would break a leg or an arm if he did. So after that he behaved.[85]

The idea that horses can be witched to bring evil to humans is a common one among the Navajo and Apache. If an illness emanating from a horse is long continued, simple retaliation may not seem to be adequate cause. A shaman may review the symptoms again with the patient and decide that although these point to "horse sickness," they suggest besides the intervention of an evil human agent. Opler writes that a common saying among the Apache is: "A witch may cause any animal to attack you or make you sick." One of his Apache informants defined sorcery as "making an individual do something evil by the power of some animal or spirit."[86] The Leightons, agreeing in general with Opler, affirm that almost every sickness among the Navajo can be traced sooner or later to witchcraft if there is any mystery at all surrounding it.[87] One Navajo observed that while a "witch can use anything to make someone sick," or "pray" that a person "be killed by anything," horses, rocks, and sheep were some of the most common instruments for carrying out a witch's schemes.[88]

When a witch wishes to cause evil influences through an animal or another being, it may call upon the appropriate power to make a certain individual sick, or even worse, to kill him or her. If the control over the power is effective, it listens and works the desired harm. If the victim is fortunate, "someone else with stronger power and good power sees it," according to an Apache, and "tells you that someone got you sick. . . ."[89] One Navajo described the routine of the witch in this way: ". . . it sets a day and says bad spells—it might say a horse will kick you, lightning hit you, snake bite you, and it happens that way."[90] Another thought that the witch could "set a date" when "a horse might roll over on you or something;" he vowed that the date of the unfortunate event "comes out just right."[91]

The Navajo and Apache also believe that a sorcerer may shoot some object, which they call an "arrow," into the body of the intended victim, and that this missile in turn has to be sucked out of the patient by a medicine person, who uses either a tube or just the lips. To witch someone by a horse a sorcerer often makes a horsehair the "arrow."[92] The Apache shaman extracts the witch's "arrow" and spits it into the fire that is always built at every Apache or Navajo curing ceremony, and as it burns, it is supposed to make a "popping" sound. While the witch's "arrow" disintegrates in the flames, all the people at the ceremony spit to rid themselves of any evil imposed by the presence of the witch's symbol.[93]

When Navajos believe that they have been witched, they will often have the Enemy Way sung over themselves. Something belonging to the witch thought responsible will be obtained, if possible, so that it can be put in the ceremonial bundle. After the first night of singing in the hogan, the bundle containing the object or objects belonging to the witch is tied to a pole and given to a man who mounts a swift horse and carries it off, followed by a number of other men on horseback. They gallop away to another hogan a good distance from where the patient is being treated, there to meet a number of other mounted men and stage a mock battle with them. "The net result of all this procedure," Kluckhohn and Leighton state, "is thought to be that evil will be turned away from the patient and back upon the witch. The Navaho theory under all circumstances is that if the intended victim is too strong or too well protected the witch's evil backfires upon himself."[94]

Because Killer-of-Enemies bestowed upon Crow, as well as upon Cowbird, curative powers over humans—assigning Crow especially those that apply to "horse sickness"—the Apache believe that Crow is capable of preventing any harm that might be in store for a person from a horse.[95] In at least one instance the power of Crow was most efficacious, when a Mescalero Apache put it to use to protect himself against witchcraft astir at a peyote meeting; his particular power was that of the Clark's crow.[96] When a Mescalero whose witching-weapon was a water beetle confronted this man, he found him more than able to take care of himself. The man carried a crow feather around with him for protection. He took it out and shot it into the mouth of his adversary, who became very angry and endeavored to shoot his water beetle into the crow-power man, casting a spell in which a horse would kill him. But the water beetle went astray and the witchcraft failed. Furthermore, the water-beetle man fell desperately ill the next morning and died before anyone could cure him. "He was shot by his own 'arrows,'" the informant said, meaning that his witchcraft had turned upon him. "But nothing happened to the Clark's crow man. He was too strong."[97]

Navajo horseman at Round Rock, Arizona. The gods taught man not only how to care for the horse, but also how, by proper procedure, the horse might care for him.

Insanity is a disease often attributed to witchcraft by the Navajo and Apache. While, on the one hand, a horsehair sucked out of a patient may be a symbol of witchcraft, on the other, the Navajo say that a "twist of hair from a wild horse's tail" can serve as a protective amulet against insanity.[98] Acts of bestiality are often identified with insanity brought about by witch-craft. An eerie Kiowa-Apache tale tells of how a stallion steals a young bride with a weak character away from her husband and bewitches her until she becomes insane and acts like a mare. Ashamed of his bride's behavior, the husband kills her.[99]

Horses are also associated with witches in various other ways. Some of the Navajo believe that witches like to ride horses on their evil excur-sions. Swiftly they ride, too, for one Navajo declared that "nobody could catch a witch on horseback."[100] However, witches are not usually described as being in motion when they actually cast their enchantments from a horse. One man has it that a witch will "sit on horseback, not moving at all, and watch his victim who can't see him," maybe from the summit of canyon walls like those of Canyon de Chelly. This man had heard tales of how witches came there frequently to scrutinize their victims "down in [the] fields below."[101] Near Chinle, Arizona, in 1939, an incident occurred that confirms those tales: "That witch used to stand still on top of Canyon de Chelly and watch someone down in the canyon. Or, he would sit still a long time on his horse and do the same thing. Then, something would happen to the people he looked at like that. So, finally, they couldn't stand it any longer and they killed him."[102]

Were-animal beliefs also exist among the Navajo. Upon donning the hides of certain animals, "goat hides" or "colt hides" among them, the witch is transformed into the beast: "the hides come right down to the wrist."[103] But horses, it seems, are especially adept at detecting the presence of the man-beasts who prowl at night and at warning humans of their proximity. Some say that when a horse gets scared at night, and a human does not see anything about that should be disturbing it, the horse senses that such witches are close by. Others say that a horse can actually smell them, and that when he does, he jumps.[104]

The power of the tiny horsehair to inflict sickness or to protect the wearer from it only reflects on a small scale the large powers that the Navajo and Apache attribute to the horse. When we consider that a horse may wreak vengeance or carry out the evil purposes of a witch, but in like manner may heal sickness and injury perpetrated by itself or other beings, we gain some understanding of the complex and forceful role that the horse has played in Navajo and Apache illness, a role that in spite of its late introduction into their societies is equal to that played by those animals or spirits of older tradition. Thus, the mutual accord that grew between Indians and their greatest domestic beast was complete: the gods taught people not only how to care for the horse, but also how, by proper procedure, the horse might care for them.

Notes

1. As noted earlier, Water Monsters are common to Southern Athapascan mythologies. Additional information on Navajo water deities is supplied in the following: Reichard, *Navaho Religion,* II, pp. 490–493; Father Berard Haile and Maud Oakes, recorders, *Beautyway: A Navaho Ceremonial,* Leland C. Wyman, ed., Bollingen Series, LIII (New York: Pantheon Books, 1957), p. 179; and Fishler, *In the Beginning,* pp. 29–30. For information on Apache water beings, see Opler, *An Apache Life-Way,* pp. 199–200; *supra,* p. 203.

2. Reichard, *Navaho Religion,* II, p. 490. See also Matthews, *Navaho Legends,* p. 168; p. 246, n. 210.

3. Wheelwright, *Hail Chant and Water Chant,* p. 222.

4. O'Bryan, p. 116.

5. Franciscan Fathers, *An Ethnologic Dictionary of the Navaho Language,* p. 358.

6. Franc J. Newcomb and Gladys A. Reichard, *Sandpaintings of the Navajo Shooting Chant* (New York: J. J. Augustin, 1937), pp. 61–62. The Shooting Way Chant is a

ceremony designed to cure illness brought about by lightning, arrows, and snakes. See ibid., p. 52.

7. Newcomb, "Navajo Symbols in Sand Paintings and Ritual Objects," p. 28.
8. Franciscan Fathers, *An Ethnologic Dictionary of the Navaho Language,* p. 359.
9. Fishler, *In the Beginning,* pp. 87–88. For another incident involving a Navajo maiden and a water horse, cf. O'Bryan, pp. 116–117.
10. Haile and Oakes, p. 8. See also p. 9, on which is mentioned the two-night short form of this ceremony. If the ceremony does not last five or nine nights, then the sweat and emetic rite is not given.
11. Ibid., p. 17.
12. Ibid., p. 8.
13. Ibid., pp. 35, 43, 97–101. Haile thinks the words have possible Pueblo or Apache origins. He says that "some verb forms suggest Jicarilla Apache, yet these parallels are too few in number to warrant a definite conclusion" (pp. 35–36).
14. Ibid., p. 44.
15 Ibid., pp. 100–102.
16. Ibid., p. 111; p. 179. Sandpaintings of the other water deities such as Water Monster, Blue Thunder, Big Otter, and Cloud Monster appear in two of the Beauty Way sandpainting reproductions. See ibid., Fig. 7, p. 175, and Plate XIII.
17. Newcomb and Reichard, p. 5.
18. Wheelwright, *Hail Chant and Water Chant,* pp. 68, 71, 76, 91, 106. See also Haile and Oakes, p. 15.
19. Wheelwright, *Hail Chant and Water Chant,* pp. 102–103.
20. See *supra,* pp. 121–122, 174–176.
21. Alexander H. Leighton and Dorothea C. Leighton, *The Navaho Door: An Introduction to Navaho Life* (Cambridge, Mass.: Harvard University Press, 1944), p. 32.
22. Ibid., p. 34.
23. Opler, *An Apache Life-Way,* p. 239; Castetter and Opler, pp. 17–18; Haile, *Navaho Flintway,* pp. 5, 8. For a book-length study of illnesses caused by the influence of the mountain animals and spirits and the ceremony used to cure them, see Leland C. Wyman, *The Mountainway of the Navajo* (Tucson: University of Arizona Press, 1975). For coyote's role in this connection, see Karl W. Luckert, *Coyoteway: A Navajo Holyway Healing Ceremonial* (Tucson: University of Arizona Press, 1979).
24. Fishler, *In the Beginning,* p. 67.
25. Opler, *An Apache Life-Way,* p. 239.
26. Opler, *Myths and Tales of the Jicarilla,* pp. 391–392.
27. See ibid., p. 392, n. 1.
28. McAllister, "Kiowa-Apache Tales," p. 52.
29. Goodwin, *The Social Organization of the Western Apache,* p. 554.
30. Haile, *Navaho Flintway,* p. 319, n. 302.
31. Ibid., pp. 7–8, 80–84.
32. For the discussion and comparison of Navajo and Apache ceremonies used to treat and care for horses, see *supra,* pp. 172–176.
33. Haile, *Navaho Flintway,* p. 10.

34. Ibid., p. 2. The home of flint, where the final arrangements concerning the Flint Way ceremony were made, is according to Navajo tradition "north of the present [Navajo) reservation and seems," Haile writes, "to correspond with the Sun Temple in Mesa Verde Park." See ibid., p. 6.

35. Reichard, *Navaho Religion*, I, p. 330.

36. Haile, *Navaho Flintway*, pp. 7–8.

37. Kluckhohn and Leighton, p. 155.

38. Reichard, *Navaho Religion*, I, p. 332.

39. Haile, *Navaho Flintway*, p. 9. In the version of Flint Way that Slim Curly recited to Haile, a nine-night ceremony is mentioned as being discontinued because of Monster Slayer's interference. Haile's other informant, also named Curly (who lived in Chinle, Arizona), referred to a discontinued nine-night ceremony too, but neither informant elaborated on the details of the nine-night Flint Way. See ibid., pp. 5–6.

40. See *supra*, pp. 121–122.

41. Haile, *Navaho Flintway*, p. 2.

42. See *supra*, p. 226.

43. Haile, *Navaho Flintway*, p. 38.

44. The sacrifice referred to in this line means that the patient has made an offering of pollen to the part of the horse's body that has caused him the injury. This offering has already been described. See *supra*, pp. 228–229.

45. Haile, *Navaho Flintway*, pp. 287, 250. It will be noted that Haile gives only the first few lines of this prayer to the horse on p. 287. He does this rather than repeat the entire prayer pattern, which is given under the Sun Carrier part of the long "Prayer to the Crane," on p. 250. I have, therefore, repeated the entire prayer pattern as it would apply to a turquoise horse, since this is the way it would be rendered in the case of injury by a gray horse. See also p. 37, where Haile says: "Flintway prayers are practically of one pattern, which has been written out in full only in the Crane prayer, par. 64 [p. 244]. Other prayers are referred to this prayer, after the changes in the invocation, the home, trail and feet have been indicated."

46. Ibid., p. 287.

47. Ibid., pp. 250–251.

48. Ibid., p. 317, n. 254; pp. 38, 287. This prayer is found in par. 64a, pp. 251–253.

49. Ibid., pp. 22, 38. See also Reichard, *Navaho Religion*, I, p. 334.

50. Haile, *Navaho Flintway*, p. 38.

51. Ibid., p. 37.

52. Ibid., pp. 9, 37.

53. See *supra*, pp. 132–133.

54. Opler, *An Apache Life-Way*, p. 295. See n. 30 too, where Opler observes that the medicine the horse gave the Apache to use in his ceremony was "possibly 'horse medicine' (*Eriogonum jamesii*). . . ." For more information concerning the many uses to which the Navaho and Apache put this popular plant medicine in curing both humans and horses of their ailments, see *supra*, pp. 180–182.

55. The four poles of the ceremonial tepee for the girl's puberty ceremony of the Chiricahua Apache are associated with long life and the cardinal horses. See *infra*, p. 253.

56. Opler, *An Apache Life-Way*, p. 295.

57. See the note by Opler in Hoijer, *Chiricahua and Mescalero Apache Texts*, p. 147, n. 35:1.

58. Although not explained by the informant, it appears that the shaman, protected by the power over horses he has received in his experience with a guardian horse, can demand things of horses that would cause them to seek revenge on ordinary men. Also, the son's action in this account implies that he is serving as a ceremonial assistant to his father and is likewise protected by his father's power. Chiricahua and Mescalero shamans often teach their sons, grandsons, or nephews their ceremonies if their powers approve of it. See Morris Edward Opler, "The Concept of Supernatural Power Among the Chiricahua and Mescalero Apaches," *American Anthropologist*, new series, XXXVII, No. 1 (January–March 1935), pp. 68–69. However, this is not true of the Jicarilla, who believe that a power of some sort chooses every Jicarilla baby at birth to be its representative during the baby's life. Since it is believed, Opler notes, that "to each man is allotted but one such ceremony, the ceremony, no matter how valuable, cannot be transmitted to another." See his "A Summary of Jicarilla Apache Culture," *American Anthropologist*, new series, XXXVIII (April–June 1936), pp. 214–215.

59. Opler, *An Apache Life-Way*, p. 296.

60. Ibid.

61. Ibid., p. 298.

62. Ibid., also n. 31. Cf. the practice in Navajo witchcraft of using the dirt from the hoof-print and saliva from a horse's mouth to weaken an opponent's racing horse. See *supra*, pp. 185–186.

63. Opler, *An Apache Life-Way*, p. 298. Cf. this Apache song with the Navajo song describing the war god's horse as being composed of similar powerful forces. See *supra*, p. 16.

64. See *supra*, p. 177.

65. Opler, *An Apache Life-Way*, pp. 296–297.

66. Ibid., p. 297.

67. Ibid., pp. 96–97, n. 5.

68. Cf. ibid., pp. 130–131, where an account is given of the Chiricahua girl's puberty ceremony.

69. Ibid., p. 297. A shorter version of the above account of the woman horse shaman's ceremony appears in Hoijer, *Chiricahua and Mescalero Apache Texts*, p. 41. In this recording, translated by Hoijer as closely as possible to the original Chiricahua speech, the woman shaman is referred to as "this woman who was holy by means of [a] horse."

70. Goodwin, *The Social Organization of the Western Apache*, p. 535.

71. Goodwin, *Myths and Tales of the White Mountain*, pp. 83–84. Regarding the symbolical journey to the "holy home of the power," see Opler, *Myths and Tales of the Chiricahua*, p. 17, n. 1, and his "A Summary of Jicarilla Apache Culture," p. 214.

72. Goodwin, *Myths and Tales of the White Mountain,* p. 84.

73. Ibid., p. 85.

74. Ibid. Sexual continence must be observed by an Apache shaman while he is learning or practicing a ceremony. In this instance, the novice who was learning the power of the horse had offended his power and had to be punished.

75. Ibid., p. 86.

76. Opler, "A Summary of Jicarilla Apache Culture," pp. 214–215. Note also Opler's examination here of the subordinate role of shamanism and the ascendancy of traditional ceremonies among the Jicarilla Apache. While it is true that the Jicarilla, like other Apache peoples, place more emphasis on shamanistic ceremonies than the Navajo do, it is also true that they, more than other Apache groups, stress their traditional or "long life" rites. This is due mainly to the fact that their religion has also been deeply influenced by those of the Pueblo Indians, though not to the heavy extent that Navajo religion has been. Jicarilla and Navajo religions also appear to have influenced each other.

77. Castetter and Opler, p. 22.

78. Opler, *An Apache Life-Way,* p. 273.

79. Castetter and Opler, p. 23.

80. Opler, *An Apache Life-Way,* p. 313.

81. See *supra,* p. 176–177.

82. Opler, *Myths and Legends of the Lipan,* p. 31.

83. Ibid., pp. 11, 75. It will be remembered from another story, which concerns the horse ceremony a Lipan shaman learned from the Cowbird's switch to use in caring for his horses, that the Cowbird is said to have stored his powers in this switch. For that story, see *supra,* pp. 166–167.

84. Opler, *Myths and Legends of the Lipan,* p. 76.

85. Ibid., pp. 76–77.

86. Opler, *An Apache Life-Way,* p. 242.

87. Ibid.; Leighton and Leighton, pp. 25–26.

88. Fishler, "Navaho Picture Writing," p. 63.

89. Opler, *An Apache Life-Way,* p. 242.

90. Kluckhohn, *Navaho Witchcraft,* p. 151.

91. Ibid., p. 150.

92. For more information on this subject, see the following works: Opler, *An Apache Life-Way,* p. 264; Castetter and Opler, p. 23; Kluckhohn, *Navaho Witchcraft,* pp. 154–157. Note especially in Opler, *An Apache Life-Way,* p. 264, where an Apache lists the following as other common objects of witchcraft: bones, sticks, needles, human hairs, spiders, and tiny buckskin pouches. Also note in Kluckhohn, *Navaho Witchcraft,* pp. 154–155, where a Navajo lists other witchcraft "arrows": ". . . porcupine quill, sharp points of yucca, charcoal from where a man died or was buried, tiny rocks from red ant house."

93. Opler, *An Apache Life-Way,* p. 264.

94. Kluckhohn and Leighton, p. 129.

95. See Opler, *Myths and Legends of the Lipan,* p. 31. Also note in this myth about Killer-of-Enemies assigning curative powers to Crow the Lipan belief that before

Crow will "take charge" of a ceremony and lend a horse shaman his aid, the person seeking the shaman's services has to give the shaman a black horse to represent Crow, who is "black all over" too. For other mythical accounts concerning Crow's association with horses, see *supra,* pp. 94–98.

96. Opler, "The Influence of Aboriginal Pattern and White Contact on a Recently Introduced Ceremony, the Mescalero Peyote Rite," p. 156. This particular kind of crow is also often called the nutcracker, or Clark's nutcracker. It is a grayish-white bird (*Nucifraga columbiana*) found in western North America.

97. Ibid.

98. Lee, "Navajo Medicine Man," p. 9.

99. For this tale, see McAllister, Kiowa-Apache Tales," pp. 97–100.

100. Kluckhohn, *Navaho Witchcraft,* p. 139.

101. Ibid., p. 151.

102. Ibid., p. 213.

103. Ibid., p. 139.

104. Ibid., pp. 139, 140.

The Horse's Role in Folk Customs and Other Ceremonies

THE ROLE OF THE HORSE IN HEALING WAS ONLY ONE OF MANY that it played in Navajo and Apache societies. Again and again, at some important juncture in a person's life, the horse filled the need for symbolic assistance. A closer look at some of these events will demonstrate the amazing extent to which the horse has penetrated Southern Athapascan folkways.

In Birth Customs

The horse entered the life of a male Navajo or Apache shortly after his birth. A Navajo mother, to assure her son's mastery over horses, would take his umbilical cord and tie it to the tail or mane of a horse, to remain there until it wore away, for it was a part of the body believed to have control over the child's destiny after it was separated from the navel.[1] An Apache mother would bury the cord in a horse track, so that her son would be always industrious and devoted to taking care of horses.[2] Babies of either sex were often fed mare's milk to bring them good health, for the Navajo in particular believed that mare's milk was superior to cow's milk for building strong and sturdy muscles, bones, and teeth.[3]

In Puberty Ceremonies

Horses again find symbolic expression in many of the puberty ceremonies that all the Southern Athapascan peoples except the Kiowa-Apache hold to initiate a girl into womanhood.[4] The cardinal horses are invoked in song by the Chiricahua and Mescalero Apache to obtain long life and good luck for a pubescent girl. Explaining the many purposes behind the

Today's Apache mothers still practice customs with the umbilical cords of tots like the tiny girl in the camp dress peering out from between the legs of her father's jeans. The rites are to assure babies of a continuing future with horses, which have always played a vital role in their parents' livelihood.

ceremonial songs, a Chiricahua Apache had these comments to make: "All the singing is supposed to work out the future life for the girl in order . . . that she have long life. The songs bring good luck. The ceremony works good luck for everyone that takes part in it. . . ."[5]

Even today, in the joint Chiricahua and Mescalero puberty ceremony, a song is sung about the blue, yellow, black, and white stallions who stand for long life.[6] It is sung at dawn while the male relatives of the girls participating in the ceremony erect four newly cut spruce poles to support the ceremonial tepee. It is called a "dwelling song" because the tepee will serve as the ceremonial home of White Painted Woman, the Apache goddess with whom the pubescent girl is identified throughout the four-day ceremony. The words are:

> Killer of Enemies and White Painted Woman have made them so,
> They have made the poles of the dwelling so,
> For long life stands the blue stallion.

> Here Killer of Enemies and White Painted Woman have made them so,
> They have made the poles of the dwelling so,
> For long life stands the yellow stallion.

> Here Killer of Enemies and White Painted Woman have made them so,
> They have made the poles of the dwelling so,
> For long life stands the black stallion.

> Here Killer of Enemies and White Painted Woman have made them so,
> They have made the poles of the dwelling so,
> For long life stands the white stallion.[7]

Inside this ceremonial tepee, an older Apache woman, following the instructions left by White Painted Woman and Killer-of-Enemies (in some versions Child-of-the-Water) at the beginning of time, attends the maturing girl in all of her various activities. Though the girl and her attendant are not necessarily relatives, they call each other "mother" and "my daughter," a custom they continue observing for the rest of their lives.[8] The woman places the girl on "the skin of a four-year-old black-tailed deer" and lays in front of her "a coiled basket tray, made of the unicorn plant, filled with bags of pollen and with ritual objects."[9] Then she performs a "molding" rite, in much the same way that the Navajo White Bead Woman molded the first horse forms. Aided by pollen and other ritual objects from the basket tray, the woman with her hands reshapes the body of the girl into the beautiful form of womanhood.[10]

According to one Chiricahua Apache, the "dwelling song" mentioning the four horses is also sung for another purpose than long life. It "is about the black horse, the stallion, the four horses, because in this ceremony a horse is given on the last day."[11] In this way he was acknowledging that the final duty of the girl is to give the singer a horse in payment for the

At Canyon Day, Arizona, 1977: the older female sponsor directs the Apache girl's acts on the required deerskin during the re-enactment of White Painted Woman's puberty cermony. Behind them, the chorus offers songs rich in supplications that the vigor and beauty of the cardinal horses bless the girl with fertility, long life, and many valuable possessions like horses.

ceremony. "A horse, any kind of a horse, is required. It always was so and has been handed down," he noted, as he described how the girl, "still dressed in her costume," walks the horse over to the singer and presents it to him.[12] Another Apache observed that even if the father of a girl who went through the puberty ceremony had only one horse, he still "had to give it to the singer. . . . He had to do it according to the Indian way."[13]

The foregoing examples are good illustrations of the way in which horses took the place of dollars in earlier days. Even now as dollars and barter goods become more plentiful among the Apache and Navajo, horses are still thought of as the only proper payment for numerous ceremonial services of singers and shamans.

The Navajo too chant horse songs at the puberty ceremony for girls, inside the ceremonial hogan on the last night of the four-day ceremony. The Navajo named Charlie Mitchell reported that the singing begins late in the night after the assembled guests have eaten a cornmeal cake the girl has especially prepared as a part of her initiation rites. The people spread out their blankets, and "an old man, one of those who knows the Blessing Rite" starts to sing it, beginning with the twelve Hogan Songs. "Along with him the men, all of them, sing and the women too."[14] And while they sing, the hogan beams that point in the four directions are smeared with pollen. Then pollen is sprinkled in a circle all around the earthen floor of the hogan, and each person present is given a pinch of it to eat. After this blessing of the hogan and the crowd, other songs are offered as "the night goes on," Mitchell said. The audience sings "the Songs of the Goods, those who know them. Those who know the Songs of Changing Woman sing them. Those who know the Mountain Songs sing them. Those who know the Horse Songs sing them. Those who know the Sheep Songs sing them. And then, in between these, those who know the Blessing Songs sing them."[15]

Mitchell offers no explanation as to why the Navajo sing horse songs at the girl's puberty ceremony. It may simply be that they wish their horses to be blessed at the same time the girl is receiving a blessing. But it may also be that the four cardinal horses, which constitute a part of Navajo fertility symbolism, are involved in the ceremony, being associated with the four roof-beams of the hogan. Earlier we saw how the Navajo erected cardinal tie-posts around their hogans to bring health and increase to their horses, as well as how they put their good luck songs for horses into constant use to increase their herds.[16] The extension of fertility beliefs from animals to man is a simple and common practice.

Unfortunately, Mitchell did not record any of these songs for Sapir and Hoijer, so that we cannot compare them with two apparently similar songs included in previous chapters—songs obtained from Sandoval and Goldtooth, which White Bead Woman sang in creating horses for the Navajo. These songs, too, seem to symbolize human as well as animal fruitfulness. Sandoval's song relates that as each of the different-colored mares emerges from the direction appropriate to her hue, she is "changed into a maiden," while Goldtooth's records that the turquoise and the jet horses become girls and the white bead and oyster shell horses become boys. We can easily see how these songs could be made to serve a dual purpose, and it may well be that they had a place in some of the puberty ceremonies.[17]

At a puberty ceremony she attended on the Navajo Reservation in 1931, Dr. Frances Gillmor noticed further evidences of horse symbolism. Her unpublished notes indicate that bridles of horses were placed before the pubescent girl along with other ceremonial equipment. I cannot determine the exact function of these trappings, but there are at least three possibilities. Considering that Apache horse shamans display trappings to insure the cooperation of their powers, the bridles here may have signified that a Navajo singer was using them for a similar purpose. Or they may merely have been payment to the singer for services rendered. Or, seeing that the reproductive powers are such an important part of the Navajo puberty ceremony, it may be that the horses from which the bridles were taken were expected to receive by transference a portion of the fertility induced by the ceremony. In describing a Blessing Rite she saw performed to assure good health to a human patient, Oakes notes that some Navajo brought saddles and bridles in and placed them before the singer so that their horses could also share the rewards of the ceremony.[18]

The association of horse symbolism with other varieties in the Navajo girls' puberty ceremonies, as well as in the Apache, is much obscured by the shiftings and borrowings at work in all ceremonies transmitted from generation to generation. A good example of this point is the horse symbolism in evidence in the Jicarilla Apache puberty ceremony. On the surface, the meaning seems obscure, but a closer examination of Jicarilla mythology helps to clarify matters.

Unlike those of other Apache groups, the Jicarilla puberty ceremony includes boys as well as girls. Under the ceremonial leadership of the Jicarilla's anthropomorphic spirit named Black Hactcin, who molded the first Jicarilla horses and other animals from clay images before the Jicarilla emerged from the underworld, the pubescent girl and boy perform ritual acts for four days to assure themselves long life.[19] Their ritual acts bring good luck not only to them, but all the people. In the first puberty ceremony the holy people held to instruct the earth people—a story related in the ceremony's origin myth—it is said that Black Hactcin gave the boy and girl "little sticks shaped like a horse's leg and hoof" to use in scratching themselves.[20] It will be recalled that Jicarilla Apache raid leaders gave their companions the same kind of hoof-shaped scratch sticks, and for novice raiders such as Dirty Boy, going on their first four expeditions as part of their initiation into manhood, the gift of the stick was equivalent to receiving the leader's power.[21] In the puberty ceremony, where the girl and boy are told "not to scratch themselves with their fingers but only with these sticks," the observance is necessary for physical wholeness: if they scratched themselves with their nails, "there would be a scar left where they scratched."[22]

To digress for a moment, we may note that rubbing, like scratching, has a powerful effect upon the state of the body. Both the Navajo and the Apache rub their bodies to resuscitate themselves. As a Chiricahua explained: "We put grease on the legs when we eat in order to 'feed' them. It makes us good runners. After we eat fat meat there is grease on our hands, and we rub them on the legs and say, 'Let me be a fast runner.' Sometimes the leg bone of an animal is broken, and the marrow is rubbed on the lower legs, the forearms, the hair, and the face while this is said."[23] A Lipan folk tale describes the same practice.[24] The Navajo went so far as to perform the rituals daily, according to Reichard: "Formerly it was customary for people to rub their legs after the evening meal with a prayer: 'May they (legs) be lively; may I be healthy.'"[25] Solomon Katchin, one of McAllister's Kiowa-Apache informants, told of how his people had once shared in the power of the horse by cutting off "the forelock and pieces of warts from the horse's legs," rubbing them first together and "then over themselves."[26]

In the Jicarilla puberty ceremony, the girl and boy have their bodies ceremonially rubbed and pressed into a new shape by Black Hactcin, assisted in this instance by White Hactcin.[27] Afterwards, these holy beings present the scratching sticks to the boy and girl, and the following order of events makes it apparent why these ritual instruments are shaped like a horse's leg and hoof. The adolescents now run four times to the east, together, so that they will "be good runners after that."[28] Clearly, the use of the scratching sticks has infused their limbs with the speed and endurance of the horse, assuring swiftness in the ceremonial races that control their future well-being and fecundity.[29]

Later in the ceremony, when Black Hactcin assigns the boy his future responsibilities, horse symbolism is again apparent. He tells him "to look after the horses of the people and to bring them to the camp early in the morning . . . to run all the time at his work and never to walk."[30] The great extent to which the Jicarilla puberty ceremony stresses the boy's duties with horses is further displayed in the four additional runs the boy completes, without the girl, toward the cardinal directions. Each time he returns to the ceremonial tent, he brings grass and horse manure to represent the cardinal horse of a quarter and to symbolize his future tending of horses.[31]

After the fourth run, the shaman advises him: "My grandson, you should practice herding horses on foot. Having roped a good horse, you will put your hand on him, saying, 'This sort, my horses will be, very fat. They will like me. They will not become poor. All sorts of property will like me.' "[32]

In Marriage Customs

Another important occasion whose customs were greatly involved with horses was the time of marriage. Horses were traditional marriage gifts from the groom's family to the bride's family among all the Southern Athapascan tribes. Sometimes other gifts would accompany the horses, but prestige and social status suffered if the gift of a horse or horses did not bless the union. Without this, the marriage was not even considered to be legitimate, and both families were disgraced. On the other hand, according to Reichard, the presentation of a horse could make legal an irregular Navajo marriage: "If two people go off and live with each other they are not considered married, but if a child is born the man may give the woman's family horses and they [will] sanction the union."[33]

In the event of an elopement between a Kiowa-Apache girl and boy, McAllister observed, "the girl's parents had the right to go to the boy's parents and take whatever they wished, even to the tepee they were living in." But even so, the groom's family was expected to give horses and saddles before the marriage became official.[34]

The Navajo and the Apache felt that a virtuous daughter would attract valuable presents to her family. The number of horses given as a marriage gift among the Navajo depended to some extent upon the social status of the families involved. As many as twelve horses might be required for a girl from a wealthy family, but one or two could be offered for a bride of less affluence.[35] Among the Chiricahua, however, Opler noted that the number of horses given by the groom's family had "little bearing on the status of the principals."[36] A member of the tribe explained: "The woman's status is not affected by the amount of the present. The man who gives a great deal is just thought of as a man who is able to give a great deal. It's considered all right, but he can't raise his position that way. About four or five horses with saddles would be a very big present. A horse or two would be normal and average."[37]

On the other hand, Goodwin, writing of such Western Apache groups as the White Mountain, Cibecue, San Carlos, and Northern and Southern Tonto, observed that the size of the marriage gift did have a bearing on the social status of the families:

The initial marriage gift made by the boy's family was supposed to be in accordance with the social status of the girl's family. That which was deemed sufficient for a poor man's daughter was not fitting for a chief's daughter, and failure to allow for this could constitute a social slight. Details concerning exchange of marriage gifts were favorite subjects for gossip and seldom failed to arouse the curiosity of neighbors.[38]

An excellent illustration of the importance of the marriage gift to social status in the White Mountain group is contained in the following account. Anna Price, daughter of the famous White Mountain chief Diablo, was nearly one hundred years old when she told Goodwin the story of her courtship. She had at first refused the boy and sent him away:

> When he got to his home, he complained to his parents that he wanted to go home with me, but I wouldn't let him. "Why did you do that?" his father and mother said to him. "That girl is the daughter of the chief. You ought not to talk that way to her. You have to give a present to her people." Later on his family gave eight horses to my father and took them to his camp at Trail between the Rocks. One man had already come to father to ask that the young man might marry me. This was the young man's maternal uncle. He was a chief also. He drove a lot of cattle to father's camp. When these horses and cattle had been given to father, I felt sorry and cried, because the others told me that after I got married I wouldn't be able to flirt with other boys. We moved our camp to Soldier's Hole. After we got there I went over to that young man's home. That made me cry, because I was going to him. That's the way it used to be.[39]

Navajo marriage preliminaries and procedures of former times were colorfully described to Sapir by Charlie Mitchell. This detailed picture further acknowledges the prestige principles and the social status involved in the arrangements made between the prospective bride's parents and the go-between sent to them by the family of the hopeful groom. As Mitchell's narration begins, the young man's father, who serves as the traditional Navajo go-between, has arrived at the hogan of a young woman who "indeed is in no way related" to the young man and is addressing the girl's father.[40]

> "Let us give our children to each other."
> "I don't know! The old woman, it is her concern, the one whose daughter it is. It is her concern," he [the girl's father] says. "Ask her to come over here." From over there the old woman comes in. "For

this purpose I have come, my mother," he [the go-between] says to her.[41] "You will give us your daughter," he says to her. At once she speaks out, the old woman. "Oh!" she says, "it is my concern, is it? It is up to the old man. Now there you are sitting," she says to her husband. Though it really is her concern, she speaks thus. If she has a son, "It is up to my son," she says, the old woman. The old man says the same thing: "It is up to my son," he says, if he has a son. If (the son) is wise, he refers (the matter) back to them.[42]

Then, at that point, the one who comes makes an offer. Horses, four or five of them, he tells the old man whose daughter it is (and) the old woman whose daughter it is. Their home is pleasant, their home is good. The old man is a well-mannered old man, the old woman is well-mannered. They live well; they being rich in sheep, they live so. So they think that their daughter is of good quality, they think that she is worth a lot. "So there are just five horses; for my daughter just five horses are not enough," he thinks. Since he thinks "My daughter is worth twelve horses," he does not want five horses. The old woman speaks thus: "For what reason of only that many horses do you speak to me? (For) my daughter I want twelve horses given to me," she says. "All right, my mother, in just that way it will be. In how many days from now are we to come, my mother?" "Well, let it be in four days. Now it will be just that way. Go then, my son. You may go back over yonder."[43]

The duties of the go-between did not end with asking permission. Mitchell said that if the girl's family consented, the agreement was then called "She Has Been Asked For."[44] And when the go-between returned home to his relatives, they had questions as to the terms of the "She Has Been Asked For" agreement. These questions again emphasize how much the number of horses was identified with the prestige principle:

At once he starts back to the hogan, the one who asked for her. There he returns, to the hogan and the people who are there, he returns. They ask him about it. "Yes! What have you been told?" they say to him. " 'All right!' I have been told. . . . 'Twelve horses,' I have been told. 'All right,' I have said," he says as he tells the people to whom he returns about it. "All right! Now it is really so," they say to him. " 'In four days you may come to us,' we were told," he says as he tells the people about it. "Now it is really so! Quite a number of us will go over there," they say. "Now at their expense, we shall eat," they say.[45]

On the day of the wedding the groom's family would set out with the horses for the dwelling place of the bride, timing their journey so as to arrive about sunset. They drove the animals into a newly built corral and assembled with the bride's family in the newly built marriage hogan for the ceremony and the feast.[46] The Navajo usually practiced distribution of the horses among the bride's relatives, her mother and father keeping only one, sometimes none. Often the go-between received a horse for his services. Sometimes shy Apache maternal uncles, or fathers (if the task had been left for them), dreading their duties, would seek out public figures, who knew "just what to do," and ask them to handle the marriage preliminaries. When such was the case, the marriage arranger was paid by the groom's family, if he was successful. As a Chiricahua Apache informed Opler: "He is given something valuable, like a buckskin or a horse, because what he has done is a very unpleasant task to the Chiricahua mind. Something holds a man back from this. I can't describe it."[47]

When a Chiricahua go-between's visit was a mere formality—and sometimes this was the case when families knew one another well and had already reached an understanding that their children would marry—he might take the horses with him when he went over to offer the proposal. In that event, he would simply leave the horses for the girl's family as soon as the consent was granted. The usual Chiricahua practice, however, was to return later with the horses after the formal consent had been given, as described in the above Navajo account.[48]

According to Goodwin, the Western Apache groups, too, were wary of sending the horses with the go-between on his first visit, for fear that the proposal might be refused and the gifts returned, creating embarrassment for the groom's family. This sometimes occurred when a girl's family was already involved in marriage negotiations with another family, and would have to say to the new bargainer: "We have already eaten another man's food and used up his property, so you better take all this back with you."[49] Even if they said this, the go-between would still leave the horses tied nearby, and the girl's mother would have to lead them back to the boy's home and tie them outside his wickiup. If the mother did not return the gifts, the boy's family understood that the girl's family had changed their minds and were going to accept the proposal. When the horses were returned, however, the boy and his family suffered from a loss of pride, since everyone saw the girl's mother return them and knew what it signified. Under such circumstances, the boy's family, "to cover their mortification and to feign unconcern," Goodwin wrote, "sometimes sent the self-same gifts immediately to another family in which there was a desirable girl."[50]

The marriage gift of horses was called "a burden has been brought" by the Chiricahua Apache.[51] Like the Navajo, the Chiricahua and the

Western Apache groups—the Kiowa-Apache, too—divided the marriage gifts among the relatives of the bride, the mother and father often receiving only a small part. This was because, in Apache societies, maternal relatives and men directly in the maternal clan line took most of the responsibility for the wedding, and property coming into the girl's family would therefore belong to them. These were the relatives who were usually consulted about her marriage, and most important among them were her maternal uncles and elder brothers.[52] In like manner, it was the groom's maternal relatives who supplied the horses, though, among the Western Apache, sometimes "a youth might add a horse" to the gifts himself.[53]

During the pre-reservation and early reservation eras, it was a common practice among many of the Southern Athapascan groups for men who could afford it to have more than one wife, quite often marrying the first wife's sister. The manner of obtaining the second wife was usually less complicated than the obtaining of the first; for instance, a Western Apache man sent "a gift of a horse, blanket and gun, or something of similar value to the girl's parents, whether they were already his parents-in-law or not, and stated that he wished another wife. If they liked him and he was able to support another wife, the gift was accepted, and the girl sent to his camp to remain there."[54]

In modern times, the role of the horse in Southern Athapascan marriage is over. The Navajo and the Apache have borrowed new customs from the white man. The death of old observances can be dated accurately among the Western Apache groups, owing to the revealing study that Goodwin made of Apache children's play habits, dividing them into three periods—old, middle, and modern—with inclusive dates from 1840 to around 1938. Remembering the games of her childhood, of between 1840 and 1850, Anna Price, Goodwin's most aged White Mountain Apache informant, said: "We played at marriage negotiations, the girl's family and boy's family exchanging large gifts of food. . . . Sometimes we would make a gift of horses to the other [the girl's] family. The horses were boys."[55] Neil Buck, a White Mountain Apache, who recalled his play habits between 1893 and 1903, in the middle period, related that while he and his companions played that they got married, they "didn't exchange gifts such as horses at these marriages," but only food and drink.[56] Thus, only twenty years after the establishment of the San Carlos Apache Reservation, the role of the horse in Western Apache marriage customs was virtually ended.

Some of the Navajo seem to have maintained this custom longer than others. When he was interviewed in 1929, Charlie Mitchell told Sapir that

While horses are no longer required as a part of the marriage gift to the bride's family, some families of Western Apache grooms will still, upon the announcement, present them with this kind of burden basket filled with gifts. Note that the Chiricahua called the gift of horses of former times "a burden has been brought."

the Navajo of the western region, living near the Hopi, still practiced the old marriage customs:

> Way over yonder, the people living on the summit of the Black Mountain on the side toward the river, they do not live like the people who live around here.[57] Only those do so still in that manner the things about which I have been telling, it seems. (They do) these things I have been telling about because, over there, they live in a fashion similar to (that of) the old days. That is all.[58]

Sapir noted that Charlie Mitchell's interpreter, Albert Sandoval, thought differently. He believed that the marriage customs of the Western Navajo at that time were the same as those of Mitchell's region on the eastern end of the Navajo Reservation.[59] However, Dr. Frances Gillmor, always a keen observer of Navajo customs on her frequent trips to the Navajo Reservation, is inclined to agree with Charlie Mitchell. She recalls going to a Navajo wedding in 1929 at Kayenta, Arizona, on the western side of the reservation, in which horses were given to the bride's family by the groom's relatives. The notes she took at the wedding record that the gifts to the bride's family were "five horses, three cows, and a string of beads."

In Rain Ceremonies

Another time in the lives of the Navajo when they can still call upon horses to play symbolic roles in ceremonies for their benefit is when they need rain. They can chant prayers in their rain ceremonies to their water horse spirits, whom we have seen earlier serving as helpers in the Beauty Way and Water Chant ceremonies to cure the sick.[60] The prayers of a rain ceremony collected by Hill address a male and a female water horse, their sex specified because the Navajo distinguish between male and female rain. Curly, a Navajo informant of Hill's from Chinle, Arizona, described male rain as follows: "When the rainy season starts a cloud appears, you hear thunder, a heavy shower with thunder and lightning follows: that is male rain." "Female rain" is "a gentle drizzle which may last all day. The thunder comes in an even roll and there is less lightning."[61]

In order to illustrate the place of the horse prayers in the rain ceremony, it is best to describe the whole context. The singer begins by spreading a sacred buckskin upon the floor and placing a prayer stick on the north edge with the tip pointing east. He then forms five ridges to represent the four directions and the zenith by pushing folds into the buckskin and filling them with such sacred objects as precious jewels and "water iron ore," blue pollen, cattail (or flag) pollen, and corn pollen. This prayer offering is made to assure the cooperation of the water deities. The next step is to carry the arranged paraphernalia out and deposit it beside "either a pile of drifted rubbish, a mud ball that water ha[s] rolled along, a bubbling spring, or a 'geyser.'" At the site the rain singer stands and draws in his mind a boundary line around the specific area in which he wishes it to rain. Next he makes a motion with the offering toward that area, and then placing the offering on the west side of the selected site he begins his chant.[62] First he addresses two chants to Male and Female Water Ox, and then two more chants to Male Water Horse followed by one to Female Water Horse.[63] The two male chants are alike, practically line for line, except that in the first, female rather than male rain is asked for, and dark fog and dark clouds instead of blue clouds and blue fog.[64] The second chant dealing with male rain follows:

> Water Horse young man the finest prayer stick I have given to you
> The finest of turquoise I offer to you
> The finest of white shell beads I offer to you
> The finest of abalone shell beads I offer to you
> The finest of jet beads I offer to you
> The finest of haliotis shell beads I offer to you
> The finest of water iron ore I offer to you
> The finest of blue pollen I offer to you
> The finest of flag pollen I offer to you
> The finest of corn pollen I offer to you
> Although there are many hardships
> Those are not for what I am making the offering
> The finest of blue clouds for that I have made an offering to you
> That is what I came after
> The finest of male rain for that I have made an offering to you
> That is what I came after
> The finest of blue fog for that I have made an offering to you
> That is what I came after
> The finest of collections of water for that I have made an offering to you
> That is what I came after
> The finest of water children for that I have made an offering to you
> That is what I came after
> The finest of vegetation for that I have made an offering to you
> That is what I came after
> The finest of flowers for that I have made an offering to you
> That is what I came after
> Good and everlasting one I being as I go about
> My front being pleasant as I go about
> My rear being pleasant as I go about
> May it be pleasant
> May it be pleasant.[65]

The third chant, directed to Female Water Horse, follows at once, identical to the one above except that "Water Horse young woman" is invoked rather than "Water Horse young man," and three of the lines refer to female rain and its elements rather than to male rain: "yellow fog" instead of "blue clouds"; "yellow clouds" instead of "blue fog."[66]

A Navajo informant told Hill that the rain singer could never be paid for his services with any kind of livestock. The reason for this, the Navajo said, was that "when he started the rain, if he had been paid in animals, the thunder and lightning would strike animals and men." The Thunder People who accompany rains are, it seems, "boys just like us, and [they] get careless and shoot animals and humans."[67]

If the Apache Controller of Water kept water horses, I have not seen a reference to them. A Chiricahua Apache once mentioned that certain individuals knew ceremonial songs and prayers enlisting aid from Controller of Water in producing rain, but the extent of his comments about these people and the ritual they practiced was:

> In those songs and in prayers they talk of Water Controller who sits at the water gate and stops the water. They hold up their hands and sing, "Controller of Water, please give us a little water." He lives up above somewhere. He is only mentioned in the ceremonies that belong to different people. Some sing that his shirt is of clouds of different colors. Some say that he wears a shirt of abalone.
>
> He holds the rain. He lets it loose or shuts it off. You sing to him if you know his song. If people believe and learn his song, they can get rain.[68]

In Death Customs

The horse had a final role to fill in a man's death, reflecting the acute dread the Southern Athapascans have always shown toward death and anything connected with the life of the deceased. In earlier times, the slaying of the person's favorite horse was a custom strictly observed by all of these people, generally according to the following pattern. The mourners would bridle and saddle the horse—at times more than one—load it with the dead person's possessions and shoot it near or over the grave. They usually cut its throat or clubbed it to death if they did not have a gun with which to kill it. The horse's body, still loaded with the possessions, which were hammered and crushed beyond use, was either buried with the man or left to waste away at the grave.

The primary reason for all this careful destruction was to prevent the spirit of the dead from returning and bringing "ghost sickness" to the living. Today, the Navajo and Apache are by no means free of their beliefs about "ghost sickness," a disease marked by extreme nervousness, faintness, and fear. The Navajo feeling on this subject is best borne out by what a Navajo named John Watchman told Sapir about the traditional Navajo mortuary customs:

> They dig a hole right inside the hogan. There are two men who bury him [a man]. Wrapping him in a good blanket, they put him in the ground. They are just naked, they (who) do the burying.
>
> And then, when the burial is all done, they tear the hogan down on top of (the grave). If he had horses, they club the horses to death at the door of the hogan. His best saddle, saddle blanket, bridle, on all of these they hammer (to destroy them). Only in this way will they be of use to (the deceased), they say. For that reason, they do so. If these belongings were not destroyed, then some Navaho wandering about would pick them up. Being hammered in that way, no one will bother them. They are called ghost's belongings. If he is buried outside away from the hogan, a hole is dug in exactly the same way. All of his belongings are similarly buried with him. . . .

> In this way, a Navaho burial is well done. When it is done so, (the deceased) is pleased with it. Right among us his spirit wanders about. For that reason, his belongings and the horse he will ride are buried with him. If this is not done, he comes back for his belongings, they say. If he possessed sheep and cattle, these are only prayed for so that they will go about safely. In this way the Navaho bury one another. . . .
>
> Women and children, when they die, even then the same things are done. (For) children, no horses are killed on them because they do not ride horses, they say.
>
> These hogans in which burials have been made are called empty hogans. They are afraid of them (and) they are not disturbed. He who dwells in it is jealous of it. They do not desecrate it, they keep it holy because (the spirits) live right among us, they say.[69]

Unless the dead man's horse were killed, then, he could not ride it in the other world. One Chiricahua Apache remembered the way his father had once described the world inhabited by the spirits as a place in the underworld where people continued to live in much the same way they had lived on earth. "If you are a bronco-buster on earth, you would be a bronco-buster in the other world. . . . Whatever a person is accustomed to do on earth he will be doing down there," the Apache's father told him when he was just a small boy.[70]

The traditional Chiricahua way of disposing of a corpse was to bury it away from the camp in some rocky crevice or cave in the mountains.[71]

As quickly as possible, the body was dressed for burial and mounted on the person's favorite horse and best saddle. Most of the possessions were loaded on, and what could not be carried was burned or destroyed at the camp. One Chiricahua gave an inimitable description of the event:

> All that a person had is destroyed. They say that whatever is thrown away with a dead person that belongs to him he carries to the underworld. They want him to have the use of these things in the other world. They don't want him to get there poor. They want to show . . . that they do not hold property above their relative. And they don't want anything that the dead person had used a great deal to be around. It would only remind people of the one who died and bring them sorrow. Also they fear that the ghost of the person who owned the article will come back to molest the one who keeps it.
>
> For the same reason they kill the horse that has carried the dead person's possessions. It is stabbed in the throat or shot, at or near the grave. If a man has several horses, sometimes they kill them all; sometimes only his favorite horse or horses, the ones he actually used all the time. It is because a person used a thing continually and it is associated with him and reminds you of him that you don't want to keep it. People don't want to see his horse. Because he used to ride it so much, to have it around reminds them of the former owner. Besides they kill the horses so they will go with the dead person. The saddles are burned.[72]

The Chiricahua felt that thwarted spirits seeking withheld goods often returned in the form of owls:

> . . . the people hear that owl calling. They say, "That person is back over there again!"
>
> They claimed that if the dead man had a horse left alive there, or if any of his clothes were there, he would come back every night until his possessions were destroyed. He would come back after his things. If you had not destroyed what belonged to the dead man, the things he had had his hands on during his life, the owl would come every now and then, perhaps often, they said. Then it might bring sickness or bad luck to that family. That's the way I heard it long ago.
>
> And so to prevent sickness, if an owl cried around the camp, they set fire to a stick of wood, carried it outside, and threw it in the direction of the owl. Then it stopped (hooting).[73]

The Chiricahua feeling about owls as unquiet ghosts was shared at least by the Navajo, and the Lipan and Mescalero Apache, and probably by other Apache groups.[74] A Navajo, who had once dreamed of visiting the dead when he was very sick, said that in his dream his dead relatives told him about the way they returned to earth: "We have a meeting before anyone goes back. We don't travel on foot, but we travel in owl or coyote. We go back in that."[75] The owl—the nocturnal bird of prey with the solemn appearance and the soft plumage that permits noiseless flight—has long been identified with death, not only by these people, but by many primitive peoples of other races, as well. That these Indians also associate Coyote with ghosts is doubtless due to this animal's habit of feeding on carrion.[76] In this man's dream, his dead relations revealed to him how they came back to this world in coyote form to claim the ghosts of the slaughtered horses, saying: "We can go into coyote and go to where the person first died and was buried. They kill a horse there, all dressed with a good saddle, blanket, and bridle. We can use that horse like it was and go back and see a squaw dance. Not there all night, only just after dark, but be there two and half or three hours [sic]. That's the way we travel."[77]

Sometime before her death in 1939, Mrs. Andrew Stanley, a very old Eastern White Mountain Apache woman who was once captured by Geronimo, told Goodwin of the customs observed after an Apache warrior had been killed in enemy territory and buried there: ". . . when the party gets home and tells his kin, they cut their hair off for him and cry and mourn just as if he had died here, and they will kill two or three of his horses or cattle for him also. They take them off a way and kill them."[78]

A Western Apache chief's suicide attempt, a story well remembered among his people and described in detail to Goodwin, shows that a man planning his own death journey would also include his favorite horse in his preparations. The events that led to the contemplated suicide were these. The chief had been a successful raider and often brought home many horses, which he delighted in giving to his son. Once while the chief was away on a raid, his son became fatally ill and died the very day his father returned home. The chief took all his son's horses and cattle to the grave and killed them. Then according to the Apache who told his story, after his son's burial,

> . . . he returned to his camp and sat there looking straight before him. He would not speak or look at any of his friends. He sat there, neither seeing nor hearing. Soon he recognized his best horse standing near by, with his finest saddle on it. He got up and went to the horse, mounted, and rode straight down toward the edge of Rocky Creek Canyon to the brink of a high cliff. He never looked back but kept facing ahead to the precipice. His friends watched his progress for a while and then followed him, turned his horse, and led

him back to his camp. All the way back no one said anything. When
they arrived at camp, his friends said to him, "We know how it is
with you, but we don't want you to do a thing like that." The chief
stood for a while, and then he spoke, "My friends, I am all right now.
A little while ago it was as if I was dead, but now I am made alive
again."[79]

The Kiowa-Apache practiced a death custom that seems to have been
unique to them. At the burial service, one or more of the deceased's
horses were killed at the graveside by being pierced in the chest. "Blood
would come out, and when the horse was about to die it would wobble,
and the widow would grab it around the neck and fall with it. Blood
would get all over her," a Kiowa-Apache related.[80] As I have noted earlier,
the Kiowa-Apache tribe follow a culture pattern with much Plains orientation. As far as my researches have shown, this custom was not observed
among other Southern Athapascan tribes. The Jicarilla and Lipan Apache,
who have the most Plains orientation next to the Kiowa-Apache, followed the more typical Apache burial procedures described above, with
some variations; for instance, the Jicarilla beheaded the horse.[81]

The number of horses killed when an Apache or Navajo died depended on the individual's wealth. If he or she owned few horses, then
all were destroyed; but what was destroyed was considered the deceased's
own personal possessions. Not all the horses of a family were considered
the property of the man; some belonged to the wife, others to the children. Even though a man was the head of a household, a Chiricahua said,
he "might not be considered to possess more than one or two horses of
his own"; these, being "his favorites and the ones he always used," had to
be killed.[82] Regarding the Western Apache, Goodwin says that while one
or two animals were killed for a man of average means, as many as eight
might be killed for a wealthy man.[83]

Some of the Apache felt, however, that something must be done about
the horses left after the favorite ones had been killed. The Chiricahua, the
Lipan, and the Kiowa-Apache cut the manes and tails of the remaining
horses as a gesture of mourning. Often a Kiowa-Apache who had a number of horses would give some to a brother if he became gravely ill and
thought he was about to die. If he died, then, according to McAllister, the
following customs became mandatory:

> The tails of these horses were bobbed and the manes cut, and they
> were given exceptionally good care. They were never ridden except
> into battle where it was a great honor to the deceased owner if they

One of the many homemade saddles that with other kinds of Apache trappings were presented to the late Eve Ball by surviving Mescalero and Chiricahua family members. The latter preferred seeing her preserve and display these possessions of their loved ones on the inner courtyard of her home's patio rather than see them destroyed or buried with those who had owned them. For more about the way Eve Ball assisted with the customs observed by these Apache at the time of death, see *infra,* p. 305.

were killed. When a man returned from battle without his deceased brother's pony, the relatives again wailed and lamented. Sometimes they did this when they saw the horse around the camp, for it reminded them of their relative.[84]

If a Lipan Apache owned no horse at the time of his death, then one of his relatives' horses carried his body to the burying site. While this horse did not have to be killed, it did have to be washed afterwards, and its mane, tail, and the section of hair over its eyes trimmed.[85]

The customs outlined above had all but disappeared during the first half of the twentieth century among modern Navajo and Apache. Yet there were still evidences of them during the latter part of it. While I was on a visit to the Navajo country in 1958, Mr. Eugene Lambson, who had spent most of his life in Ramah, New Mexico, told me some of the Navajo still adhered to the old ways. When a Navajo friend of his died, the Navajo's son took his horse to the graveyard, not far from Lambson's restaurant in Ramah, shot it, and buried it with his father. After the burial was over, Lambson said, the son, realizing that white men often kept remembrances of their friends, came up to him with his father's whip, gave it to him and said, "Here, this is all that's left of the old man."

Nevertheless, the role of the horse in the death customs of the Navajo and the Apache has seen its day. American burial customs are replacing those of the Indian. ". . . now, the American doctors, they alone, in the hospital, fix up the Navaho who die," John Watchman told Sapir as he ended his recountal of the traditional mortuary customs of his people.[86] He was referring to another custom, a very common one these days among the Navajo. Having still their deep-rooted horror of death or anything touching it, the Navajo often welcome the convenient exit the American hospital door provides from the dreaded duties imposed on them by their traditional death customs. Nowadays they will take a dying relative to the hospital to avoid having him or her die in the hogan, which would then have to be abandoned. Often, too, they ask the nearest white man to bury their dead for them rather than go through the old ceremonies of purification, bathing, and the four-day avoidance that are necessary ritual for any Navajo who has buried anyone.[87]

The Apache's death customs are changing too. Commenting on these things, a White Mountain Apache observed: "Nowadays when we get back to camp after a burial, we don't bathe in smoke or wash all over. Some will go to the store before going home and not bother to wash until it is time to eat. But before they eat next time they will have to wash their hands, that is all."[88]

Although this Apache seemed disdainful of these particular changes, he had come to feel as the white man does about the horses and other livestock that had been the property of the deceased. "In the old days it was customary to kill the stock that a man owned, but now they save the stock for the children. It is better that way," he said.[89]

Notes

1. Newcomb, *Navajo Omens and Taboos,* p. 29.
2. Goodwin, *Social Organization of the Western Apache,* p. 435.
3. Newcomb, *Navajo Omens and Taboos,* p. 30.
4. The Kiowa-Apache do not have a girl's puberty ceremony, but they have traditions announcing adolescence, which they still observe. These traditions have
   Plains orientation and are not representative of Southern Athapascan patterns.
   A Kiowa-Apache girl is given social recognition when she makes her first piece
   of handiwork. A crier makes a public announcement of her accomplishments
   and displays her handiwork before all her neighbors. A grandfather or a maternal uncle of hers gives the crier a horse in payment for his services. See J. Gilbert
   McAllister, "Kiowa-Apache Social Organization," in *Social Anthropology of the
   North American Tribes,* Fred Eggan, ed., The University of Chicago Publications in
   Anthropology, Social Anthropology Series (Chicago: University of Chicago Press,
   1937), pp. 119, 142–143.
5. Opler, *An Apache Life-Way,* p. 91.
6. As noted in the preceding chapter, the Chiricahua and Mescalero Apache, who
   now live together on the Mescalero Apache Reservation, act together to hold
   one big puberty ceremony for all the pubescent girls on the reservation instead
   of the individual ceremonies held by each family during earlier times. This
   celebration is held annually on the reservation in early July.
7. Opler, *An Apache Life-Way,* p. 95. It has been explained earlier that Child-of-the-
   Water rather than Killer-of-Enemies has come to be considered the chief protagonist for the Chiricahua and Mescalero Apache. See *supra,* pp. 59–60, 89, 94.
   Opler explains the reference to Killer-of-Enemies in the above song as a persis-
   tence of the older Apache heritage. Concerning this point, he writes: "The
   older heritage persists, however, in the songs of the girl's puberty rite, which
   mention only Killer of Enemies. The Chiricahua simply accept these references
   as concerned with Child of the Water." See his *Apache Life-Way,* p. 95, n. 3.
8. Ibid., pp. 85, 89–90. Unlike the ceremonies that Apache shamans learn through
   supernatural experiences, the woman attending the pubescent girl has learned
   her ceremonial role from another older woman at some point in her life. However, as Opler notes, sometimes "the purely shamanistic premise persists, for
   women ... who have had a supernatural experience with White Painted Woman
   are thought to carry on this ceremony with best results" (p. 84).
9. Ibid., p. 97.
10. Ibid., pp. 97–99. The girl is thought to be a source of supernatural power at this
    time, and Opler observes that "definite curative powers are attributed" to her (p.
    97).
11. Ibid., p. 95.
12. Ibid., p. 133.
13. Ibid., p. 87.
14. Sapir and Hoijer, p. 289. For more information on Hogan Songs, see *infra,* pp.
    293–294.
15. Ibid., pp. 289, 291.

16. See *supra*, pp. 190–192, 197. For further findings on why horse songs are sung at the girl's puberty rite, see *infra*, pp. 294–297.

17. For these horse songs, see *supra*, pp. 79, 191.

18. Oakes and Campbell, p. 45. For later findings concerning the function of these trappings in the ceremony, see *infra*, p. 297.

19. See *supra*, pp. 87–88.

20. Opler, *Myths and Tales of the Jicarilla*, p. 89.

21. See *supra*, pp. 142–143.

22. Opler, *Myths and Tales of the Jicarilla*, p. 89.

23. Opler, *An Apache Life-Way*, p. 429. For a similar account, see Opler, *Myths and Tales of the Chiricahua*, p. 91.

24. See Opler, *Myths and Legends of the Lipan*, p. 288. In connection with this Lipan tale, Opler states that the Jicarilla and Mescalero Apache tell this story too.

25. Reichard, *Navaho Religion*, II, p. 594.

26. McAllister, "Kiowa-Apache Tales," p. 52.

27. Opler, *Myths and Tales of the Jicarilla*, p. 89.

28. Ibid.

29. Besides the races that are a part of their puberty ceremony, one of the most important of all the Jicarilla "long life ceremonies" is the separate ceremonial relay race, still held annually on September 15 at Horse and Stone Lakes in northern New Mexico, for the purpose of blessing humans as well as animals and plants with fertility. For a detailed account of this race, see Morris Edward Opler, "The Jicarilla Apache Ceremonial Relay Race" *American Anthropologist*, new series, XLVI, No. 1 (January–March 1944), pp. 75–97.

30. Opler, *Myths and Tales of the Jicarilla*, p. 90.

31. In and out of mythology, grasses and horse manure often symbolize horses to the Apache, as well as to the Navajo. For example, there is a White Mountain tale in which horse dung found under a cottonwood tree signifies the cardinal horses for an Apache learning the ceremony of the horse. See Goodwin, *Myths and Tales of the White Mountain*, p. 86. Another story recounts the way in which an Apache actually used horse manure on one occasion to symbolize a horse. See Opler, *An Apache Life-Way*, p. 129.

32. Goddard, *Jicarilla Apache Texts*, pp. 267–268. For a similar account, see Opler, *Myths and Tales of the Jicarilla*, p. 90.

33. Reichard, *Social Life of the Navajo*, p. 140.

34. McAllister, "Kiowa-Apache Social Organization," pp. 146, 147.

35. Reichard, *Social Life of the Navajo*, p. 139. Sapir and Hoijer, p. 532, n. 24; p. 10, state that twelve horses were considered the limit for the marriage gift; the Navajo believed that more than twelve brought bad luck.

36. Opler, *An Apache Life-Way*, p. 161.

37. Ibid.

38. Goodwin, *The Social Organization of the Western Apache*, p. 322.

39 Ibid., p. 331.

40. Though the maternal uncle serves as the go-between in the foregoing Apache account, an Apache father could also act as go-between. See ibid., p. 316; Opler,

An Apache Life-Way, p. 157.The Navajo usually leave the task to the young man's father. However, Reichard observes: "If the boy's father is not interested in getting his son married his [the boy's] father's father would take the lead.The father does so more often than the mother's brother...." See her *Social Life of the Navajo,* p. 139. Sapir's informant endorses Reichard, saying:"The old man, the very one whose son it is, goes over there." See Sapir and Hoijer, p. 309.

41. Sometimes the young man's father will call the prospective bride's mother a term of relationship, signifying that he hopes the families will unite through their children; however, in this case, the narrator implies that "my mother" is merely a term of respect. See Sapir and Hoijer, p. 532, n. 24:7, n. 24:8.

42. Sapir and Hoijer note that this "'passing of the buck' is a sign ... the old folks are prepared to accept the boy. If they don't want him, they say so at once.The girl is not consulted at all, nor was the boy in the old days." See *Navaho Texts,* p. 532, n. 24:9.

43. Ibid., pp. 309, 311.Though Mitchell describes the marriage procedures in terms of the boy's father asking the girl's parents for the hand of their daughter, neither Hoijer nor Sapir explains why the girl's mother addresses the boy's father as "my son."

44. Ibid., p. 311.

45. Ibid.

46. Ibid., pp. 311, 313.The Navajo wedding ceremony centers around a ritualistic feast. The bride and groom pour water over one another's hands, dipping it from a small pot with a gourd ladle.They eat from a basket filled with ceremonial (unflavored) gruel. Following this ritual, the general feasting begins, and the guests spend the whole night celebrating and giving the young couple advice. See Reichard, *Social Life of the Navajo,* pp. 140–141.

47. Opler, *An Apache Life-Way,* p. 158; Sapir and Hoijer, p. 532, n. 24:10.

48. Opler, *An Apache Life-Way,* p. 161.

49. Goodwin, *The Social Organization of the Western Apache,* p. 323.

50. Ibid., pp. 323–324.

51. Opler, *An Apache Life-Way,* p. 161.

52. See ibid., p. 162; Goodwin, *Social Organization of the Western Apache,* p. 319; McAllister, "Kiowa-Apache Social Organization," p. 146. I have found no representative accounts of the division of the marriage gifts among the Jicarilla, Lipan, and Mescalero Apache.

53. Goodwin, *Social Organization of the Western Apache,* p. 326.

54. Ibid., p. 354. Opler states that the Lipan Apache did not practice polygamy. See his *Myths and Legends of the Lipan,* p. 43, n. 1.

55. Goodwin, *Social Organization of the Western Apache,* p. 482. It should also be noted that in most Apache societies, there was an exchange of gifts between the bride's and groom's families.The bride's family usually sent such things as food and clothing to the groom's family. They did not include horses among their gifts to the groom's family, however.

56. Ibid., p. 486.

57. Charlie Mitchell lived at Crystal, New Mexico.

58. Sapir and Hoijer, pp. 315, 317.

59. Ibid., p. 533, n. 24:19.

60. See *supra*, pp. 223–225.

61. Hill, *The Agricultural and Hunting Methods of the Navaho Indians*, p. 72.

62. Ibid., pp. 84, 88.

63. Water Ox is identified with Water Monster by Reichard. See her *Navaho Religion*, II, p. 491.

64. Hill, *The Agricultural and Hunting Methods of the Navaho Indians*, pp. 90–91.

65. Ibid., The translation of the last four lines of this chant distressed Gladys Reichard, who commented on them in her study of Navajo prayer, *Prayer: The Compulsive Word*, Monograph of the American Ethnological Society, VII (New York: J. J. Augustin, 1944). See p. 39, where she notes: "...the Navajo prayers are beautiful in a serious sense even to an English-speaking person. It seems to me, therefore, irreverent and offensive, if not even vulgar, to be satisfied with translations like the following: 'My front shall be pleasant, my rear shall be pleasant, my below shall be pleasant, my above shall be pleasant.'"

66. Hill, *The Agricultural and Hunting Methods of the Navaho Indians*, pp. 91–92.

67. Ibid., p. 74.

68. Opler, *An Apache Life-Way*, p. 199.

69. Sapir and Hoijer, pp. 431, 433.

70. Opler, *An Apache Life-Way*, p. 42. Cf. this Chiricahua Apache's ideas concerning the world of the dead with a Jicarilla Apache's statement about the afterworld being an "existence . . . of pleasure and plenty." See Opler, "A Summary of Jicarilla Apache Culture," p. 222. Cf. his ideas also with a White Mountain Apache's belief that the afterworld was a place exactly like earth but where "little or no labor" was required. See Grenville Goodwin, "White Mountain Apache Religion," *American Anthropologist*, new series, XL, No. 1 (January–March 1938), p. 36.

71. Newcomb, *Navajo Omens and Taboos*, p. 75, describes a Navajo burial in a high place among the rocks, similar to the above Apache custom. She says that the horse that transported the corpse was "killed near the grave still wearing its bridle and saddle."

72. Opler, *An Apache Life-Way*, p. 474.

73. Ibid., p. 42.

74. The Lipan, Mescalero, and Chiricahua Apache also had the belief that Apache who were considered sorcerers in life turned themselves into owls after death. See Opler, *Myths and Legends of the Lipan*, p. 39, n. 1; also his "The Lipan Apache Death Complex and Its Extensions," *Southwestern Journal of Anthropology*, I, No. 1 (Spring 1945), pp. 134–135. See, too, Castetter and Opler, p. 33.

75. Leland C. Wyman, W. W. Hill, and Iva Ósanai, *Navajo Eschatology*, Bulletin of the University of New Mexico, Anthropological Series, IV, No. 1 (Albuquerque: University of New Mexico Press, 1942), p. 34.

76. See also *supra*, pp. 97–98, where Owl and Coyote, accompanied by Crow, Magpie, and Vulture, appear in a myth as the five traditional horse thieves whom the Navajo associate with death.

77. Wyman, Hill, and Ósanai, p. 34.

78. Goodwin, *The Social Organization of the Western Apache*, p. 520.

79. Ibid., pp. 209–210.

80. McAllister, "Kiowa-Apache Social Organization," p. 159.

81. See Goddard, *Jicarilla Apache Texts*, p. 270; Opler, "A Summary of Jicarilla Apache Culture," p. 223; Opler, "The Lipan Apache Death Complex and Its Extensions," p. 125.

82. Opler, *An Apache Life-Way*, p. 474.

83. Goodwin, *The Social Organization of the Western Apache*, p. 377.

84. McAllister, "Kiowa-Apache Social Organization," p. 158. For the Chiricahua practice of this custom, see Opler, *An Apache Life-Way*, p. 474.

85. Opler, "The Lipan Apache Death Complex and Its Extensions," p. 125.

86. Sapir and Hoijer, p. 433.

87. Leighton and Leighton, p. 76.

88. Goodwin, *The Social Organization of the Western Apache*, p. 520.

89. Ibid., p. 521.

Epilogue

I F I WERE WRITING *They Sang for Horses* today, my approach to understanding the pre-eminent place of the horse in Navajo and Apache myths, ceremonies, beliefs, customs, and traditions would be fundamentally the same. Such a study would still necessitate, first of all, heavy research in libraries to cover thoroughly an impact like the acquisition that the Spanish horse made on these wide-ranging peoples. Not only have they occupied an area covering an extensive portion of the Southwest, but the period the animal flourished in these societies covers from three hundred and fifty to three hundred and eighty years. And simultaneously the project would also demand comparable firsthand knowledge of all the different Native American groups that together make up these linguistically related Southern Athapascan peoples, for in order to make such an assessment, it would be essential that the researcher obtain a close familiarity with each of their individual homelands, lifeways, and practices.

While all these things can presently still be accomplished, it is in this latter connection that I feel particularly fortunate in having begun the primary study for this work as a term paper for a folklore class of Frances Gillmor's at the University of Arizona in the mid-1950s and to have completed it in the mid-1960s—the time when it also first went to press after I had revised and enlarged it from its thesis form. More importantly, what these dates have turned out to mean is that I had the good fortune of being able to take a major influence, which such a European introduction as the horse had on the Navajo and Apache, and then investigate its adoption into their cultures during the period it was still exerting a considerable influence. Moreover, I could finish by the time—the mid-1960s—

when things changed significantly: the period when with the rapid spread of pickups and the beginning of the individual ownership of them in large numbers by the people themselves brought about the horse's decline from many aspects of their lifeways, and with that the redefining of its role from what it had been. Thus, by the time this book appeared in 1966, the major changes had come about and the whole period could already be investigated in such a way that even now—thirty-five years later—the main themes it encompasses have not continued to change enough to discredit the picture presented here. Which means in turn that the work still stands—that it is credible and viable as it is. While I am grateful to have this the case, I am nevertheless happy to have a chance now to bring to light material I have meanwhile uncovered about certain of the topics I treat, all of which better rounds them out. By and large I am referring to points concerning ceremonies involving either horses or else substantial symbolism about them, as well as to the myths and songs the rites incorporate, about which prior to this book's publication little in-depth source material was available.

The purpose, then, of this epilogue is to provide information that either gives a clearer understanding of a topic treated or else puts it into a more appropriate context for consideration than was possible before. As I go about my mission, I wish not only to survey the source material now at hand, but to note other scholarly work, too, that like it has appeared in the interim, and that contains further pertinent information. As I proceed, I intend to point out a work's contribution or how it relates to this study. Additionally, I want to take advantage of the opportunity afforded me to share many of my own discoveries and firsthand experiences in connection with various related matters. The latter will incorporate a number of gleanings I have had in days subsequent to publication, too, along the long trail I have continued from time to time to travel with an eye still on horses as I went about other projects in Navajo and Apache country. Many of my more recent findings are accompanied by photographs I have taken, mostly from the 1960s forward. Considering that all of them appear in these pages for the first time, they should widen considerably the vista the words provide.

The new material I want first to take up deals largely with the Navajo and source material focusing on their rituals. With its accessibility in published form, a number of puzzles were promptly illuminated that had plagued my researches on rituals involving or surrounding the horse. Lacking it, I had been forced to deal either with fragmentary information or else with material taken out of its proper context, and sometimes with both.

St. Michael's Franciscan Mission, Window Rock, Arizona: Fr. Berard Haile served, and painstakingly recorded Navajo lore, here for over fifty years. In the first half of the twentieth century, especially before the organization of the tribal council, the place was also one where leaders met and discussed matters of tribal concern. The first Navajo dictionary was published here by the Fathers, too.

By far the most significant of the primary material related to Navajo ceremonial matters in which a goodly portion of horse lore is also associated is the joint production of Fr. Berard Haile and Leland C. Wyman— the volume *Blessingway*. The ceremony known by that name, and the related rites it encompasses, have been referred to frequently enough in my foregoing text that readers may have already surmised that the ceremony holds a unique place in Navajo society—that it constitutes, in fact, what these people call the backbone of their religion. The foundations for the basic study of this ceremony, which is performed for so many purposes, lie in the dedicated efforts of Fr. Haile, the Franciscan priest from St. Michael's Mission on the Navajo Reservation. He collected, assembled, and translated with the aid of interpreters, themselves singers and informants, the fundamental research beginning in the late 1920s. While he continued his investigations, he produced numerous other important ceremonial studies, never ceasing his endeavors until his health failed him in the mid-1950s.

In studying the Blessing Way, he worked mainly with three singers—Slim Curly, Frank Mitchell, and River Junction Curly—recording a version of the ceremony from each and emerging with an exhaustive rendering not likely to be surpassed of its myth and the procedures for the accompanying ritual that Frank Mitchell appropriately maintained, like various other singers, is the most important of all Navajo ceremonials. In fact, other ceremonials always include blessing portions from it and must always close with one of its songs.[1]

Haile's toils are testimony not only to the perseverance of a dedicated scholar but also to his special affiliation with the Navajo. As priest of a religion that when compared with theirs had been recently established among the people, he was yet a scholar passionately interested in preserving the beliefs and practices of the superseded faith—not unlike Sahagun among the Aztecs in the sixteenth century. As such, he enjoyed the friendship and respect of his informants to a degree that probably led them to be more open with him than they would have been with an inquirer of lesser status. Like many other Navajo conversions Haile must have witnessed along the way, Frank Mitchell's was marked by the traditional aspects of his culture that he maintained. He was buried a Catholic but with his bridle and saddle in the grave. His son, like that of many another Navajo in keeping with an elder's wishes, carried out his father's requests as late as 1967, shooting his favorite horse in the traditional manner and leaving its carcass in an arroyo near the grave to insure his parent a way of getting about in the afterlife.[2]

For all the length and thoroughness of Haile's work, he died before he recovered his health enough to finish it. Fortunately the great accumulation of his papers—including substantial drafts and translations for the volume he projected on the Blessing Way, along with voluminous notes and other data of his on the lifeways of the Navajo—is now housed in Special Collections at the University of Arizona. After its acquisition some years following his death, it was put into the expert hands of the great Navajo scholar Leland Wyman, who then took over the task of shaping into publishable form the core of Haile's vast body of research, going on to produce the book that appeared as *Blessingway* in 1970. Nevertheless I was unable to make use of this great offering for *They Sang for Horses* until the latter's third printing (1983), and even then was allowed only space enough to alert readers to the study's importance by way of a footnote.

Before the publication of the work by Haile and Wyman, no one could easily take into close account the paramount position that the horse had come to truly command in Blessing Way, and thus to consider more fully its adoption into Navajo ceremonies and religion. I found the study helped shed light on and clarify the complex relationships and overlapping I had already touched on several times in the text between Blessing Way and its related subcategory of rituals. I found the work particularly illuminating in providing contexts for the myths involving the creating of horses and for the horse songs. For instance, in connection with the horse songs, I can now by way of the study identify them as belonging to the ceremony whereas they were not readily identifiable in that connection beforehand. At the time I was collecting and arranging a number of them, as well as some segments of myths from widespread sources, much of the material I was assembling had become separated from its original ceremonial context and had been presented rather in publications as separate entities complete in themselves. And while I sometimes found clues, or suspected that the songs or mythical segments I was working with were related in some manner to the Blessing Way, without the text of the complete ceremony itself to refer to and compare my findings with, I had no direct evidence to support me in any firm conclusions.[3] As a matter of fact, such parallels turned out to go beyond anything I could have imagined. For what Haile recorded reveals that the Blessing Way is actually the direct source of all the horse songs in Navajo mythology! More than that, the Blessing Way and the creation of the horse are conjoined and inseparable, stemming as they do from the origin legends of the people and thus from the myth that governs the ceremony itself. Though previous to having the study before me, I had not discovered this, with it, I could see that this was logical, for since the myth always determines the procedure that a ceremony follows, it then would likewise determine the order and nature of the songs included in it.

Also, with the Haile and Wyman study at hand, I could now look more closely at, and consider more exactly, the roles of Changing Woman and the other Holy Beings that I had touched on in the text in connection with the creation of horses, and could then additionally see what further came to light about them and the ceremony. What I found was that the three versions of Blessing Way in the Haile and Wyman volume presented the following story. Changing Woman herself, as the principal goddess of the Navajo, had created the People by rolling up little balls of wasted skin from her breasts and shoulders, and afterwards had called together a great conclave of Holy Ones at the rim of the Emergence. Among them were the Sunray People, the Rock Crystal People, the Wind and Lightning and Star People, and more yet. Later, as I had shown in the text, with their assistance, she performed the first Blessing Way for the

Some versions of the stories about Changing Woman's creation of the Navajo mention places like the famous Shiprock landmark, especially in the parts of them that
contain the migration legends about the Navajo's movements across Dinétah into
the Four Corners.

everlasting benefit of the People—to employ the name the Navajo call
themselves. At the end of the ceremony the Holy Ones departed for
invisible realms and warned against anyone ever trying to see them again.
They surrendered their power of speech, too, even for communicating
with one another. They affirmed, though, that they would be present in
the rocks and the mountains, where one could appeal for their help by
leaving offerings in the right spots, and as further consolation they promised to be heard in the wind, in the sound of eagle feathers, in bird songs,
and in the growing of the corn.[4]

Now this original Blessing Way was above all an act of creation and a
culminating product of it was—as the many mythical segments included
in my book have already shown—the horse. But then, by extension, what
we learn from Haile and Wyman is that this noble creature could also
stand for other domestic creatures, like the sheep and cattle also essential
to the People's existence, and, further, sometimes even beyond that for all
good things, as well, by which the People were to live. But again, like
we've seen before, Changing Woman did not make the transition of the
horse from sky to earth easy. In the way of divinities she put Enemy

Slayer and Younger Brother, who went in search of mounts for humans, through the motions of a pair of visits to their father the Sun. We are familiar, too, with how Sun also removed the supernatural powers of the ideal horse before actually bestowing upon the visiting boys the gift of ceremonial objects with which their mother could create the earthly models of the supernatural creature he possessed. But, to go back now to the primordial occasion of the Blessing Way, we remember further how Changing Woman laid down the rules for continuance of the manifold blessings she had by then created for the People. On this occasion, we need to keep in mind, too, the way she likewise emphasized the responsibility she charged the Navajo with—that of celebrating the sacredness of birth as the multiplying process of all good things, including the exact procedures by which the Blessing Way could be utilized in a never-failing production of horses. What the Haile and Wyman study made clear to me, and what I wish now to point out in this epilogue about this pattern of the mythical story I'd earlier pieced together from various sources and presented in *They Sang for Horses*, is that with the new study I could see, too, how all the segments I'd utilized in making up my version had turned out also to actually belong to the origin myth of the Blessing Way![5]

The significance of this myth in connection with the horse songs—songs that Haile and Wyman are the first to present in their ceremonial context—and to the study of the ceremony cannot be overemphasized. Songs addressed to other religious entities may originate in other rituals, but that invocations of the horse originally belong only to this, the fundamental ceremony of Navajo belief, confirms the total extent to which Navajo society and its religion were transformed by the introduction of the animal—the arrival, in their mythic view, of this supreme gift of gods that determined their way of life from then on—or at least until a further transformation was forced on them to cope with the contemporary world.

What first strikes the reader about any one of the three versions of the Blessing Way that Haile gathered is the dazzling and intricate nature of Navajo myth: the often homely but always mysterious details of the adventures and exploits of various humans and gods—such as their moving about on rainbows and how the power of speech encompassing the sacredness of the word itself would come to be identified as a rainbow the gods put into the mouths of humans.[6] We find one natural stone or substance after another infused with the supernatural power of the divine—with holiness attributed to certain places the Navajo hold sacred, each given in compelling geographical particulars, down to the holy attributes even of the soil surrounding them. Best of all, in reading Haile and Wyman's *Blessingway,* one has the privilege of a rewarding use of contrast and comparison, with each of the gifted singers providing a version and rendering the mythology according to what might appear to be a pure freedom of invention, though actually the marvelous nuances are dictated by long tradition. For example, while Slim Curly's version concentrates on the gods' jealous possession of that magnificent creature the horse and their reluctance to part with it, Frank Mitchell's version stresses the search for horses of the Twin War Gods. His version resembles that of a variant of the story that we have earlier seen of Elder Brother (Enemy Slayer or Turquoise Boy) going alone, instead of both boys. Still it agrees with both Curly's and many others in taking them to such holy places as mountain tops and inside the rooms and corrals next to impressive hogans belonging to their father, Sun, or to their mother, Changing Woman.[7]

The foregoing examples of the many variants in the three accounts will hint, I hope, at the effects wrought by the intricate expanse of the Blessing Way. Suffice it to say that the many facets of the myth and its ceremonies—this combination of prayer, chant, invocation, and sacred narrative—intermingled as they are, arrive yet in the end at a rounded conception, without contradiction, into a believable narrative whole. I need say no more, for there is no way to appreciate this remarkable story except to read and absorb the entire text of it that *Blessingway* provides. One precaution is perhaps necessary, though. As I have suggested, readers who might expect consistency among the elements of story will not find it. Even outright contradictions do occur between the particulars of one version and those of another, the most glaring of which will be that although each of these male singers is well aware of prominent differences between his rendering of the myth and that of other singers, he will frequently claim that they are all telling the same story and even insist, paradoxically, that the obvious distinctions do not exist, a denial often stated even when the modifications are related by the same narrator from one session to the next.

Another great boon for the study of Navajo culture—an invaluable complement to *Blessingway* as well as an eminent contribution in its own right—comes to us from two scholars who established close ties with Frank Mitchell, the second of Haile's informants: Charlotte Frisbie and David McAllester. They collected a wealth of material from him, on his life as well as his standing as a medicine man and ritual singer. He recorded first for McAllester, who after beginning the project alone in 1957 was joined in 1963 by his student, Frisbie, providing them with his version of the Blessing Way, just as he originally had for Haile. Though his recording for them of the ceremony was marked by numerous instances in which he either left out information, or else varied it somewhat from what he had provided Haile with, he always supplied the variations without any sense of violating the integrity of the sacred narrative. In any case, the outcome of Frisbie and McAllester's work is invaluable, for it produced *Navajo Blessingway Singer: The Autobiography of Frank Mitchell, 1881–1967* (1978). Fortunately, in addition to their other talents, Frisbie and McAllester are musicologists as well as scholars whose particular emphases is on poetry and ceremonialism—specialties that enabled them to add greatly to the dimensions of the songs among their various contributions to this work. In addition to McAllester's increasing abilities with the Navajo language over the years, they had line-for-line translations of the Mitchell tapes recorded by Albert G. (Chic) Sandoval, Sr. This interpreter had once assisted the great linguist Edward Sapir in his work with Navajo texts, and the editors had further additional help from his son, Albert, Jr., and Mitchell's daughter Augusta, the wife of Cecil Sandoval.

Taken together, *Blessingway* and *Navajo Blessingway Singer* constitute a body of work the like of which will not likely be surpassed. The three traditional singers whose texts appear lived out their lives in a transitional time when they could still learn and perform the key rites of their people, before they had much faded or been corrupted by the intrusion of modern times. As the calendar moves on, such men cannot ever appear on the scene again. Navajo ceremonialism may be yet some time in vanishing, but the probability of its survival in anything near the form it had for Haile's three singers is slight. These two volumes then jointly represent a precious and irreplaceable heritage for the study of one of the principal branches of Native American culture, invaluable not only for the Navajo themselves but for all Americans. Without these three versions much of the true meaning of the Blessing Way, and with it knowledge of the place of the horse in Navajo culture, would be lost forever—lost not only to scholars, we may add, but also to modern-day practitioners. We should not forget that in the current revivals of ceremonialism among numerous Native American tribes, practitioners must frequently go to the writings of ethnologists to recover the means of performing the rites they have lost but once again feel are essential to their heritage. If the loss has not yet reached a critical degree among the Navajo, we should yet bear in mind that Frank Mitchell was already troubled by the deterioration of ceremonial knowledge among singers of the Blessing Way that had come about in the 1960s near the end of his life.[8]

Another key contribution to understanding the complexity of Navajo ceremonialism published since *They Sang for Horses* came out is Charlotte Frisbie's *Kinaaldá: A Study of the Navaho Girl's Puberty Ceremony* (1967). Her principal informant—though not her only one—was also Frank Mitchell. Further, she was able to work with four versions of the Kinaaldá myth that had been collected—not just by herself but by others also— from him over a thirty-two-year period, and then to compare his contributions as well with accounts of the ceremony by other people.[9] A like situation with variants that turned up exists here as with the Blessing Way. Yet, in spite of easily recognizable disparities, Mitchell maintained to Frisbie that they were all actually one version. Of course he may have considered by this apparent inconsistency that the central body of the myth and the ritual remained intact even though a variety of excrescences had surrounded it. For another and more intriguing reason, he may have been rejecting strict conformity as a precaution against a serious risk. Among the Navajo, a belief prevails that a singer must always keep back a part of what he or she knows. If singers put into the ceremony the whole store of their learning, the consequence may well be the loss of their powers. Or their lives may be shortened.[10]

There are obviously strong motivations for limiting not only the number of elements put into a specific ceremony, but also for preventing a singer from sharing knowledge with other practitioners, even perhaps with an apprentice, as when Frank Mitchell's mentor, Man Who Shouts, declined to teach him his Corn Bundle songs, declaring he would not survive the sharing of them.[11] And it may well be that the practice is not merely self-imposed but stands as a cultural prohibition against passing on too much of tribal lore to outsiders. In any case, the practice poses special problems for the scholar and collector. It may leave gaps in a body of material that lead to flawed conclusions about the substance and structure of Navajo ceremonialism. All the singers who served as informants to Haile, and to Frisbie and McAllester, admitted keeping a number of their chants secret, their reluctance diminishing only in the later years of friendship and collaboration, when they did share further songs. However, in spite of the long friendship between them, Frank Mitchell never did turn over his horse songs to Haile. Perhaps the reason was he thought they were too sacred, for he often mentioned his reluctance in giving up various songs because of such connections. The exception here is Slim Curly, who did let Haile record his. Of course, Curly had worked with Haile on various other ceremonials, and was doubtless a closer friend of his than Mitchell ever was. In any case, Curly declared to the priest, when he had finished recording his horse songs that now accompany his version of the Blessing Way, and had also helped Haile arrange all of them in their proper ceremonial contexts, that because of their long friendship, he had delivered over to him every single thing that he knew of the ceremony.[12]

Another reason that may be behind the singers guarding their horse songs as closely as they have in times past is the Navajo belief in the power of the word. Even when spoken in ordinary parlance—as stated above, the gods gave mankind speech through the magic of the rainbow—words are considered potent beyond being a vehicle for simple communication. But when certain word forms are uttered in a context of chant and prayer, their creative power is extraordinary because they are suffused with their supernatural origin. As such these divinely inspired words possess the power of direct creation, a power that flows over into the singer within the magic circle of the ceremony being performed.[13] The necessity to handle this holy language with the greatest of care is evident. There is a natural explanation here, too, as to why repetition is such a prominent feature in ceremonial chants, as, for example, the invocation "Come, come" intoned as a key word in the lines of one of Slim Curly's horse songs. It is not that the gods are hard of hearing, but that the reiterated chant is believed to be a translation, so to speak, of putting human words back into their divine original contexts.[14] Little wonder, then—with all these restrictions against culminating ritual chants without displaying the proper respect for them—that Navajo singers are so wary and protective of their own particular versions of songs used ceremonially.

Only after seeing what these scholars had recovered, did I come to understand why, in my research for *They Sang for Horses*, I had come across so many references to horse songs, yet with nothing more than very general and limited descriptions accompanying the references—why so few if any of the specific songs themselves were presented—and besides that why almost no context was ever provided for them. Even now, with the prohibitions imposed on the singers, it is likely that horse songs are being lost while a greater portion are gone forever, the memory of them having died with their possessors. For instance, as noted in the text, O'Bryan's informant who was referred to only as Sandoval told her he knew eighty-five horse chants, but to my knowledge none of them were ever recorded or written down. We must be grateful, therefore, for those that were recorded and passed on to us in no matter how fragmentary a form or how out of context they have come to us, for it's probable that their collectors had little opportunity to learn more about their true ritualistic settings.

Frank Mitchell, singing the Blessing Way as he conducts the 1957 puberty ceremony
for his granddaughter, Isabelle Mitchell, who is seated beside him in the family hogan.
Cf. also *infra,* pp. 296–297. (Photo by Mabel Bosch Denton, courtesy Charlotte J. Frisbie
and David P. McAllester, eds., *Navajo Blessing Way Singers: The Autobiography of Frank
Mitchell* [University of Arizona Press, 1978, p. 301])

The total recorded in connection with Blessing Way is seventy-eight songs: seventeen from Frank Mitchell and sixty-one from Slim Curly. When Mitchell finally decided to record his horse songs, he did so initially for McAllester, then later for Frisbie, and she included some of them in her *Kinaaldá*. While McAllester had employed his knowledge of the Navajo tongue along with his expertise in musicology, poetry, and ceremony to translating them, and had the help of the several Navajos mentioned, particularly that of Albert Sandoval, Sr., the whole text has lamentably not been published yet. He does seem to have included at least one horse song, though, in *Hogans: Navajo Houses and House Poems,* a work he edited, which contains photos by his late wife, Susan. Also the tapes of the original recordings are on file in several places: the Laboratory of Ethnomusicology at Wesleyan University, the Museum of Navajo Ceremonial Arts in Santa Fe, and the Library of Congress. The 1963 and 1964 recordings Frisbie made of Blessing Way horse songs, which she translated with the help principally of the Navajo interpreter William Morgan and the aid additionally of Albert G. Sandoval, Sr., are also at the Archives of Fine Arts at the University of New Mexico.[15]

Let me mention at this point an interesting attempt by Jerome Rothenberg to bring the seventeen Mitchell songs into the mainstream of American poetry. For his small book *The Seventeen Horse Songs of Frank Mitchell, Nos. X–XIII,* and others of the songs he published in the magazine *Alcheringa,* for which he was a co-editor, he modified McAllester's texts into what he calls "total translations." What I like about his scattered renderings are that they do make Mitchell's horse songs more readily available for use than the recorded audio material is. Upon examining the Mitchell songs they offer, I found that despite the presence of both Twins in the myth Mitchell had earlier recorded for Haile, the songs focus on the quest of Enemy Slayer alone, the search that eventually led him to the house of his father, Sun. In the tenth song he arrives. The eleventh takes up his seeing the sacred horses and other wondrous possessions of Sun, whereas the twelfth treats the boy's journey home. In the next, Enemy Slayer sings about the horses as if they had already become his. The last six songs center on the ceremony wrought by Changing Woman and the Holy Ones to deliver the Blessing Way and therefore the horses, too, to the people on earth.

What I dislike most about the offerings that Rothenberg has termed "total translations" are—at least for my purposes—their abstractness. True, Rothenberg has described his reworkings and renditions of these translations in an introduction to them in the magazine as "sound poetry," and has offered there some theorizing about his intent for them—one admittedly quite different from mine. Yet as grateful as I am for some of his earlier renderings of Indian poetry, for instance that of the Aztecs, this particular experiment of his does not strike me as highly successful. First to be noted is that since Mitchell was skillful in the Navajo singer practice of abbreviating and abstracting lines for ceremonial use, the meaning of his songs had already become somewhat partially obscured. Second, as far as poetry goes, further loss may have resulted from the very act itself of the translation of them, and despite McAllester's considerable and proven skills in such a capacity. Still, even so, Rothenberg's additional work on the songs could hardly be described as what I think of in connection with the word "total," not to mention the distortions he notes as making in order to fit the songs into the "sound frames" in English that he had in mind. To me, somewhere along the way we get too far from Mitchell's originals for the renderings resulting to retain much of their original import. For the best sense of this, I think we must go back to McAllester's direct translations instead—that is, where we have them. And lacking them, I think it still preferable to turn to Slim Curly's horse songs and rely on the very adequate and equally appropriate renderings of Haile's that are presented in *Blessingway*. But before leaving the particular matter of the problems involved in translating and interpreting Native American materials, let me say in passing that both McAllester and W. Beavis have each, in articles cited in the note appended here, treated the subject with discernment and at more length than I can now.[16]

While the pattern of the songs of Slim Curly does not vary greatly from that of Frank Mitchell, the emphasis does, and in Curly's a wealth of more elaborate details are also assembled. Much is made in Curly's songs of how the principal seeker, who identifies himself with the son of the Sun and Changing Woman, is enthralled by his first sight of the horse in his father's dwelling, its beauty and magnificence fashioned from a miraculous assortment of elements and substances: such as ears of the Sun's pollen, eyes of great dark stars, legs of lightning, and tail formed from a shower of white rain—the latter two being some of its evident fertility attributes. The last several of Slim Curly's songs treat the gradual approach of the culture hero to the miraculous animal, alternating between going forward to claim it and waiting hopefully to receive it, but all the while pleading for the favor of the gift and always addressing the animal as the "beautiful one." In summing up Curly's horse songs, I must agree with David McAllester, who once told me he thought they represented some of the best offerings available of Navajo poetry.[17]

In other horse songs contained in the two Blessing Way books and in Frisbie's *Kinaaldá,* the symbolism of semiprecious stones and rare minerals in the physical make-up of the animal are again much elaborated on. In addition to what we knew before, substances making horses up range from the familiar turquoise to mirage stone (a banded aragonite) down to a sampling of earth itself, which has come from one of the four sacred mountains. All these substances that are considered as part of the composition of the horse's body, with turquoise often being prominent among them, are moreover things that these later sources reveal go into the composition of the Mountain Soil Bundle, without which a Blessing Way cannot be performed. But while anyone who has read *They Sang for Horses* will be familiar with the sacred and transcendent elements out of which the horse was created, still it was not until after the book's publication that I knew the extent of the wondrous intelligence certain Navajo attributed to the creatures: some saying, like various of the myths attest, that horses were really human beings in a different form, and others, like the case of the Navajo medicine man Curly Mustache, that they were far superior since they had been created with more values than a person had. Some even said that they had magic powers above those of any shaman, which fleeing riders could petition for and get—down to sensing the precise location of enemies. Yet in order to acquire these abilities, petitioners did need to demonstrate proper respect first to the mounts believed to have them.[18]

To consider two of the subcategories of ceremonies springing from Blessing Way that frequently contain horse symbolism, let's turn to the hogan blessing rites as well as to the girl's puberty ceremony, both of which can employ horse songs in their own specific fashions. Again, Frisbie is the main authority on either ceremony, with Frank Mitchell the major informant. She wrote her Ph.D. dissertation on the hogan rite and published an article that has become a valuable source on the subject. It, "Ritual Drama in the Navajo House Blessing Ceremony," is included in the collection titled *Southwestern Indian Ritual Drama,* which she edited (1980.) The hogan rite is conducted chiefly to bless a private home—a mythic parallel is the hogan of Changing Woman afloat in the far Pacific—with horse chants offered at corrals or other homestead structures that shelter horses and other livestock. However, this ceremony and its songs may be offered to bless public structures, too, in the wider context of stadiums, including arenas and corrals where horses and other livestock are presented or held. On the other hand, even though the horse songs occur very often, the ceremony need not always include them.

Many of the decisions regarding the songs for the private rite are left up to what the owner of the dwelling wishes included, thus Frisbie found quite a bit of variation as to the number or type of songs used.

The two types of songs that must always make up hogan rites are the Chief Hogan Songs and the Talking God Songs. Both song cycles can also contain references to sacred horses and others of the valued possessions associated with them, depending mostly on the practitioner's version of the ceremony performed. Such is the case with a song prayer Gladys Reichard collected in 1940 at the public rite given in Gallup, New Mexico, to dedicate that city's Indian Ceremonial stadium. The pertinent line from it goes: "Horses of all kinds, those will I accumulate." Like in the case of the singing of all such lines, the singer offered it as a general petition for the increase and continuation of the animals belonging to all the participants attending the rite. Reichard reported he later told her he didn't receive any objections for using this song at such a public event because "the song belonged to everyone." However, Frisbie notes that as more and more public hogan rites are held, the Navajos in charge of arranging them decide which songs containing sacred references are okay for singing before an audience that will likely contain non-Navajos or at least people who cannot be expected to be aware of the need to show proper respect when they are sung.

One of River Junction Curly's songs recorded by Haile offers lines associated with Talking and Calling Gods. It extends, too, the theme in the song just cited from Reichard, featuring as it does these lines of repeated song-prayer: "With the idea of a beautiful horse following me, I go around." The immediate lines following this statement vary from it only by mentioning rock crystal in the first stanza. This is a substance identified in myths with Talking God's possessions and that in the song is said to be what the head of the horse is formed from. The reference is replaced in the next stanza where the rainbow takes the place of rock crystal in the wording. Likewise, the first of Slim Curly's horse songs describes the last home of Changing Woman, picturing it in the familiar way of "floating on the Pacific Ocean," and mentioning some of the precious things that the singer envisions as being attached to the white shell and turquoise "uprights" that are said to be a feature of the place. If only these features can be transferred to the rear corners of the household that is being blessed, then its owners will "be winners," for through their associations with the sacred horses, they have thus become "partners" with them. Therein they are the proud recipients of "possessions of all kinds," including the handsome earthly forms of these beautiful horses that promise those lucky enough to possess them "long and happy lives." Along with this blessing, there will be plenty of sheep and other domestic animals at the new home that, as mentioned, the term "horse" can in a song be made to stand for. Moreover, in Curly's eighth horse song, a number of lines in its stanzas offer references to "the common sound" that the horses coming from Changing Woman's and Sun's home are making "very close by, behind my hogan." The singer affirms the deities' horses can be heard through the "tingling of their hoofs," the "pounding of their bodies," and through "their leg movements in unison," and their "neighing," which accompanies the motion of their legs. The reference to the white shell and turquoise uprights in the rear of the petitioner's house found in Curly's first song probably refers either to the rear poles supporting the house or to the "tie-posts" behind it. Haile renders the word for the object to which horses are attached at Navajo dwellings throughout the references to them as "uprights." Like Goddard, who also uses the word "poles" in connection with the "tie-posts" of a White Mountain Apache myth provided earlier, Haile implies that the Navajo uprights can likewise serve as the poles do for these Apache: as fetishes for producing horses. In fact, Goddard's text indicates that the words for "tie-posts" and "directional poles" are, like their purposes, used interchangably, and that both allude to directional fixtures for increasing horses as well as trappings. Further, it should also be mentioned, as a point of general interest, that two of the Chief Hogan Songs recorded by Frank Mitchell are to be found in *Navajo Blessingway Singer,* though neither makes any mention of horses, sacred or otherwise.[19]

A great portion of the blessing for the hogan as a dwelling is devoted to the four main support poles of the structure, and stresses how the strength of these typify a long and secure life. And the songs used in this particular part of the hogan Blessing Way rite call to mind those the Mescalero and Chiricahua Apache call "dwelling songs," in which long life and happiness are associated with the horses of the four directions. One such song has been presented in the text as also being used in connection with a song these Apache sing, too, at their puberty rites. The song centers on how these same blessings were provided by Killer-of-Enemies and White Painted Woman at the time when they put the four directional poles in place to support the ceremonial tepee in which the girl's rite is held. The lines specifically point out how each of the cardinal horses featured in them stands "for long life." Wyman says of the Navajo that the Chief Hogan Songs can, in fact, be used to identify a ceremony as belonging to Blessing Way or to one of its subcategory rites because only these rites mention the dwelling's poles and its stone slabs. We

Because the hogan blessing rite begins with the blessing of the four main directional supports of the structure—an act then followed by the singing of songs entreating assistance from the cardinal horses identified with them—Frisbie aptly referred to the animal's Navajo ceremonial role as being that of "a creature of directions and deities."

need to recall also at this point that even today, the Mescalero and Chiricahua Apache male relatives of the celebrant girl always erect four newly cut spruce poles to support the conical-shaped ceremonial tepee that represents the home of White Painted Woman, the deity with whom we've seen the Apache pubescent girl identified. Further, like in the case of the Navajo girl and the equivalent goddess, Changing Woman, whose adolescent rite the myth governing the Navajo ceremony concerns, it should be noted that the Navajo goddess's father, First Man, had built her first hogan atop Spruce Hill. The latter is a name the Navajo frequently substitute for Gobernador Knob, and the name came into existence due to the abundance of the spruce growing there. What we should bear in mind besides is that the Mescalero style of tepee used for the puberty rite has a resemblance to the conical-shaped hogan of the Navajo. I want to mention in passing here additionally that this style of tepee is said to have come into greater use by the Mescalero when with the coming of the horse, they were then able to hunt buffalo on the plains. Thus, the animal not only was to assist them in the hunt, but also in moving a tepee of this style. The tepee became feasible then as a dwelling because of its portability on a travois.[20]

Although Frisbie's *Kinaaldá* is the definitive study so far of the Navajo girl's puberty ceremony, information about the ceremony in general is much enhanced by Shirley M. Begay's *Kinaaldá: A Navajo Puberty Ceremony* (1983), illustrated with sketches by a Navajo artist concerning each ritual act and providing a richness in other details. Above all, Begay's work presents the unique perspective of a Navajo female author for whom the ceremony was performed, and who for years has likewise participated in the rites of other girls. As I've mentioned, a number of the motifs developed in the hogan rites carry over to the girl's puberty ceremony, and I have found other close parallels between the practices among the Navajo and those of the Apache. In this connection, I want to remind readers how "dwelling songs" are again sung by the Mescalero and Chiricahua while the four support poles for the ceremonial tepee are being raised—the structure within which the puberty ceremony will be celebrated—and where the poles have the symbolic connection with the horses of the four directions. In one case I've presented, a closer affinity between the maiden and the mythic dimension is expressed in a horse song that makes me feel more than ever, and in view of the available sources now, that it is one belonging to the Navajo puberty rite. The words tell of how a maiden is ritually transformed into a large black mare—an animal of her own sex—which then may be said to transfer to her from the sacred region of the east, the powers of endurance and speed, and the blessing of a long life. The inclusion of horse songs on the last night of the kinaaldá, as well as for the presence of horse symbolism at various times in some of the other ritual offered in it, is for the same purpose as that shown in the text for the Apache: to bring the blessings of increase and health to the girl's family's animals and those belonging to the participants attending. Likewise the ritual involving fertility symbolism occurs so that the girl herself will be able to reproduce and also count many animals like those in the songs among her possessions. Of its place in the ceremonial framework, Frisbie notes that "the horse is a creature of directions and deities." While the offering of the horse songs themselves is again optional, she says they are a very popular item belonging to the "free song" periods occurring at specific points in the ceremony when those attending who know them can sing them if the audience decides to include them.[21]

Now about the bridles that the text speculates about in connection with their placement before the girl and alongside the other articles at the 1931 rite Frances Gillmor saw. Frisbie, Begay, and the field notes of Dorothea Leighton all note at ceremonies they've witnessed over the years the presence of similar trappings representing those of the ceremonial guests' personal possessions. This is done, Begay specifically states, so that if in the future the person the particular item represents wants more valuable possessions like it, the wish will be granted.[22]

Painting the girl with white clay is supposed to insure a never-failing increase in the blessings of life, especially in horses and other valuable possessions and beneficial gifts, again not just for the girl, who is supposed to be praying for these things at the time, but also for the guests who are simultaneously expected to be offering prayers for themselves to that effect.[23]

According to Begay, the final act of a girl's ceremony carries through the link with horses that the other acts have demonstrated. She goes to a family corral and blesses the horses that are penned there with corn pollen for the purpose of transferring to them at this time some of her powers to bring health and increase to all that she blesses.[24]

In light of all this additional information provided by the publications concerning the kinaaldá, we can see that the Navajo, like we saw earlier was the case with the Apache, accorded their horses a similarly exalted position in their puberty rites. Imagine their shock, then, when, as was also mentioned, the federal government set up a livestock reduction program for them and the Western Apaches in the 1930s that continued into the 1940s for the Navajo and into the 1950s among the Apache. Overgrazing—due in part to the huge number of stray horses left uncontrolled—was depleting the ranges of the Navajo and those of the San Carlos and White Mountain people. But to the Navajo, the Blessing Way injunction of "increase with no decrease" meant just what it said: assurance from the gods that if the traditional ceremonial life was conducted according to form, supply and demand would take care of themselves. So to take up a matter only briefly touched on before, the Navajo particularly fought the killing off of superfluous horses in every way they could, with reasoning that made the best of sense to them. Drought from time to time exacerbated the problem. Yet to them, as the songs and prayers from Blessing Way that once were used in the now obsolete rain ceremony affirmed, the supply of rain was in the hands of the Water Horse Spirits that are mentioned in some of the songs and in others, to horses formed of the supernatural forces that Slim Curly's horse songs describe. An example of the latter is Curly's forty-sixth song from the Blessing Way cycle. It clearly shows how the horse could be directly associated by the Navajo with rain and fertile, growing plants and also serves as a typical song pertaining to this now abandoned ceremony. As further noted in the text, this rite belongs, like the hogan and puberty rites do, to the subcategory ceremonies that stem from Blessing Way. At this point, I want to call attention to the supernatural attributes for moisture-making that Curly's rain horse possesses. These are: the "straight lightning" produced from the sound the animal makes, the "vegetation," which is caused by its face, and the "white drooping rain" sent by its tail. This song of Curly's, then, as well as material in some of the other works published since my book's appearance literally spell out how the lack of rain can be directly tied in with the Blessing Way, therein making the kind of concrete connection between horses and the rain rites possible that was not as easily demonstrated earlier.[25]

The offense for destroying the creatures that were truly the earthly forms of these water spirits and supernatural horses was obvious to everybody but Washington: hence this punishment of little rain. And the immortals who had planted the wild medicinal plants for the people's use could be offended likewise and, as a consequence, cause the plants they nurtured, and on which the tribe depended, to die off. But back to the matter of resolving the problems the program itself created. The government finally in desperation turned the matter of livestock control over to the Navajo Tribe, who through their chapter houses and grazing committees did eventually cope with the problem commendably and effectively. This troublesome chapter in tribal animal husbandry is fully explored, with sufficient reference to ceremonialism, in a valuable work containing interviews with many Navajo leaders and horse owners as well as with medicine people. Published by the Navajo Community College in 1974, it was edited by Broderick Johnson and Ruth Roessel, and is entitled *Navajo Livestock Reduction: A National Disgrace.* Similar subject matter is touched upon, too, by James F. Downs, whose work, *Animal Husbandry in Navajo Society and Culture,* appeared just after mine had in 1964 first gone to the publishers. Today, the Downs work still makes a fine and substantial contribution to the subject of the husbandry of horses and other domestic animals among the Navajo. Considering that the work does not include anything about the esoteric practices of these people, and in view of the focus on such practices in my book, the two do not overlap, but as far as the Navajo are concerned make fine companions instead in providing a total picture of the procedures the latter have practiced within modern times in their daily care of horses.

In connection with the Western Apache, the best and basic source of information on the various cattle industries and the accompanying herding operations for them that involve horses remains the concise but solid *The San Carlos Indian Cattle Industry* (1963), written by my former professor and guide in Apache studies at the University of Arizona, the late Harry T. Getty, Professor of Anthropology. Fine glimpses of the Navajo attitudes about their homeland's natural grasslands, ranges, plants, and herbs are offered in a book with the title *Navajo Sacred Places* by Klara Bonseck Kelley and Harris Francis, published as recently as 1994. In a few places, the work contains other material more directly related to horse lore, too. For instance, mention is made of the fact that even nowadays, the Navajo say prayers and offer the four stones most commonly associated with the cardinal directions for the well-being of their horses and livestock at various sacred spots on hilltops. Such high places on the reservation are favored for the sighting of straying stock.[26]

To round out the subject of Blessing Way's subrituals that contain horse symbolism, I want now to turn to another abandoned Navajo rite— the one associated with raiding. Two books subsequent to mine by Karl W. Luckert give new understanding of hunting rituals, and furnish welcome glimpses into former rites for raiding, particularly those featuring the use of Blessing Way hogan songs in sweat houses: *The Navajo Hunter Tradition* (1975) and *Navajo Mountain and Rainbow Bridge Religion* (1977). In these sources, and again in Downs's book on husbandry, I found proof after my book's publication that Navajo raiders, like those who went on forays among the Apache, purified themselves with sweat lodge sessions they held in connection with raid preparations. At such times they offered horse songs in the lodges among others. Likewise, a comparative look at a similar practice among the Western Apache is now more readily accessible than before through an interview Grenville Goodwin did with an aged raider in the early 1930s. According to his elderly informant, these Apache observed another cherished tradition in connection with the singing: that of feasting on a couple of horses in the sweat lodges while they sang the sets of songs, among which were those for horses. Another of Goodwin's informants claimed, in fact, that while they steamed themselves in the lodges, they never sang anything but horse songs. These informants were among the aged Apaches possessing firsthand raiding experience and knowledge whose unique accounts, including the lengthy

and especially informative one by John Rope, Goodwin had the fore-
sight to put down. Published first in a western history magazine no longer
circulated, the accounts are now easily obtained for they are part of a
landmark work on the subject of Apache raiding that Keith H. Basso
expertly edited and annotated. I refer to his one-of-a-kind edition of
Goodwin's notes that appeared in 1971 under the title of *Western Apache
Raiding and Warfare*.[27]

In view of the fact that less has come to light on Apache horse lore
than on that of the Navajo since *They Sang for Horses* was published, the
Basso and Goodwin offering merits special attention here, as do several
other outstanding additions I now want to turn to: Morris E. Opler's
Apache Odyssey: A Journey Between Two Worlds (1969), Keith Basso's *The
Cibecue Apache* (1970), Eve Ball's *In the Days of Victorio* (1970) and her
Indeh: An Apache Odyssey (1980), as well as Richard J. Perry's *Apache Reservation: Indigenous Peoples and the American State* (1993). These books all
offer an array of fresh insights, but Ball's two have the added advantage of
coming to us directly from the oral histories she took down from Mescalero
and Chiricahua leaders, men who had been children in the raiding days,
yet who had the advantage of intimate acquaintance with their fathers'
and uncles' experiences. One of these Apaches was James Kaywaykla, a
nephew of Victorio's and a grand nephew of chief Nana's, both of whom
belonged to the Warm Springs Apache who now live at Mescalero. Another was Ace Daklugie, the nephew of Geronimo and son of the
Chiricahua leader Juh. Besides these family ties, Daklugie had taken part,
too, in directing matters concerning the successful buildup of the fore-
runner of what is now the tribal cattle industry at Mescalero. Of particular
interest here in the works of Ball, and especially in the Basso and Goodwin
title, is the material containing examples of the ritual the Apache practiced on raids that involved the use of supernatural powers to control
horses, and all of which in turn add new vistas to what is already included
on that subject in this study. As we have seen, the medicine people who
possessed such talents were held in high regard and, of course, deemed
especially valuable on raids. One report now introduces us to another
tactic not yet discussed that a certain medicine man practiced. He would
rope a tree in enemy territory, say Mexico, then the whole party would
gather around and sing what he specified as a "horse song." If they repeated
this ceremony four times along the way, they would find and escape with
all the horses they wanted. Other men were reported to have the power
to make the horses of their enemies balk, disrupting any chase after a raid.
Basso's notes to Goodwin's accounts further indicate a wider utilization

in Apache puberty rites and raid rituals of the good luck or "happiness songs"—those songs of the Apache that possess a marked resemblance to many of the Navajo horse songs. Basso and Goodwin provide new insights, too, into the magical creative power of words that are so empowered through speech as to assure success in getting horses. As shown in an earlier chapter, these powers were frequently related to the altered language.

Basso and Goodwin affirm that the Western Apache, like the Chiricahua and Mescalero, referred to horses and other things associated with the raid and warpath only by certain terms while engaged in such activities. While a Western Apache informant of Goodwin's would only say that "a horse" was known by a "different word," he gave the name for a mule or burro as "shakes his tail." Such terms, he maintained, had to be used "properly" to prevent "something bad" from besetting the speaker or the mission itself. Additionally, the old Navajo warrior Gus Bighorse, who had seen raiding days himself, suggested that using the sacred names and songs for horses would affect the animal in certain ways that would be beneficial to the men engaged in such an exploit. These included alerting the animal to the fact that the enemy was close by, or providing it with the stamina to stand quietly in one spot for a protracted time while awaiting its master's return. When spoken, the sacred name itself enabled the animal to increase its strength and provided it with the ability to go great distances without water. While the sacred names for horses that certain Navajos possessed went on from generation to generation in a family, Bighorse, like others who have been cited previously, insisted that they had to be kept secret and as magical ritual to be used strictly among family members. Basso and Goodwin give further examples of how raiders, trusting in the potency of certain words, could in using them actually attract horses out of the herds of their victims.[28]

Basso's *The Cibecue Apache* does not contain much more on horses than a few accounts about witchcraft practices—incidents where owners suspect the working of it on their animals. The accounts provided duplicate moreover those contained in his *Western Apache Witchcraft* (1969). Opler's *Apache Odyssey*, on the other hand, does supply a number of accounts that concern horse power and the use of it, with all of them coming from Mescalero informants. However, these are so similar to those of the Chiricahua recorded in his *An Apache Life-Way* that since the latter have already been examined here, the more recent information does not strike me as warranting further investigation now. The accounts could still be used, nevertheless, to provide beneficial comparative data for researchers interested in weighing it with regard to these two different Apache peoples. My prime purpose, though, in calling attention to both the Basso title and the more recent one of Opler's is because each provides other excellent and definitive supplemental material about two important divisions of Apache people, especially the Cibecue, about whom comparatively little is otherwise available. And as for the contribution Perry's recent book makes: it presents material that furnishes a welcome 1990s updating of the cattle industry as an economic focus for the San Carlos people, therein producing much for consideration about a livelihood that still utilizes horses in herding operations and one further that has seen a decided economic decline since Getty's work appeared.[29]

As I mentioned in several places in the text, there were women singers among the Apaches. Though they were always in the minority, some did use the ceremonial privileges provided by their various powers beneficially. However, there were restrictions; women could not impersonate the Mountain Spirits, nor could they use sweat lodges. Among the Navajo, women were traditionally restricted from being ceremonialists until after menopause. Nevertheless, the custom seems to have changed among these people. Frisbie reports that since 1973 a growing number of women have conducted the public hogan rite and other literature, dating mostly since the 1980s, brings up instances of the kinaaldá being directed by women.[30] It is likely that Frisbie's forthcoming work, *Tall Woman: The Life Story of Rose Mitchell,* a biography of Frank Mitchell's wife, will contribute further to this area of investigation. Currently the book is in production at the University of New Mexico Press and not scheduled to appear until around the time this edition does.

Also, while I have attended numerous puberty rites among the Apache over the years, I have never seen or heard of a woman singer conducting one. As for the Blessing Way, in *Women in Navajo Society* (1981), Ruth Roessel, herself a well-informed Navajo author with considerable contributions about her people now to her credit, writes of studying the Blessing Way with her father. She states that both of her grandmothers were medicine women—one of them even instructed a number of male leaders.[31]

To go further back, I now know from Eve Ball's writings the name of the remarkable Apache woman I mentioned, who was known to whites as "Dexterous Horse Thief." She was Lozen, Victorio's sister, highly honored in her Warm Springs Apache tribe not only for her uncanny ability during raids in locating the enemy and horses to steal, but also as a medicine woman admired and trusted among the raiders. A great-niece of hers, Virginia Gayton, whose ancestral line and background appear in Narcissus Duffy Gayton's book with Ruth McDonald Boyer, *Apache Mothers and Daughters,* has been influential in recent times among the Mescalero Apaches in deciding many of the issues considered by the tribal council of which she has been a member. Though she could not properly be called a medicine woman in the ceremonial sense, she has worked in hospital administration and with health issues most of her life, and has helped legislate and have a say about many important health matters involving her people.

While Eve Ball's writings on Lozen serve as a major source for two books published during the last decade offering new insights on Apache women—Henrietta Stockel's *Women of the Apache Nation* (1991) and Kimberly Moore Buchanan's *Apache Women Warriors* (1996)—both titles go beyond Ball's findings to offer data from other sources that, taken together, make for a fine and clearer portrait of the role this unusual Apache female leader played. Moreover, Stockel's work provides welcome information about a number of other contemporary Mescalero and Chiricahua female leaders. Though none of these women of today could in any way be called horse ceremonialists, I, like Stockel, am grateful to Eve Ball for first providing me with introductions, and in my case for arranging for me to photograph them as well. I might point out, however, that in connection with horses, some of them like Ruey Darrow, Blossom Haozous, and Mildred Cleghorn know much of the history of their ancestor George Wratten that might have been helpful. As an Anglo interpreter for the military who had married an Apache wife, and who often proved himself a decided help and loyal friend to the Apaches, he was present at many negotiations with their leaders that involved horses. Thus, as Eve pointed out to me, they could have been women who knew stories of Apaches individuals who professed having power with horses, though as it turned out those they recalled were all men.[32]

As far as the subject of past Apache medicine women is concerned, Joseph C. Porter's *Paper Medicine Man: John Gregory Bourke and His American West,* a 1986 publication, offers, like Buchanan's later book, interesting sketches of Apache women who dealt with horses all their lives. First, there is Francesca (or Huera), a Warm Springs Apache whose husband—and there were apparently others—was the chief named Mangus. She was a practitioner who befriended Bourke during his military assignment among the Western Apache. This woman, whom Buchanan refers to as "Pretty Mouth" (Tse-go-juni), and whom she, like Porter, also notes was struck by lightning and mauled by a mountain lion, was known, too, for her successes in effecting a series of miraculous escapes from enemies. Eve Ball's writings additionally include a few brief mentions of her and her adventures. But the longer sketches about her activities provided by Porter furnish information besides about Captain Jack, the female leader of a small band of Western Apache, whom Buchanan mentions too, crediting Bourke, like Porter, as her source. Porter, who also has the advantage of being familiar with Bourke's diary, in addition to his writing on Apache medicine men, notes how Bourke described Captain Jack as being advanced in years, "feeble," yet "bright in intellect," and a woman who could hold her own when it came to medicine.[33]

Study of the intricacies of life among the Navajo and Apache has been highly active, as you see, during the years since I finished *They Sang for Horses,* producing quite a number of notable additions to the literature already in existence. For this reason, besides the studies taking up the horse lore that I have mentioned in this epilogue, I am also including in the bibliography additional supplemental works that contain substantial mention of matters peripheral to the subject investigated here, in the hope that these sources will likewise be helpful to those readers interested in related topics.

At this point, I would like to go briefly into certain aspects of the culture in which horses were once deeply involved—practices that since the 1960s have undergone significant changes. The first is the horse's role in customs relating to death and burial. In 1967, while changes were well underway, the killing of a favorite horse was still frequently practiced, as witnessed by the composite of Navajo and Christian traditions observed at Frank Mitchell's funeral. The lack of conformity about such matters and a good review of many different Navajo death customs that were still in transition by 1978 was the subject of a special issue that year of *American Indian Quarterly,* edited by Charlotte Frisbie. Though it is now over twenty years old, the group of articles it presents remain the most up-to-date collection on the subject. Mary Shepardson, a contributor, noted elsewhere that the first Christian burial held in the Navajo Mountain area took place in 1970. She affirms in the article that in this same area, the shooting of the favorite horse of the deceased was continuing to be prevalent in 1978. But like Joyce Griffen in her contribution to the issue, she referred to how the surviving relatives often agonized together in coming to a decision about whether or not to kill the animal. Griffen reported interviewing sixteen funeral home directors in Navajo country who had witnessed a number of times the killing of a horse associated with the dead person near the grave. In Shepardson's case, she, like Jerrold Levy, still another well-known authority in the issue—and one moreover who has written elsewhere on suicide—had even heard of a Navajo who shot his mount before putting the gun to his own head. An article appears, too, by Albert E. Ward, who has since added further meaningful data about the changing death practices by way of his *Navajo Graves: An Archaeological Reflection of Ethnographic Reality* (1980). Lastly, as concerns the Navajo practice, let me note that the son of my friend Esta Tso Klade died at Blue Gap on the reservation around 1980. His sister told me afterwards that the horse he shared with his father in sheep herding was killed. However, I want to point out that the killing of the horse at the grave only takes place when the burial occurs on the reservation, not in the city cemeteries of towns bordering it where there are ordinances against such practices.[34]

Now about the Apaches. In the late 1970s, I went with Eve Ball to the funeral home service of a Mescalero man in Ruidoso, New Mexico. He was a friend of hers who loved horses, and she had introduced me to him some time before. His daughter told Eve that his horse was not to be shot: like many Apaches in these changing times, he had given it to a favorite grandson. But he still wanted Eva, as so many of the Apaches called her, to bake him a pumpkin pie—a thing I watched her do the morning of his service—to put in the coffin for "his journey." It was not the first or last pie either that this remarkable woman who counted so many of the Apache among her friends baked and carried over to that funeral home to be put inside a coffin. But to go back in history, there are several accounts of death practices in her book *Indeh* that involve Mescalero and Chiricahua horses and the disposition of them and their owners' trappings, including those of Geronimo. And additionally, before leaving the subject of funeral homes and the Apache, I want to point out that Perry's study confirms a similar popularity these days for burials from such establishments among the Western Apache, though information regarding recent practices of theirs in connection with the favorite horse is not provided.[35]

While the amazing extent to which the horse penetrated Navajo and Apache folkways is steadily on the wane, some notable exceptions still prevail, as for example in birth customs. Dorothy Smith, a Navajo friend of mine from Chinle, Arizona, told me in 1980 that she buried the umbilical cords of her three youngest children—two sons and a daughter—near their corral. The sons would thus be sure to take to horses, and the daughter was already accomplished at barrel racing. Western Apache mothers at Bylas and Whiteriver, Arizona, informed me around 1985 that they still held to that same custom, as well as to usually having a woman shaman in attendance as a midwife at a birth. Maureen Schwarz found that the burial of umbilical cords near corrals remained a prevalent custom,

San Carlos Apache cattle graze on the range at Black River Crossing, Arizona, 1970.

too, among some of her informants on the Navajo Reservation in the early 1990s. While the horse had disappeared for all practical purposes from the marriage customs before this book appeared, conversely, it has managed to sometimes cling in an extended way to a few of those practiced in connection with divorce and separation. Among the Navajo, from time to time a wife is mentioned who continues to put her husband's saddle outside the hogan door to indicate he's no longer welcome. And as late as 1993, a Western Apache woman could still announce her separation from her husband by crossing two poles before the doorway of their dwelling and tossing his things outside. Among these people, an unwanted mate's possessions usually include at least a few items of horse gear.[36]

In bringing this epilogue to a close, let me turn to further personal experiences among the people to trace shifts in horse lore and related issues, beginning with my first visit to the Navajo country. It came in 1956 when I went to a squaw dance at Cow Springs, near Red Lake, just north of Kayenta, Arizona. The reservation roads in those days were mainly dirt washboard affairs along which you often had to pull to the shoulder to avoid a mudhole or to let a buckboard full of colorfully dressed inhabitants pass. You saw a great many riders across the wide expanses too. And far out of the small settlements and towns just mentioned, you saw hardly any buildings except hogans and corrals in little huddles where extended families lived. Ceremonial grounds were always packed with a random gathering of the ubiquitous wagons, a rare pickup, and numerous tethered horses. By and large, the women wore plush velvet blouses with roomy satin skirts, and the men, rough range clothing like that of white ranchers—both the Navajo and the Apache having turned into livestock cultures, though after the raiding days, of course. So things looked much as they would have in the nineteenth century. Yet not quite. Many of the corrals were low on horses then, or without them at all, and the tribe was likewise suffering from the shrinkage of their herds of sheep, their basic form of subsistence at that time. Because of the stock reduction program, they and the San Carlos and White Mountain Apache had lost those animals along with a heavy percentage of their range horses, and they were all bitter about it. At the time, one could not help questioning whether horses in any great number would ever roam the high desert valleys and canyons of all these people again. Still, in those days the horses were yet the basic means of travel, either carrying riders or else pulling wagons, and they were additionally the main animal helping with herding or other tasks.

As my visits to these areas proceeded on into the 1960s, I was usually accompanied by my husband, L.D. Clark. In Navajoland as in the mountainous regions of central Arizona that surround the Apache living on the adjacent San Carlos and Fort Apache reservations, we began to encounter newly paved and widened roads. Yet the homes around us were still mainly grass wickiups with surrounding brush arbors, or at most cabin-size frame houses. The physical layouts of these dwellings demonstrated the Apaches' preference to cluster together in little groups composed of relatives inside the small towns that made up their population centers rather than in isolated small groups on the range. This was a trait of theirs, in fact, that Harry Getty often lamented about to students of his like me, promptly explaining that in the long run, this tendency might one day work against

Today the rodeo, which goes back to the 1920s on the Navajo and Apache reservations, has helped thrust the horse's place to the top of the list as being, with its rider the chief performer in the favorite competitive sport of all the different Southern Athapascan groups.

what was then their flourishing cattle industry. He was engrossed in doing the history of the one at San Carlos at that time and thought the only way these people could depend on its remaining a successful venture was for them in particular to adapt their lives like Anglo cowboys and ranchers did and live with their families out on their ranges. These afforded good grazing, and by living close to the cattle, they would better be able to supervise and care for them. His particular concern about their failure to do so is one, by the way, that Richard Perry's *Apache Reservation* demonstrates the wisdom of through its picture of the decline in recent years that this tribal industry has been experiencing. However, this is by no means to imply that Perry has ever known of the conjectures Getty made to his classes, but only to note that what he feared has been shown by Perry as now having come to pass.

But back to my own picture of the Western Apache whom L.D. and I visited with in the 1960s. Younger women were starting to wear slack suits, saving their camp dresses for ceremonies, but older women still wore them daily. And half the mothers continued to carry their babies on cradleboards. Apache men, like the Navajo, were most often seen in western clothes, their hair usually short, though sometimes long and hanging straight down, while various of the Navajo men of the same period did wear theirs proudly in a traditional bun or pulled back with a hair-tie.

As pointed out, range management during the stock reduction days was never truly successful. But a revitalized ranching economy—with the Navajo as well as the Jicarilla Apache increasingly turning away from sheep to cattle—has been on the rise in recent decades, which has meant of course a greater use for horses. So these days we are beginning to see an appreciable comeback of the equine population after all among the majority of Southern Athapascans.

Presently in addition to ranching chores, horses of course figure extensively in the Navajo and Apache passion for the rodeo. The latter goes back to the 1920s when Indian rodeos began evolving in places like Gallup, Flagstaff, and Phoenix. By the 1930s they were flourishing enough among the Western Apache that Grenville Goodwin applauded the sport for the needed cash it was bringing in, and they were getting popular then among the Navajo, too, with the Rodeo of the Navajo Nation becoming since 1946 an annual, well-attended event. Today rodeos are in full swing on nearly every weekend of the late spring, summer, and early fall in practically every town or sizeable rural community throughout the Navajo and Apache reservations. As such, they provide a ready cash flow to all the people, not just through participation in the arenas for the purses offered there, but in the stands for fast foods, jewelry, handicrafts, and even in the spontaneous tailgate flea markets that surround them and supply like them other welcome avenues for making money.

Among both the Navajo and Apache, the rodeo, as the most popular sport of any these days, has helped thrust the horse's place in Southern Athapascan societies to the top of the list as being with its rider the chief performer in the competitions most admired and attended by all the people. Calf roping, bull riding, bronc riding, bareback riding, and steer wrestling are the standard offerings, as in Anglo rodeos. The ready cash offered in the various competitions continues having its impact on the

This Navajo chicken pull of 1913, photographed by Dwight Franklin, features the horsemen starting off from the line where they have been waiting for the opportunity to dash out and seize the chicken from the rider on the mottled white horse. (Courtesy Special Collections, University of Arizona Library/Tucson)

economy while the events requiring skills in horsemanship in turn also produce their share of role models among the people.

One unusual feature once common but less so today is horse racing—in former days mustang racing. But if now rare at rodeos, horse races are still often staged at Navajo squaw dances, with betting very much a part of the activities. The Jicarilla Apache continue to hold them in connection with their annual, traditional relay races at Horse and Stone Lakes on September 15. A recent work offering a good summary of the rodeo and its events along with cattle ranching—not only among the Navajo and some of the Apache, but of many other western Indian groups—is Peter Iverson's *When Indians Became Cowboys: Native People and Cattle Ranching in the American West* (1994). The work extends a theme James Downs first sketched with discernment in his article "The Cowboy and the Lady," which focuses on the reasons why the role model of today's Navajo male is the American cowboy.[37]

Another once popular activity that has faded considerably from the rodeo scene is the chicken pull. In a big open space a chicken is buried up to the neck. Suddenly out of a group of waiting horsemen, one of the riders darts forward in hell-for-leather fashion, then leans low while sweeping past the chicken anchored in a hole to grab it by the head and pull it out of the ground. If the rider succeeds, the others, who have been waiting in a line, rush in to seize the prize, while the one with the chicken—dead by now—resists by beating them on the shoulders with it. Among some of the Navajo, a bag of money used to be buried with the chicken. If you got hold of that, you had to fight even harder to retain it. The best chicken pulls I ever saw were in the 1970s and took place at Zia, New Mexico. Some of the other pueblos like San Juan sometimes held good ones too, and at all of them, as was the case at Zia, the chicken was customarily a rooster. I loved to listen to my friend Juan Pino, a former governor at Zia who then was around sixty years old, recall for a number of his customary Navajo guests and myself at his and his wife Vicentita's feast table, the stories of rooster pulls there in which visiting Navajos from the Torreon area participated when he was a young man. The rivalry was fierce. He would laugh and tell about how he and others from Zia would pursue the Navajo riders all the way out from the pueblo to around Cabezon Peak, and how the rider with the rooster would be slapping it against the shoulders of those who came close enough, and of how they in turn fought in their saddles to grab and carry it away. Ruth Roessel wrote of watching chicken pulls as a little girl on the Navajo Reservation. Her father always said that if all the people took part, the chicken pull could bring rain.[38] My friends at Zia also regarded the chicken pull as part of the rain-making rituals. However that may be, these Southwestern Indians adopted this sport from the Spaniards: from riding feats *a la jineta*. I encountered several such exhibitions in Spain in the late 1960s and early 1970s after seeing them as well during the 1960s at times when I was in Mexico.[39]

Now, while I feel fortunate in my research and blessed in my association with Navajo and Apache friends and acquaintances, my luck has been sporadic, as I suspect is the case with most researchers. One great disappointment was that I never succeeded in getting to meet Father Berard Haile. Bolstered with an introduction from my friend and mentor Frances Gillmor, I went in 1956 to the St. Michael's Mission outside Window Rock to seek him out. Sadly I found that he was in the hospital in Santa Fe—and alas, he remained there for a long time, never recovering his health until his death in 1961. I was not allowed to talk with him later either because those who took care of him thought he was too weak to stand the excitement of discussing the Blessing Way with visiting students.

They felt this way—and I've come to think justifiably so—because they saw how he lived in constant anxiety for fear he could never finish his work on this, the Navajo ceremony that he was doubtless the most attached to, and despite the many other contributions he had made previously in interpreting the various, different ceremonies he collected and happily saw published.

In 1970 I met Frank Mitchell's grandson Douglas. He was about to leave for Wesleyan University to help David McAllester with Frank's recordings. He sang one of Frank's horse songs for my husband and me under the cliffs of Tse Bonito Park in Window Rock. That remains for me an unforgettable and irreplaceable moment. When David and Susan McAllester visited with me one afternoon while they were in Tucson seeing about the publication of Frank's autobiography, I learned about Douglas's untimely death. According to the autobiography, some of his family thought he had a voice much like his grandfather's. They had even once felt he might become a Blessing Way singer himself.

Another sorrow comes to mind concerning Phillip Cassadore, a gifted San Carlos Apache medicine man whose ancestors were leaders. He seemed to be in the prime of his life when he invited me to work with him on the beautiful Changing Woman puberty ceremony that he was so adept at conducting. I was eager to do so but I was about to go abroad, and when I came home—alas, I found that he too had met with an untimely death.

But I need not conclude with a litany of woes. For one joy is remembering how I once acquired a Navajo horse song, even though it came from a Hopi-Tewa, T. Pavetea of Seba Dalkai, Arizona. He had learned it from a male relative of his Navajo wife—a person who was a singer—though not in order to conduct a ceremony himself, but to sing on occasion for the good of the family horses, which he, following Navajo custom, helped his wife's extended family care for. Yet, in keeping with another Navajo tradition, he looked on even the singing of the song for me as a form of teaching it—that is in the sense of transferring the knowledge of it to me. For this reason, he asked me for ceremonial payment, not in money, but in items useful to the Blessing rites the song was associated with: white shell, turquoise, abalone, and a loggerhead turtle shell. I had no trouble locating any of these except that particular kind of turtle shell. Even so I held out for it, knowing that only it and it alone would do. When I finally got my hands on one, and my husband and I went to deliver it, Pavetea was not at his reservation home but at his wife's nephew's house in Holbrook.

We found the family gathered around a television set watching the manned flight to the moon. He took the shell and thanked me matter-of-factly, then went on watching the astronauts in their moon walk. A minute later, still in an unassuming voice, he said: "That trip's nothing to us, my friend. Maybe it was long ago, but I think you know: we were there before this." I only nodded then, but I want to conclude by saying that as we move forward in this new millennium, I frequently find his words returning.

One reason is because of a thought I've had earlier, too, in connection with the myths concerning horse creation, and of how I am more and more fascinated by an idea Claire Farrer presented in her fine study, *Living Life's Circle: Mescalero Apache Cosmovision*. As she noted: "If the Athapascan speakers originated in the Asian steppes, as some scholars aver, then it is quite possible, indeed probable, that they did have the horse and lost it, as some of their stories relate." She goes on to point out how such a theory also "lends credence to the idea that the Apachean ancestors were affiliated at one time with the people we today term Mongols, who, of course, are renowned horsemen and have been for millennia." With these thoughts in mind, let me say, too, that with regard to the evidence of Apachean forebears being as close to the Asian steppes as the Bering Straits are, the proof of them in the Straits area that excites me most are the finds there by archaeologists of the same kinds of scratch sticks that the different groups of Apaches here in the Southwest still use ceremonially, and which the Jicarilla of the last century even went so far as to shape into the form of a horse's hoof. True, today's Athapascan boys no longer use these sticks with ritual on raids in the way novice raiders were formerly required to do, still we know beyond a doubt how important their ritualistic use remains in all the modern-day girls' puberty rites of the various Apaches and that some Navajo ceremonialists insist on their use in a Kinaaldá performance likewise.[40]

Regardless of what the case may be about a previous acquaintance with horses centuries ago by Athapascan peoples, another reason why my friend's words come to mind is that as this new millennium proceeds, I am further reminded of several things about the horse and its importance to the people within the more recent times of the last century. That century began while the majority of people in this country were starting to conclude our own horse age, and then the latter half of it ended with the Navajo and Apache also concluding theirs, and at a time, too, when a space station was already spanning the sky. On the other hand, even now as capsules zoom back and forth to reach that station and plans continue for a visit to a planet overhead, I have also witnessed how here on earth the story of the horse and its importance to the Navajo and Apache is far from ended. Even though its role among them has changed drastically, this remains a time when most of the Southern Athapascans are beginning to bring back to their ranges—and in noticeable numbers again—the descendants of the hearty Spanish horses. Also, by and large, the horses I saw last summer grazing on scattered grasses—though mostly grama—from Whitetail to Dulce, and from Dinnehotso to down below Bylas, looked strong and sturdy enough to have had something resembling the speed and stamina of Sun's stallions infused in them from this nutritious forage, if not from vibrant ceremony and song alone. Yet what was most evident to me about them was their splendid reinvigoration. It conveyed a spirit of the rare sort I had to see before I could assess their future and make this final projection. The zest I glimpsed of their spirits was enough to assure me that whether they came to the Navajo and Apache from the gods, the Asian steppes, the Spaniards, or—as is still a possibility—from all of them, they will endure well past this year of 2001, among these people for whom they became and unquestionably still remain so extraordinary.

Notes

1. Father Berard Haile, trans. and recorder, and Leland C. Wyman, ed. and anno., *Blessingway,* (Tucson: University of Arizona Press, 1970), pp. 3–9. Incidentally, Frank Mitchell always said that he learned much from his lifelong friend, Navajo leader Charles Mitchell. His regard for Charlie Mitchell was such, in fact, that when he needed an English name under which to enroll in school, he took the name of Mitchell at Charlie's suggestion.

2. Charlotte J. Frisbie and David P. McAllester, eds., *Navajo Blessingway Singer: The Autobiography of Frank Mitchell, 1881–1967* (Tucson: University of Arizona Press, 1978), p. 335.

3. Cf. *supra,* pp. 16, 36, 79–81, 170–172, 191–192. My further study of the various songs, prayers, and mythical segments found here indicates that they belong to Blessing Way rites, though they are not presented in this context by the sources that provide them.

4. Haile and Wyman, pp. 621–634.

5. Ibid., pp. 234–240.

6. Maureen Trudelle Schwarz, *Modeled in the Image of Changing Woman: Navajo Views on the Human Body and Personhood* (Tucson: University of Arizona Press, 1997), p. 81.

7. Haile and Wyman, pp. 109–340, 343–492.

8. Frisbie and McAllester, pp. 2–3, 7–8, 227–228, 237–238.

9. Charlotte J. Frisbie, *Kinaaldá: A Study of the Navajo Girl's Puberty Ceremony.* (Middletown, Ct.: Wesleyan University Press, 1967), pp. 16–17—hereafter cited as *Kinaaldá;* Haile and Wyman, p. xxiii, n.7; p. 9, n. 21.

10. Kluckhohn and Leighton, p. 226.

11. Frisbie and McAllester, pp. 204, 214, 237.

12. Haile and Wyman, p. xxii.

13. Frisbie and McAllester, pp. 210–211.

14. For more extended treatments concerning the power of words and repetitions, see Sam D. Gill, *Native American Religious Action: A Performance Approach to Religion* (Columbia: University of South Carolina Press, 1987), p. 18, and N. Scott Momaday, "The Man Made of Words," in *Indian Voices: The First Convocation of American Indian Scholars* (San Francisco: Indian Historian Press, 1970), pp. 49–62.

15. David P. McAllester, ed. and trans. *Hogans: Navajo Houses and House Poems.* Photographs by Susan W. McAllester (Middletown, Ct.: Wesleyan University Press, 1980), pp. 105–106. Note that I feel the song rendered here is one of McAllester's translations of the horse songs that Frank Mitchell recorded for him. Cf. with the similar song of Slim Curly in Haile and Wyman, p. 252, and see also ibid., pp. xxiii, 33, 249–264; *supra,* p. 175; Frisbie and McAllester, pp. 4, 6–7.

16. Jerome Rothenberg, "A Note to Accompany the 'First Horse Song of Frank Mitchell,'" *Alcheringa: Ethnopoetics* I (Fall 1970), p. 63. Note that the small book of Mitchell's horse songs appeared in London: Tetrad Press, 1969. See also David P. McAllester, "A Different Drum: A Consideration of Music in Native American Humanities," in *The Religious Character of Native American Humanities,* ed. Sam D. Gill (Tempe: Department of Religion, Arizona State University, 1977), pp. 170–172, and W. Beavis, "American Indian Verse Translations," *College English* XXXV, No. 6 (March 1964), pp. 693–703.

17. Haile and Wyman, pp. 249–264. Cf. also pp. 250–251, the turquoise horse as it is pictured in Curly's songs with the turquoise horse described in the Leightons' summary in *supra,* p. 226.

18. Tina Bighorse, *Bighorse: The Warrior,* ed. Noel Bennett (Tucson: University of Arizona Press, 1990), pp. 90, 93, 96; Robert S. McPherson, *Sacred Land, Sacred Views: Navajo Perceptions of the Four Corners Region,* Charles Redd Monograph in Western History, XIX (Provo: Brigham Young University, 1992), p. 62; Ruth Roessel, *Women in Navajo Society* (Rough Rock, Az.: Navajo Resources Center, 1981), pp. 49, 144.

19. Charlotte J. Frisbie, "Ritual Drama in the Navajo House Blessing Ceremony," in *Southwestern Indian Ritual Drama,* ed. Charlotte J. Frisbie (Albuquerque: University of New Mexico Press, 1980), pp. 175, 188—hereafter cited as "House Blessing." See also Frisbie and McAllester, pp. 171–174; Haile and Wyman, pp. 113–118; 114, n. 99; 245; 247, n. 178; 251–252; 384, n. 280; 523; Reichard, *Navaho Religion,* I, p. 290. For a review of the Navajo and White Mountain Apache use of terms "uprights" and "tie-posts," see *supra,* pp. 197–198, Goddard, *Myths and Tales from the White Mountain,* pp. 105–106.

20. *Supra,* pp. 251–254; Haile and Wyman, pp. 13–14; Opler, *An Apache Life-Way,* p. 13. See also Morris Edward Opler, *Apache Odyssey: A Journey Between Two Worlds* (New York: Holt, Rinehart & Winston, 1969), p. 156.

21. *Supra,* pp. 79, 253; Frisbie, *Kinaaldá,* pp . 69, 203, 260, 269, 299, 348, 372; Shirley M. Begay, *Kinaaldá: A Navajo Puberty Ceremony* (Rough Rock, Az.:

Navajo Curriculum Center, 1982), pp. 127, 131, 135. See also Schwarz, pp. 218–219.

22. Begay, p. 127; Frisbie, *Kinaaldá*, pp. 48, 370–371, 381, 396–399.

23. Frisbie, *Kinaaldá*, p. 368. See also LaVerne Harrell Clark, "The Girl's Puberty Ceremony of the San Carlos Apaches," *Journal of Popular Culture* 10 (1976), pp. 303–328. The article is illustrated with numerous of Clark's photographs of the stages of the ceremony.

24. Begay, pp. 163, 169. Cf. *supra,* p. 190.

25. Haile and Wyman, pp. 8–9; *supra,* pp. 265–266.

26. See Downs, pp. 21, 50, 89. His book, hereafter cited as *Husbandry,* appeared in the University of California Publications in Anthropology, I (Berkeley: University of California Press, 1964). The Kelley and Francis title was published by Indiana University Press, Bloomington. See pp. 81, 102–103, 201–203.

27. Basso's edition of Goodwin's notes was published in Tucson by the University of Arizona Press. See pp. 193, 215, 247, 275, 319, n. 6. Cf. also Frisbie and McAllester, p. 84.

28. Basso and Goodwin, pp. 48, 101–103, 115, 148–150, 176, 178, 253, 265, 274; p. 302, n. 11 and n. 12; p. 319, n. 6; Bighorse, p. 91; *supra,* pp. 142, 146–147, 148, 195–196. Ball's *In the Days of Victorio* was published by the University of Arizona Press, Tucson. See pp. 11, 20–21, 38–48, 68–70, 104–106, 128. Her *Indeh: An Apache Odyssey*—hereafter cited as *Indeh*—was published by the Brigham Young University Press, Provo. See pp. 9, 13, 25, 60–64; p. 87, n. 111; pp. 153, 162–164, 173, 206, 278–280, 297, 311, 313.

29. Basso's book on the Cibecue was published by Holt, Rinehart & Winston in New York. See pp. 76, 83–84. His witchcraft study is Vol. XV of the Anthropological Papers of the University of Arizona, Tucson. Opler's 1969 work on the Mescalero Apache was published by Holt, Rinehart & Winston in New York. See pp. 46, 124–125, 144–145, 152, 156, 189, 199–200, 238.

30. *Supra,* pp. 177, 190, 235–238; Opler, *An Apache Life-Way,* p. 201; Schwarz, p. 169; Frisbie, "House Blessing," pp. 169; 196, n. 5.

31. Roessel, pp. 121–125, 157.

32. *Supra,* p. 219, n. 149. See also Ball, *Indeh,* pp. 54, 62; Ball, *In the Days of Victorio,* pp. 9–10, 21, 38–41, 115–120, 128, 150; Ruth McDonald Boyer and Narcissus Duffy Gayton, *Apache Mothers and Daughters: Four Generations of a Family* (Norman: University of Oklahoma Press, 1992), p. 54; H. Henrietta Stockel, *Women of the Apache Nation: Voices of Truth* (Reno: University of Nevada Press, 1990), pp. 47–48; Kimberly Moore Buchanan, *Apache Women Warriors* (El Paso: Texas Western Press, 1996), p. 36.

33. John G. Bourke, "Diary," as cited in Joseph C. Porter, *Paper Medicine Man: John Gregory Bourke and His American West* (Norman: University of Oklahoma Press, 1986), pp. 170–171, 196–197. Note, too, the photo of Francisca in Porter's work, p. 246. See also Buchanan, p. 36; Ball, *In the Days of Victorio,* pp. 169, 172–173, 176, 208; *Indeh,* pp. 45–47, 179. Note Ball's mention in *In the Day of Victorio* of a Huera as the wife of Chihuahua. This could indicate a marriage of the Huera known as Francisca later than the one to Mangus. Likewise, as Ball's *Indeh* shows, under

the name of Francisca, she was said to have become one of Geronimo's wives not long before his death.

34. Mary Shephardson and Blodwen Hammond, *The Navajo Mountain Community* (Berkeley: University of California Press, 1992). The articles by Shephardson and Griffen that are cited appear in *American Indian Quarterly* IV, No. 4 (1978). See Mary Shephardson, "Changes in Navajo Mortuary Practices and Beliefs," p. 389, and Joyce Griffen, "Variations on a Rite of Passage: Some Recent Navajo Funerals," pp. 370, 372, 374, 377, 378, n.10. See also Jerrold E. Levy, "Navajo Suicide," *Human Organization* 24, No. 4 (Winter 1965), pp. 308–318, and note, too, *supra,* pp. 269–270, where details about a White Mountain Apache suicide attempt are furnished. Ward's book was published in the Ethnohistorical Report Series, II (Albuquerque: Center for Anthropological Studies, 1980).

35. *Indeh,* pp. 58, 181–182; Perry's book was published by the University of Texas Press in Austin. See pp. 174–175, 200–201. For practices observed in connection with the Apache leader Cochise's horse and the trappings at his burial, see Edwin R. Sweeney, *Cochise: A Chiricahua Apache Chief* (Norman: University of Oklahoma Press, 1991), pp. 396–397.

36. Schwarz, pp. 138–141; Perry p. 168; Clarence G. Salsbury, with Paul Hughes, *The Salsbury Story* (Tucson: University of Arizona Press, 1969), p. 184; cf. also *supra,* pp. 258–264.

37. Downs's article appears in *Native Americans Today: Sociological Perspectives,* ed. Howard M. Bahr, Bruce A. Chadwick, and Robert C. Day (New York: Harper & Row, 1972), pp. 284–287. The article appeared originally in 1963. Iverson's book was published by the University of Oklahoma Press in Norman.

38. Roessel, pp. 148–149.

39. For more details regarding Spanish influences on Navajo riding practices, see Downs, *Husbandry,* pp. 3, 50, 89.

40. Claire R. Farrer, *Living Life's Circle: Mescalero Apache Cosmovision* (Albuquerque: University of New Mexico Press, 1991), p. 236, n. 6. For a review of the Jicarilla's use of the horse's hoof-stick ceremonially, see *supra,* p. 142.

Bibliography

Aberle, David F. "A Plan for Navaho Economic Development." In *Toward Economic Development for Native American Communities.* Compendium of Papers Submitted to the Subcommittee in Economy in Government of the Joint Economic Committee. 91st Congress, 1st Session, 223–276. Washington, D.C.: Joint Committee Print, 1969.

———. "Navajo Exogamic Rules and Preferred Marriages." In *The Versatility of Kinship,* ed. Linda Cordell and Stephen Beckman, 105–143. New York: Academic, 1980.

Adair, John. *The Navajo and Pueblo Silversmiths.* Norman: University of Oklahoma Press, 1946.

Alexander, Hartley B. "The Horse in American Indian Culture." In *So Live the Works of Men,* ed. Donald D. Brand and Fred E. Harvey, 65–74. Albuquerque: University of New Mexico Press, 1939.

Allen, T. D. *Navahos Have Five Fingers.* Norman: University of Oklahoma Press, 1963.

Anonymous, 1763. *Rudo Ensayo,* trans. in 1894 by Eusebio Guitéras. Tucson: Arizona Silhouettes, 1951.

Arizona Highways (December 1958), centerfold.

———. (July 1959), cover.

Ball, Eve. *Indeh: An Apache Odyssey.* Provo: Brigham Young University Press, 1980.

———. *In the Days of Victorio.* Tucson: University of Arizona Press, 1970.

Bartlett, John Russell. *Personal Narrative of the Explorations and Incidents in Texas, New Mexico, California, Sonora and Chihuahua.* 2 vols. New York: D. Appleton and Co., 1854.

Basso, Keith H. *The Cibecue Apache.* Case Studies in Cultural Anthropology. New York: Holt, Rinehart & Winston, 1970.

———. *Western Apache Witchcraft.* Anthropological Papers of the University of Arizona, XV. Tucson: University of Arizona Press, 1969.

———. *Wisdom Sits in Places: Landscape and Language.* Albuquerque: University of New Mexico, 1996.

————, ed., and Grenville Goodwin, recorder. *Western Apache Raiding and Warfare.* From the notes of Grenville Goodwin. Tucson: University of Arizona Press, 1969.

————, and Morris E. Opler, eds. *Apachean Culture, History and Ethnology.* Tucson: University of Arizona Press, 1971.

————, eds. *Western Apache Language and Culture: Essays in Linguistic Anthropology.* Tucson: University of Arizona Press, 1989.

Beavis, W. "American Indian Verse Translations." *College English* XXXV (March 1964), 693–703.

Begay, Shirley M. *Kinaaldá: A Navajo Puberty Ceremony.* Rough Rock, Az.: Navajo Curriculum Center, 1983.

Bell, John R. *The Journal of Captain John R. Bell, Official Journalist for the Stephen H. Long Expedition to the Rocky Mountains, 1820,* ed. Harlin M. Fuller and LeRoy R. Hafen. The Far West and the Rockies Historical Series, 1820–1875, VI. Glendale: Arthur H. Clark Co., 1957.

Benavides, Fray Alonso de. *Memorial of 1630,* trans. Peter P. Forrestal. Washington, D.C.: The Academy of American Franciscan History, 1954.

————. *Fray Alonso de Benavides' Revised Memorial of 1634.* See Hodge et al.

Benson, Lyman, and Robert A. Darrow. *The Trees and Shrubs of the Southwestern Deserts.* Tucson and Albuquerque: University of Arizona Press and University of New Mexico Press, 1954.

Bighorse, Tina. *Bighorse: The Warrior,* ed. Noel Bennett. Tucson: University of Arizona Press, 1990.

Bloom, Lansing B., and Lynn B. Mitchell. "The Chapter Elections in 1672." *New Mexico Historical Review* XIII (January 1938), 85–119.

Bolton, Herbert E. *Coronado on the Turquoise Trail: Knight of Pueblos and Plains.* Albuquerque: University of New Mexico Press, 1949.

————, ed. *Spanish Explorations in the Southwest, 1542–1706: Original Narratives of Early American History.* New York: Charles Scribner's Sons, 1916.

Bourke, John G. "The Medicine-Men of the Apache." *Annual Report of the Bureau of American Ethnology,* IX, 443–603. Washington, D.C.: Government Printing Office, 1892.

Boyer, Ruth McDonald, and Narcissus Duffy Gayton. *Apache Mothers and Daughters: Four Generations of a Family.* Norman: University of Oklahoma Press, 1992.

Brant, Charles S., ed. *Jim Whitewolf: The Life of a Kiowa Apache Indian.* New York: Dover Publications, 1969.

Brugge, David. "A Comparative Study of Navajo Mortuary Practices." *American Indian Quarterly* IV, No. 4 (1978), 309–328.

Buchanan, Kimberly Moore. *Apache Women Warriors.* El Paso: Texas Western Press, 1996.

Castañeda, Pedro de. "History of the Expedition." In *Narratives of the Coronado Expedition of 1540–1542,* ed. and trans. George P. Hammond and Agapito Rey. Coronado Cuatro Centennial Publications, 1540–1940, II, 191–283. Albuquerque: University of New Mexico Press, 1940.

Castetter, Edward F., and Morris E. Opler. *The Ethnobiology of the Chiricahua and Mescalero Apache.* The University of New Mexico Bulletin, Biological Series, IV, No. 5. Albuquerque: University of New Mexico Press, 1936.

Catlin, George. *Episodes from "Life Among the Indians" and "Last Rambles," with 152 Scenes and Portraits by the Artist,* ed. Marvin C. Ross. Norman: University of Oklahoma Press, 1959.

Clark, LaVerne Harrell. "Early Horse Trappings of the Navajo and Apache Indians," *Arizona and the West* V (Autumn 1963), 233–248.

———. "The Girl's Puberty Ceremony of the San Carlos Apaches." *Journal of Popular Culture* 10 (1976), 431–448.

———. "The Mythical Horse of the Navajo and Apache Indians." In *The Western Folklore Conference: Selected Papers,* ed. Austin E. Fife and J. Golden Taylor. Monograph Series of the Utah State University Press, XI, No. 3, 33–51. Logan, 1964.

Coolidge, Dane, and Mary Roberts Coolidge. *The Navajo Indians.* Boston and New York: Houghton Mifflin Co., 1930.

Coronado, Francisco Vázquez de. "Letter of Francisco Vázquez de Coronado to His Majesty, Giving an Account of the Discovery of the Province of Tiguex. October 20, 1541." In *Narratives of the Coronado Expedition of 1540–1542,* ed. and trans. George P. Hammond and Agapito Rey. Coronado Cuatro Centennial Publications, 1540–1940, II, 185–190. Albuquerque: University of New Mexico Press, 1940.

Correll, J. Lee. *Bai-A-Lil-Le: Medicine Man—Witch.* Biographical Series of Navajo Parks and Recreation, III. Window Rock, Az.: Navajo Historical Publications, 1970.

Cremony, John C. *Life Among the Apaches.* Tucson: Arizona Silhouettes, 1951.

Curtis, Natalie. *The Indians' Book.* New York and London: Harper and Brothers, 1907.

Debo, Angie. *Geronimo: The Man, His Times, His Place.* Norman: University of Oklahoma Press, 1976.

Denhardt, Robert Moorman. *The Horse of the Americas.* Norman: University of Oklahoma Press, 1948.

Dennis, T. S., and Mrs. T. S. Dennis, eds. *Life of F. M. Buckelew, the Indian Captive as Related by Himself.* Bandera, Texas, 1925.

Dobie, J. Frank. "Indian Horses and Horsemanship." *Southwest Review* XXXV (Autumn 1950), 265–275.

———. *The Mustangs.* Boston: Little, Brown and Co., 1952.

Dodge, Richard Irving. *The Plains of the Great West and Their Inhabitants, Being a Description of the Plains, Game, Indians, &c. of the Great North American Desert.* New York: Archer House, 1959.

Downs, James F. *Animal Husbandry in Navajo Society and Culture.* University of California Publications in Anthropology, I. Berkeley: University of California Press, 1964.

———. "The Cowboy and the Lady: Models as a Navajo Determinant of the Rate of Acculturation Among the Piñon Navajo." In *Native Americans Today: Sociological Perspectives,* ed. Howard M. Bahr, Bruce A. Chadwick, and Robert C. Day, 284–287. New York: Harper & Row, 1972. (Downs's article was published originally in 1963.)

Dunn, William Edward. "Apache Relations in Texas, 1718–1750." *The Quarterly of the Texas State Historical Association,* XIV (January 1911), 198–274.

Dyk, Walter. *Son of Old Man Hat: A Navaho Autobiography.* New York: Harcourt, Brace and Co., 1938.

Emerson, Dorothy. *Among the Mescalero Apaches: The Story of Father Albert Braun.* Tucson: University of Arizona Press, 1973.

Farella, John. *The Main Stalk: A Synthesis of Navajo Philosophy.* Tucson: University of Arizona Press, 1984.

Farrer, Claire R. *Living Life's Circle: Mescalero Apache Cosmovision.* Albuquerque: University of New Mexico Press, 1991.

———. "Singing for Life: The Mescalero Girl's Puberty Ceremony." In *Southwestern Indian Ritual Drama,* ed. Charlotte J. Frisbie, 125–159. Albuquerque: University of New Mexico Press, 1980.

———, and Ray A. Williamson, eds. *Earth and Sky: Visions of the Cosmos in Native American Folklore.* Albuquerque: University of New Mexico Press, 1992.

Ferg, Alan, ed. *Western Apache Material Culture: The Goodwin and Guenther Collections,* with contributions by William B. Kessel, Morris E. Opler, Grenville Goodwin, and Jan Bell. Tucson: For Arizona State Museum by University of Arizona Press, 1987.

Fishler, Stanley A. *In the Beginning, a Navaho Creation Myth.* Anthropological Papers of the University of Utah, No. 13. Salt Lake City: University of Utah Press, 1953.

———. "Navaho Picture Writing." In Franc Johnson Newcomb, Stanley A. Fishler, and Mary C. Wheelwright, *A Study of Navajo Symbolism.* Papers of the Peabody Museum of Archaeology and Ethnology at Harvard University, XXXII, No. 3, 51–80. Cambridge, Mass.: Peabody Museum, 1956.

Forbes, Jack D. *Apache, Navaho and Spaniard.* Norman: University of Oklahoma Press, 1960.

———. "The Appearance of the Mounted Indian in Northern Mexico and the Southwest to 1680." *Southwestern Journal of Anthropology* XV (Summer 1959), 189–208.

Franciscan Fathers. *An Ethnologic Dictionary of the Navaho Language.* Saint Michaels, Az.: Navajo Indian Mission, 1910.

———. *A Vocabulary of the Navaho Language.* 2 vols. Saint Michaels, Az.: Navajo Indian Mission, 1912.

Frisbie, Charlotte J. "Discussion." *Symposium on Navajo Mortuary Practices.* Special issue, *American Indian Quarterly* IV, No. 4 (1978), 407–443.

———. "Introduction." *Symposium on Navajo Mortuary Practices.* Special issue, *American Indian Quarterly* IV, No. 4 (1978), 303–308.

———. *Kinaaldá: A Study of the Navajo Girl's Puberty Ceremony.* Middletown, Ct.: Wesleyan University Press, 1967.

———. "The Navajo House Blessing Ceremonial," *El Palacio* 75, No. 3 (1968), 26–35.

———. *The Navajo House Blessing Ceremonial: A Study of Cultural Change.* Ph.D. dissertation for Department of Anthropology, University of New Mexico. Ann Arbor: University Microfilms, 1970.

———. "Ritual Drama in the Navajo House Blessing Ceremony." In *Southwestern Indian Ritual Drama,* ed. Charlotte J. Frisbie, 161–198. Albuquerque: University of New Mexico Press, 1980.

————. *Tall Woman: The Life Story of Rose Mitchell*. Albuquerque: University of New Mexico Press, forthcoming, 2001.

————, ed. *Southwestern Indian Ritual Drama*. Albuquerque: University of New Mexico Press, 1980.

————, and David P. McAllester, eds. *Navajo Blessingway Singer: The Autobiography of Frank Mitchell, 1881–1967*. Tucson: University of Arizona Press, 1978.

Getty, Harry T. *The San Carlos Indian Cattle Industry*. University of Arizona Anthropological Papers, VII. Tucson: University of Arizona Press, 1963.

Gill, Sam D. *Native American Religions: An Introduction*. Belmont, Ca.: Wadsworth, 1982.

————. *Native American Religious Action: A Performance Approach to Religion*. Columbia: University of South Carolina Press, 1987.

————, ed. *The Religious Character of Native American Humanities*. Tempe: Department of Religious Studies, Arizona State University, 1977.

————. *Sacred Words: A Study of Navajo Religion and Prayer*. Contributions in Intercultural and Comparative Studies, IV. Westport, Ct.: Greenwood Press, 1981.

Goddard, Pliny Earle. *Jicarilla Apache Texts*. Anthropological Papers of the American Museum of Natural History, VIII. New York: The American Museum of Natural History, 1911.

————. *Myths and Tales from the San Carlos Apache*. Anthropological Papers of the American Museum of Natural History, XXIV, Part I. New York: The American Museum of Natural History, 1918.

————. *Myths and Tales from the White Mountain Apache*. Anthropological Papers of the American Museum of Natural History, XXIV, Part II. New York: The American Museum of Natural History, 1919.

————. *Navajo Texts*. Anthropological Papers of the American Museum of Natural History, XXXIV, Part I. New York: The American Museum of Natural History, 1934.

Goodwin, Grenville. *Myths and Tales of the White Mountain Apache*. Memoirs of the American Folklore Society, XXXIII. New York: J. J. Augustin, 1939.

————. "The Social Divisions and Economic Life of the Western Apache." *American Anthropologist*, new series, XXXVII (January–March 1935), 55–64.

————. *The Social Organization of the Western Apache*. University of Chicago Publications in Anthropology, Ethnological Series. Chicago: University of Chicago Press, 1942.

————. "White Mountain Apache Religion." *American Anthropologist*, new series, XL (January–March 1938), 24–37.

————, recorder, and Keith H. Basso, ed. *Western Apache Raiding and Warfare*. Tucson: University of Arizona Press, 1971.

Gregg, Josiah. *Commerce of the Prairies*, ed. Milo Milton Quaife. Lakeside Classics. Chicago: R. R. Donnelley and Sons Co., 1926.

Griffen, Joyce. "Variations on a Rite of Passage: Some Recent Navajo Funerals." *American Indian Quarterly* IV, No. 4 (1978), 367–382.

Griffin, P. Bion, Mark P. Leone, and Keith H. Basso. "Western Apache Ecology." In *Apachean Culture, History, and Ethnology*, ed. Keith H. Basso and Morris E. Opler, 69–73. Tucson: University of Arizona Press, 1971.

Griffin-Pierce, Trudy. *Earth Is My Mother, Sky Is My Father: Space, Time and Astronomy in Navajo Sandpainting*. Albuquerque: University of New Mexico Press, 1992.

Gunnerson, Dolores A. *The Jicarilla Apaches: A Study in Survival.* DeKalb: Northern Illinois University Press, 1974.

———, and James H. Gunnerson. "Apachean Culture: A Study in Unity and Diversity." In *Apachean Culture, History and Ethnology*, ed. Keith H. Basso and Morris E. Opler, 7–27. Tucson: University of Arizona Press, 1971.

Haile, Father Berard. *Origin Legend of the Navaho Enemy Way.* Yale University Publications in Anthropology, No. 17. New Haven, Conn.: Yale University Press, 1938.

———. *Origin Legend of the Navaho Flintway.* University of Chicago Publications in Anthropology, Linguistic Series. Chicago: University of Chicago Press, 1943.

———, trans. and recorder, and Leland C. Wyman, ed. and anno. *Blessingway.* Tucson: University of Arizona Press, 1970.

———, and Maud Oakes. *Beautyway: A Navaho Ceremonial*, ed. with commentaries by Leland C. Wyman and with sandpaintings recorded by Laura A. Armer, Franc J. Newcomb, and Maud Oakes. Bollingen Series, LIII. New York: Pantheon Books, 1957.

Haines, Francis. *Appaloosa: The Spotted Horse in Art and History.* Publication of the Amon Carter Museum of Western Art at Fort Worth. Austin: University of Texas Press, 1963.

———. "Where Did the Plains Indians Get Their Horses?" *American Anthropologist,* new series, XL (January–March 1938), 112–117.

Hall, Edward Twitchell, Jr. *Early Stockaded Settlements in the Governador, New Mexico.* Columbia University Studies in Archaeology and Ethnology, II, Part 1. New York: Columbia University Press, 1944.

Hammond, George P., and Agapito Rey, eds. and trans. *Don Juan de Oñate: Colonizer of New Mexico, 1595–1628.* 2 vols. Coronado Cuatro Centennial Publications, 1540–1940, V. Albuquerque: University of New Mexico Press, 1953.

Hannum, Alberta. *Paint the Wind,* illustrated with paintings by Beatien Yazz. New York: The Viking Press, 1958.

———. *Spin a Silver Dollar: The Story of a Desert Trading Post,* illustrated with paintings by Little No-Shirt (Beatien Yazz). New York: The Viking Press, 1946.

Harrington, John P. "The Ethnogeography of the Tewa Indians." In *Annual Report of the Bureau of American Ethnology,* XXIX, 37–618. Washington, D.C.: Government Printing Office, 1916.

———. "Southern Peripheral Athapaskawan Origins, Divisions, and Migrations." In *Essays in Historical Anthropology of North America.* Smithsonian Miscellaneous Collections, Vol. 100, 503–532. Washington, D.C., 1940.

Hartmann, Horst. *George Catlin Und Balduin Möllhausen: Zwei Interpreten Der Indianer Und Des Alten Westens.* Berlin: Dietrich Reimer Verlag, 1963.

Hester, James J. "Navajo Culture Changes: 1550 to 1960 and Beyond." In *Apachean Culture, History and Ethnology,* ed. Keith H. Basso and Morris E. Opler, 51–67. Tucson: University of Arizona Press, 1971.

Hill, Gertrude. "Turquoise and the Zuñi Indian." *The Kiva* XII (May 1947), 42–52.

Hill, W[illard] W. *Navaho Warfare.* Yale University Publications in Anthropology, No. 5. New Haven: Yale University Press, 1936.

———. "Navajo Salt Gathering." *The University of New Mexico Bulletin,* Anthropological Series, III (February 1940), 3–25.

———. *The Agricultural and Hunting Methods of the Navaho Indians.* Yale University Publications in Anthropology, No. 18. New Haven, Conn.: Yale University Press, 1938.

Hinton, Leanne. "Vocables in Havasupai Song." In *Southwestern Indian Ritual Drama,* ed. Charlotte J. Frisbie, 275–305. Albuquerque: University of New Mexico Press, 1980.

Hodge, Frederick Webb, George P. Hammond, and Agapito Rey, eds. and trans. *Fray Alonso de Benavides' Revised Memorial of 1634,* annotated by F. W. Hodge. Coronado Cuatro Centennial Publications, 1540–1940, IV. Albuquerque: University of New Mexico Press, 1945.

Hoijer, Harry. *Chiricahua and Mescalero Apache Texts,* with ethnological notes by Morris Edward Opler. University of Chicago Publications in Anthropology, Linguistic Series. Chicago: University of Chicago Press, 1938.

———. "The Southern Athapaskan Languages." *American Anthropologist,* new series, XL (January–March 1938), 75–87.

Holder, Preston. *The Hoe and the Horse on the Plains: A Study of Cultural Development among North American Indians.* Lincoln: University of Nebraska Press, 1970.

Iverson, Peter. *The Navajos.* Indians of North America Series. New York: Chelsea House Publishers, 1990.

———. *When Indians Became Cowboys: Native People and Cattle Ranching in the American West.* Norman: University of Oklahoma Press, 1994.

James, Edwin, ed. *Account of an Expedition from Pittsburgh to the Rocky Mountains, Performed in the Years, 1819, 1820, under the Command of Major S. H. Long.* 3 vols. London: Longman, Hurst, Rees, Orme, and Brown, 1823.

Johnson, Broderick H. *Denetsosie,* ed. Sydney M. Calloway et al. Rough Rock, Az.: Navajo Curriculum Center, 1969.

———, and Ruth Roessel, eds. *Navajo Livestock Reduction: A National Disgrace.* Tsaile, Az.: Navajo Community College Press, 1974.

Kearney, Thomas H., Robert H. Peebles, and collaborators. *Arizona Flora.* Berkeley: University of California Press, 1951.

Kelley, Klara Bonseck, and Harris Francis. *Navaho Sacred Places.* Bloomington: Indiana University Press, 1994.

Klah, Hasteen, *Navajo Creation Myth,* recorded by Mary C. Wheelwright. Santa Fe: Museum of Navajo Ceremonial Art, 1942.

Kluckhohn, Clyde. *Navaho Witchcraft.* Boston: Beacon Press, 1962.

———, and Dorothea Leighton. *The Navaho.* Cambridge, Mass.: Harvard University Press, 1956.

———, and Leland C. Wyman. *An Introduction to Navaho Chant Practice.* Memoirs of the American Anthropological Association, No. 53. Menasha, Wis.: American Anthropological Association, 1940.

Lamphere, Louise. *To Run After Them: Cultural and Social Bases of Cooperation in a Navajo Community.* Tucson: University of Arizona Press, 1977.

Lee, Joseph G. "Navajo Medicine Man." *Arizona Highways* XXXVII (August 1961), 2–9.

Leighton, Alexander H., and Dorothea C. Leighton. *The Navaho Door: An Introduction to Navaho Life*. Cambridge, Mass.: Harvard University Press, 1944.

Levy, Jerrold E. "Changing Burial Practices of the Western Navajo: A Consideration of the Relationships Between Attitudes and Behaviors." *American Indian Quarterly* IV, No. 4 (1978), 397–406.

————. "Navajo Suicide." *Human Organization* 24, No. 4 (Winter 1965), 308–318.

Luckert, Karl W. *Coyoteway: A Navajo Holyway Healing Ceremonial*. Tucson: University of Arizona Press, 1979.

————. *Navajo Mountain and Rainbow Bridge Religion*. American Tribal Religion Series, I. Flagstaff: Museum of Northern Arizona, 1977.

————. *A Navajo Bringing Home Ceremony: The Claus Chee Sonny Version of Deerway Aji Lee*. American Tribal Religion Series, III. Flagstaff: Museum of Northern Arizona, 1978.

————. *The Navajo Hunter Tradition*. Tucson: University of Arizona Press, 1975.

Mails, Thomas E. *The People Called Apache*, revised edition. New York: BDD Promotional Book Co., 1993.

Margry, Pierre. *Découvertes et établissements des Français dans l'Ouest et dans le sud de l'Amérique Septentrionale (1614–1754), Mémoires et documents originaux*. Vols. II and VI. Paris: Imprimerie Jouaust et Sigaux, 1876–1886.

Matthews, Washington. *Navaho Legends*. Memoirs of the American Folklore Society, V. New York: G. E. Stechert and Co., 1897.

————. "Navaho Myths, Prayers and Songs," ed. P. E. Goddard. In *The University of California Publications in American Archaeology and Ethnology*, V, No. 2, 21–63. Berkeley: University of California Press, 1907–1910.

————. "Navajo Names for Plants." *American Naturalist* XX (September 1886), 767–777.

McAllester, David P. "A Different Drum: A Consideration of Music in Native American Humanities." In *The Religious Character of Native American Humanities*, ed. Sam D. Gill, 155–183. Tempe: Department of Religion, Arizona State University, 1977.

———— *Enemy Way Music: A Study of Social and Esthetic Values as Seen in Navaho Music*. Papers of the Peabody Museum of Archaeology and Ethnology at Harvard University, XLI, No. 3. Cambridge, Mass.; Peabody Museum, 1954.

————, ed. and trans. *Hogans: Navajo Houses and House Poems*. Photographs by Susan W. McAllester. Middletown, Ct.: Wesleyan University Press, 1980.

————, and Charlotte J. Frisbie, eds. *Navajo Blessingway Singer: The Autobiography of Frank Mitchell, 1881–1967*. Tucson: University of Arizona Press, 1978.

McAllister, J. Gilbert. *Daveko: Kiowa-Apache Medicine Man*. Texas Memorial Museum Bulletin, XVII. Austin: University of Texas, 1970.

————. "Kiowa-Apache Social Organization." In *Social Anthropology of the North American Tribes*, ed. Fred Eggan. The University of Chicago Publications in Anthropology, Social Anthropology Series, 99–169. Chicago: University of Chicago Press, 1937.

————. "Kiowa-Apache Tales." In *The Sky Is My Tipi*, ed. Mody C. Boatright. Publication of the Texas Folklore Society, No. 22, 1–141. Dallas: University Press, 1949.

McNeely, James Kale. *Holy Wind in Navajo Philosophy.* Tucson: University of Arizona Press, 1981.

McPherson, Robert S. *Sacred Land, Sacred View: Navajo Perceptions of the Four Corners Region.* Charles Redd Monograph in Western History, XIX. Provo: Brigham Young University, 1992.

Melody, Michael E. *The Apaches.* Indians of North America Series. New York: Chelsea House, 1989.

Miskin, Bernard. *Rank and Warfare among the Plains Indians.* Monograph of the American Ethnological Society, III. New York: J. J. Augustin, 1940.

Momaday, N. Scott. "The Man Made of Words." In *Indian Voices: The First Convocation of American Indian Scholars,* 45–62. San Francisco: The Indian Historian Press, 1970.

Newcomb, Franc Johnson. *Hosteen Klah: Navajo Medicine Man.* New York: Holt, Rinehart & Winston, 1969.

———. *Navajo Omens and Taboos.* Santa Fe: The Rydal Press, 1940.

———. "Navajo Symbols in Sand Paintings and Ritual Objects." In Franc Johnson Newcomb, Stanley A. Fishler, and Mary C. Wheelwright, *A Study of Navajo Symbolism.* Papers of the Peabody Museum of Archaeology and Ethnology at Harvard University, XXXII, No. 3, 3–48. Cambridge, Mass.: Peabody Museum, 1956.

———, and Gladys A. Reichard. *Sandpaintings of the Navajo Shooting Chant.* New York: J. J. Augustin, 1937.

Newcomb, W. W., Jr. *The Indians of Texas from Prehistoric to Modern Times.* Austin: University of Texas Press, 1961.

———. "A Summary of Kiowa-Apache History and Culture" (Introduction.) In *Daveko: Kiowa-Apache Medicine Man* by J. Gilbert McAllister, 1–28. Texas Memorial Museum Bulletin, XVII. Austin: University of Texas, 1970.

Nye, Wilbur Sturtevant. *Bad Medicine and Good: Tales of the Kiowas.* Norman: University of Oklahoma Press, 1962.

Oakes, Maud, and Joseph Campbell. *Where the Two Came to Their Father: A Navaho War Ceremonial,* with sandpaintings recorded by Maud Oakes. 2 vols. Bollingen Series, I. New York: Pantheon Books, 1943.

O'Bryan, Aileen. *The Diné: Origin Myths of the Navaho Indians.* Smithsonian Institution Bureau of American Ethnology Bulletin, No. 163. Washington, D.C.: Government Printing Office, 1956.

Opler, Morris Edward. *An Apache Life-Way: The Economic, Social, and Religious Institutions of the Chiricahua Indians.* Chicago: University of Chicago Press, 1941.

———. *Apache Odyssey: A Journey Between Two Worlds.* New York: Holt, Rinehart & Winston, 1969.

———. "The Concept of Supernatural Power among the Chiricahua and Mescalero Apaches." *American Anthropologist,* new series, XXXVII (January–March 1935), 65–70.

———. *Dirty Boy: A Jicarilla Tale of Raid and War.* Memoirs of the American Anthropological Association, No. 52. Menasha, Wis.: American Anthropological Association, 1938.

————. "The Influence of Aboriginal Pattern and White Contact on a Recently Introduced Ceremony, the Mescalero Peyote Rite." *The Journal of American Folklore*, XLIX (January–June 1936), 143–166.

————. "The Jicarilla Apache Ceremonial Relay Race." *American Anthropologist,* new series, XLVI (January–March 1944), 75–97.

————. "Lipan and Mescalero Apaches in Texas." In *Apache Indians X,* ed. Verne F. Ray and Morris E. Opler, 1–285. New York: Garland Publishing, Inc., 1974.

————. "The Lipan Apache Death Complex and Its Extensions." *Southwestern Journal of Anthropology* I (Spring 1945), 122–141.

————. *Myths and Legends of the Lipan Apache Indians.* Memoirs of the American Folklore Society, XXXVI. New York: J. J. Augustin, 1940.

————. *Myths and Tales of the Chiricahua Apache Indians,* with an appendix of Apache and Navajo comparative references by David French. Memoirs of the American Folklore Society, XXXVII. New York: The American Folklore Society, 1942.

————. *Myths and Tales of the Jicarilla Apache Indians.* Memoirs of the American Folklore Society, XXXI. New York: G. E. Stechert and Co., 1938.

————. "An Outline of Chiricahua Apache Social Organization." In *Social Anthropology of the North American Tribes,* ed. Fred Eggan. The University of Chicago Publications in Anthropology, Social Anthropology Series, 173–239. Chicago: University of Chicago Press, 1937.

————. "A Summary of Jicarilla Apache Culture." *American Anthropologist,* new series, XXXVIII (April–June 1936), 202–223.

————, and Harry Hoijer. "The Raid and Warpath Language of the Chiricahua Apache." *American Anthropologist,* new series, XLII (October–December 1940), 617–634.

————, and Keith H. Basso, eds. *Apachean Culture, History and Ethnography.* Tucson: University of Arizona Press, 1971.

————, and Keith H. Basso, eds. *Western Apache Language and Culture: Essays in Linguistics Anthropology.* Tucson: University of Arizona Press, 1989.

————, and Verne F. Ray, eds. *Apache Indians X.* New York: Garland Publishing, Inc., 1974.

Parsons, Elsie Clews. *Tewa Tales.* Memoirs of the American Folklore Society, XIX. New York: G. E. Stechert and Co., 1926.

Perry, Richard John. *Apache Reservation: Indigenous Peoples and the American State.* Austin: University of Texas Press, 1993.

Pfefferkorn, Ignaz. *Sonora: A Description of the Province,* trans. and anno. Theodore E. Treutlein. Coronado Cuatro Centennial Publications, 1540–1940, XII. Albuquerque: University of New Mexico Press, 1949.

Porter, Joseph C. *Paper Medicine Man: John Gregory Bourke and His American West.* Norman: University of Oklahoma Press, 1986.

Prada, Father Juan de. "Petition of September 26, 1638." *Historical Documents Relating to New Mexico, Nueva Vizcaya and Approaches Thereto, to 1773,* recorded by Adolph F. Bandelier and Fanny R. Bandelier, ed. and trans. Charles Wilson Hackett. Vol. III, 108–110. Washington, D.C.: Carnegie Institution, 1923–1927.

Ray, Verne Frederick. "Ethnohistorical Analysis of Documents Relating to the Apache Indians of Texas." In *Apache Indians X*, ed. Verne F. Ray and Morris E. Opler, 1–198. New York: Garland Publishing, Inc., 1974.

————, and Morris E. Opler, eds. *Apache Indians* X. New York: Garland Publishing, Inc., 1974.

Reichard, Gladys A. *Navaho Religion: A Study of Symbolism*. 2 vols. Bollingen Series, XVIII. New York: Pantheon Books, 1950.

————. *Prayer: The Compulsive Word*. Monograph of the American Ethnological Society, VII. New York: J. J. Augustin, 1944.

————. *Social Life of the Navajo Indians, with Some Attention to Minor Ceremonies*. Columbia University Contributions to Anthropology, VII. New York: Columbia University Press, 1928.

Roessel, Ruth. *Women in Navajo Society*. Rough Rock, Az.: Navajo Resource Center, 1981.

————, and Broderick H. Johnson, eds. *Navajo Livestock Reduction: A National Disgrace*. Tsaile, Az.: Navajo Community College, 1974.

Rothenberg, Jerome. "A Note to Accompany the 'First Horse Song of Frank Mitchell.'" *Alcheringa: Ethnopoetics* I, No. 1 (Fall 1970), 63.

————, ed. *The Seventeen Horse Songs of Frank Mitchell, Nos. X–XIII*. London: Tetrad Press, 1969.

Salsbury, Clarence G., with Paul Hughes. *The Salsbury Story*. Tucson: University of Arizona Press, 1969.

Sandner, Donald. *Navaho Symbols of Healing*. New York: Harcourt, Brace Jovanovich, 1977.

Sapir, Edward, and Harry Hoijer. *Navaho Texts*, ed. Harry Hoijer. William Dwight Whitney Linguistic Series. Iowa City: University of Iowa, 1942.

Scholes, France V. "Juan Martínez de Montoya, Settler and Conquistador of New Mexico." *New Mexico Historical Review* XIX (October 1944), 337–342.

Schwarz, Maureen Trudelle. *Modeled in the Image of Changing Woman: Navajo Views on the Human Body and Personhood*. Tucson: University of Arizona Press, 1997.

Shepardson, Mary. "Changes in Navajo Mortuary Practices and Beliefs." *American Indian Quarterly* IV, No. 4 (1978), 383–396.

————, and Blodwen Hammond. *The Navajo Mountain Community*. Berkeley: University of California Press, 1992.

Sonnichsen, C. L. *The Mescalero Apaches*. Norman: University of Oklahoma Press, 1958.

Stockel, H. Henrietta. *Women of the Apache Nation: Voices of Truth*. Reno: University of Nevada Press, 1991.

Storm, Joe. "Sons of the Devil." In *Puro Mexicano*, ed. J. Frank Dobie. Publication of the Texas Folklore Society, No. 12, 190–193. Austin: Texas Folklore Society, 1935.

Swanton, John R. *Source Material on the History and Ethnology of the Caddo Indians*. Smithsonian Institution Bureau of American Ethnology Bulletin, No. 132. Washington, D.C.: Government Printing Office, 1942.

Sweeney, Edwin R. *Cochise: A Chiricahua Apache Chief*. Norman: University of Oklahoma Press, 1991.

Tanner, Clara Lee. *Southwest Indian Painting.* Tucson: University of Arizona Press and Arizona Silhouettes, 1957.

Terrell, John Upton. *Apache Chronicle.* New York: World Publishing, 1972.

Thrapp, Dan L. *The Conguest of Apacheria.* Norman: University of Oklahoma Press, 1974.

————. *Victorio and the Mimbres Apaches.* Norman: University of Oklahoma Press, 1974.

Tiller, Veronica E. Velarde. *The Jicarilla Apache Tribe: A History.* Lincoln: University of Nebraska Press, 1992.

Van Valkenburg, Richard, and John C. McPhee. *A Short History of the Navajo People.* Window Rock, Az.: Department of the Interior, Navajo Service, 1938.

Ward, Albert E. *Navajo Graves: An Archaeological Reflection of Ethnographic Reality.* Ethnohistorical Report Series, II. Albuquerque: Center for Anthropological Studies, 1980.

————. "Navajo Graves: Some Preliminary Considerations for Recording and Classifying Reservation Burials." *American Indian Quarterly* IV, No. 4 (1978), 329–346.

Wheelwright, Mary C. *Hail Chant and Water Chant.* Navajo Religion Series, II. Santa Fe: Museum of Navajo Ceremonial Art, 1946.

————. *Myth of Mountain Chant, Told by Hasteen Klah, and Beauty Chant, Told by Hasteen Gahni.* Bulletin of the Museum of Navajo Ceremonial Art, No. 5. Santa Fe, 1951.

————. *Navajo Creation Myth.* See Klah.

Wilken, Robert L. *Anselm Weber, O.F.M.: Missionary to the Navaho.* Milwaukee: Bruce Publishing Co., 1955.

Wissler, Clark. "The Influence of the Horse in the Development of Plains Culture." *American Anthropologist,* new series, XVI (January–March 1914), 1–25.

Witherspoon, Gary. *Language and Art in the Navajo Universe.* Ann Arbor: University of Michigan Press, 1977.

————. *Navajo Kinship and Marriage.* Chicago: University of Chicago Press, 1975.

————. "The Central Concepts of Navajo World View." Part I, in *Linguistics* 119 (January 1, 1974), 41–59; and Part II, in *Linguistics* 161 (October 1, 1975), 69–87.

————, and Glen Peterson. *Dynamic Symmetry and Asymmetry in Navajo and Western Art and Holistic Cosmology.* New York: P. Lang, 1995.

Wooster, David, ed. and trans. "A Ride with the Apaches: The Unpublished Narrative of José Mendivil." *Overland Monthly* VI (April 1871), 341–345.

Worcester, Donald Emmet. *The Apaches: Eagles of the Southwest.* Norman: University of Oklahoma Press, 1979.

————. "Spanish Horses among the Plains Tribes." *The Pacific Historical Review* XIV (December 1945), 409–417.

————. "The Spread of Spanish Horses in the Southwest." *New Mexico Historical Review* XIX (July 1944), 225–232.

Wyman, Leland C. *The Mountainway of the Navajo.* Tucson: University of Arizona Press, 1975.

————, and Stuart K. Harris. *Navajo Indian Medical Ethnobotany.* The University of New Mexico Bulletin, Anthropological Series, III, No. 5. Albuquerque: University of New Mexico Press, 1941.

————,W. W. Hill, and Iva Osanai. *Navajo Eschatology.* The University of New Mexico Bulletin, Anthropological Series, IV, No. 1. Albuquerque: University of New Mexico Press, 1942.

————, and Clyde Kluckhohn. *Navaho Classification of their Song Ceremonials.* Memoirs of the American Anthropological Association, No. 50. Menasha, Wis.: American Anthropological Association, 1938.

————, ed. and anno., and Father Berard Haile, trans. and recorder. *Blessingway.* Tucson: University of Arizona Press, 1970.

Wyman, Walker D. *The Wild Horse of the West.* Caldwell, Idaho: The Caxton Printers, Ltd., 1945.

Young, Robert W., ed. *The Navajo Yearbook 8* (1951–1961). Window Rock, Az.: Navajo Agency, 1961.

————. *The Role of the Navajo in the Southwestern Drama.* Gallup: The Gallup Independent, 1967.

Zárate-Salmerón, Fray Gerónimo de. "Relaciones de Todas Las Cosas Que en El Nuevo México Se Han Visto y Sabido, Así por Mar Como por Tierra Desde El Año 1538 Hasta El de 1626." In *Obras Inéditas De José Fernando Ramírez,* ed. por Vargas Rea. Segunda Serie, 9–72. México, D. F.: Biblioteca Aportación Histórica, 1949.

Zolbrod, Paul G. *Diné Bahane: The Navajo Creation Story.* Albuquerque: University of New Mexico Press, 1984.

Personal Correspondence:

Eve Ball. Letters to LaVerne Harrell Clark: 1970–1983. LaVerne H. Clark Collection of Special Collections, Main Library of Texas Woman's University, Denton, Texas.

Frances Gillmor. Letters to LaVerne H. Clark: 1956–1986. Clark Collection of Special Collections, Main Library of Texas Woman's University, Denton, Texas.

Index

Page numbers in italics indicate illustrations.

Abalone Shell, 20, 40, 44, *312*
Acoma Indians, 2
Agate, 18
Air Spirit, 64, 66
Albino: *see* White horses
Altered Language, 128–129, 149–150, 301
Amulets, 147, 148, *173, 205*
Apache Indians: archery ability, 210–211; dates of acquisition of horses, 4–10, *9*; divination, 134–139; linguistic divisions of Southern Athapascans (chart), xix; maps, xxi, xxiv–xxv; present locations (chart), xx; raiding practices: *see* Raids; reaction to first horses, 1–3, trading journey to Zuñi described, 203–204
Apache myths: black horses in, 31–33; raiding, 129–130; turquoise horses in, 34–38, 40; white horses in, 28, 30–31; *see also* Chiricahua Apache myths; Jicarilla Apache myths; Kiowa-Apache myths; Lipan Apache myths; Mescalero Apache myths; San Carlos Apache myths; White Mountain Apache myths
Appaloosa horses, 46–47
"Arrows" in witchcraft, 243

Bat, 91–92, 177, 202
Bear, powers of, 122, 123–128
Bear Way, 121, 122
Beauty Way, 223–225
Begay, Harrison, 48
Békotsidi (Begochiddy), 60, 212; as creator of horses, 22–24
Big Sheep Mountain: *65*, 107n27; *see also* Debentsa and La Plata Mountains
Big Snake, powers of, 124ff, 129–130
Big Snake Way, 121, 122–123, 129
Birth customs, horses in, 190, 251, *252*, 305–306
Black Bear: *see* Bear
Black horses: associated with east (Apache myth), 32–33; associated with north (Navajo myth), 66; in Indian art, 33; in Navajo myth, 33–34; preferred steed (Apache myth), 31–32
Blessing Way: *25,* 73, 121–122, 280, 284, 285–286, 287–292, 297–298, 299, 302, 312; importance of horse songs in, 282, 284; in other ceremonies, 122, 174–175, 230, 280, 282, 289, 292, 294, *295,* 297–298, 299; rites for horses, 175–176, *187,*

282, 284, 297; and singer Frank
Mitchell, *25, 289;* used against
witchcraft, 186–187
Blood, magic properties of, 21
Blue horses: *see* Turquoise horses
Body painting, 148–149, 297
Born-of-Water: *see* Child-of-the-Water
Botany, medical, 180ff; *see also* Plants
Breaking of horses, 176–177
Breeding: *see* Horses, care and breeding of
Bridles: *see* Trappings

Cardinal horses: *see* Color and direction
Carnelian: *see* Red horses
Castañeda, Pedro de, 1–3
Catlin, George, 210
Center of the earth, 66, 74, 85, 88
Ceremonial equipment, 75, 80, 178, 179
Changing Woman, 18, 41–42, 123, 170,
191, 292, 293, 294, 295, 312; and
creation of horses (Navajo myth),
62–66, 72–82, 283–284, 285, 290,
291; and yellow horses, 40–42; as
creator of horses for the Navajo,
72–82ff; Sun's courtship of, 29
Chants: *see* Bear Way; Beauty Way; Big
Snake Way; Blessing Way; Enemy
Way; Flint Way; Frog Way, Night
Chant; Turtle Way, Water Chant
Chicken Pull, *310,* 310–311
Child-of-the-Water, 24, 30, 42, 60, 89–
90, 284
Chiricahua Apache, dates of acquisition
of horses, 9–10
Chiricahua Apache myths, guardian
horse in, 132–133; liberation of
domestic animals, 94–96
Chuska Mountains, 77, *78,* 109n72
Chuska (Chush gaeye, White Spruce)
Peak, 77, 109n72
Cibecue Apache, 17, 193, 238, 302
Color and direction, 27–28ff
Color sequence, 27; Navajo, 29, 35;
Apache, 32 f, 87–88
Comanche Indians, 151–152
Controller of Waters, 266; *see also* Water
Monsters

Coral: *see* Red horses
Corn in process of maturing in Navajo
myth, 283
Cornstalk in creation myth, 17, 75–76, 197
Coronado, 1, 3–4
Corrals, Navajo, *187;* Sun's mythical, 26,
40, 285; customs and taboos
connected with, 202, 292, 297, 305
Cowbird, 91–94, 241–242; as teacher of
care and breeding of horses
(Apache myth), 165–167, 176–177
Coyote, 269; in Apache creation myths,
89, 95–97; in Navajo myth, 97–98
"Coyote dun" horses, 43, 44
Creation myths, 61ff; gods' creation of
horses, 21–24, 282; Apache myths,
bat, cowbird and crow in, 91–96;
Black Hactcin as creator of horses,
87–88; Child-of-the-Water as
creator of horses, 89–90; Coyote's
role in, 89; culture hero as sole
creator of horses, 89–90; Elder
Brother or culture hero as creator
of horses for earth (Goddard and
Goodwin versions), 82–87;
guardian horse in (Kiowa-Apache
myths), 98; Killer-of-Enemies as
liberator of domestic animals, 94–
96; lakes and water in, 99; Mole as
liberator of horses, 98–99; The
Twins as liberators of horses, 98;
Navajo myths: Changing Woman in
(Goddard version), 75, 76–80;
Changing Woman in (O'Bryan
version), 75, 76–78, 79, 80–82;
Changing Woman in (Sapir
version), 62–66, 69–70 72–74;
Changing Woman in (Fishler
version), 70–71, 72–73, 75–76, 82;
Changing Woman in (Haile and
Wyman version), 282–284; first
horse medicine man as bringer of
horses, 81–82; Frog Man in (Fishler
version), 70–72; Nohoílpi (Gambler) as giver of horses, 61;
Turquoise Boy and creation of
horses (Sapir version), 62–75

Crossing of the waters, 169
Crow, 91–92, 94–96, 97–98, 243
Crown Point, 22
Cures: see Medicines
Curly, Slim, 119, 123, 149, 229, 231, 232, 281, 287, 290, 291, 293–294, 298, 315n15

Datura, 184, 189, 198
Death Customs, horses in, 266–272, 281, 304–305
Debentsa, 64, 65, 107n27
Dinétah, 66–67
Directions and colors, 26, 28ff, 34ff, 125, 294, 295, 296, 299. See also Color sequence
Dirty Boy, 31, 42–43, 46, 140, 144–145, 150–151, 152, 155–156
Divination, Apache, 134–137
Divination, Navajo, 137–139
Dodge, Adee, 33, 39, 48–49; cover painting, description of, 48–49
Dotso, 169; see also Fly
Drinking tube, 146; 147

Eagle feathers, 39, 205, 240, 283
Elder Brother: see Killer-of-Enemies; Monster Slayer; Enemy Slayer; Twin War Gods; Turquoise Boy; Naiyenezgani
Emergence legend, 89. See also Creation myths
Enemy Slayer, 67, 69ff, 119, 123, 208, 283–284, 289, 290; see also Killer-of-Enemies; Elder Brother; Monster Slayer; Twin War Gods; Turquoise Boy; Naiyenezgani
Enemy Way, 57, 119–120, 123–124, 143, 149, 232, 243; as Squaw Dance, 307, 310
Entrails, magic properties of, 20, 146

"Female River," see Rio Grande River
Fetishes: see Horse fetishes
Fire Boy, 60, 98
Flint Way, 30, 231–232
Fly, 26, 38, 41, 86–87, 168–169; see also Dotso

Foolish People, 101–105
Fort Sumner, New Mexico, Navajo captivity at, 208
Frog Man, 46, 195; in creation myths, 70–72
Frog, powers of, 128–129
Frog Way, 121, 122

Gambler, 61
Gans (Gahe), 87
Gods, use of horses by, 24–49
Gods, possession of horses by, 21ff, 26ff
Gods: see Sun; Changing Woman; Békotsidi; Moon; Twin War Gods
Good luck songs, 36, 190–193, 301
Grasses: grama grass, 168, 188, 314; "jack-rabbit" grass, 188; mountain rice, 168, 187; rice grass, 188; rush-grass, 168, 188; salt-weed, 168, 188; sheep-grass, 167, 168
Grasses as horse symbols, 168–169, 187–188, 257
Grazing, 105, 188, 209, 257, 298, 306, 307, 314
Grooming, 203–204
Ground-drawings, 153–154
Grullo horse, 35–36
Guadalupe Mountains in creation myths, 90, 91, 93, 118

Hactcin, 87–88, 256–257
Hesperus Peak, 65; see also Debentsa and La Plata Range
Hail, 17, 202
Haliotis shell, 44
Hand-trembling, 137–138
Harness: see Trappings
Hogan, 81
Hogan Blessing Rite, 165, 292, 293, 294–296; 295
Hogan Gods, 63–64
Holy Beings, Navajo, 282–283
Hopi Indians, 100, 172, 176, 205
Hopi-Tewa Indians, 312
Horse ceremonies, Apache and Navajo compared, 172–174
Horse fetishes, 57, 66, 72, 75–76, 79, 167,

168, 172, 294; as ceremonial paraphernalia, 175–176

Horse racing: *see* Racing

Horse raiding: *see* Raids

Horse shamans, Apache: *see* Shamans

Horse thievery, punishment for, 32, 97, 120

Horseback riding, learning (Apache tale), 101–105

Horsehair in witchcraft, 245

Horsemanship: *see* Riding ability

Horses, effect on Indian way of life, 10–12; creation of: *see* Creation myths; dates of Indian acquisition, 4–10, 278, 313, 314; lack of among Indians, explanation for, 57–58; supernatural creation belief, 69ff

Horses as cause of Navajo-Apache separation, 100

Horses as payment, for puberty rites, 253–254; in marriages, 258–264; to shamans for cures, 239–240

Horses, care and breeding of, 165ff, 200, 208–210, *244*, 266, 292, 298–299; Navajo ceremonies for, 174–176, 286; Navajo songs for increase or benefit of herds, 191–196, 292; powers of Apache shamans over, *19*, 176–180; sacred names, 195–196, 301; taboos and customs, 199–203; witchcraft, plants for, 198–201

Horses, colors of (Navajo myth), 26ff; names of colors, 28

Horses, deformed, 200–201

Horses, elements in body of, 16, 18, 19, 20, 291–292, 293; according to Lipan myth, 17

Horses, Indian, as seen by whites, 206–208, 209–211

Horses, injuries caused by and treatment for, 227, 229ff, 244

Horses, introduction of, 1–10

Horses, jealousy of, 238–239

Horses, marked with spot on forehead, 32, 38, 39

Horses, as doers of good, 221, 223–226, 228–238

Horses, as doers of harm, 223, 242–243

Horses, organs of magical powers (Apache tales), 19–21

Horses, powers of essential for raid leader, 133–134, 300, 302

Horses, powers of bestowed on shamans, 33, 131, 134, 156, *178*, 238ff, 301, 303–304

Horses, Apache reduction program, 297, 307, 309

Horses, Navajo reduction program, 297, 298, 307, 309

Horses, as animals representing or including other domestic animals, 283

Horses, as property representing other prized possessions, 283

Horses, retaliatory powers of for ill treatment, 227, 228–229

Horses, spread of in Southwest, 4–10, 278

Horses, treatment of by Indians, 206–207, 227ff; as viewed by whites, 209–211

Horses, treatment by whites as seen by Indians, 211–213

Horseshoes, 182–183

Huerfano Mountain, 22, 64, 107n28

Illness and injuries of humans, horse ceremonies for (Apache), 232–238

Illness of horses, treatments for, 180ff; *see also* Medicines; Plants, medicinal

Jackasses, 23–24

Jemez Indians, 6–7, 67

Jet-stone, 79, 109n76; 231; *see also* Black horses

Jicarilla Apache myths, black horses in, 32; creation myth, 87–89; Foolish People, 101–105; spotted horses in, 46; white horses in, 31; yellow horses in, 43

Jumano Apache, 7–8

Killer-of-Enemies, 24, 32, 38, 42, 59, 60, 294; as slayer of eagle, 20–21; as teacher of raiding, 118–119; *see also* Creation myths

Kinaaldá: *see* Puberty Ceremony (Navajo)
Kiowa-Apache Indians, date of acquisition of horses, 8–9; creation myth, 98–99

Lakes, 98–99
Lameness, 183
Language, altered or sacred, 128–129, 149–150; 301
La Plata Mountains, *65,* 107n27
Life Way: *see* Flint Way
Lightning, 201–202, 222, 225, 282, 291, 298; in creation myth, 17, 20
Lipan Apache, date of acquisition of horses, 8, 10
Lipan Apache myths, creation of horses, 17, 90–93; feeding of horses, 105, 167, 209; raiding, 118–119, 131–132
Little Breeze, 169

Magical powers: *see* Raids
"Male River": *see* San Juan River
Manure as horse symbol, 257
Marriage customs, horses in, 258–264, 306
Medicine bags, 175–176
Medicine bundle, 148, 292
Medicine people, Apache: *173,* 312
Medicine people, Navajo: creation of horses, 82, 167–172; importance of fetishes to, 175–176; medicine men, *25, 68,* 172, *222, 289;* medicine women, *165,* 302, 303–304; *see also* Shamans; Slim Curly; Charlie Mitchell; Frank Mitchell
Medicines, 179ff
Mescalero Apache myths, creation of horses, 89–90, 93–94
Mexicans, 61
Mirage Man, 26–27, 46, 69–70
Mirage stones, 18, 44, 292
Mitchell, Charlie, 65, 67, *68,* 73, 78, 82, 108n56; 109n63; 255, 259, 260, 262, 264, 275n57; 314n1
Mitchell, Frank, *25,* 281, 285, 286, *289,* 291, 292, 312
Mole, 98–99
Monster Slayer as teacher of raiding, 119–120; *see also* Killer-of-Enemies

Möllhausen, H. Balduin, 211
Moon, 24, 30, 38, 41, 73, 313
Mount Taylor, 63, 169
Mountain-around-which-moving-was-done, 107n28; *see also* Huerfano Mountain
Mountains (Apache sacred), *see* Guadalupe Mountains; "Old Baldy" (Sierra Blanca Peak)
Mountains (Navajo sacred): *see* Chuska Mountains; Chuska (White Spruce) Peak; Debentsa (Big Sheep, Hesperus); Huerfano; La Plata Mountains; Mountain-around-which-moving-was-done; Mt. Taylor; Pelado Peak; Reversible Mountain; San Francisco Peaks; Sísnajíní; Wide Belt Mountain
Mustangs, 48, 94, 206–207

Nailor, Gerald, 47–48
Naiyenezgani: *see* Killer-of-Enemies
Names, sacred, 195–196, 301
Natay, Ed Lee, 43
Navajo Indians, dates of acquisition of horses: 6–7, 10; divination: 137–139; first mention of: 5–6; linguistic divisions of Southern Athapascans (chart), xix; maps: xxii–xxiii; xxiv–xxv; present locations of (chart), xx; raiding practices: *see* Raids
Navajo myths: black horses in, 33; cardinal horse myth, 26–27; creation of horses, 18–19, 22–23, 24, *25,* 61, 62–82, *68,* 285ff; horse power brought to people, 167–172; raiding, 119–120, 121–130; spotted horses in, 46; Sun and White Shell Woman, 29, 30; turquoise horse in, 34, 37, 38; Water Horse, 221–222, 223–226, 264–265; white horses in, 29–30; yellow horses in, 40
Night Chant, 77, 167; *see also* Yeibitchai
Nohoílpi, 61

"Old Baldy" (Sierra Blanca Peak), 94
Owl, 97, 268–269

Pack Horses, 193–195
Palomino horses, *16,* 43, 48
Pelado Peak, 63, 71, 88, 108n46
Pinto horses: *see* Spotted horses
Plains Indians and Apache acquisition
    of horses, 102–103
Plants, beneficial, 187–189, 299
Plants, injurious, 189–190
Plants, medicinal, 180ff, 298
Pollen, 69, 108n42, 127, 148, 184, 291, 297
Prayers for increasing horses, Navajo,
    192–193, 297
Prayers for pack horses, 194, 195
Puberty ceremony, 235, 236, 237;
    Apache, *104, 147, 237,* 251–254,
    254, 256–258, 294, 301, 312, 313;
    horses in, 253–258, 292; Navajo
    (Kinaaldá), *165,* 255–256, 287, *289,*
    290, 292, 296, 297, 313
Pueblo Indians, reaction to first horses,
    1–3; influence on Navajo myths, 67,
    69, 172; influence on Navajo religion,
    172; *see also* Acoma; Hopi; Jemez;
    San Juan; Tewa; Zia; Zuñi Indians

Querecho Indians, 1, 3

Racing, 23–24, 31–32, 36, 305, 310;
    foot-racing, 257; medicines and
    customs of, 183–185; witchcraft
    and, 184–187
Raids, 114ff; clothing and weapons, 142;
    customs: *see* Taboos and customs in
    raids; distribution of captured
    horses, 155–156; groups on, 120–
    121; magical powers, origins of,
    118–119; magical powers used by
    Navajos, Tewa tales of, 116–117;
    mythical and economic reasons for,
    114; precautions on, 150–151;
    pursuit, precautions against, *136,*
    151–155; return from, obstacles
    and dangers, 154–155; taboos: *see*
    Taboos and customs in raids;
    victory dances, 156
Raids, Apache, altered language on,
    149–150, 301; ceremonies, 129ff;

divination rites, 134–136; magic
    powers used in, 136ff, 300, 301;
    magic role of Bear, Snake, and
    Turtle in, 129–130; origins of, 118–
    119; powers of horses essential for
    leaders, 133–134, 300, 302; prepara-
    tions for, 140–141, 299; size of
    parties, 120–121; supernatural
    powers of youths, 146; training for,
    139–140; Yaqui magic and, 117–118
Raids, Navajo, ceremonies, 121ff;
    divination rites, 137–139; magic
    role of Bear, Snake, Turtle, and
    Frog in, 122ff; on Tewa Indians,
    116–117; origins, 118–119; size of
    parties, 120–121
Rain ceremonies, horses in, 264–266,
    297–298, 311
Rain in creation myths, 17, 18, 291
Rainbow, 17, 18, 20, 24, 288, 293
Red horses, 33–34
Regalia: *see* Trappings
Remedies: *see* Medicines; Plants,
    medicinal
Repetition (power of), 288
Reversible Mountain, 107n28; *see also*
    Huerfano Mountain
Riding ability, 38–39, 43, 48, 93–94, 105,
    177, 204, 209, 210–211, 305, 309–
    310, 311
Riding, Apache tale of Foolish People,
    101–105
Riding Taboos, 202
Rio Grande River, 170, 214n18
Rock Crystal, 282, 293
Rodeo, *308,* 309–310
Rooster Pull: *see* Chicken Pull
Roping, 309
Rubbing rituals, 257

Saddles, mythical elements of
    (Chiricahua song), 20
Saddles, sores and galls, treatment, 182
Saddles, 26, 47, 102, *178,* 179, 198, 202,
    204, *271*
Salt gathering, 193–194, 203
Salt Woman, 193, 194

San Carlos Apache myth, black horse in, 31, turquoise horse in, 37
San Francisco Peaks, 64
San Juan Indians, 116, 117
San Juan River, 169, 214n18
Sandpainting, horses in, 29, 222, 223, 225
Scratching and scratch sticks, 142–143, 147, 256–257, 313
Shamans, Apache, 131–134, 135–137, 172–174, 176–180, 232–243; payments to, 177–178, 239–240, 253–255; women, 177, 235–238, 302–303, 304
Shields, 128, 142
Shirts, 142
Singers: see Medicine Men; see also Charlie Mitchell, Frank Mitchell, Slim Curly, Sam Yazzie
Singing for horses, 15, 73–74ff, 177, 190–193
Sísnajíní (Wide Belt Mountain), 70–71, 108n46; see also Pelado Peak
Sisna.te.l (Sis ná dzil), 66–67, 74, 167–168, 172, 213n9
Sister goddesses: see Changing Woman and White Shell (or White Bead) Woman
Sky Opening, 25–26, 169
Snake: see Big Snake
Songs: Bear songs, 126, 127, 154; creation songs, 79–80, 170–172; dwelling songs, 253, 294, 296; "Happiness" songs: see Good luck songs; Horse songs, for beautiful horses, 15–16, 293; for curing injuries from horses, 235; for increase and the benefit and protection of horses, 191–193, 282, 288, 290, 291, 292, 293, 294, 296, 299, 300, 301, 312; importance of horse songs in Blessing Way, 284, 291; of turquoise horse, 36, 170, 192; racing, 170; salt gathering, 194; to Water Horse, 265, 298; White Water Horse, 224–225
Spotted horses, 27, 44ff, 45; as folk hero favorites, 45–46; associated with north, 44; in Indian art, 47–48
Spotted Wood People, 101; see also Foolish People

Squaw Dance: see Enemy Way
Star in creation myth, 17, 18
Star-gazing, 138
Star symbolism, 20, 39, 44, 291
"Steelduster" horse, 35
Sucking, by Big Snake, 124–125
Sun, and black horses, 31, 32–33; and his Apache corral, 40–41; cardinal horses of, 16, 294; courtship of Changing Woman, 29, 37; as creator of horses, 21–22, 24; and his daughter, 29; and his Navajo corral, 26–27, 294; and his wives, 71, see also Changing Woman; and red horses, 34; and spotted horses, 46; and turquoise horses, 36, 38, 65–66; and white horses, 28, 29; and yellow horses, 16, 40–41, 42; role in bringing horses to Apaches, 57ff, 58, 82ff; role in bringing horses to Navajos, 57ff, 66, 284, 290–291; use of horses by, 24–26, 28ff
Sweat Lodge, 142, 299–300, 302

Taboos in horseback riding, 202
Taboos and customs in care of horses, 199–203
Taboos and customs in raids, 139ff, 300–301; altered language, 128–129, 149–150, 301; food and water, 145, 146; mental attitudes, 144; ritual painting, 148–149; scratching, 142–143, 145, 313; sexual restrictions, 141; sleeping postures, 143; taboos for women, 144–145
Tahoma, Quincy, 39–40, 43–44
Talking Gods, 63–64, 293
Taylor, Mount, 64, 169
Tewa Indians, 116–117
Thunder People, 266
Tie posts, 197–198, 293–294
Tobatc'istcini (Born-of-Water), 60; See also Child-of-the-Water
Tonto Apache, Northern Tonto, 17, 238; Southern Tonto, 17, 100, 238
Trappings, 37, 47–48, 136, 177–179, 178, 198, 202–203, 204–206, 271, 305

Tsinajinie, Andy, 38–39
Tsínihanoai (Sun Bearer), 22
Turquoise Boy, 26–27, 285; and creation of horses (Navajo myth), 62–74; see also Killer-of-Enemies
Turquoise horses, 27–28, 34–40; and moon god, 38; as Sun's horses, 34, 36–38; associated with south, 34–35; in Apache myth, 35, 37–38; in cure of illness, 226; in Indian art, 38–40, 54n95; preferred steed in Navajo myths, 34, 36–37
Turtle, powers of, 128–130
Turtle Dove and altered language, 129
Turtle Way, 121, 122
Twin horses, 201
Twin War Gods, 24, 57–60, 58, 70–73, 82, 85–86, 98; and black horse, 31, 32, 41, 42; and spotted horse, 46, 72; and turquoise horse, 37–38, 85; and white horse, 29, 31; and yellow horse, 41, 42–43; as bringers of horses (Apache myths), 85–87, 97–98; as bringers of horses (Navajo myth), 70–73, 290; as personification of struggle of Indian and white, 59–60; horses of, 30, 31–32; mistake in refusing horses for people, 57–59; see also Child-of-the-Water; Fire Boy; Killer-of-Enemies; Monster Slayer; Naiyenezgani; Turquoise Boy; Tobatc'istcini; Water Boy

Vigil, Frank, 43

Water Boy, 60, 98
Water Chant, 129, 225
Water horse, 222, 224, 225, 264, 265, 298
Water monsters, 203, 224–225, 245n1
Were-animals, 245
Western Apache Indians: date of acquisition of horses, 9–10, 17; map of, ca. 1850, xxi; see also Cibecue Apache; San Carlos Apache; Tonto Apache; White Mountain Apache
White, symbolism of, 29
White Bead Woman, see Changing Woman

White beads, 28
White horses, 26, 28–31; and Sun deity (Navajo myths), 28–29, 38; as moon symbol, 30; associated with east, 28; associated with west, 30; in Indian art, 29; position of in Apache mythology, 30–31
White man's god, 60, 61; see also Békotsidi
White Mountain Apache myths, black horse in, 32, 41, 83–85; creation of horses, 82–87; turquoise horse in, 37–38, 85, 87; white horse in, 30; wrong choice of gifts in, 59; yellow horse in, 40–43
White Painted Woman, 40–42, 104, 253, 254, 294; see also Changing Woman
White shell, 28, 69f, 312; see also White horses
White Shell Woman: see Changing Woman
"White stockings," 33, 39, 43, 49
Wide Belt (Sísnajíní) Mountain, 70–71, 72, 108n46; see also Pelado Peak
Winds, 17, 201, 282
Witchcraft, horses as instruments in, 242–245; plants for, 198–199; practiced on horses, 184–185, 301; cures for horses suffering from witchcraft practices, 186
Words (Belief about empowering them through speech), 288, 301

Yaqui Indians and Chiricahua Apache, 117–118
Yazz, Beatien, 44, 47–48
Yazzie, Sam, 222
Yeibitchai, 77, 167; see also Night Chant
Yel-Ha-Yah, 39–40, 44
Yellow horses, 27, 40–44; associated with west, 40; associated with moon and earth (Apache myth), 41; in Indian art, 43–44
Yoɫgaiesdzan, 75; see also White Shell Woman; Changing Woman
Younger Brother: see Child-of-the-Water

Zia Pueblo, 311
Zuñi Indians, 2, 172, 203–204, 215n49